The
Little
Data
Book
2001

April 2001

The Little Data Book 2001 is a product of the Development
Data Group of the World Bank's Development Economics Vice
Presidency.

CONTENTS

The Little Data Book 2001 is a pocket edition of the *World Development Indicators*. It is intended as a quick reference for users of the *World Development Indicators 2001* book and CD-ROM and of the *World Bank Atlas*, which between them cover more than 600 indicators spanning more than 30 years.

The 207 country pages in **The Little Data Book** present the latest available data for World Bank members and other economies with populations of more than 30,000. The 14 summary pages cover regional and income group aggregates.

For more information about these data or other World Bank data publications, call our hotline 800 590 1906 or 202 473 7824; fax 202 522 1498; or visit our data web site at www.worldbank.org/data. Our e-mail address is info@worldbank.org.

To order the *World Development Indicators 2001*, the *World Development Indicators 2001 CD-ROM* or the *World Bank Atlas*, call 800 645 7247 or 703 661 1580, fax 703 661 1501; or visit the publications website at www.worldbank.org/publications.

DATA NOTES

The data in this book are for 1990, 1998, and 1999 or the most recent year unless otherwise noted in the glossary.

Growth rates are proportional changes from the previous year unless otherwise noted.

Regional aggregates include data for low- and middle-income economies only. The aggregates are shown only if data are available for 66% of the economies in the regional or income group.

Figures in italics indicate data for years or periods other than those specified.

Symbols used:

..	means that data are not available or that aggregates cannot be calculated because of missing data.
0 or **0.0**	means zero or less than half the unit shown.
$	means current U.S. dollars.

Data are shown for economies with populations greater than 30,000 or less if they are members of the World Bank. The term "country" (used interchangeably with economy) does not imply political independence or official recognition by the World Bank but refers to any economy for which the authorities report separate social or economic statistics.

In keeping with the *World Development Indicators 2001*, this edition of *The Little Data Book 2001* uses terminology in line with the 1993 system of National Accounts (SNA). In particular, Gross National Product (GNP) is replaced by Gross National Income (GNI).

REGIONAL TABLES

WORLD

Population (millions)	5,978	Population growth (%)	1.4
Surface area (1,000 sq km)	133,432	Population per sq km	46
GNI ($ millions)	29,994,602	GNI per capita ($)	5,020

	1990	1998	1999
People			
Life expectancy (years)	65	66	66
Fertility rate (births per woman)	3.1	2.8	2.7
Infant mortality rate (per 1,000 live births)	61	56	54
Under 5 mortality rate (per 1,000 children)	86	83	78
Child malnutrition (% of children under 5)	..	..	..
Urban population (% of total)	43	46	46
Rural population density (per km^2 arable land)	496	520	..
Illiteracy male (% of people 15 and above)	..	..	..
Illiteracy female (% of people 15 and above)	..	..	..
Net primary enrollment (% of relevant age group)	..	..	..
Net secondary enrollment (% of relevant age group)	..	..	..
Girls in primary school (% of enrollment)	46	46	..
Girls in secondary school (% of enrollment)	44	44	..

	1990	1998	1999
Environment			
Forests (1,000 sq. km.)	39,513	..	38,609
Deforestation (% change 1990-2000)			0.2
Water use (% of total resources)	..	..	
CO_2 emissions (metric tons per capita)	3.5	4.1	..
Access to improved water source (% of urban pop.)	94	..	93
Access to sanitation (% of urban population)	78	..	84
Energy use per capita (kg of oil equivalent)	1,501	1,659	..
Electricity use per capita (kWh)	1,757	2,085	..

	1990	1998	1999
Economy			
GDP ($ millions)	21,728,147	29,430,162	30,876,254
GDP growth (annual %)	2.7	1.9	2.6
GDP implicit price deflator (annual % growth)	..	..	..
Value added in agriculture (% of GDP)	6.1	5.2	..
Value added in industry (% of GDP)	34.4	31.4	..
Value added in services (% of GDP)	59.0	63.4	..
Exports of goods and services (% of GDP)	19.3	22.7	26.8
Imports of goods and services (% of GDP)	19.5	22.1	25.1
Gross domestic investment (% of GDP)	24.0	22.4	22.9
Central government revenues (% of GDP)	23.0	26.6	..
Overall budget deficit (% of GDP)	-3.0	-1.5	..
Money and quasi money (annual % growth)	..	..	..

	1990	1998	1999
Technology and infrastructure			
Telephone mainlines (per 1,000 people)	100	144	158
Cost of 3 min local call ($)	0.05	0.06	0.06
Personal computers (per 1,000 people)	25.0	60.8	68.3
Internet users (thousands)	45	154,120	241,864
Paved roads (% of total)	39	55	..
Aircraft departures (thousands)	14,641	19,685	20,645

	1990	1998	1999
Trade and finance			
Trade as share of PPP GDP (%)	24.3	27.3	27.4
Trade growth less GDP growth (average %, 1989-99)			..
High-technology exports (% of manufactured exports)	20	21	21
Net barter terms of trade (1995=100)	..	..	..
Foreign direct investment ($ millions)	..	..	..
Present value of debt ($ millions)			..
Total debt service ($ millions)	..	..	..
Short term debt ($ millions)	..	..	..
Aid per capita ($)	11	10	10

Population (millions)	1,837	Population growth (%)	1.1
Surface area (1,000 sq km)	16,385	Population per sq km	115
GNI ($ millions)	1,854,509	GNI per capita ($)	1,010

	1990	1998	1999
People			
Life expectancy (years)	67	69	69
Fertility rate (births per woman)	2.4	2.2	2.1
Infant mortality rate (per 1,000 live births)	40	37	35
Under 5 mortality rate (per 1,000 children)	55	47	44
Child malnutrition (% of children under 5)	19	12	..
Urban population (% of total)	30	34	34
Rural population density (per km^2 arable land)	665	691	..
Illiteracy male (% of people 15 and above)	13	9	8
Illiteracy female (% of people 15 and above)	29	22	22
Net primary enrollment (% of relevant age group)	98	100	..
Net secondary enrollment (% of relevant age group)	..	..	..
Girls in primary school (% of enrollment)	47	48	48
Girls in secondary school (% of enrollment)	43	50	..
Environment			
Forests (1,000 sq. km.)	4,412	..	4,341
Deforestation (% change 1990-2000)			0.2
Water use (% of total resources)	..	..	..
CO_2 emissions (metric tons per capita)	2.1	2.8	..
Access to improved water source (% of urban pop.)	96	93	93
Access to sanitation (% of urban population)	63	59	74
Energy use per capita (kg of oil equivalent)	737	857	..
Electricity use per capita (kWh)	466	787	..
Economy			
GDP ($ millions)	927,038	1,682,712	1,894,945
GDP growth (annual %)	7.1	-1.3	6.8
GDP implicit price deflator (annual % growth)	..	..	..
Value added in agriculture (% of GDP)	19.8	14.6	14.1
Value added in industry (% of GDP)	40.5	44.8	44.9
Value added in services (% of GDP)	39.7	40.5	41.0
Exports of goods and services (% of GDP)	26.0	41.3	38.1
Imports of goods and services (% of GDP)	25.7	32.6	31.7
Gross domestic investment (% of GDP)	34.6	29.1	29.8
Central government revenues (% of GDP)	13.3	10.1	..
Overall budget deficit (% of GDP)	-0.8	-3.0	..
Money and quasi money (annual % growth)	..	..	..
Technology and infrastructure			
Telephone mainlines (per 1,000 people)	16	70	82
Cost of 3 min local call ($)	0.04	0.03	0.03
Personal computers (per 1,000 people)	1.9	14.2	17.0
Internet users (thousands)	0	6,878	23,593
Paved roads (% of total)	24	17	..
Aircraft departures (thousands)	924	1,381	1,350
Trade and finance			
Trade as share of PPP GDP (%)	15.4	14.9	15.3
Trade growth less GDP growth (average %, 1989-99)			..
High-technology exports (% of manufactured exports)	20	29	31
Net barter terms of trade (1995=100)	..	..	..
Foreign direct investment ($ millions)	11,135	63,297	56,041
Present value of debt ($ millions)			..
Total debt service ($ millions)	39,766	83,644	111,689
Short term debt ($ millions)	49,176	125,160	113,365
Aid per capita ($)	5	5	5

EUROPE AND CENTRAL ASIA

Population (millions)	474	Population growth (%)	0.1
Surface area (1,000 sq km)	24,106	Population per sq km	20
GNI ($ millions)	1,023,895	GNI per capita ($)	2,160

	1990	1998	1999
People			
Life expectancy (years)	69	69	69
Fertility rate (births per woman)	2.3	1.7	1.6
Infant mortality rate (per 1,000 live births)	28	23	21
Under 5 mortality rate (per 1,000 children)	34	29	26
Child malnutrition (% of children under 5)	..	..	
Urban population (% of total)	63	66	67
Rural population density (per km^2 arable land)	114	125	..
Illiteracy male (% of people 15 and above)	2	2	2
Illiteracy female (% of people 15 and above)	6	5	5
Net primary enrollment (% of relevant age group)	..	92	..
Net secondary enrollment (% of relevant age group)	..	..	..
Girls in primary school (% of enrollment)	49	48	..
Girls in secondary school (% of enrollment)	..	..	..

	1990	1998	1999
Environment			
Forests (1,000 sq. km.)	9,383	..	9,464
Deforestation (% change 1990-2000)			-0.1
Water use (% of total resources)	..	..	..
CO_2 emissions (metric tons per capita)	8.9	6.9	..
Access to improved water source (% of urban pop.)	..	..	95
Access to sanitation (% of urban population)	..	..	..
Energy use per capita (kg of oil equivalent)	3,454	2,637	..
Electricity use per capita (kWh)	3,327	2,652	..

	1990	1998	1999
Economy			
GDP ($ millions)	1,244,658	1,010,339	1,097,780
GDP growth (annual %)	-1.9	0.1	1.0
GDP implicit price deflator (annual % growth)	..	..	..
Value added in agriculture (% of GDP)	16.8	10.3	10.1
Value added in industry (% of GDP)	43.6	33.3	33.4
Value added in services (% of GDP)	39.7	56.4	56.4
Exports of goods and services (% of GDP)	22.8	34.1	40.4
Imports of goods and services (% of GDP)	23.7	35.7	36.7
Gross domestic investment (% of GDP)	27.6	21.5	20.9
Central government revenues (% of GDP)	..	25.4	26.8
Overall budget deficit (% of GDP)	..	-4.7	-3.7
Money and quasi money (annual % growth)	..	..	..

	1990	1998	1999
Technology and infrastructure			
Telephone mainlines (per 1,000 people)	125	201	213
Cost of 3 min local call ($)	0.01	0.05	0.07
Personal computers (per 1,000 people)	4.3	33.7	39.3
Internet users (thousands)	2	5,927	10,184
Paved roads (% of total)	74	87	87
Aircraft departures (thousands)	..	781	754

	1990	1998	1999
Trade and finance			
Trade as share of PPP GDP (%)	..	19.8	17.7
Trade growth less GDP growth (average %, 1989-99)			..
High-technology exports (% of manufactured exports)	..	8	11
Net barter terms of trade (1995=100)	..	..	..
Foreign direct investment ($ millions)	1,051	24,997	26,534
Present value of debt ($ millions)			..
Total debt service ($ millions)	32,060	56,240	60,902
Short term debt ($ millions)	40,857	67,982	71,360
Aid per capita ($)	8	18	23

LATIN AMERICA AND CARIBBEAN

Population (millions)	508	Population growth (%)	1.5
Surface area (1,000 sq km)	20,461	Population per sq km	25
GNI ($ millions)	1,932,869	GNI per capita ($)	3,800

	1990	1998	1999
People			
Life expectancy (years)	68	70	70
Fertility rate (births per woman)	3.1	2.7	2.6
Infant mortality rate (per 1,000 live births)	41	32	30
Under 5 mortality rate (per 1,000 children)	49	41	38
Child malnutrition (% of children under 5)	..	9	..
Urban population (% of total)	71	75	75
Rural population density (per km^2 arable land)	213	252	..
Illiteracy male (% of people 15 and above)	14	11	11
Illiteracy female (% of people 15 and above)	17	13	13
Net primary enrollment (% of relevant age group)	89	91	..
Net secondary enrollment (% of relevant age group)	29	33	..
Girls in primary school (% of enrollment)	50	..	..
Girls in secondary school (% of enrollment)	..	..	..
Environment			
Forests (1,000 sq. km.)	9,899	..	9,440
Deforestation (% change 1990-2000)			0.5
Water use (% of total resources)	..	..	..
CO$_2$ emissions (metric tons per capita)	2.3	2.8	..
Access to improved water source (% of urban pop.)	92	..	93
Access to sanitation (% of urban population)	85	..	87
Energy use per capita (kg of oil equivalent)	1,050	1,183	..
Electricity use per capita (kWh)	1,141	1,452	..
Economy			
GDP ($ millions)	1,136,103	2,036,653	2,052,720
GDP growth (annual %)	-0.6	1.9	0.0
GDP implicit price deflator (annual % growth)	..	..	..
Value added in agriculture (% of GDP)	8.7	7.9	7.7
Value added in industry (% of GDP)	36.4	29.2	30.0
Value added in services (% of GDP)	54.9	63.0	62.3
Exports of goods and services (% of GDP)	14.1	14.6	16.5
Imports of goods and services (% of GDP)	12.0	17.7	17.7
Gross domestic investment (% of GDP)	19.3	21.8	20.3
Central government revenues (% of GDP)	23.2	20.5	..
Overall budget deficit (% of GDP)	-3.5	-4.2	..
Money and quasi money (annual % growth)	..	..	..
Technology and infrastructure			
Telephone mainlines (per 1,000 people)	64	119	130
Cost of 3 min local call ($)	0.05	0.06	0.09
Personal computers (per 1,000 people)	5.9	32.0	37.7
Internet users (thousands)	0	5,928	9,687
Paved roads (% of total)	22	20	..
Aircraft departures (thousands)	1,213	1,911	1,930
Trade and finance			
Trade as share of PPP GDP (%)	11.4	18.5	18.2
Trade growth less GDP growth (average %, 1989-99)			..
High-technology exports (% of manufactured exports)	7	13	16
Net barter terms of trade (1995=100)	..	..	..
Foreign direct investment ($ millions)	8,188	72,052	90,352
Present value of debt ($ millions)			..
Total debt service ($ millions)	45,579	121,566	162,327
Short term debt ($ millions)	77,429	126,789	120,068
Aid per capita ($)	12	11	12

MIDDLE EAST AND NORTH AFRICA

Population (millions)	290	Population growth (%)	1.9
Surface area (1,000 sq km)	11,024	Population per sq km	26
GNI ($ millions)	598,379	GNI per capita ($)	2,060

	1990	1998	1999
People			
Life expectancy (years)	65	67	68
Fertility rate (births per woman)	4.8	3.7	3.5
Infant mortality rate (per 1,000 live births)	60	47	44
Under 5 mortality rate (per 1,000 children)	71	58	56
Child malnutrition (% of children under 5)	..	..	..
Urban population (% of total)	54	58	58
Rural population density (per km^2 arable land)	523	534	..
Illiteracy male (% of people 15 and above)	33	26	25
Illiteracy female (% of people 15 and above)	59	48	47
Net primary enrollment (% of relevant age group)	..	87	..
Net secondary enrollment (% of relevant age group)	..	62	..
Girls in primary school (% of enrollment)	45	45	..
Girls in secondary school (% of enrollment)	43	44	..
Environment			
Forests (1,000 sq. km.)	165	..	168
Deforestation (% change 1990-2000)			-0.1
Water use (% of total resources)	..	..	..
CO_2 emissions (metric tons per capita)	3.5	4.0	..
Access to improved water source (% of urban pop.)	93	..	96
Access to sanitation (% of urban population)	92	..	94
Energy use per capita (kg of oil equivalent)	1,126	1,344	..
Electricity use per capita (kWh)	939	1,263	..
Economy			
GDP ($ millions)	402,940	589,371	613,765
GDP growth (annual %)	7.0	3.6	2.6
GDP implicit price deflator (annual % growth)	..	..	..
Value added in agriculture (% of GDP)	14.8	13.7	..
Value added in industry (% of GDP)	38.4	38.1	..
Value added in services (% of GDP)	46.8	48.2	..
Exports of goods and services (% of GDP)	33.5	26.4	29.7
Imports of goods and services (% of GDP)	35.3	29.3	27.2
Gross domestic investment (% of GDP)	24.5	22.1	21.8
Central government revenues (% of GDP)	..	..	..
Overall budget deficit (% of GDP)	..	..	..
Money and quasi money (annual % growth)	..	..	..
Technology and infrastructure			
Telephone mainlines (per 1,000 people)	38	74	87
Cost of 3 min local call ($)	0.03	0.03	0.03
Personal computers (per 1,000 people)	..	21.5	25.4
Internet users (thousands)	0	461	1,153
Paved roads (% of total)	67	52	..
Aircraft departures (thousands)	346	423	428
Trade and finance			
Trade as share of PPP GDP (%)	23.5	17.3	16.8
Trade growth less GDP growth (average %, 1989-99)			..
High-technology exports (% of manufactured exports)	2	2	..
Net barter terms of trade (1995=100)	..	..	..
Foreign direct investment ($ millions)	2,504	6,576	1,461
Present value of debt ($ millions)			..
Total debt service ($ millions)	24,303	23,346	25,574
Short term debt ($ millions)	44,368	40,577	50,622
Aid per capita ($)	43	19	18

Population (millions)	1,329	Population growth (%)	1.9
Surface area (1,000 sq km)	5,140	Population per sq km	278
GNI ($ millions)	581,295	GNI per capita ($)	440

	1990	1998	1999
People			
Life expectancy (years)	59	62	63
Fertility rate (births per woman)	4.1	3.5	3.4
Infant mortality rate (per 1,000 live births)	87	76	74
Under 5 mortality rate (per 1,000 children)	121	104	99
Child malnutrition (% of children under 5)	64	47	..
Urban population (% of total)	25	28	28
Rural population density (per km^2 arable land)	472	537	..
Illiteracy male (% of people 15 and above)	41	35	34
Illiteracy female (% of people 15 and above)	66	59	58
Net primary enrollment (% of relevant age group)	..	..	..
Net secondary enrollment (% of relevant age group)	..	..	..
Girls in primary school (% of enrollment)	40	43	..
Girls in secondary school (% of enrollment)	37	39	..
Environment			
Forests (1,000 sq. km.)	790	..	782
Deforestation (% change 1990-2000)			0.1
Water use (% of total resources)	..	..	..
CO_2 emissions (metric tons per capita)	0.7	0.9	..
Access to improved water source (% of urban pop.)	93	..	92
Access to sanitation (% of urban population)	63	..	76
Energy use per capita (kg of oil equivalent)	391	445	..
Electricity use per capita (kWh)	228	341	..
Economy			
GDP ($ millions)	404,001	554,035	581,186
GDP growth (annual %)	5.6	6.0	6.0
GDP implicit price deflator (annual % growth)	..		
Value added in agriculture (% of GDP)	30.6	28.4	27.4
Value added in industry (% of GDP)	26.7	25.4	25.7
Value added in services (% of GDP)	42.7	46.1	46.8
Exports of goods and services (% of GDP)	9.1	13.0	13.4
Imports of goods and services (% of GDP)	13.0	16.2	16.9
Gross domestic investment (% of GDP)	23.7	21.4	21.9
Central government revenues (% of GDP)	13.9	12.8	13.6
Overall budget deficit (% of GDP)	-7.3	-5.1	-4.2
Money and quasi money (annual % growth)	..	..	..
Technology and infrastructure			
Telephone mainlines (per 1,000 people)	6	19	23
Cost of 3 min local call ($)	0.04	0.02	0.02
Personal computers (per 1,000 people)	0.4	2.8	3.2
Internet users (thousands)	0	1,538	3,034
Paved roads (% of total)	38	43	..
Aircraft departures (thousands)	245	304	282
Trade and finance			
Trade as share of PPP GDP (%)	4.3	4.7	4.6
Trade growth less GDP growth (average %, 1989-99)			..
High-technology exports (% of manufactured exports)	3	4	..
Net barter terms of trade (1995=100)	..	..	..
Foreign direct investment ($ millions)	464	3,549	3,070
Present value of debt ($ millions)			..
Total debt service ($ millions)	11,466	15,947	14,588
Short term debt ($ millions)	12,371	7,120	7,146
Aid per capita ($)	5	4	3

13

SUB-SAHARAN AFRICA

Population (millions)	643	Population growth (%)	2.5
Surface area (1,000 sq km)	24,267	Population per sq km	27
GNI ($ millions)	315,834	GNI per capita ($)	490

	1990	1998	1999
People			
Life expectancy (years)	50	49	47
Fertility rate (births per woman)	6.0	5.5	5.3
Infant mortality rate (per 1,000 live births)	101	94	92
Under 5 mortality rate (per 1,000 children)	155	159	161
Child malnutrition (% of children under 5)	..	..	..
Urban population (% of total)	28	33	34
Rural population density (per km^2 arable land)	315	369	..
Illiteracy male (% of people 15 and above)	40	32	31
Illiteracy female (% of people 15 and above)	60	49	47
Net primary enrollment (% of relevant age group)	..	..	..
Net secondary enrollment (% of relevant age group)	..	..	..
Girls in primary school (% of enrollment)	45	45	..
Girls in secondary school (% of enrollment)	42	..	..
Environment			
Forests (1,000 sq. km.)	6,965	..	6,436
Deforestation (% change 1990-2000)			0.8
Water use (% of total resources)	..	..	..
CO$_2$ emissions (metric tons per capita)	0.9	0.8	..
Access to improved water source (% of urban pop.)	81	..	82
Access to sanitation (% of urban population)	80	..	81
Energy use per capita (kg of oil equivalent)	717	700	..
Electricity use per capita (kWh)	454	454	..
Economy			
GDP ($ millions)	297,444	322,338	324,097
GDP growth (annual %)	1.1	2.0	2.0
GDP implicit price deflator (annual % growth)	..		
Value added in agriculture (% of GDP)	18.1	18.4	15.3
Value added in industry (% of GDP)	34.2	28.9	29.2
Value added in services (% of GDP)	47.9	52.6	55.5
Exports of goods and services (% of GDP)	27.2	29.0	28.7
Imports of goods and services (% of GDP)	25.7	31.7	30.9
Gross domestic investment (% of GDP)	14.7	18.6	17.6
Central government revenues (% of GDP)	24.2	..	..
Overall budget deficit (% of GDP)	-3.5	..	..
Money and quasi money (annual % growth)	..	..	..
Technology and infrastructure			
Telephone mainlines (per 1,000 people)	10	14	..
Cost of 3 min local call ($)	0.09	0.08	0.07
Personal computers (per 1,000 people)	..	7.5	8.4
Internet users (thousands)	0	1,530	2,357
Paved roads (% of total)	17	15	..
Aircraft departures (thousands)	317	318	331
Trade and finance			
Trade as share of PPP GDP (%)	17.3	16.0	16.3
Trade growth less GDP growth (average %, 1989-99)			..
High-technology exports (% of manufactured exports)	..	5	9
Net barter terms of trade (1995=100)	..	..	..
Foreign direct investment ($ millions)	923	6,294	7,949
Present value of debt ($ millions)			..
Total debt service ($ millions)	10,896	13,981	14,250
Short term debt ($ millions)	20,895	42,606	44,280
Aid per capita ($)	36	23	20

INCOME GROUP TABLES

LOW INCOME

Population (millions)	2,417	Population growth (%)		1.9
Surface area (1,000 sq km)	34,227	Population per sq km		73
GNI ($ millions)	1,008,397	GNI per capita ($)		420

	1990	1998	1999
People			
Life expectancy (years)	58	*59*	59
Fertility rate (births per woman)	4.4	*3.8*	3.7
Infant mortality rate (per 1,000 live births)	88	*79*	77
Under 5 mortality rate (per 1,000 children)	126	*118*	116
Child malnutrition (% of children under 5)	..	..	
Urban population (% of total)	28	31	31
Rural population density (per km^2 arable land)	458	507	..
Illiteracy male (% of people 15 and above)	35	30	29
Illiteracy female (% of people 15 and above)	56	49	48
Net primary enrollment (% of relevant age group)	..	..	..
Net secondary enrollment (% of relevant age group)	..	..	..
Girls in primary school (% of enrollment)	*43*	*44*	..
Girls in secondary school (% of enrollment)	*39*	*40*	..
Environment			
Forests (1,000 sq. km.)	9,554	..	*8,840*
Deforestation (% change 1990-2000)			*0.8*
Water use (% of total resources)	..	..	..
CO$_2$ emissions (metric tons per capita)	0.8	*1.1*	..
Access to improved water source (% of urban pop.)	89	..	88
Access to sanitation (% of urban population)	68	..	79
Energy use per capita (kg of oil equivalent)	429	550	..
Electricity use per capita (kWh)	189	362	..
Economy			
GDP ($ millions)	878,364	959,510	1,033,244
GDP growth (annual %)	3.4	0.9	4.1
GDP implicit price deflator (annual % growth)	..	..	..
Value added in agriculture (% of GDP)	28.9	26.6	25.8
Value added in industry (% of GDP)	30.7	30.2	30.4
Value added in services (% of GDP)	40.5	43.1	43.8
Exports of goods and services (% of GDP)	17.2	26.3	24.1
Imports of goods and services (% of GDP)	20.0	27.8	25.5
Gross domestic investment (% of GDP)	24.3	22.3	21.7
Central government revenues (% of GDP)	15.5	14.2	15.4
Overall budget deficit (% of GDP)	-4.8	-4.0	-3.0
Money and quasi money (annual % growth)	..	..	..
Technology and infrastructure			
Telephone mainlines (per 1,000 people)	11	22	27
Cost of 3 min local call ($)	0.05	0.06	0.05
Personal computers (per 1,000 people)	..	3.8	4.4
Internet users (thousands)	0	2,410	4,766
Paved roads (% of total)	17	*19*	..
Aircraft departures (thousands)	681	814	730
Trade and finance			
Trade as share of PPP GDP (%)	8.0	8.1	7.8
Trade growth less GDP growth (average %, 1989-99)			..
High-technology exports (% of manufactured exports)	..	6	..
Net barter terms of trade (1995=100)	..	..	..
Foreign direct investment ($ millions)	2,201	13,380	9,830
Present value of debt ($ millions)			..
Total debt service ($ millions)	32,215	48,221	47,223
Short term debt ($ millions)	50,010	62,393	62,437
Aid per capita ($)	12	9	9

Population (millions)	2,665	Population growth (%)	1.1
Surface area (1,000 sq km)	67,155	Population per sq km	40
GNI ($ millions)	5,285,017	GNI per capita ($)	1,980

	1990	1998	1999
People			
Life expectancy (years)	68	69	69
Fertility rate (births per woman)	2.6	2.2	2.2
Infant mortality rate (per 1,000 live births)	38	33	31
Under 5 mortality rate (per 1,000 children)	49	41	39
Child malnutrition (% of children under 5)	..	14	..
Urban population (% of total)	45	49	50
Rural population density (per km^2 arable land)	586	584	..
Illiteracy male (% of people 15 and above)	13	10	9
Illiteracy female (% of people 15 and above)	26	20	20
Net primary enrollment (% of relevant age group)	95	98	..
Net secondary enrollment (% of relevant age group)	..	..	..
Girls in primary school (% of enrollment)	47	48	..
Girls in secondary school (% of enrollment)	43	46	..
Environment			
Forests (1,000 sq. km.)	22,060	..	21,791
Deforestation (% change 1990-2000)			0.1
Water use (% of total resources)	..	..	..
CO_2 emissions (metric tons per capita)	2.7	3.8	..
Access to improved water source (% of urban pop.)	95	..	94
Access to sanitation (% of urban population)	75	..	82
Energy use per capita (kg of oil equivalent)	1,012	1,311	..
Electricity use per capita (kWh)	872	1,367	..
Economy			
GDP ($ millions)	3,520,734	5,222,690	5,518,746
GDP growth (annual %)	1.7	1.1	3.0
GDP implicit price deflator (annual % growth)	..	..	..
Value added in agriculture (% of GDP)	13.5	10.2	9.9
Value added in industry (% of GDP)	39.4	35.7	35.9
Value added in services (% of GDP)	47.1	54.1	54.2
Exports of goods and services (% of GDP)	21.3	27.3	28.8
Imports of goods and services (% of GDP)	20.5	26.2	26.3
Gross domestic investment (% of GDP)	25.9	24.0	23.6
Central government revenues (% of GDP)	19.6	19.4	..
Overall budget deficit (% of GDP)	-2.5	-3.0	..
Money and quasi money (annual % growth)	..	..	..
Technology and infrastructure			
Telephone mainlines (per 1,000 people)	46	108	121
Cost of 3 min local call ($)	0.04	0.05	0.05
Personal computers (per 1,000 people)	3.2	22.8	27.1
Internet users (thousands)	0	19,853	45,241
Paved roads (% of total)	50	48	..
Aircraft departures (thousands)	2,595	4,305	4,345
Trade and finance			
Trade as share of PPP GDP (%)	14.9	17.3	16.9
Trade growth less GDP growth (average %, 1989-99)			..
High-technology exports (% of manufactured exports)	..	18	21
Net barter terms of trade (1995=100)	..	..	..
Foreign direct investment ($ millions)	22,064	163,384	175,577
Present value of debt ($ millions)			..
Total debt service ($ millions)	131,855	266,504	342,109
Short term debt ($ millions)	195,086	347,840	344,404
Aid per capita ($)	10	8	9

17

LOWER MIDDLE INCOME

Population (millions)	2,093	Population growth (%)		1.0
Surface area (1,000 sq km)	44,649	Population per sq km		48
GNI ($ millions)	2,508,312	GNI per capita ($)		1,200

	1990	1998	1999
People			
Life expectancy (years)	68	69	69
Fertility rate (births per woman)	2.5	2.2	2.1
Infant mortality rate (per 1,000 live births)	38	34	32
Under 5 mortality rate (per 1,000 children)	50	42	40
Child malnutrition (% of children under 5)	18	9	..
Urban population (% of total)	39	42	43
Rural population density (per km^2 arable land)	633	631	..
Illiteracy male (% of people 15 and above)	13	10	9
Illiteracy female (% of people 15 and above)	29	23	22
Net primary enrollment (% of relevant age group)	96	99	..
Net secondary enrollment (% of relevant age group)	..	..	..
Girls in primary school (% of enrollment)	47	48	..
Girls in secondary school (% of enrollment)	42	50	..

	1990	1998	1999
Environment			
Forests (1,000 sq. km.)	13,863	..	13,966
Deforestation (% change 1990-2000)			-0.1
Water use (% of total resources)		..	..
CO$_2$ emissions (metric tons per capita)	2.2	3.4	..
Access to improved water source (% of urban pop.)	96	..	94
Access to sanitation (% of urban population)	70	..	80
Energy use per capita (kg of oil equivalent)	797	1,116	..
Electricity use per capita (kWh)	566	1,064	..

	1990	1998	1999
Economy			
GDP ($ millions)	1,808,310	2,447,133	2,608,902
GDP growth (annual %)	1.9	2.4	3.6
GDP implicit price deflator (annual % growth)	..		
Value added in agriculture (% of GDP)	20.9	14.9	14.3
Value added in industry (% of GDP)	39.2	39.0	39.3
Value added in services (% of GDP)	39.9	46.1	46.4
Exports of goods and services (% of GDP)	21.3	28.4	31.4
Imports of goods and services (% of GDP)	22.1	27.0	27.6
Gross domestic investment (% of GDP)	30.4	26.8	26.0
Central government revenues (% of GDP)	12.9	14.5	..
Overall budget deficit (% of GDP)	-1.5	-4.0	..
Money and quasi money (annual % growth)	..	..	..

	1990	1998	1999
Technology and infrastructure			
Telephone mainlines (per 1,000 people)	32	90	102
Cost of 3 min local call ($)	0.02	0.03	0.05
Personal computers (per 1,000 people)	1.2	14.4	17.7
Internet users (thousands)	0	6,285	17,942
Paved roads (% of total)	51	46	..
Aircraft departures (thousands)	1,079	2,028	2,001

	1990	1998	1999
Trade and finance			
Trade as share of PPP GDP (%)	11.6	12.2	11.7
Trade growth less GDP growth (average %, 1989-99)			..
High-technology exports (% of manufactured exports)	..	17	18
Net barter terms of trade (1995=100)	..	..	..
Foreign direct investment ($ millions)	9,584	76,298	66,214
Present value of debt ($ millions)			..
Total debt service ($ millions)	73,209	103,395	116,830
Short term debt ($ millions)	88,772	166,020	161,789
Aid per capita ($)	11	8	9

18

UPPER MIDDLE INCOME

Population (millions)	571	Population growth (%)	1.3
Surface area (1,000 sq km)	22,506	Population per sq km	26
GNI ($ millions)	2,782,483	GNI per capita ($)	4,870

	1990	1998	1999
People			
Life expectancy (years)	69	69	69
Fertility rate (births per woman)	2.9	2.5	2.4
Infant mortality rate (per 1,000 live births)	35	28	27
Under 5 mortality rate (per 1,000 children)	46	36	34
Child malnutrition (% of children under 5)	..	..	..
Urban population (% of total)	71	75	75
Rural population density (per km^2 arable land)	202	193	..
Illiteracy male (% of people 15 and above)	11	9	9
Illiteracy female (% of people 15 and above)	14	11	11
Net primary enrollment (% of relevant age group)	91	94	..
Net secondary enrollment (% of relevant age group)	41	43	..
Girls in primary school (% of enrollment)	50	..	..
Girls in secondary school (% of enrollment)	..	..	..
Environment			
Forests (1,000 sq. km.)	8,197	..	7,825
Deforestation (% change 1990-2000)			0.5
Water use (% of total resources)	..	..	
CO$_2$ emissions (metric tons per capita)	4.4	5.5	..
Access to improved water source (% of urban pop.)	..	..	94
Access to sanitation (% of urban population)	..	..	87
Energy use per capita (kg of oil equivalent)	1,748	2,025	..
Electricity use per capita (kWh)	1,917	2,482	..
Economy			
GDP ($ millions)	1,728,727	2,781,290	2,915,898
GDP growth (annual %)	1.6	0.0	2.6
GDP implicit price deflator (annual % growth)	..	..	..
Value added in agriculture (% of GDP)	8.1	6.7	6.4
Value added in industry (% of GDP)	39.5	33.3	33.2
Value added in services (% of GDP)	52.4	60.0	60.4
Exports of goods and services (% of GDP)	21.4	26.5	26.8
Imports of goods and services (% of GDP)	19.2	25.7	25.3
Gross domestic investment (% of GDP)	22.7	21.9	21.9
Central government revenues (% of GDP)	23.9	22.6	..
Overall budget deficit (% of GDP)	-3.1	-3.5	..
Money and quasi money (annual % growth)	..	..	..
Technology and infrastructure			
Telephone mainlines (per 1,000 people)	100	177	190
Cost of 3 min local call ($)	0.04	0.06	0.07
Personal computers (per 1,000 people)	9.9	52.8	60.9
Internet users (thousands)	0	13,568	27,299
Paved roads (% of total)	50	50	..
Aircraft departures (thousands)	1,516	2,277	2,344
Trade and finance			
Trade as share of PPP GDP (%)	18.8	25.8	26.0
Trade growth less GDP growth (average %, 1989-99)			..
High-technology exports (% of manufactured exports)	13	19	24
Net barter terms of trade (1995=100)	..	..	..
Foreign direct investment ($ millions)	12,480	87,087	109,364
Present value of debt ($ millions)			..
Total debt service ($ millions)	58,646	163,109	225,279
Short term debt ($ millions)	106,314	181,820	182,615
Aid per capita ($)	8	7	7

19

Population (millions)	5,082	Population growth (%)	1.4
Surface area (1,000 sq km)	101,382	Population per sq km	46
GNI ($ millions)	6,292,072	GNI per capita ($)	5,020

	1990	1998	1999
People			
Life expectancy (years)	63	65	64
Fertility rate (births per woman)	3.4	3.0	2.9
Infant mortality rate (per 1,000 live births)	66	60	59
Under 5 mortality rate (per 1,000 children)	91	87	85
Child malnutrition (% of children under 5)	..	..	..
Urban population (% of total)	37	41	41
Rural population density (per km^2 arable land)	519	542	..
Illiteracy male (% of people 15 and above)	22	18	18
Illiteracy female (% of people 15 and above)	39	33	32
Net primary enrollment (% of relevant age group)	..	..	..
Net secondary enrollment (% of relevant age group)	..	..	..
Girls in primary school (% of enrollment)	45	46	..
Girls in secondary school (% of enrollment)	42	43	..
Environment			
Forests (1,000 sq. km.)	31,614	..	30,630
Deforestation (% change 1990-2000)			0.3
Water use (% of total resources)	..	..	..
CO_2 emissions (metric tons per capita)	1.8	2.5	..
Access to improved water source (% of urban pop.)	93	..	92
Access to sanitation (% of urban population)	72	..	81
Energy use per capita (kg of oil equivalent)	753	967	..
Electricity use per capita (kWh)	569	913	..
Economy			
GDP ($ millions)	4,393,226	6,181,957	6,551,527
GDP growth (annual %)	2.0	1.1	3.2
GDP implicit price deflator (annual % growth)	..	..	..
Value added in agriculture (% of GDP)	15.8	12.7	12.4
Value added in industry (% of GDP)	38.1	34.8	35.0
Value added in services (% of GDP)	46.1	52.4	52.6
Exports of goods and services (% of GDP)	20.7	27.1	28.1
Imports of goods and services (% of GDP)	20.4	26.5	26.2
Gross domestic investment (% of GDP)	25.7	23.8	23.3
Central government revenues (% of GDP)	19.0	18.8	..
Overall budget deficit (% of GDP)	-2.8	-3.1	..
Money and quasi money (annual % growth)	..	..	..
Technology and infrastructure			
Telephone mainlines (per 1,000 people)	30	67	79
Cost of 3 min local call ($)	0.04	0.05	0.05
Personal computers (per 1,000 people)	2.2	14.1	16.6
Internet users (thousands)	0	22,263	50,006
Paved roads (% of total)	29	30	..
Aircraft departures (thousands)	3,276	5,118	5,074
Trade and finance			
Trade as share of PPP GDP (%)	13.2	15.1	14.7
Trade growth less GDP growth (average %, 1989-99)			..
High-technology exports (% of manufactured exports)	..	17	20
Net barter terms of trade (1995=100)	..	..	..
Foreign direct investment ($ millions)	24,265	176,764	185,408
Present value of debt ($ millions)			..
Total debt service ($ millions)	164,070	314,725	389,332
Short term debt ($ millions)	245,096	410,234	406,841
Aid per capita ($)	12	9	10

Population (millions)	293	Population growth (%)	0.2
Surface area (1,000 sq km)	2,436	Population per sq km	122
GNI ($ millions)	6,513,106	GNI per capita ($)	22,250

	1990	1998	1999
People			
Life expectancy (years)	76	78	78
Fertility rate (births per woman)	1.5	1.4	1.4
Infant mortality rate (per 1,000 live births)	8	5	5
Under 5 mortality rate (per 1,000 children)	9	6	5
Child malnutrition (% of children under 5)	..	..	
Urban population (% of total)	76	78	78
Rural population density (per km^2 arable land)	137	141	..
Illiteracy male (% of people 15 and above)	..	..	..
Illiteracy female (% of people 15 and above)	..	..	..
Net primary enrollment (% of relevant age group)	93	94	..
Net secondary enrollment (% of relevant age group)	88	91	..
Girls in primary school (% of enrollment)	49	48	..
Girls in secondary school (% of enrollment)	50	49	..
Environment			
Forests (1,000 sq. km.)	872	..	898
Deforestation (% change 1990-2000)			-0.3
Water use (% of total resources)	..	..	
CO_2 emissions (metric tons per capita)	7.2	8.2	..
Access to improved water source (% of urban pop.)	..	..	
Access to sanitation (% of urban population)	..		
Energy use per capita (kg of oil equivalent)	3,628	3,834	..
Electricity use per capita (kWh)	4,841	5,504	..
Economy			
GDP ($ millions)	5,656,919	6,585,993	6,535,484
GDP growth (annual %)	1.5	2.7	2.4
GDP implicit price deflator (annual % growth)	..	..	..
Value added in agriculture (% of GDP)	2.7	2.3	2.0
Value added in industry (% of GDP)	29.6	26.8	27.3
Value added in services (% of GDP)	67.0	71.0	70.7
Exports of goods and services (% of GDP)	27.5	32.8	32.8
Imports of goods and services (% of GDP)	27.7	30.4	30.9
Gross domestic investment (% of GDP)	23.4	21.0	21.3
Central government revenues (% of GDP)	34.8	37.3	..
Overall budget deficit (% of GDP)	-3.7	-2.3	..
Money and quasi money (annual % growth)	..	..	..
Technology and infrastructure			
Telephone mainlines (per 1,000 people)	415	514	526
Cost of 3 min local call ($)	0.15	0.12	0.13
Personal computers (per 1,000 people)	64.1	212.7	234.9
Internet users (thousands)	494	23,185	41,280
Paved roads (% of total)	94	90	99
Aircraft departures (thousands)	1,714	3,021	3,186
Trade and finance			
Trade as share of PPP GDP (%)	45.2	51.5	52.7
Trade growth less GDP growth (average %, 1989-99)			..
High-technology exports (% of manufactured exports)	13	17	19
Net barter terms of trade (1995=100)	..	..	..
Foreign direct investment ($ millions)	..	..	..
Present value of debt ($ millions)			..
Total debt service ($ millions)	..	..	..
Short term debt ($ millions)	..	..	..
Aid per capita ($)	..	..	..

HIGH INCOME

Population (millions)	896	Population growth (%)		0.7
Surface area (1,000 sq km)	32,050	Population per sq km		29
GNI ($ millions)	23,701,691	GNI per capita ($)		26,440

	1990	1998	1999
People			
Life expectancy (years)	76	77	78
Fertility rate (births per woman)	1.8	1.7	1.7
Infant mortality rate (per 1,000 live births)	8	6	6
Under 5 mortality rate (per 1,000 children)	9	7	6
Child malnutrition (% of children under 5)	..	..	
Urban population (% of total)	75	77	77
Rural population density (per km^2 arable land)	176	175	..
Illiteracy male (% of people 15 and above)	..	..	..
Illiteracy female (% of people 15 and above)	..	..	..
Net primary enrollment (% of relevant age group)	98	95	..
Net secondary enrollment (% of relevant age group)	88	90	..
Girls in primary school (% of enrollment)	49	49	..
Girls in secondary school (% of enrollment)	49	49	..

	1990	1998	1999
Environment			
Forests (1,000 sq. km.)	7,899	..	7,979
Deforestation (% change 1990-2000)			-0.1
Water use (% of total resources)	..	..	..
CO$_2$ emissions (metric tons per capita)	12.3	12.8	..
Access to improved water source (% of urban pop.)	..	..	..
Access to sanitation (% of urban population)	..	..	..
Energy use per capita (kg of oil equivalent)	4,991	5,366	..
Electricity use per capita (kWh)	7,300	8,353	..

	1990	1998	1999
Economy			
GDP ($ millions)	17,320,028	23,244,648	24,323,287
GDP growth (annual %)	2.8	2.1	2.4
GDP implicit price deflator (annual % growth)	..	..	..
Value added in agriculture (% of GDP)	..	..	..
Value added in industry (% of GDP)	..	..	..
Value added in services (% of GDP)	..	..	..
Exports of goods and services (% of GDP)	18.9	21.6	..
Imports of goods and services (% of GDP)	19.2	21.0	..
Gross domestic investment (% of GDP)	23.5	22.0	..
Central government revenues (% of GDP)	23.9	28.9	..
Overall budget deficit (% of GDP)	-3.0	-1.1	..
Money and quasi money (annual % growth)	..	..	..

	1990	1998	1999
Technology and infrastructure			
Telephone mainlines (per 1,000 people)	465	572	583
Cost of 3 min local call ($)	0.13	0.10	0.10
Personal computers (per 1,000 people)	115.1	306.5	345.8
Internet users (thousands)	45	131,857	191,857
Paved roads (% of total)	86	90	..
Aircraft departures (thousands)	11,365	14,566	15,571

	1990	1998	1999
Trade and finance			
Trade as share of PPP GDP (%)	31.1	37.0	37.4
Trade growth less GDP growth (average %, 1989-99)			..
High-technology exports (% of manufactured exports)	21	22	22
Net barter terms of trade (1995=100)	..	..	..
Foreign direct investment ($ millions)	..	..	..
Present value of debt ($ millions)			..
Total debt service ($ millions)	..	..	..
Short term debt ($ millions)	..	..	..
Aid per capita ($)	3	2	2

COUNTRY TABLES

AFGHANISTAN

South Asia   Low income

Population (millions)	25,869	Population growth (%)		3.2
Surface area (1,000 sq km)	652.1	Population per sq km		40
GNI ($ millions)	..	GNI per capita ($)		..

	1990	1998	1999
People			
Life expectancy (years)	43	45	46
Fertility rate (births per woman)	6.9	6.9	6.7
Infant mortality rate (per 1,000 live births)	164	151	147
Under 5 mortality rate (per 1,000 children)	257	226	220
Child malnutrition (% of children under 5)	..	49	..
Urban population (% of total)	18	21	22
Rural population density (per km^2 arable land)	183	250	..
Illiteracy male (% of people 15 and above)	59	50	50
Illiteracy female (% of people 15 and above)	88	81	80
Net primary enrollment (% of relevant age group)	..	29	..
Net secondary enrollment (% of relevant age group)	..	14	..
Girls in primary school (% of enrollment)	34	32	..
Girls in secondary school (% of enrollment)	32	25	..
Environment			
Forests (1,000 sq. km.)	14	..	14
Deforestation (% change 1990-2000)			0.0
Water use (% of total resources)	..	..	40.2
CO$_2$ emissions (metric tons per capita)	0.2	0.0	..
Access to improved water source (% of urban pop.)	..	39	19
Access to sanitation (% of urban population)	..	38	25
Energy use per capita (kg of oil equivalent)	..	..	..
Electricity use per capita (kWh)	..	..	..
Economy			
GDP ($ millions)	..	..	..
GDP growth (annual %)	..	..	..
GDP implicit price deflator (annual % growth)	..	..	..
Value added in agriculture (% of GDP)	..	..	..
Value added in industry (% of GDP)	..	..	..
Value added in services (% of GDP)	..	..	..
Exports of goods and services (% of GDP)	..	..	..
Imports of goods and services (% of GDP)	..	..	..
Gross domestic investment (% of GDP)	..	..	..
Central government revenues (% of GDP)	..	..	..
Overall budget deficit (% of GDP)	..	..	..
Money and quasi money (annual % growth)	..	..	..
Technology and infrastructure			
Telephone mainlines (per 1,000 people)	2	1	1
Cost of 3 min local call ($)	..	..	..
Personal computers (per 1,000 people)	..	..	..
Internet users (thousands)	..	..	..
Paved roads (% of total)	13	13	..
Aircraft departures (thousands)	5	2	3
Trade and finance			
Trade as share of PPP GDP (%)	..	..	..
Trade growth less GDP growth (average %, 1989-99)			..
High-technology exports (% of manufactured exports)	..	..	..
Net barter terms of trade (1995=100)	99	100	..
Foreign direct investment ($ millions)	..	..	..
Present value of debt ($ millions)			..
Total debt service ($ millions)	..	..	..
Short term debt ($ millions)	..	..	..
Aid per capita ($)	7	6	6

Europe & Central Asia   **Lower middle income**

Population (millions)	3	Population growth (%)		1.1
Surface area (1,000 sq km)	29	Population per sq km		123
GNI ($ millions)	3,146	GNI per capita ($)		930

	1990	1998	1999
People			
Life expectancy (years)	72	72	72
Fertility rate (births per woman)	3.0	2.5	2.4
Infant mortality rate (per 1,000 live births)	28	26	24
Under 5 mortality rate (per 1,000 children)	42	31	..
Child malnutrition (% of children under 5)	..	8	..
Urban population (% of total)	36	40	41
Rural population density (per km² arable land)	362	345	..
Illiteracy male (% of people 15 and above)	14	9	9
Illiteracy female (% of people 15 and above)	32	24	23
Net primary enrollment (% of relevant age group)	..	102	..
Net secondary enrollment (% of relevant age group)	..	..	..
Girls in primary school (% of enrollment)	48	48	..
Girls in secondary school (% of enrollment)	45	49	..
Environment			
Forests (1,000 sq. km.)	11	..	10
Deforestation (% change 1990-2000)			0.8
Water use (% of total resources)			3.3
CO_2 emissions (metric tons per capita)	2.3	0.5	..
Access to improved water source (% of urban pop.)	..	97	..
Access to sanitation (% of urban population)	..	97	..
Energy use per capita (kg of oil equivalent)	811	284	..
Electricity use per capita (kWh)	810	678	..
Economy			
GDP ($ millions)	2,102	3,058	3,676
GDP growth (annual %)	-9.6	8.0	7.2
GDP implicit price deflator (annual % growth)	-0.5	24.8	2.5
Value added in agriculture (% of GDP)	35.9	54.4	52.6
Value added in industry (% of GDP)	48.2	24.5	26.0
Value added in services (% of GDP)	15.9	21.0	21.4
Exports of goods and services (% of GDP)	14.9	9.2	11.4
Imports of goods and services (% of GDP)	23.2	31.9	29.9
Gross domestic investment (% of GDP)	29.3	16.0	16.8
Central government revenues (% of GDP)	..	19.4	..
Overall budget deficit (% of GDP)	..	-8.5	..
Money and quasi money (annual % growth)	..	20.6	22.3
Technology and infrastructure			
Telephone mainlines (per 1,000 people)	12	31	36
Cost of 3 min local call ($)	0.01	0.01	0.02
Personal computers (per 1,000 people)	..	4.0	5.2
Internet users (thousands)	..	2	3
Paved roads (% of total)	..	39	39
Aircraft departures (thousands)	..	1	1
Trade and finance			
Trade as share of PPP GDP (%)	6.7	10.7	13.9
Trade growth less GDP growth (average %, 1989-99)			10.9
High-technology exports (% of manufactured exports)	..	1	..
Net barter terms of trade (1995=100)	..	..	..
Foreign direct investment ($ millions)	0	45	41
Present value of debt ($ millions)			665
Total debt service ($ millions)	3	36	37
Short term debt ($ millions)	313	35	29
Aid per capita ($)	3	77	142

ALGERIA

Population (millions)	30	Population growth (%)		1.5
Surface area (1,000 sq km)	2,382	Population per sq km		13
GNI ($ millions)	46,548	GNI per capita ($)		1,550

	1990	1998	1999
People			
Life expectancy (years)	67	70	71
Fertility rate (births per woman)	4.5	3.6	3.4
Infant mortality rate (per 1,000 live births)	46	35	34
Under 5 mortality rate (per 1,000 children)	55	39	39
Child malnutrition (% of children under 5)	9	13	..
Urban population (% of total)	52	59	60
Rural population density (per km^2 arable land)	168	159	..
Illiteracy male (% of people 15 and above)	32	24	23
Illiteracy female (% of people 15 and above)	59	46	44
Net primary enrollment (% of relevant age group)	93	94	..
Net secondary enrollment (% of relevant age group)	54	56	..
Girls in primary school (% of enrollment)	45	46	..
Girls in secondary school (% of enrollment)	43	48	..
Environment			
Forests (1,000 sq. km.)	19	..	21
Deforestation (% change 1990-2000)			-1.3
Water use (% of total resources)			31.5
CO_2 emissions (metric tons per capita)	3.3	3.4	..
Access to improved water source (% of urban pop.)	86	..	98
Access to sanitation (% of urban population)	..	..	90
Energy use per capita (kg of oil equivalent)	938	898	..
Electricity use per capita (kWh)	449	563	..
Economy			
GDP ($ millions)	61,902	47,362	47,872
GDP growth (annual %)	-1.3	5.1	3.3
GDP implicit price deflator (annual % growth)	34.4	-4.1	10.9
Value added in agriculture (% of GDP)	13.7	12.1	11.4
Value added in industry (% of GDP)	45.5	47.3	50.7
Value added in services (% of GDP)	40.8	40.6	37.9
Exports of goods and services (% of GDP)	23.3	22.9	27.6
Imports of goods and services (% of GDP)	25.1	23.5	23.3
Gross domestic investment (% of GDP)	29.3	27.7	27.4
Central government revenues (% of GDP)	..	27.8	29.8
Overall budget deficit (% of GDP)	..	-3.6	-0.4
Money and quasi money (annual % growth)	11.4	18.9	13.7
Technology and infrastructure			
Telephone mainlines (per 1,000 people)	32	49	52
Cost of 3 min local call ($)	0.07	0.02	..
Personal computers (per 1,000 people)	1.0	5.3	5.8
Internet users (thousands)	..	2	20
Paved roads (% of total)	67	69	..
Aircraft departures (thousands)	44	44	36
Trade and finance			
Trade as share of PPP GDP (%)	19.9	13.7	14.3
Trade growth less GDP growth (average %, 1989-99)			-1.3
High-technology exports (% of manufactured exports)	1	1	4
Net barter terms of trade (1995=100)	126	117	..
Foreign direct investment ($ millions)	0	5	7
Present value of debt ($ millions)			29,011
Total debt service ($ millions)	8,803	5,136	5,332
Short term debt ($ millions)	791	186	195
Aid per capita ($)	10	13	3

AMERICAN SAMOA

Population (thousands)	64	Population growth (%)		..
Surface area (1,000 sq km)	0.2	Population per sq km		320
GNI ($ millions)	..	GNI per capita ($)		..

	1990	1998	1999
People			
Life expectancy (years)	..	..	..
Fertility rate (births per woman)	..	..	..
Infant mortality rate (per 1,000 live births)	..	..	..
Under 5 mortality rate (per 1,000 children)	..	..	..
Child malnutrition (% of children under 5)	..	..	..
Urban population (% of total)	48	52	52
Rural population density (per km^2 arable land)	..	..	..
Illiteracy male (% of people 15 and above)	..	..	..
Illiteracy female (% of people 15 and above)	..	..	..
Net primary enrollment (% of relevant age group)	..	..	..
Net secondary enrollment (% of relevant age group)	..	..	..
Girls in primary school (% of enrollment)	*48*	..	..
Girls in secondary school (% of enrollment)	*46*	..	..
Environment			
Forests (1,000 sq. km.)	0	..	*0*
Deforestation (% change 1990-2000)			*0.0*
Water use (% of total resources)	..	..	..
CO$_2$ emissions (metric tons per capita)	..	..	..
Access to improved water source (% of urban pop.)	100	..	*100*
Access to sanitation (% of urban population)	..	..	..
Energy use per capita (kg of oil equivalent)	..	..	..
Electricity use per capita (kWh)	..	..	..
Economy			
GDP ($ millions)	..	..	..
GDP growth (annual %)	..	..	..
GDP implicit price deflator (annual % growth)	..	..	..
Value added in agriculture (% of GDP)	..	..	..
Value added in industry (% of GDP)	..	..	..
Value added in services (% of GDP)	..	..	..
Exports of goods and services (% of GDP)	..	..	..
Imports of goods and services (% of GDP)	..	..	..
Gross domestic investment (% of GDP)	..	..	..
Central government revenues (% of GDP)	..	..	..
Overall budget deficit (% of GDP)	..	..	..
Money and quasi money (annual % growth)	..	..	..
Technology and infrastructure			
Telephone mainlines (per 1,000 people)	118	214	212
Cost of 3 min local call ($)	..	..	..
Personal computers (per 1,000 people)	..	..	..
Internet users (thousands)	..	..	..
Paved roads (% of total)	..	..	..
Aircraft departures (thousands)	..	..	..
Trade and finance			
Trade as share of PPP GDP (%)	..	..	..
Trade growth less GDP growth (average %, 1989-99)			..
High-technology exports (% of manufactured exports)	..	..	..
Net barter terms of trade (1995=100)	..	..	..
Foreign direct investment ($ millions)	..	..	..
Present value of debt ($ millions)			..
Total debt service ($ millions)	..	..	..
Short term debt ($ millions)	..	..	..
Aid per capita ($)	..	..	..

27

ANDORRA

Population (thousands)	66	Population growth (%)		..
Surface area (1,000 sq km)	0.5	Population per sq km		147
GNI ($ millions)	..	GNI per capita ($)		..

	1990	1998	1999
People			
Life expectancy (years)	..	..	..
Fertility rate (births per woman)	..	..	..
Infant mortality rate (per 1,000 live births)	..	..	..
Under 5 mortality rate (per 1,000 children)	..	..	..
Child malnutrition (% of children under 5)	..	..	..
Urban population (% of total)	95	93	93
Rural population density (per km^2 arable land)	..	..	..
Illiteracy male (% of people 15 and above)	..	..	..
Illiteracy female (% of people 15 and above)	..	..	..
Net primary enrollment (% of relevant age group)	..	..	..
Net secondary enrollment (% of relevant age group)	..	..	..
Girls in primary school (% of enrollment)	..	..	..
Girls in secondary school (% of enrollment)	..	..	..
Environment			
Forests (1,000 sq. km.)	..	..	..
Deforestation (% change 1990-2000)			..
Water use (% of total resources)	..	..	..
CO_2 emissions (metric tons per capita)	..	..	..
Access to improved water source (% of urban pop.)	..	..	*100*
Access to sanitation (% of urban population)	..	..	*100*
Energy use per capita (kg of oil equivalent)	..	..	..
Electricity use per capita (kWh)	..	..	..
Economy			
GDP ($ millions)	..	..	..
GDP growth (annual %)	..	..	..
GDP implicit price deflator (annual % growth)	..	..	..
Value added in agriculture (% of GDP)	..	..	..
Value added in industry (% of GDP)	..	..	..
Value added in services (% of GDP)	..	..	..
Exports of goods and services (% of GDP)	..	..	..
Imports of goods and services (% of GDP)	..	..	..
Gross domestic investment (% of GDP)	..	..	..
Central government revenues (% of GDP)	..	..	..
Overall budget deficit (% of GDP)	..	..	..
Money and quasi money (annual % growth)	..	..	..
Technology and infrastructure			
Telephone mainlines (per 1,000 people)	414	439	447
Cost of 3 min local call ($)	*0.03*	0.10	0.10
Personal computers (per 1,000 people)	..	..	..
Internet users (thousands)	..	5	5
Paved roads (% of total)	..	..	..
Aircraft departures (thousands)	..	..	..
Trade and finance			
Trade as share of PPP GDP (%)	..	..	..
Trade growth less GDP growth (average %, 1989-99)			..
High-technology exports (% of manufactured exports)	..	..	..
Net barter terms of trade (1995=100)	..	..	..
Foreign direct investment ($ millions)	..	..	..
Present value of debt ($ millions)			..
Total debt service ($ millions)	..	..	..
Short term debt ($ millions)	..	..	..
Aid per capita ($)	..	..	..

Sub-Saharan Africa   **Low income**

Population (millions)	12	Population growth (%)		2.9
Surface area (1,000 sq km)	1,247	Population per sq km		10
GNI ($ millions)	3,276	GNI per capita ($)		270

	1990	1998	1999
People			
Life expectancy (years)	45	46	47
Fertility rate (births per woman)	7.2	6.8	6.7
Infant mortality rate (per 1,000 live births)	130	125	127
Under 5 mortality rate (per 1,000 children)	..	209	208
Child malnutrition (% of children under 5)	20	41	..
Urban population (% of total)	28	33	34
Rural population density (per km² arable land)	230	268	..
Illiteracy male (% of people 15 and above)	..	..	..
Illiteracy female (% of people 15 and above)	..	..	..
Net primary enrollment (% of relevant age group)	..	..	..
Net secondary enrollment (% of relevant age group)	..	..	..
Girls in primary school (% of enrollment)	48	47	..
Girls in secondary school (% of enrollment)	..	..	..
Environment			
Forests (1,000 sq. km.)	710	..	698
Deforestation (% change 1990-2000)			0.2
Water use (% of total resources)	..	..	0.3
CO_2 emissions (metric tons per capita)	0.5	0.5	..
Access to improved water source (% of urban pop.)	..	..	34
Access to sanitation (% of urban population)	..	..	70
Energy use per capita (kg of oil equivalent)	681	595	..
Electricity use per capita (kWh)	64	60	..
Economy			
GDP ($ millions)	10,260	6,449	8,545
GDP growth (annual %)	-0.3	3.2	2.7
GDP implicit price deflator (annual % growth)	10.8	39.9	501.3
Value added in agriculture (% of GDP)	17.9	13.0	6.9
Value added in industry (% of GDP)	40.8	55.7	77.1
Value added in services (% of GDP)	41.2	31.3	16.1
Exports of goods and services (% of GDP)	38.9	56.8	..
Imports of goods and services (% of GDP)	20.9	48.4	..
Gross domestic investment (% of GDP)	11.7	24.0	32.8
Central government revenues (% of GDP)	..	..	..
Overall budget deficit (% of GDP)	..	..	..
Money and quasi money (annual % growth)	..	57.6	526.0
Technology and infrastructure			
Telephone mainlines (per 1,000 people)	8	6	8
Cost of 3 min local call ($)	0.12	0.14	0.06
Personal computers (per 1,000 people)	..	0.8	1.0
Internet users (thousands)	..	3	10
Paved roads (% of total)	25	25	10
Aircraft departures (thousands)	7	7	6
Trade and finance			
Trade as share of PPP GDP (%)	37.3	18.2	16.0
Trade growth less GDP growth (average %, 1989-99)			..
High-technology exports (% of manufactured exports)	..	..	..
Net barter terms of trade (1995=100)	145	70	..
Foreign direct investment ($ millions)	-335	1,114	2,471
Present value of debt ($ millions)			8,494
Total debt service ($ millions)	326	1,128	1,144
Short term debt ($ millions)	989	1,710	1,624
Aid per capita ($)	29	28	31

ANTIGUA AND BARBUDA

Latin America & Caribbean   **Upper middle income**

Population (thousands)	67	Population growth (%)	0.8
Surface area (1,000 sq km)	0.4	Population per sq km	153
GNI ($ millions)	606	GNI per capita ($)	8,990

	1990	1998	1999
People			
Life expectancy (years)	74	75	75
Fertility rate (births per woman)	1.8	1.7	1.7
Infant mortality rate (per 1,000 live births)	21	17	16
Under 5 mortality rate (per 1,000 children)	..	21	20
Child malnutrition (% of children under 5)	..	..	..
Urban population (% of total)	35	36	37
Rural population density (per km^2 arable land)	517	532	..
Illiteracy male (% of people 15 and above)	..	..	..
Illiteracy female (% of people 15 and above)	..	..	..
Net primary enrollment (% of relevant age group)	..	..	..
Net secondary enrollment (% of relevant age group)	..	..	..
Girls in primary school (% of enrollment)	49	..	..
Girls in secondary school (% of enrollment)	50	..	..
Environment			
Forests (1,000 sq. km.)	0	..	0
Deforestation (% change 1990-2000)			0.0
Water use (% of total resources)	..	..	10.0
CO$_2$ emissions (metric tons per capita)	4.7	5.1	..
Access to improved water source (% of urban pop.)	..	..	95
Access to sanitation (% of urban population)	..	..	98
Energy use per capita (kg of oil equivalent)	..	..	..
Electricity use per capita (kWh)	..	..	..
Economy			
GDP ($ millions)	392	617	640
GDP growth (annual %)	2.5	4.4	4.6
GDP implicit price deflator (annual % growth)	2.3	1.8	-0.9
Value added in agriculture (% of GDP)	4.2	4.0	3.9
Value added in industry (% of GDP)	20.1	18.9	19.2
Value added in services (% of GDP)	75.7	77.1	76.8
Exports of goods and services (% of GDP)	89.0	72.0	71.1
Imports of goods and services (% of GDP)	87.0	83.5	87.2
Gross domestic investment (% of GDP)	32.4	32.2	29.8
Central government revenues (% of GDP)	..	..	..
Overall budget deficit (% of GDP)	..	..	..
Money and quasi money (annual % growth)	4.8	15.7	9.9
Technology and infrastructure			
Telephone mainlines (per 1,000 people)	253	468	489
Cost of 3 min local call ($)	0.05	0.05	0.05
Personal computers (per 1,000 people)	..	..	..
Internet users (thousands)	..	3	4
Paved roads (% of total)	..	..	..
Aircraft departures (thousands)	58	70	68
Trade and finance			
Trade as share of PPP GDP (%)	49.7	54.5	..
Trade growth less GDP growth (average %, 1989-99)			-1.5
High-technology exports (% of manufactured exports)	..	..	..
Net barter terms of trade (1995=100)	..	..	..
Foreign direct investment ($ millions)	..	..	..
Present value of debt ($ millions)			..
Total debt service ($ millions)	..	..	..
Short term debt ($ millions)	..	..	..
Aid per capita ($)	73	148	159

Latin America & Caribbean   **Upper middle income**

Population (millions)	37	Population growth (%)	1.3
Surface area (1,000 sq km)	2,780	Population per sq km	13
GNI ($ millions)	276,097	GNI per capita ($)	7,550

	1990	1998	1999
People			
Life expectancy (years)	72	73	74
Fertility rate (births per woman)	2.9	2.6	2.5
Infant mortality rate (per 1,000 live births)	25	19	18
Under 5 mortality rate (per 1,000 children)	28	24	22
Child malnutrition (% of children under 5)	..	2	..
Urban population (% of total)	87	89	90
Rural population density (per km^2 arable land)	18	15	..
Illiteracy male (% of people 15 and above)	4	3	3
Illiteracy female (% of people 15 and above)	4	3	3
Net primary enrollment (% of relevant age group)	..	104	..
Net secondary enrollment (% of relevant age group)	..	..	..
Girls in primary school (% of enrollment)	..	49	..
Girls in secondary school (% of enrollment)	..	52	..
Environment			
Forests (1,000 sq. km.)	375	..	346
Deforestation (% change 1990-2000)			0.8
Water use (% of total resources)	..	..	7.9
CO_2 emissions (metric tons per capita)	3.4	3.9	..
Access to improved water source (% of urban pop.)	..	71	85
Access to sanitation (% of urban population)	..	80	89
Energy use per capita (kg of oil equivalent)	1,385	1,726	..
Electricity use per capita (kWh)	1,241	1,891	..
Economy			
GDP ($ millions)	141,352	298,444	283,166
GDP growth (annual %)	-2.4	3.9	-3.2
GDP implicit price deflator (annual % growth)	2,076.8	-2.0	-2.0
Value added in agriculture (% of GDP)	8.1	5.7	4.6
Value added in industry (% of GDP)	36.0	28.7	28.2
Value added in services (% of GDP)	55.9	65.6	67.1
Exports of goods and services (% of GDP)	10.4	10.4	9.8
Imports of goods and services (% of GDP)	4.6	12.9	11.5
Gross domestic investment (% of GDP)	14.0	19.9	18.8
Central government revenues (% of GDP)	10.5	13.8	..
Overall budget deficit (% of GDP)	-0.4	-1.5	..
Money and quasi money (annual % growth)	1,113.3	10.5	4.1
Technology and infrastructure			
Telephone mainlines (per 1,000 people)	93	197	201
Cost of 3 min local call ($)	0.10	0.10	0.09
Personal computers (per 1,000 people)	7.2	41.6	49.2
Internet users (thousands)	1	200	900
Paved roads (% of total)	29	30	29
Aircraft departures (thousands)	114	166	184
Trade and finance			
Trade as share of PPP GDP (%)	6.5	12.8	10.9
Trade growth less GDP growth (average %, 1989-99)			8.3
High-technology exports (% of manufactured exports)	8	6	8
Net barter terms of trade (1995=100)	94	104	..
Foreign direct investment ($ millions)	1,836	6,670	23,929
Present value of debt ($ millions)			154,362
Total debt service ($ millions)	6,158	21,486	25,723
Short term debt ($ millions)	10,473	30,956	31,515
Aid per capita ($)	5	2	2

31

ARMENIA

Europe & Central Asia — Low income

Population (millions)	4	Population growth (%)	0.4
Surface area (1,000 sq km)	30	Population per sq km	135
GNI ($ millions)	1,878	GNI per capita ($)	490

	1990	1998	1999
People			
Life expectancy (years)	72	74	74
Fertility rate (births per woman)	2.6	1.3	1.3
Infant mortality rate (per 1,000 live births)	19	15	14
Under 5 mortality rate (per 1,000 children)	24	18	18
Child malnutrition (% of children under 5)	..	3	..
Urban population (% of total)	68	69	70
Rural population density (per km^2 arable land)	245	234	..
Illiteracy male (% of people 15 and above)	1	1	1
Illiteracy female (% of people 15 and above)	4	3	3
Net primary enrollment (% of relevant age group)	..	..	..
Net secondary enrollment (% of relevant age group)	..	..	..
Girls in primary school (% of enrollment)	..	51	..
Girls in secondary school (% of enrollment)	..	..	..
Environment			
Forests (1,000 sq. km.)	3	..	4
Deforestation (% change 1990-2000)			-1.3
Water use (% of total resources)	..	..	27.6
CO_2 emissions (metric tons per capita)	1.1	0.8	..
Access to improved water source (% of urban pop.)	..	..	..
Access to sanitation (% of urban population)	..	..	..
Energy use per capita (kg of oil equivalent)	1,166	511	..
Electricity use per capita (kWh)	1,692	930	..
Economy			
GDP ($ millions)	4,124	1,894	1,845
GDP growth (annual %)	-11.7	7.2	3.3
GDP implicit price deflator (annual % growth)	79.3	10.8	0.1
Value added in agriculture (% of GDP)	17.4	34.0	28.7
Value added in industry (% of GDP)	52.0	30.8	32.6
Value added in services (% of GDP)	30.7	35.2	38.7
Exports of goods and services (% of GDP)	35.0	19.0	21.0
Imports of goods and services (% of GDP)	46.3	52.8	49.7
Gross domestic investment (% of GDP)	47.1	19.1	19.5
Central government revenues (% of GDP)	..	..	..
Overall budget deficit (% of GDP)	..	..	..
Money and quasi money (annual % growth)	..	36.7	14.0
Technology and infrastructure			
Telephone mainlines (per 1,000 people)	157	157	155
Cost of 3 min local call ($)	0.00	0.11	0.11
Personal computers (per 1,000 people)	..	4.2	5.7
Internet users (thousands)	..	4	30
Paved roads (% of total)	99	96	96
Aircraft departures (thousands)	..	5	4
Trade and finance			
Trade as share of PPP GDP (%)	..	13.3	..
Trade growth less GDP growth (average %, 1989-99)			-11.7
High-technology exports (% of manufactured exports)	..	6	2
Net barter terms of trade (1995=100)	..	..	..
Foreign direct investment ($ millions)	0	221	122
Present value of debt ($ millions)			662
Total debt service ($ millions)	..	61	58
Short term debt ($ millions)	..	45	49
Aid per capita ($)	1	38	55

ARUBA

Population (thousands)	98	Population growth (%)		..
Surface area (1,000 sq km)	0.2	Population per sq km		516
GNI ($ millions)	..	GNI per capita ($)		..

	1990	1998	1999
People			
Life expectancy (years)	..	..	..
Fertility rate (births per woman)	..	..	..
Infant mortality rate (per 1,000 live births)	..	..	..
Under 5 mortality rate (per 1,000 children)	..	..	..
Child malnutrition (% of children under 5)	..	..	..
Urban population (% of total)	..	..	..
Rural population density (per km^2 arable land)	..	..	..
Illiteracy male (% of people 15 and above)	..	..	..
Illiteracy female (% of people 15 and above)	..	..	..
Net primary enrollment (% of relevant age group)	..	..	..
Net secondary enrollment (% of relevant age group)	..	..	..
Girls in primary school (% of enrollment)	..	..	..
Girls in secondary school (% of enrollment)	..	..	..
Environment			
Forests (1,000 sq. km.)		..	..
Deforestation (% change 1990-2000)			..
Water use (% of total resources)		..	..
CO$_2$ emissions (metric tons per capita)	..	..	..
Access to improved water source (% of urban pop.)		..	..
Access to sanitation (% of urban population)		..	..
Energy use per capita (kg of oil equivalent)	..	..	..
Electricity use per capita (kWh)	..	..	..
Economy			
GDP ($ millions)	865	1,728	..
GDP growth (annual %)	12.0	6.0	..
GDP implicit price deflator (annual % growth)	5.4	3.7	..
Value added in agriculture (% of GDP)	..	..	..
Value added in industry (% of GDP)	..	..	..
Value added in services (% of GDP)	..	..	..
Exports of goods and services (% of GDP)	..	..	..
Imports of goods and services (% of GDP)	..	..	..
Gross domestic investment (% of GDP)	..	..	..
Central government revenues (% of GDP)	..	..	..
Overall budget deficit (% of GDP)	..	..	..
Money and quasi money (annual % growth)	17.2	13.6	10.2
Technology and infrastructure			
Telephone mainlines (per 1,000 people)	282	373	372
Cost of 3 min local call ($)	0.08	0.08	..
Personal computers (per 1,000 people)		..	..
Internet users (thousands)		2	4
Paved roads (% of total)		..	..
Aircraft departures (thousands)	..	..	..
Trade and finance			
Trade as share of PPP GDP (%)	..	..	..
Trade growth less GDP growth (average %, 1989-99)			..
High-technology exports (% of manufactured exports)	..	..	..
Net barter terms of trade (1995=100)	..	..	..
Foreign direct investment ($ millions)	..	..	..
Present value of debt ($ millions)			..
Total debt service ($ millions)	..	..	..
Short term debt ($ millions)	..	..	..
Aid per capita ($)	..	..	-75

AUSTRALIA

Population (millions)	19	Population growth (%)	1.1
Surface area (1,000 sq km)	7,741	Population per sq km	2
GNI ($ millions)	397,345	GNI per capita ($)	20,950

	1990	1998	1999
People			
Life expectancy (years)	77	79	79
Fertility rate (births per woman)	1.9	1.8	1.8
Infant mortality rate (per 1,000 live births)	8	5	5
Under 5 mortality rate (per 1,000 children)	10	7	5
Child malnutrition (% of children under 5)	..	0	..
Urban population (% of total)	85	85	85
Rural population density (per km^2 arable land)	5	5	..
Illiteracy male (% of people 15 and above)	..	..	..
Illiteracy female (% of people 15 and above)	..	..	..
Net primary enrollment (% of relevant age group)	99	95	..
Net secondary enrollment (% of relevant age group)	79	89	..
Girls in primary school (% of enrollment)	49	49	..
Girls in secondary school (% of enrollment)	50	50	..
Environment			
Forests (1,000 sq. km.)	1,581	..	1,581
Deforestation (% change 1990-2000)			0.0
Water use (% of total resources)	..	..	4.3
CO_2 emissions (metric tons per capita)	15.8	17.2	..
Access to improved water source (% of urban pop.)	100	..	100
Access to sanitation (% of urban population)	100	..	100
Energy use per capita (kg of oil equivalent)	5,107	5,600	..
Electricity use per capita (kWh)	7,572	8,717	..
Economy			
GDP ($ millions)	310,041	372,723	404,033
GDP growth (annual %)	-0.2	4.5	4.4
GDP implicit price deflator (annual % growth)	3.4	0.3	1.1
Value added in agriculture (% of GDP)	3.1	3.1	..
Value added in industry (% of GDP)	26.5	24.7	..
Value added in services (% of GDP)	70.5	72.3	..
Exports of goods and services (% of GDP)	16.7	18.8	..
Imports of goods and services (% of GDP)	16.9	21.3	..
Gross domestic investment (% of GDP)	22.0	24.6	..
Central government revenues (% of GDP)	25.0	23.9	24.2
Overall budget deficit (% of GDP)	2.0	2.8	1.4
Money and quasi money (annual % growth)	12.8	8.4	11.7
Technology and infrastructure			
Telephone mainlines (per 1,000 people)	456	526	520
Cost of 3 min local call ($)	0.18	0.15	0.16
Personal computers (per 1,000 people)	149.7	411.8	469.2
Internet users (thousands)	190	3,000	6,000
Paved roads (% of total)	35	39	..
Aircraft departures (thousands)	256	378	338
Trade and finance			
Trade as share of PPP GDP (%)	27.8	27.7	26.9
Trade growth less GDP growth (average %, 1989-99)			3.7
High-technology exports (% of manufactured exports)	12	12	11
Net barter terms of trade (1995=100)	117	100	95
Foreign direct investment ($ millions)	..	..	..
Present value of debt ($ millions)			..
Total debt service ($ millions)	..	..	..
Short term debt ($ millions)	..	..	..
Aid per capita ($)	..	..	..

34

AUSTRIA

High income

Population (millions)	8	Population growth (%)	0.2
Surface area (1,000 sq km)	84	Population per sq km	98
GNI ($ millions)	205,743	GNI per capita ($)	25,430

	1990	1998	1999
People			
Life expectancy (years)	76	78	78
Fertility rate (births per woman)	1.5	1.3	1.3
Infant mortality rate (per 1,000 live births)	8	5	4
Under 5 mortality rate (per 1,000 children)	9	7	5
Child malnutrition (% of children under 5)	..	..	..
Urban population (% of total)	65	65	65
Rural population density (per km^2 arable land)	192	205	..
Illiteracy male (% of people 15 and above)	..	..	..
Illiteracy female (% of people 15 and above)	..	..	..
Net primary enrollment (% of relevant age group)	90	88	..
Net secondary enrollment (% of relevant age group)	91	88	..
Girls in primary school (% of enrollment)	49	48	..
Girls in secondary school (% of enrollment)	47	47	..
Environment			
Forests (1,000 sq. km.)	38	..	39
Deforestation (% change 1990-2000)			-0.2
Water use (% of total resources)	..	..	2.7
CO_2 emissions (metric tons per capita)	7.8	7.8	..
Access to improved water source (% of urban pop.)	100	..	100
Access to sanitation (% of urban population)	100	..	100
Energy use per capita (kg of oil equivalent)	3,322	3,567	..
Electricity use per capita (kWh)	5,587	6,175	..
Economy			
GDP ($ millions)	162,288	210,913	208,173
GDP growth (annual %)	4.6	2.9	2.1
GDP implicit price deflator (annual % growth)	3.4	0.6	0.9
Value added in agriculture (% of GDP)	4.8	2.2	2.1
Value added in industry (% of GDP)	30.9	29.5	29.1
Value added in services (% of GDP)	64.2	68.3	68.7
Exports of goods and services (% of GDP)	39.6	44.9	45.3
Imports of goods and services (% of GDP)	38.7	45.4	45.7
Gross domestic investment (% of GDP)	24.3	24.7	24.2
Central government revenues (% of GDP)	33.9	37.5	37.7
Overall budget deficit (% of GDP)	-4.4	-5.7	..
Money and quasi money (annual % growth)	..	..	..
Technology and infrastructure			
Telephone mainlines (per 1,000 people)	418	491	472
Cost of 3 min local call ($)	0.17	0.17	0.17
Personal computers (per 1,000 people)	64.8	233.4	256.8
Internet users (thousands)	20	1,230	1,840
Paved roads (% of total)	100	100	100
Aircraft departures (thousands)	42	128	127
Trade and finance			
Trade as share of PPP GDP (%)	61.6	67.7	65.1
Trade growth less GDP growth (average %, 1989-99)			3.3
High-technology exports (% of manufactured exports)	8	12	13
Net barter terms of trade (1995=100)	..	..	..
Foreign direct investment ($ millions)	..	..	..
Present value of debt ($ millions)			..
Total debt service ($ millions)	..	..	..
Short term debt ($ millions)	..	..	..
Aid per capita ($)	..	..	..

35

AZERBAIJAN

Population (millions)	8	Population growth (%)	0.9
Surface area (1,000 sq km)	87	Population per sq km	92
GNI ($ millions)	3,705	GNI per capita ($)	460

	1990	1998	1999
People			
Life expectancy (years)	71	71	71
Fertility rate (births per woman)	2.7	2.0	2.0
Infant mortality rate (per 1,000 live births)	23	17	16
Under 5 mortality rate (per 1,000 children)	..	23	21
Child malnutrition (% of children under 5)	..	10	..
Urban population (% of total)	54	57	57
Rural population density (per km² arable land)	222	205	..
Illiteracy male (% of people 15 and above)	..	..	..
Illiteracy female (% of people 15 and above)	..	..	..
Net primary enrollment (% of relevant age group)	..	..	..
Net secondary enrollment (% of relevant age group)	..	..	..
Girls in primary school (% of enrollment)	49	48	..
Girls in secondary school (% of enrollment)	49	49	..
Environment			
Forests (1,000 sq. km.)	10	..	11
Deforestation (% change 1990-2000)			-1.3
Water use (% of total resources)			54.6
CO₂ emissions (metric tons per capita)	6.4	4.1	..
Access to improved water source (% of urban pop.)	..	..	..
Access to sanitation (% of urban population)	..	67	..
Energy use per capita (kg of oil equivalent)	2,269	1,564	..
Electricity use per capita (kWh)	1,645	1,584	..
Economy			
GDP ($ millions)	9,837	4,181	4,004
GDP growth (annual %)	-11.7	10.0	7.4
GDP implicit price deflator (annual % growth)	7.5	-6.9	-5.1
Value added in agriculture (% of GDP)	..	21.4	23.3
Value added in industry (% of GDP)	..	42.6	35.4
Value added in services (% of GDP)	..	36.0	41.3
Exports of goods and services (% of GDP)	..	24.1	33.8
Imports of goods and services (% of GDP)	..	58.0	50.6
Gross domestic investment (% of GDP)	..	45.8	39.6
Central government revenues (% of GDP)	..	19.0	20.1
Overall budget deficit (% of GDP)	..	-3.9	-2.9
Money and quasi money (annual % growth)	..	-17.4	21.5
Technology and infrastructure			
Telephone mainlines (per 1,000 people)	86	89	95
Cost of 3 min local call ($)	..	0.12	..
Personal computers (per 1,000 people)	..	..	..
Internet users (thousands)	..	3	8
Paved roads (% of total)	..	92	92
Aircraft departures (thousands)	..	10	9
Trade and finance			
Trade as share of PPP GDP (%)	..	8.9	8.6
Trade growth less GDP growth (average %, 1989-99)			24.9
High-technology exports (% of manufactured exports)	..	..	..
Net barter terms of trade (1995=100)	..	..	..
Foreign direct investment ($ millions)	0	1,023	510
Present value of debt ($ millions)			744
Total debt service ($ millions)	..	24	85
Short term debt ($ millions)	..	2	29
Aid per capita ($)	1	11	20

THE BAHAMAS

Population (thousands)	298	Population growth (%)	1.4
Surface area (1,000 sq km)	13.9	Population per sq km	30
GNI ($ millions)	..	GNI per capita ($)	..

	1990	1998	1999
People			
Life expectancy (years)	72	74	73
Fertility rate (births per woman)	2.1	2.3	2.2
Infant mortality rate (per 1,000 live births)	28	17	18
Under 5 mortality rate (per 1,000 children)	29	21	21
Child malnutrition (% of children under 5)	..	..	..
Urban population (% of total)	84	88	88
Rural population density (per km^2 arable land)	524	603	..
Illiteracy male (% of people 15 and above)	6	5	5
Illiteracy female (% of people 15 and above)	5	4	4
Net primary enrollment (% of relevant age group)	96	98	..
Net secondary enrollment (% of relevant age group)	88	86	..
Girls in primary school (% of enrollment)	49	49	..
Girls in secondary school (% of enrollment)	50	49	..
Environment			
Forests (1,000 sq. km.)	8	..	8
Deforestation (% change 1990-2000)			0.0
Water use (% of total resources)	..	..	..
CO_2 emissions (metric tons per capita)	7.6	6.0	..
Access to improved water source (% of urban pop.)	99	97	98
Access to sanitation (% of urban population)	100	100	93
Energy use per capita (kg of oil equivalent)	..	..	..
Electricity use per capita (kWh)	..	..	..
Economy			
GDP ($ millions)	3,105	3,742	..
GDP growth (annual %)	1.1	3.0	5.5
GDP implicit price deflator (annual % growth)	3.2	3.2	3.2
Value added in agriculture (% of GDP)	..	..	..
Value added in industry (% of GDP)	..	..	..
Value added in services (% of GDP)	..	..	..
Exports of goods and services (% of GDP)	..	..	..
Imports of goods and services (% of GDP)	..	..	..
Gross domestic investment (% of GDP)	..	..	..
Central government revenues (% of GDP)	16.1	18.2	19.1
Overall budget deficit (% of GDP)	-2.5	-1.9	-1.1
Money and quasi money (annual % growth)	16.8	16.2	10.6
Technology and infrastructure			
Telephone mainlines (per 1,000 people)	274	358	369
Cost of 3 min local call ($)	0.00	0.00	..
Personal computers (per 1,000 people)	..	..	..
Internet users (thousands)	..	7	11
Paved roads (% of total)	52	57	..
Aircraft departures (thousands)	19	29	31
Trade and finance			
Trade as share of PPP GDP (%)	75.4	68.7	..
Trade growth less GDP growth (average %, 1989-99)			..
High-technology exports (% of manufactured exports)	..	..	..
Net barter terms of trade (1995=100)	..	..	..
Foreign direct investment ($ millions)	..	..	..
Present value of debt ($ millions)			..
Total debt service ($ millions)	..	..	..
Short term debt ($ millions)	..	..	..
Aid per capita ($)	10	77	39

BAHRAIN

Population (thousands)	666	Population growth (%)	3.6
Surface area (1,000 sq km)	0.7	Population per sq km	966
GNI ($ millions)	..	GNI per capita ($)	..

	1990	1998	1999
People			
Life expectancy (years)	71	73	73
Fertility rate (births per woman)	3.8	3.4	3.3
Infant mortality rate (per 1,000 live births)	23	9	8
Under 5 mortality rate (per 1,000 children)	23	11	12
Child malnutrition (% of children under 5)	7	..	..
Urban population (% of total)	88	91	92
Rural population density (per km^2 arable land)	3,119	1,835	..
Illiteracy male (% of people 15 and above)	13	10	10
Illiteracy female (% of people 15 and above)	25	19	18
Net primary enrollment (% of relevant age group)	99	98	..
Net secondary enrollment (% of relevant age group)	85	83	..
Girls in primary school (% of enrollment)	49	49	..
Girls in secondary school (% of enrollment)	50	51	..
Environment			
Forests (1,000 sq. km.)	..	..	..
Deforestation (% change 1990-2000)			..
Water use (% of total resources)			..
CO$_2$ emissions (metric tons per capita)	23.4	24.1	..
Access to improved water source (% of urban pop.)	100	100	..
Access to sanitation (% of urban population)	100	100	..
Energy use per capita (kg of oil equivalent)	9,590	9,718	..
Electricity use per capita (kWh)	5,964	7,645	..
Economy			
GDP ($ millions)	4,006	5,350	..
GDP growth (annual %)	1.3	2.1	..
GDP implicit price deflator (annual % growth)	6.8	-4.9	..
Value added in agriculture (% of GDP)	0.9	0.9	..
Value added in industry (% of GDP)	45.7	39.9	..
Value added in services (% of GDP)	53.3	59.2	..
Exports of goods and services (% of GDP)	122.0	115.4	..
Imports of goods and services (% of GDP)	99.7	79.3	..
Gross domestic investment (% of GDP)	20.0	6.0	..
Central government revenues (% of GDP)	31.1	25.7	..
Overall budget deficit (% of GDP)	-6.8	-5.8	..
Money and quasi money (annual % growth)	-9.6	16.8	4.1
Technology and infrastructure			
Telephone mainlines (per 1,000 people)	192	245	249
Cost of 3 min local call ($)	0.07	0.05	0.05
Personal computers (per 1,000 people)	..	93.5	139.8
Internet users (thousands)	..	20	30
Paved roads (% of total)	75	77	77
Aircraft departures (thousands)	11	12	13
Trade and finance			
Trade as share of PPP GDP (%)	128.3	76.5	..
Trade growth less GDP growth (average %, 1989-99)			..
High-technology exports (% of manufactured exports)	..	4	..
Net barter terms of trade (1995=100)	..	..	..
Foreign direct investment ($ millions)	..	..	..
Present value of debt ($ millions)			..
Total debt service ($ millions)	..	..	..
Short term debt ($ millions)	..	..	..
Aid per capita ($)	272	73	6

Population (millions)	128	Population growth (%)		1.6
Surface area (1,000 sq km)	144	Population per sq km		981
GNI ($ millions)	47,071	GNI per capita ($)		370

	1990	1998	1999
People			
Life expectancy (years)	55	60	61
Fertility rate (births per woman)	4.1	3.3	3.2
Infant mortality rate (per 1,000 live births)	91	66	61
Under 5 mortality rate (per 1,000 children)	136	94	89
Child malnutrition (% of children under 5)	66	56	..
Urban population (% of total)	19	23	24
Rural population density (per km^2 arable land)	975	1,204	..
Illiteracy male (% of people 15 and above)	54	49	48
Illiteracy female (% of people 15 and above)	77	71	71
Net primary enrollment (% of relevant age group)	64	..	..
Net secondary enrollment (% of relevant age group)	18	..	..
Girls in primary school (% of enrollment)	45	..	..
Girls in secondary school (% of enrollment)	33	..	..
Environment			
Forests (1,000 sq. km.)	12	..	13
Deforestation (% change 1990-2000)			-1.3
Water use (% of total resources)	..	..	1.2
CO_2 emissions (metric tons per capita)	0.1	0.2	..
Access to improved water source (% of urban pop.)	98	..	99
Access to sanitation (% of urban population)	78	77	82
Energy use per capita (kg of oil equivalent)	145	159	..
Electricity use per capita (kWh)	43	81	..
Economy			
GDP ($ millions)	30,129	44,092	45,961
GDP growth (annual %)	6.6	5.2	4.9
GDP implicit price deflator (annual % growth)	4.9	5.3	4.6
Value added in agriculture (% of GDP)	29.4	24.5	25.3
Value added in industry (% of GDP)	20.9	24.8	24.3
Value added in services (% of GDP)	49.7	50.7	50.5
Exports of goods and services (% of GDP)	6.2	13.3	13.2
Imports of goods and services (% of GDP)	13.6	18.3	18.7
Gross domestic investment (% of GDP)	17.1	21.6	22.2
Central government revenues (% of GDP)	8.3	..	..
Overall budget deficit (% of GDP)	-0.3	..	..
Money and quasi money (annual % growth)	10.4	11.4	15.5
Technology and infrastructure			
Telephone mainlines (per 1,000 people)	2	3	3
Cost of 3 min local call ($)	0.04	0.03	0.03
Personal computers (per 1,000 people)	..	1.0	1.0
Internet users (thousands)	..	5	50
Paved roads (% of total)	7	10	..
Aircraft departures (thousands)	13	5	6
Trade and finance			
Trade as share of PPP GDP (%)	4.5	6.8	6.8
Trade growth less GDP growth (average %, 1989-99)			6.9
High-technology exports (% of manufactured exports)	0	0	..
Net barter terms of trade (1995=100)	115	103	..
Foreign direct investment ($ millions)	3	190	179
Present value of debt ($ millions)			10,988
Total debt service ($ millions)	776	681	788
Short term debt ($ millions)	156	150	255
Aid per capita ($)	19	10	9

Latin America & Caribbean   **Upper middle income**

Population (thousands)	267	Population growth (%)	0.4
Surface area (1,000 sq km)	0.4	Population per sq km	620
GNI ($ millions)	2,294	GNI per capita ($)	8,600

	1990	1998	1999
People			
Life expectancy (years)	75	76	76
Fertility rate (births per woman)	1.7	1.8	1.8
Infant mortality rate (per 1,000 live births)	12	14	14
Under 5 mortality rate (per 1,000 children)	13	17	18
Child malnutrition (% of children under 5)	..	..	..
Urban population (% of total)	45	49	49
Rural population density (per km^2 arable land)	890	848	..
Illiteracy male (% of people 15 and above)	..	..	..
Illiteracy female (% of people 15 and above)	..	..	..
Net primary enrollment (% of relevant age group)	78	..	..
Net secondary enrollment (% of relevant age group)	75	..	..
Girls in primary school (% of enrollment)	49	..	..
Girls in secondary school (% of enrollment)	47	..	..
Environment			
Forests (1,000 sq. km.)	0	..	0
Deforestation (% change 1990-2000)			0.0
Water use (% of total resources)	..	..	80.0
CO_2 emissions (metric tons per capita)	4.6	3.7	..
Access to improved water source (% of urban pop.)	100	100	100
Access to sanitation (% of urban population)	100	100	100
Energy use per capita (kg of oil equivalent)	..	..	..
Electricity use per capita (kWh)	..	..	..
Economy			
GDP ($ millions)	1,710	2,365	2,476
GDP growth (annual %)	-4.8	4.1	1.3
GDP implicit price deflator (annual % growth)	5.5	3.6	3.4
Value added in agriculture (% of GDP)	7.4	5.8	6.1
Value added in industry (% of GDP)	19.7	21.6	21.5
Value added in services (% of GDP)	72.9	72.6	72.4
Exports of goods and services (% of GDP)	49.1	53.9	50.4
Imports of goods and services (% of GDP)	51.7	56.1	55.4
Gross domestic investment (% of GDP)	18.8	18.5	19.4
Central government revenues (% of GDP)	32.7	..	..
Overall budget deficit (% of GDP)	-1.0	..	..
Money and quasi money (annual % growth)	13.8	7.6	12.1
Technology and infrastructure			
Telephone mainlines (per 1,000 people)	281	422	427
Cost of 3 min local call ($)	0.00	0.00	0.00
Personal computers (per 1,000 people)	..	74.6	78.1
Internet users (thousands)	..	5	6
Paved roads (% of total)	87	99	99
Aircraft departures (thousands)	1	..	..
Trade and finance			
Trade as share of PPP GDP (%)	31.2	34.1	32.7
Trade growth less GDP growth (average %, 1989-99)			2.6
High-technology exports (% of manufactured exports)	20	21	25
Net barter terms of trade (1995=100)	90	96	..
Foreign direct investment ($ millions)	11	16	17
Present value of debt ($ millions)			596
Total debt service ($ millions)	141	87	96
Short term debt ($ millions)	178	220	230
Aid per capita ($)	11	59	-8

Population (millions)	10	Population growth (%)		-0.9
Surface area (1,000 sq km)	208	Population per sq km		48
GNI ($ millions)	26,299	GNI per capita ($)		2,620

	1990	1998	1999
People			
Life expectancy (years)	71	68	68
Fertility rate (births per woman)	1.9	1.3	1.3
Infant mortality rate (per 1,000 live births)	12	11	11
Under 5 mortality rate (per 1,000 children)	16	14	14
Child malnutrition (% of children under 5)	..	..	..
Urban population (% of total)	66	70	71
Rural population density (per km^2 arable land)	55	49	..
Illiteracy male (% of people 15 and above)	0	0	0
Illiteracy female (% of people 15 and above)	1	1	1
Net primary enrollment (% of relevant age group)	..	85	..
Net secondary enrollment (% of relevant age group)	..	..	..
Girls in primary school (% of enrollment)	..	48	..
Girls in secondary school (% of enrollment)	..	50	..
Environment			
Forests (1,000 sq. km.)	68	..	94
Deforestation (% change 1990-2000)			-3.2
Water use (% of total resources)	..	..	4.7
CO_2 emissions (metric tons per capita)	9.3	6.1	..
Access to improved water source (% of urban pop.)	..	..	100
Access to sanitation (% of urban population)	..	..	..
Energy use per capita (kg of oil equivalent)	3,867	2,614	..
Electricity use per capita (kWh)	3,309	2,761	..
Economy			
GDP ($ millions)	34,911	24,798	26,815
GDP growth (annual %)	-2.2	8.3	3.4
GDP implicit price deflator (annual % growth)	10.6	74.2	322.0
Value added in agriculture (% of GDP)	23.8	12.5	12.9
Value added in industry (% of GDP)	47.2	43.0	42.1
Value added in services (% of GDP)	29.0	44.4	45.0
Exports of goods and services (% of GDP)	46.3	62.0	61.8
Imports of goods and services (% of GDP)	44.1	68.0	64.7
Gross domestic investment (% of GDP)	26.8	26.1	24.0
Central government revenues (% of GDP)	31.8	31.2	30.3
Overall budget deficit (% of GDP)	-5.1	-0.9	-2.1
Money and quasi money (annual % growth)	..	276.0	132.7
Technology and infrastructure			
Telephone mainlines (per 1,000 people)	153	243	257
Cost of 3 min local call ($)	..	0.00	0.01
Personal computers (per 1,000 people)	..	..	..
Internet users (thousands)	..	8	50
Paved roads (% of total)	96	96	95
Aircraft departures (thousands)	..	6	6
Trade and finance			
Trade as share of PPP GDP (%)	..	23.8	18.2
Trade growth less GDP growth (average %, 1989-99)			-5.2
High-technology exports (% of manufactured exports)	..	4	4
Net barter terms of trade (1995=100)	..	..	..
Foreign direct investment ($ millions)	0	144	225
Present value of debt ($ millions)			1,093
Total debt service ($ millions)	..	157	219
Short term debt ($ millions)	..	111	93
Aid per capita ($)	18	3	2

41

BELGIUM

Population (millions)	10	Population growth (%)	0.2
Surface area (1,000 sq km)	33	Population per sq km	312
GNI ($ millions)	252,051	GNI per capita ($)	24,650

	1990	1998	1999
People			
Life expectancy (years)	76	78	78
Fertility rate (births per woman)	1.6	1.6	1.6
Infant mortality rate (per 1,000 live births)	8	6	5
Under 5 mortality rate (per 1,000 children)	9	7	6
Child malnutrition (% of children under 5)	..	..	..
Urban population (% of total)	97	97	97
Rural population density (per km^2 arable land)	46	35	..
Illiteracy male (% of people 15 and above)	..	..	..
Illiteracy female (% of people 15 and above)	..	..	..
Net primary enrollment (% of relevant age group)	97	98	..
Net secondary enrollment (% of relevant age group)	88	88	..
Girls in primary school (% of enrollment)	49	49	..
Girls in secondary school (% of enrollment)	49	51	..
Environment			
Forests (1,000 sq. km.)	7	..	7
Deforestation (% change 1990-2000)			
Water use (% of total resources)	..	..	..
CO_2 emissions (metric tons per capita)	10.1	10.5	..
Access to improved water source (% of urban pop.)	..	..	..
Access to sanitation (% of urban population)	..	..	..
Energy use per capita (kg of oil equivalent)	4,858	5,719	..
Electricity use per capita (kWh)	5,817	7,249	..
Economy			
GDP ($ millions)	197,787	250,391	248,404
GDP growth (annual %)	3.0	2.7	2.5
GDP implicit price deflator (annual % growth)	3.1	1.6	0.9
Value added in agriculture (% of GDP)	2.4	1.3	1.2
Value added in industry (% of GDP)	28.5	25.7	25.3
Value added in services (% of GDP)	69.1	73.0	73.5
Exports of goods and services (% of GDP)	71.1	75.6	76.1
Imports of goods and services (% of GDP)	69.5	71.5	72.1
Gross domestic investment (% of GDP)	23.1	21.1	21.2
Central government revenues (% of GDP)	42.6	43.9	..
Overall budget deficit (% of GDP)	-5.5	-1.8	..
Money and quasi money (annual % growth)	..	..	..
Technology and infrastructure			
Telephone mainlines (per 1,000 people)	393	500	502
Cost of 3 min local call ($)	0.17	0.16	0.16
Personal computers (per 1,000 people)	87.9	287.1	315.2
Internet users (thousands)	2	800	1,400
Paved roads (% of total)	81	81	..
Aircraft departures (thousands)	67	213	233
Trade and finance			
Trade as share of PPP GDP (%)	..	..	129.6
Trade growth less GDP growth (average %, 1989-99)			2.6
High-technology exports (% of manufactured exports)	5	8	..
Net barter terms of trade (1995=100)	..	101	98
Foreign direct investment ($ millions)	..	..	..
Present value of debt ($ millions)			..
Total debt service ($ millions)	..	..	..
Short term debt ($ millions)	..	..	..
Aid per capita ($)			

42

Latin America & Caribbean — **Lower middle income**

Population (thousands)	247	Population growth (%)		3.4
Surface area (1,000 sq km)	23.0	Population per sq km		11
GNI ($ millions)	673	GNI per capita ($)		2,730

	1990	1998	1999
People			
Life expectancy (years)	71	73	72
Fertility rate (births per woman)	4.4	3.7	3.5
Infant mortality rate (per 1,000 live births)	34	29	28
Under 5 mortality rate (per 1,000 children)	49	40	37
Child malnutrition (% of children under 5)	6	..	..
Urban population (% of total)	48	53	53
Rural population density (per km^2 arable land)	199	176	..
Illiteracy male (% of people 15 and above)	10	7	7
Illiteracy female (% of people 15 and above)	12	8	7
Net primary enrollment (% of relevant age group)	94	99	..
Net secondary enrollment (% of relevant age group)	29	..	..
Girls in primary school (% of enrollment)	48	49	..
Girls in secondary school (% of enrollment)	53	52	..
Environment			
Forests (1,000 sq. km.)	17	..	13
Deforestation (% change 1990-2000)			2.3
Water use (% of total resources)			0.6
CO$_2$ emissions (metric tons per capita)	1.6	1.7	..
Access to improved water source (% of urban pop.)	..	..	83
Access to sanitation (% of urban population)	..	23	59
Energy use per capita (kg of oil equivalent)	..	..	..
Electricity use per capita (kWh)	..	..	..
Economy			
GDP ($ millions)	403	676	730
GDP growth (annual %)	10.6	4.5	4.5
GDP implicit price deflator (annual % growth)	0.3	-0.3	3.5
Value added in agriculture (% of GDP)	20.7	18.9	18.6
Value added in industry (% of GDP)	25.4	25.5	25.0
Value added in services (% of GDP)	53.8	55.6	56.3
Exports of goods and services (% of GDP)	63.8	50.0	48.8
Imports of goods and services (% of GDP)	61.6	57.2	58.4
Gross domestic investment (% of GDP)	28.4	23.0	24.2
Central government revenues (% of GDP)	..	..	..
Overall budget deficit (% of GDP)	..	..	..
Money and quasi money (annual % growth)	15.2	5.9	15.8
Technology and infrastructure			
Telephone mainlines (per 1,000 people)	92	138	156
Cost of 3 min local call ($)	0.07	0.07	0.07
Personal computers (per 1,000 people)	..	87.0	106.4
Internet users (thousands)	..	10	12
Paved roads (% of total)	..	17	..
Aircraft departures (thousands)	..	..	..
Trade and finance			
Trade as share of PPP GDP (%)	43.6	41.6	43.5
Trade growth less GDP growth (average %, 1989-99)			-2.2
High-technology exports (% of manufactured exports)	..	0	..
Net barter terms of trade (1995=100)	..	..	..
Foreign direct investment ($ millions)	17	18	4
Present value of debt ($ millions)			329
Total debt service ($ millions)	20	46	43
Short term debt ($ millions)	6	55	57
Aid per capita ($)	160	63	186

43

BENIN

Population (millions)	6	Population growth (%)	2.7
Surface area (1,000 sq km)	113	Population per sq km	55
GNI ($ millions)	2,320	GNI per capita ($)	380

	1990	1998	1999
People			
Life expectancy (years)	52	53	53
Fertility rate (births per woman)	6.6	5.8	5.6
Infant mortality rate (per 1,000 live births)	104	88	87
Under 5 mortality rate (per 1,000 children)	185	149	145
Child malnutrition (% of children under 5)	..	29	..
Urban population (% of total)	35	41	42
Rural population density (per km^2 arable land)	192	207	..
Illiteracy male (% of people 15 and above)	59	46	45
Illiteracy female (% of people 15 and above)	84	77	76
Net primary enrollment (% of relevant age group)	49	63	..
Net secondary enrollment (% of relevant age group)	..	..	..
Girls in primary school (% of enrollment)	33	38	..
Girls in secondary school (% of enrollment)	..	..	..
Environment			
Forests (1,000 sq. km.)	33	..	27
Deforestation (% change 1990-2000)			2.3
Water use (% of total resources)			0.6
CO_2 emissions (metric tons per capita)	0.2	0.2	..
Access to improved water source (% of urban pop.)	..	41	74
Access to sanitation (% of urban population)	46	54	46
Energy use per capita (kg of oil equivalent)	354	377	..
Electricity use per capita (kWh)	37	46	..
Economy			
GDP ($ millions)	1,845	2,306	2,369
GDP growth (annual %)	3.2	4.5	5.0
GDP implicit price deflator (annual % growth)	1.6	4.2	2.1
Value added in agriculture (% of GDP)	36.1	38.6	37.9
Value added in industry (% of GDP)	13.2	13.5	13.8
Value added in services (% of GDP)	50.7	47.9	48.3
Exports of goods and services (% of GDP)	14.3	17.3	16.7
Imports of goods and services (% of GDP)	26.3	27.8	28.0
Gross domestic investment (% of GDP)	14.2	17.1	17.6
Central government revenues (% of GDP)	..	..	..
Overall budget deficit (% of GDP)	..	..	..
Money and quasi money (annual % growth)	28.6	-3.6	34.8
Technology and infrastructure			
Telephone mainlines (per 1,000 people)	3	7	..
Cost of 3 min local call ($)	0.22	0.11	..
Personal computers (per 1,000 people)	..	1.2	1.5
Internet users (thousands)	..	2	10
Paved roads (% of total)	20	20	..
Aircraft departures (thousands)	1	2	2
Trade and finance			
Trade as share of PPP GDP (%)	16.6	20.3	18.1
Trade growth less GDP growth (average %, 1989-99)			-1.5
High-technology exports (% of manufactured exports)	..	0	..
Net barter terms of trade (1995=100)	100	95	..
Foreign direct investment ($ millions)	1	38	31
Present value of debt ($ millions)			950
Total debt service ($ millions)	38	61	70
Short term debt ($ millions)	55	86	122
Aid per capita ($)	57	35	34

44

BERMUDA

Population (thousands)	64	Population growth (%)	..
Surface area (1,000 sq km)	0.1	Population per sq km	1,280
GNI ($ millions)	..	GNI per capita ($)	..

	1990	1998	1999
People			
Life expectancy (years)	..	..	..
Fertility rate (births per woman)	..	..	..
Infant mortality rate (per 1,000 live births)	..	..	..
Under 5 mortality rate (per 1,000 children)	..	..	..
Child malnutrition (% of children under 5)	..	..	..
Urban population (% of total)	100	100	100
Rural population density (per km^2 arable land)	..	..	..
Illiteracy male (% of people 15 and above)	..	..	..
Illiteracy female (% of people 15 and above)	..	..	..
Net primary enrollment (% of relevant age group)	..	..	..
Net secondary enrollment (% of relevant age group)	..	..	..
Girls in primary school (% of enrollment)	..	*49*	..
Girls in secondary school (% of enrollment)	..	..	..
Environment			
Forests (1,000 sq. km.)	..	..	
Deforestation (% change 1990-2000)			..
Water use (% of total resources)	..	..	
CO_2 emissions (metric tons per capita)	..	..	..
Access to improved water source (% of urban pop.)	..	..	..
Access to sanitation (% of urban population)	..	..	..
Energy use per capita (kg of oil equivalent)	..	..	..
Electricity use per capita (kWh)	..	..	..
Economy			
GDP ($ millions)	1,592	*2,370*	..
GDP growth (annual %)	0.0	1.5	..
GDP implicit price deflator (annual % growth)	6.0	2.2	..
Value added in agriculture (% of GDP)	..	..	..
Value added in industry (% of GDP)	..	..	..
Value added in services (% of GDP)	..	..	..
Exports of goods and services (% of GDP)	..	..	..
Imports of goods and services (% of GDP)	..	..	..
Gross domestic investment (% of GDP)	..	..	..
Central government revenues (% of GDP)	..	..	..
Overall budget deficit (% of GDP)	..	..	..
Money and quasi money (annual % growth)	..	..	..
Technology and infrastructure			
Telephone mainlines (per 1,000 people)	617	840	857
Cost of 3 min local call ($)	0.14	*0.15*	..
Personal computers (per 1,000 people)	..	406.3	436.8
Internet users (thousands)	..	20	25
Paved roads (% of total)	..	..	..
Aircraft departures (thousands)	..	..	..
Trade and finance			
Trade as share of PPP GDP (%)	..	..	..
Trade growth less GDP growth (average %, 1989-99)			..
High-technology exports (% of manufactured exports)	..	..	..
Net barter terms of trade (1995=100)	..	..	..
Foreign direct investment ($ millions)	..	..	..
Present value of debt ($ millions)			..
Total debt service ($ millions)	..	..	..
Short term debt ($ millions)	..	..	..
Aid per capita ($)	..	..	1

BHUTAN

Population (thousands)	782	Population growth (%)	2.9
Surface area (1,000 sq km)	47.0	Population per sq km	17
GNI ($ millions)	399	GNI per capita ($)	510

	1990	1998	1999
People			
Life expectancy (years)	58	61	61
Fertility rate (births per woman)	5.8	5.8	5.7
Infant mortality rate (per 1,000 live births)	75	63	59
Under 5 mortality rate (per 1,000 children)	..	..	..
Child malnutrition (% of children under 5)	38	..	19
Urban population (% of total)	5	7	7
Rural population density (per km² arable land)	503	506	..
Illiteracy male (% of people 15 and above)	..	..	..
Illiteracy female (% of people 15 and above)	..	..	..
Net primary enrollment (% of relevant age group)	..	..	..
Net secondary enrollment (% of relevant age group)	..	..	..
Girls in primary school (% of enrollment)	37	43	..
Girls in secondary school (% of enrollment)	..	..	..
Environment			
Forests (1,000 sq. km.)	30	..	30
Deforestation (% change 1990-2000)			0.0
Water use (% of total resources)	..		0.0
CO_2 emissions (metric tons per capita)	0.2	0.6	..
Access to improved water source (% of urban pop.)	..	75	86
Access to sanitation (% of urban population)	..	66	65
Energy use per capita (kg of oil equivalent)	..	..	..
Electricity use per capita (kWh)	..	..	..
Economy			
GDP ($ millions)	285	398	440
GDP growth (annual %)	7.7	7.1	7.0
GDP implicit price deflator (annual % growth)	5.6	5.9	7.8
Value added in agriculture (% of GDP)	43.2	38.2	37.7
Value added in industry (% of GDP)	25.3	36.5	36.7
Value added in services (% of GDP)	31.5	25.4	25.6
Exports of goods and services (% of GDP)	28.3	33.2	33.0
Imports of goods and services (% of GDP)	32.3	42.6	42.0
Gross domestic investment (% of GDP)	36.1	47.3	48.5
Central government revenues (% of GDP)	19.0	19.1	19.3
Overall budget deficit (% of GDP)	-7.8	0.9	-1.6
Money and quasi money (annual % growth)	10.5	13.9	32.0
Technology and infrastructure			
Telephone mainlines (per 1,000 people)	4	16	18
Cost of 3 min local call ($)	0.03	0.02	..
Personal computers (per 1,000 people)	..	3.9	4.6
Internet users (thousands)	..	..	1
Paved roads (% of total)	77	61	..
Aircraft departures (thousands)	1	1	1
Trade and finance			
Trade as share of PPP GDP (%)	34.4	24.9	..
Trade growth less GDP growth (average %, 1989-99)			..
High-technology exports (% of manufactured exports)	..	..	..
Net barter terms of trade (1995=100)	..	..	..
Foreign direct investment ($ millions)	0	0	0
Present value of debt ($ millions)			138
Total debt service ($ millions)	5	9	7
Short term debt ($ millions)	3	0	2
Aid per capita ($)	78	73	85

46

BOLIVIA

Latin America & Caribbean   **Lower middle income**

Population (millions)	8	Population growth (%)		2.3
Surface area (1,000 sq km)	1,099	Population per sq km		8
GNI ($ millions)	8,092	GNI per capita ($)		990

	1990	1998	1999
People			
Life expectancy (years)	58	*61*	62
Fertility rate (births per woman)	4.8	*4.2*	4.0
Infant mortality rate (per 1,000 live births)	80	*62*	59
Under 5 mortality rate (per 1,000 children)	120	*85*	83
Child malnutrition (% of children under 5)	11	8	..
Urban population (% of total)	56	61	62
Rural population density (per km² arable land)	154	156	..
Illiteracy male (% of people 15 and above)	13	9	8
Illiteracy female (% of people 15 and above)	30	22	21
Net primary enrollment (% of relevant age group)	91	..	..
Net secondary enrollment (% of relevant age group)	29	..	..
Girls in primary school (% of enrollment)	47	..	..
Girls in secondary school (% of enrollment)	46	..	..
Environment			
Forests (1,000 sq. km.)	547	..	*531*
Deforestation (% change 1990-2000)			*0.3*
Water use (% of total resources)	..	..	0.4
CO_2 emissions (metric tons per capita)	0.9	*1.4*	..
Access to improved water source (% of urban pop.)	92	..	*93*
Access to sanitation (% of urban population)	77	77	*82*
Energy use per capita (kg of oil equivalent)	441	581	..
Electricity use per capita (kWh)	274	409	..
Economy			
GDP ($ millions)	4,868	8,515	8,323
GDP growth (annual %)	4.6	5.5	0.6
GDP implicit price deflator (annual % growth)	16.3	7.0	2.8
Value added in agriculture (% of GDP)	25.6	18.9	18.4
Value added in industry (% of GDP)	20.0	18.7	18.1
Value added in services (% of GDP)	54.4	62.4	63.5
Exports of goods and services (% of GDP)	22.8	20.0	17.4
Imports of goods and services (% of GDP)	23.9	32.4	27.1
Gross domestic investment (% of GDP)	12.5	23.1	18.9
Central government revenues (% of GDP)	13.7	17.7	17.8
Overall budget deficit (% of GDP)	-1.7	-2.3	-2.3
Money and quasi money (annual % growth)	52.8	12.9	5.7
Technology and infrastructure			
Telephone mainlines (per 1,000 people)	28	57	62
Cost of 3 min local call ($)	..	0.09	0.09
Personal computers (per 1,000 people)	2.2	7.5	12.3
Internet users (thousands)	..	17	78
Paved roads (% of total)	4	6	..
Aircraft departures (thousands)	16	30	24
Trade and finance			
Trade as share of PPP GDP (%)	13.4	16.6	14.6
Trade growth less GDP growth (average %, 1989-99)			1.9
High-technology exports (% of manufactured exports)	..	..	..
Net barter terms of trade (1995=100)	115	110	..
Foreign direct investment ($ millions)	27	957	1,016
Present value of debt ($ millions)			2,974
Total debt service ($ millions)	385	467	494
Short term debt ($ millions)	154	1,262	1,402
Aid per capita ($)	83	79	70

47

BOSNIA AND HERZEGOVINA

Population (millions)	4	Population growth (%)	3.0
Surface area (1,000 sq km)	51	Population per sq km	76
GNI ($ millions)	4,706	GNI per capita ($)	1,210

	1990	1998	1999
People			
Life expectancy (years)	71	73	73
Fertility rate (births per woman)	1.7	1.6	1.6
Infant mortality rate (per 1,000 live births)	15	13	13
Under 5 mortality rate (per 1,000 children)	21	..	18
Child malnutrition (% of children under 5)	..	..	..
Urban population (% of total)	39	42	43
Rural population density (per km^2 arable land)	354	436	..
Illiteracy male (% of people 15 and above)	..	..	..
Illiteracy female (% of people 15 and above)	..	..	..
Net primary enrollment (% of relevant age group)	..	..	..
Net secondary enrollment (% of relevant age group)	..	..	..
Girls in primary school (% of enrollment)	..	..	..
Girls in secondary school (% of enrollment)	..	..	..
Environment			
Forests (1,000 sq. km.)	23	..	23
Deforestation (% change 1990-2000)			0.0
Water use (% of total resources)	..	..	..
CO_2 emissions (metric tons per capita)	1.2	1.2	..
Access to improved water source (% of urban pop.)	..	..	..
Access to sanitation (% of urban population)	..	71	..
Energy use per capita (kg of oil equivalent)	1,093	517	..
Electricity use per capita (kWh)	2,962	539	..
Economy			
GDP ($ millions)	..	4,058	4,387
GDP growth (annual %)	..	14.9	12.8
GDP implicit price deflator (annual % growth)	..	1.6	-0.2
Value added in agriculture (% of GDP)	..	15.8	15.5
Value added in industry (% of GDP)	..	27.5	26.7
Value added in services (% of GDP)	..	56.7	57.8
Exports of goods and services (% of GDP)	..	31.0	27.4
Imports of goods and services (% of GDP)	..	70.0	62.2
Gross domestic investment (% of GDP)	..	38.0	34.9
Central government revenues (% of GDP)	..	..	..
Overall budget deficit (% of GDP)	..	..	..
Money and quasi money (annual % growth)	..	..	..
Technology and infrastructure			
Telephone mainlines (per 1,000 people)	140	91	96
Cost of 3 min local call ($)	..	0.03	..
Personal computers (per 1,000 people)	..	..	..
Internet users (thousands)	..	1	4
Paved roads (% of total)	54	52	..
Aircraft departures (thousands)	..	1	4
Trade and finance			
Trade as share of PPP GDP (%)	..	..	..
Trade growth less GDP growth (average %, 1989-99)			-0.7
High-technology exports (% of manufactured exports)	..	..	..
Net barter terms of trade (1995=100)	..	..	..
Foreign direct investment ($ millions)	..	..	0
Present value of debt ($ millions)			1,627
Total debt service ($ millions)	..	..	416
Short term debt ($ millions)	..	81	40
Aid per capita ($)	..	238	274

48

Population (millions)	2	Population growth (%)	1.7
Surface area (1,000 sq km)	582	Population per sq km	3
GNI ($ millions)	5,139	GNI per capita ($)	3,240

	1990	1998	1999
People			
Life expectancy (years)	57	47	39
Fertility rate (births per woman)	5.1	4.3	4.1
Infant mortality rate (per 1,000 live births)	55	58	58
Under 5 mortality rate (per 1,000 children)	62	88	95
Child malnutrition (% of children under 5)	..	17	..
Urban population (% of total)	42	49	50
Rural population density (per km^2 arable land)	179	231	..
Illiteracy male (% of people 15 and above)	34	27	26
Illiteracy female (% of people 15 and above)	30	22	21
Net primary enrollment (% of relevant age group)	93	81	..
Net secondary enrollment (% of relevant age group)	34	45	..
Girls in primary school (% of enrollment)	52	50	..
Girls in secondary school (% of enrollment)	53	52	..
Environment			
Forests (1,000 sq. km.)	136	..	124
Deforestation (% change 1990-2000)			0.9
Water use (% of total resources)	..	..	0.7
CO_2 emissions (metric tons per capita)	1.7	2.2	..
Access to improved water source (% of urban pop.)	100	100	100
Access to sanitation (% of urban population)	84	91	..
Energy use per capita (kg of oil equivalent)	..	..	..
Electricity use per capita (kWh)	..	..	..
Economy			
GDP ($ millions)	3,766	4,876	5,996
GDP growth (annual %)	7.2	3.5	4.5
GDP implicit price deflator (annual % growth)	5.6	7.9	7.5
Value added in agriculture (% of GDP)	4.6	3.6	3.6
Value added in industry (% of GDP)	56.4	46.1	45.4
Value added in services (% of GDP)	39.0	50.4	51.0
Exports of goods and services (% of GDP)	55.4	35.0	27.5
Imports of goods and services (% of GDP)	50.1	33.8	33.1
Gross domestic investment (% of GDP)	31.7	20.6	19.7
Central government revenues (% of GDP)	51.3	44.4	..
Overall budget deficit (% of GDP)	11.3	8.4	..
Money and quasi money (annual % growth)	-14.0	39.4	26.3
Technology and infrastructure			
Telephone mainlines (per 1,000 people)	21	65	77
Cost of 3 min local call ($)	0.04	0.03	0.02
Personal computers (per 1,000 people)	..	25.5	31.0
Internet users (thousands)	0	10	12
Paved roads (% of total)	32	56	55
Aircraft departures (thousands)	6	5	6
Trade and finance			
Trade as share of PPP GDP (%)	59.3	42.3	44.0
Trade growth less GDP growth (average %, 1989-99)			-3.6
High-technology exports (% of manufactured exports)	..	..	..
Net barter terms of trade (1995=100)	110	91	..
Foreign direct investment ($ millions)	95	95	37
Present value of debt ($ millions)			385
Total debt service ($ millions)	106	77	83
Short term debt ($ millions)	6	7	20
Aid per capita ($)	115	68	38

BRAZIL

Latin America & Caribbean · Upper middle income

Population (millions)	168	Population growth (%)	1.3
Surface area (1,000 sq km)	8,547	Population per sq km	20
GNI ($ millions)	730,424	GNI per capita ($)	4,350

	1990	1998	1999
People			
Life expectancy (years)	65	67	67
Fertility rate (births per woman)	2.7	2.3	2.2
Infant mortality rate (per 1,000 live births)	48	34	32
Under 5 mortality rate (per 1,000 children)	58	44	40
Child malnutrition (% of children under 5)	7	6	..
Urban population (% of total)	75	80	81
Rural population density (per km^2 arable land)	82	62	..
Illiteracy male (% of people 15 and above)	18	16	15
Illiteracy female (% of people 15 and above)	20	16	15
Net primary enrollment (% of relevant age group)	86	90	..
Net secondary enrollment (% of relevant age group)	16	20	..
Girls in primary school (% of enrollment)	51	..	..
Girls in secondary school (% of enrollment)	..	..	..
Environment			
Forests (1,000 sq. km.)	5,547	..	5,325
Deforestation (% change 1990-2000)			0.4
Water use (% of total resources)	..	..	1.0
CO$_2$ emissions (metric tons per capita)	1.5	1.9	..
Access to improved water source (% of urban pop.)	93	..	95
Access to sanitation (% of urban population)	84	74	85
Energy use per capita (kg of oil equivalent)	893	1,055	..
Electricity use per capita (kWh)	1,425	1,793	..
Economy			
GDP ($ millions)	464,989	774,967	751,505
GDP growth (annual %)	-4.3	-0.1	0.8
GDP implicit price deflator (annual % growth)	2,509.5	3.9	5.9
Value added in agriculture (% of GDP)	8.1	8.4	8.6
Value added in industry (% of GDP)	38.7	28.8	30.6
Value added in services (% of GDP)	53.2	62.8	60.8
Exports of goods and services (% of GDP)	8.2	7.4	10.6
Imports of goods and services (% of GDP)	7.0	10.1	11.7
Gross domestic investment (% of GDP)	20.2	21.3	20.4
Central government revenues (% of GDP)	31.4	24.6	..
Overall budget deficit (% of GDP)	-5.8	-7.3	..
Money and quasi money (annual % growth)	1,289.2	10.0	7.4
Technology and infrastructure			
Telephone mainlines (per 1,000 people)	65	121	149
Cost of 3 min local call ($)	..	0.08	0.03
Personal computers (per 1,000 people)	3.1	30.1	36.3
Internet users (thousands)	5	2,500	3,500
Paved roads (% of total)	10	9	10
Aircraft departures (thousands)	416	666	678
Trade and finance			
Trade as share of PPP GDP (%)	6.5	9.8	8.4
Trade growth less GDP growth (average %, 1989-99)			6.2
High-technology exports (% of manufactured exports)	7	10	13
Net barter terms of trade (1995=100)	60	105	..
Foreign direct investment ($ millions)	989	31,913	32,659
Present value of debt ($ millions)			242,739
Total debt service ($ millions)	8,168	45,403	67,522
Short term debt ($ millions)	23,716	30,122	29,521
Aid per capita ($)	1	2	1

50

High income

Population (thousands)	322	Population growth (%)	2.1
Surface area (1,000 sq km)	5.8	Population per sq km	61
GNI ($ millions)	..	GNI per capita ($)	..

	1990	1998	1999
People			
Life expectancy (years)	74	76	76
Fertility rate (births per woman)	3.2	2.8	2.7
Infant mortality rate (per 1,000 live births)	9	9	9
Under 5 mortality rate (per 1,000 children)	..	11	11
Child malnutrition (% of children under 5)	..	..	..
Urban population (% of total)	66	71	72
Rural population density (per km² arable land)	2,930	3,044	..
Illiteracy male (% of people 15 and above)	9	6	6
Illiteracy female (% of people 15 and above)	21	13	13
Net primary enrollment (% of relevant age group)	91	91	..
Net secondary enrollment (% of relevant age group)	71	68	..
Girls in primary school (% of enrollment)	47	47	..
Girls in secondary school (% of enrollment)	50	52	..
Environment			
Forests (1,000 sq. km.)	5	..	4
Deforestation (% change 1990-2000)			0.2
Water use (% of total resources)	..	..	1.1
CO_2 emissions (metric tons per capita)	22.6	17.7	..
Access to improved water source (% of urban pop.)	..	100	..
Access to sanitation (% of urban population)	..	71	..
Energy use per capita (kg of oil equivalent)	5,741	6,610	..
Electricity use per capita (kWh)	3,934	7,676	..
Economy			
GDP ($ millions)	3,591	4,846	..
GDP growth (annual %)	2.7	1.0	..
GDP implicit price deflator (annual % growth)	8.4	-0.2	..
Value added in agriculture (% of GDP)	2.4	2.8	..
Value added in industry (% of GDP)	54.8	44.4	..
Value added in services (% of GDP)	42.9	52.7	..
Exports of goods and services (% of GDP)	..	..	..
Imports of goods and services (% of GDP)	..	..	..
Gross domestic investment (% of GDP)	..	..	..
Central government revenues (% of GDP)	..	..	..
Overall budget deficit (% of GDP)	..	..	..
Money and quasi money (annual % growth)	..	..	..
Technology and infrastructure			
Telephone mainlines (per 1,000 people)	136	247	246
Cost of 3 min local call ($)	0.00	0.00	0.00
Personal computers (per 1,000 people)	11.2	54.0	62.1
Internet users (thousands)	..	20	25
Paved roads (% of total)	31	75	..
Aircraft departures (thousands)	4	14	16
Trade and finance			
Trade as share of PPP GDP (%)	..	..	..
Trade growth less GDP growth (average %, 1989-99)			..
High-technology exports (% of manufactured exports)	..	9	..
Net barter terms of trade (1995=100)	127	82	..
Foreign direct investment ($ millions)	..	..	..
Present value of debt ($ millions)			..
Total debt service ($ millions)	..	..	..
Short term debt ($ millions)	..	..	..
Aid per capita ($)	15	1	4

51

BULGARIA

Population (millions)	8	Population growth (%)	-0.6
Surface area (1,000 sq km)	111	Population per sq km	74
GNI ($ millions)	11,572	GNI per capita ($)	1,410

	1990	1998	1999
People			
Life expectancy (years)	71	71	71
Fertility rate (births per woman)	1.8	1.1	1.1
Infant mortality rate (per 1,000 live births)	15	14	14
Under 5 mortality rate (per 1,000 children)	19	15	17
Child malnutrition (% of children under 5)	..	..	..
Urban population (% of total)	67	69	69
Rural population density (per km^2 arable land)	76	60	..
Illiteracy male (% of people 15 and above)	2	1	1
Illiteracy female (% of people 15 and above)	4	2	2
Net primary enrollment (% of relevant age group)	86	92	..
Net secondary enrollment (% of relevant age group)	63	74	..
Girls in primary school (% of enrollment)	48	48	..
Girls in secondary school (% of enrollment)	50	48	..
Environment			
Forests (1,000 sq. km.)	35	..	37
Deforestation (% change 1990-2000)			-0.6
Water use (% of total resources)			..
CO_2 emissions (metric tons per capita)	8.9	6.1	..
Access to improved water source (% of urban pop.)	..	..	100
Access to sanitation (% of urban population)	..	..	100
Energy use per capita (kg of oil equivalent)	3,111	2,418	..
Electricity use per capita (kWh)	4,046	3,166	..
Economy			
GDP ($ millions)	20,726	12,258	12,403
GDP growth (annual %)	-9.1	3.5	2.4
GDP implicit price deflator (annual % growth)	26.2	22.2	3.1
Value added in agriculture (% of GDP)	17.7	18.7	15.1
Value added in industry (% of GDP)	51.3	25.5	23.4
Value added in services (% of GDP)	31.0	55.7	61.5
Exports of goods and services (% of GDP)	33.1	45.2	44.1
Imports of goods and services (% of GDP)	36.7	46.3	51.9
Gross domestic investment (% of GDP)	25.6	14.7	19.0
Central government revenues (% of GDP)	49.1	34.2	35.2
Overall budget deficit (% of GDP)	-8.3	2.8	1.5
Money and quasi money (annual % growth)	53.8	11.6	11.9
Technology and infrastructure			
Telephone mainlines (per 1,000 people)	242	329	354
Cost of 3 min local call ($)	0.09	0.00	..
Personal computers (per 1,000 people)	10.5	24.0	26.6
Internet users (thousands)	..	150	235
Paved roads (% of total)	92	92	92
Aircraft departures (thousands)	37	15	15
Trade and finance			
Trade as share of PPP GDP (%)	20.0	23.3	22.9
Trade growth less GDP growth (average %, 1989-99)			-4.9
High-technology exports (% of manufactured exports)	..	4	..
Net barter terms of trade (1995=100)	100	..	..
Foreign direct investment ($ millions)	4	537	806
Present value of debt ($ millions)			9,508
Total debt service ($ millions)	1,374	1,296	1,156
Short term debt ($ millions)	1,056	419	376
Aid per capita ($)	2	29	32

BURKINA FASO

Population (millions)	11	Population growth (%) 2.4
Surface area (1,000 sq km)	274	Population per sq km 40
GNI ($ millions)	2,602	GNI per capita ($) 240

	1990	1998	1999
People			
Life expectancy (years)	45	*45*	45
Fertility rate (births per woman)	7.0	*6.8*	6.6
Infant mortality rate (per 1,000 live births)	111	*105*	105
Under 5 mortality rate (per 1,000 children)	*229*	*219*	210
Child malnutrition (% of children under 5)	..	*33*	..
Urban population (% of total)	14	17	18
Rural population density (per km^2 arable land)	218	260	..
Illiteracy male (% of people 15 and above)	75	68	67
Illiteracy female (% of people 15 and above)	92	87	87
Net primary enrollment (% of relevant age group)	27	*31*	..
Net secondary enrollment (% of relevant age group)	7	7	..
Girls in primary school (% of enrollment)	*38*	40	..
Girls in secondary school (% of enrollment)	34	..	..
Environment			
Forests (1,000 sq. km.)	72	..	*71*
Deforestation (% change 1990-2000)			*0.2*
Water use (% of total resources)	..	..	2.2
CO$_2$ emissions (metric tons per capita)	0.1	*0.1*	..
Access to improved water source (% of urban pop.)	74	..	84
Access to sanitation (% of urban population)	88	*78*	88
Energy use per capita (kg of oil equivalent)	..	..	..
Electricity use per capita (kWh)	..	..	..
Economy			
GDP ($ millions)	2,765	2,580	2,580
GDP growth (annual %)	-1.5	6.2	5.8
GDP implicit price deflator (annual % growth)	1.4	3.2	-1.4
Value added in agriculture (% of GDP)	32.3	32.0	31.3
Value added in industry (% of GDP)	22.3	27.8	28.3
Value added in services (% of GDP)	45.3	40.1	40.4
Exports of goods and services (% of GDP)	12.7	14.0	11.3
Imports of goods and services (% of GDP)	25.6	30.9	29.4
Gross domestic investment (% of GDP)	20.6	29.6	27.8
Central government revenues (% of GDP)	11.2	*17.1*	..
Overall budget deficit (% of GDP)	-1.3	*3.8*	..
Money and quasi money (annual % growth)	-0.5	1.0	2.6
Technology and infrastructure			
Telephone mainlines (per 1,000 people)	2	4	4
Cost of 3 min local call ($)	..	0.10	0.10
Personal computers (per 1,000 people)	0.1	0.9	1.0
Internet users (thousands)	..	1	4
Paved roads (% of total)	17	*16*	..
Aircraft departures (thousands)	2	3	3
Trade and finance			
Trade as share of PPP GDP (%)	11.0	10.9	8.7
Trade growth less GDP growth (average %, 1989-99)			-1.4
High-technology exports (% of manufactured exports)	..	..	..
Net barter terms of trade (1995=100)	91	91	..
Foreign direct investment ($ millions)	0	10	10
Present value of debt ($ millions)			631
Total debt service ($ millions)	34	53	63
Short term debt ($ millions)	84	59	103
Aid per capita ($)	37	37	36

BURUNDI

Population (millions)	7	Population growth (%)		2.0
Surface area (1,000 sq km)	28	Population per sq km		260
GNI ($ millions)	823	GNI per capita ($)		120

	1990	1998	1999
People			
Life expectancy (years)	44	*42*	42
Fertility rate (births per woman)	6.8	*6.3*	6.1
Infant mortality rate (per 1,000 live births)	119	*110*	105
Under 5 mortality rate (per 1,000 children)	180	*177*	176
Child malnutrition (% of children under 5)	..	..	..
Urban population (% of total)	6	8	9
Rural population density (per km^2 arable land)	631	779	..
Illiteracy male (% of people 15 and above)	50	45	44
Illiteracy female (% of people 15 and above)	73	63	61
Net primary enrollment (% of relevant age group)	*52*	..	..
Net secondary enrollment (% of relevant age group)	*5*	..	..
Girls in primary school (% of enrollment)	*46*	45	44
Girls in secondary school (% of enrollment)	37	..	..
Environment			
Forests (1,000 sq. km.)	2	..	*1*
Deforestation (% change 1990-2000)			*9.0*
Water use (% of total resources)	..	..	2.8
CO$_2$ emissions (metric tons per capita)	0.0	*0.0*	..
Access to improved water source (% of urban pop.)	94	..	96
Access to sanitation (% of urban population)	67	..	79
Energy use per capita (kg of oil equivalent)	..	..	..
Electricity use per capita (kWh)	..	..	..
Economy			
GDP ($ millions)	1,132	878	714
GDP growth (annual %)	3.5	4.8	-1.0
GDP implicit price deflator (annual % growth)	6.0	11.2	3.4
Value added in agriculture (% of GDP)	55.9	54.2	52.2
Value added in industry (% of GDP)	19.0	16.4	17.3
Value added in services (% of GDP)	25.2	29.5	30.5
Exports of goods and services (% of GDP)	7.9	8.1	8.8
Imports of goods and services (% of GDP)	27.8	19.8	18.3
Gross domestic investment (% of GDP)	14.5	8.8	9.1
Central government revenues (% of GDP)	*18.2*	16.9	17.9
Overall budget deficit (% of GDP)	*-3.3*	-4.6	-4.7
Money and quasi money (annual % growth)	9.6	-3.7	47.3
Technology and infrastructure			
Telephone mainlines (per 1,000 people)	2	3	3
Cost of 3 min local call ($)	0.07	0.02	0.03
Personal computers (per 1,000 people)	..	..	..
Internet users (thousands)	..	0	2
Paved roads (% of total)	..	..	..
Aircraft departures (thousands)	1	1	0
Trade and finance			
Trade as share of PPP GDP (%)	7.7	5.9	4.5
Trade growth less GDP growth (average %, 1989-99)			4.1
High-technology exports (% of manufactured exports)	..	..	..
Net barter terms of trade (1995=100)	75	74	..
Foreign direct investment ($ millions)	1	1	0
Present value of debt ($ millions)			677
Total debt service ($ millions)	42	30	29
Short term debt ($ millions)	13	20	70
Aid per capita ($)	48	12	11

CAMBODIA

Population (millions)	12	Population growth (%)	2.2
Surface area (1,000 sq km)	181	Population per sq km	67
GNI ($ millions)	3,023	GNI per capita ($)	260

	1990	1998	1999
People			
Life expectancy (years)	50	54	54
Fertility rate (births per woman)	4.9	4.6	4.4
Infant mortality rate (per 1,000 live births)	122	103	100
Under 5 mortality rate (per 1,000 children)	..	147	143
Child malnutrition (% of children under 5)	..	47	..
Urban population (% of total)	13	15	16
Rural population density (per km^2 arable land)	216	263	..
Illiteracy male (% of people 15 and above)	49	43	41
Illiteracy female (% of people 15 and above)	86	80	79
Net primary enrollment (% of relevant age group)	..	100	..
Net secondary enrollment (% of relevant age group)	..	..	..
Girls in primary school (% of enrollment)	..	45	46
Girls in secondary school (% of enrollment)	..	35	..
Environment			
Forests (1,000 sq. km.)	99	..	93
Deforestation (% change 1990-2000)			0.6
Water use (% of total resources)	..	..	0.1
CO$_2$ emissions (metric tons per capita)	0.0	0.0	..
Access to improved water source (% of urban pop.)	..	..	53
Access to sanitation (% of urban population)	..	..	58
Energy use per capita (kg of oil equivalent)	..	..	..
Electricity use per capita (kWh)	..	..	..
Economy			
GDP ($ millions)	1,115	2,871	3,117
GDP growth (annual %)	1.2	1.0	4.5
GDP implicit price deflator (annual % growth)	145.6	17.0	5.7
Value added in agriculture (% of GDP)	55.6	50.6	..
Value added in industry (% of GDP)	11.2	14.8	..
Value added in services (% of GDP)	33.2	34.6	..
Exports of goods and services (% of GDP)	6.1	34.1	..
Imports of goods and services (% of GDP)	12.8	43.6	..
Gross domestic investment (% of GDP)	8.2	15.0	..
Central government revenues (% of GDP)	..	..	..
Overall budget deficit (% of GDP)	..	..	..
Money and quasi money (annual % growth)	..	15.7	17.3
Technology and infrastructure			
Telephone mainlines (per 1,000 people)	0	2	3
Cost of 3 min local call ($)	0.00	0.09	0.03
Personal computers (per 1,000 people)	..	1.0	1.2
Internet users (thousands)	..	2	4
Paved roads (% of total)	8	8	..
Aircraft departures (thousands)	..	..	..
Trade and finance			
Trade as share of PPP GDP (%)	2.8	6.7	..
Trade growth less GDP growth (average %, 1989-99)			..
High-technology exports (% of manufactured exports)	..	..	..
Net barter terms of trade (1995=100)	..	..	..
Foreign direct investment ($ millions)	0	121	126
Present value of debt ($ millions)			1,872
Total debt service ($ millions)	30	13	33
Short term debt ($ millions)	140	42	53
Aid per capita ($)	5	29	24

CAMEROON

Population (millions)	15	Population growth (%)	2.7
Surface area (1,000 sq km)	475	Population per sq km	32
GNI ($ millions)	8,798	GNI per capita ($)	600

	1990	1998	1999
People			
Life expectancy (years)	54	53	51
Fertility rate (births per woman)	6.0	5.1	4.9
Infant mortality rate (per 1,000 live births)	81	80	77
Under 5 mortality rate (per 1,000 children)	141	151	154
Child malnutrition (% of children under 5)	15	22	..
Urban population (% of total)	40	47	48
Rural population density (per km^2 arable land)	115	127	..
Illiteracy male (% of people 15 and above)	28	20	19
Illiteracy female (% of people 15 and above)	46	33	31
Net primary enrollment (% of relevant age group)	76	..	..
Net secondary enrollment (% of relevant age group)	..	..	..
Girls in primary school (% of enrollment)	46	45	..
Girls in secondary school (% of enrollment)	41	..	..
Environment			
Forests (1,000 sq. km.)	261	..	239
Deforestation (% change 1990-2000)			0.9
Water use (% of total resources)	..	..	0.1
CO_2 emissions (metric tons per capita)	0.2	0.2	..
Access to improved water source (% of urban pop.)	76	..	82
Access to sanitation (% of urban population)	99	..	99
Energy use per capita (kg of oil equivalent)	439	432	..
Electricity use per capita (kWh)	204	185	..
Economy			
GDP ($ millions)	11,152	8,703	9,187
GDP growth (annual %)	-6.1	5.0	4.4
GDP implicit price deflator (annual % growth)	1.6	1.1	-1.2
Value added in agriculture (% of GDP)	24.6	42.4	43.5
Value added in industry (% of GDP)	29.5	20.9	18.6
Value added in services (% of GDP)	46.0	36.6	37.8
Exports of goods and services (% of GDP)	20.2	26.5	24.4
Imports of goods and services (% of GDP)	17.3	25.0	24.9
Gross domestic investment (% of GDP)	17.8	18.4	19.5
Central government revenues (% of GDP)	15.4	16.5	16.0
Overall budget deficit (% of GDP)	-5.9	1.6	0.1
Money and quasi money (annual % growth)	-1.7	7.8	13.3
Technology and infrastructure			
Telephone mainlines (per 1,000 people)	3	7	6
Cost of 3 min local call ($)	..	0.06	..
Personal computers (per 1,000 people)	1.3	2.4	2.7
Internet users (thousands)	..	2	20
Paved roads (% of total)	11	13	..
Aircraft departures (thousands)	7	6	5
Trade and finance			
Trade as share of PPP GDP (%)	18.8	14.7	12.7
Trade growth less GDP growth (average %, 1989-99)			1.8
High-technology exports (% of manufactured exports)	3	2	..
Net barter terms of trade (1995=100)	88	102	..
Foreign direct investment ($ millions)	-113	50	40
Present value of debt ($ millions)			6,601
Total debt service ($ millions)	522	533	549
Short term debt ($ millions)	960	1,398	1,278
Aid per capita ($)	39	30	30

56

CANADA

High income

Population (millions)	30	Population growth (%)	0.8
Surface area (1,000 sq km)	9,971	Population per sq km	3
GNI ($ millions)	614,003	GNI per capita ($)	20,140

	1990	1998	1999
People			
Life expectancy (years)	77	79	79
Fertility rate (births per woman)	1.8	1.5	1.5
Infant mortality rate (per 1,000 live births)	7	6	5
Under 5 mortality rate (per 1,000 children)	8	8	6
Child malnutrition (% of children under 5)	..	..	..
Urban population (% of total)	77	77	77
Rural population density (per km^2 arable land)	14	15	..
Illiteracy male (% of people 15 and above)	..	..	..
Illiteracy female (% of people 15 and above)	..	..	..
Net primary enrollment (% of relevant age group)	97	95	..
Net secondary enrollment (% of relevant age group)	89	91	..
Girls in primary school (% of enrollment)	48	49	..
Girls in secondary school (% of enrollment)	49	49	..
Environment			
Forests (1,000 sq. km.)	2,446	..	2,446
Deforestation (% change 1990-2000)			0.0
Water use (% of total resources)	..	..	1.6
CO$_2$ emissions (metric tons per capita)	15.5	16.6	..
Access to improved water source (% of urban pop.)	100	..	100
Access to sanitation (% of urban population)	100	..	100
Energy use per capita (kg of oil equivalent)	7,524	7,747	..
Electricity use per capita (kWh)	15,042	15,071	..
Economy			
GDP ($ millions)	572,673	598,249	634,898
GDP growth (annual %)	0.2	3.3	4.6
GDP implicit price deflator (annual % growth)	3.1	-0.6	1.6
Value added in agriculture (% of GDP)	2.4	2.5	..
Value added in industry (% of GDP)	28.6	28.6	..
Value added in services (% of GDP)	69.0	68.9	..
Exports of goods and services (% of GDP)	26.1	41.8	43.7
Imports of goods and services (% of GDP)	26.0	40.5	40.8
Gross domestic investment (% of GDP)	20.7	20.3	20.2
Central government revenues (% of GDP)	21.6	21.8	..
Overall budget deficit (% of GDP)	-4.8	0.4	..
Money and quasi money (annual % growth)	7.8	2.3	5.0
Technology and infrastructure			
Telephone mainlines (per 1,000 people)	565	638	655
Cost of 3 min local call ($)	0.00	0.00	..
Personal computers (per 1,000 people)	107.0	331.1	360.8
Internet users (thousands)	160	7,500	11,000
Paved roads (% of total)	35	35	..
Aircraft departures (thousands)	347	318	310
Trade and finance			
Trade as share of PPP GDP (%)	44.7	55.9	57.3
Trade growth less GDP growth (average %, 1989-99)			5.5
High-technology exports (% of manufactured exports)	14	16	15
Net barter terms of trade (1995=100)	100	96	98
Foreign direct investment ($ millions)	..	..	..
Present value of debt ($ millions)			..
Total debt service ($ millions)	..	..	..
Short term debt ($ millions)	..	..	..
Aid per capita ($)	..	..	..

57

CAPE VERDE

Population (thousands)	428	Population growth (%)	3.0
Surface area (1,000 sq km)	4.0	Population per sq km	106
GNI ($ millions)	569	GNI per capita ($)	1,330

	1990	1998	1999
People			
Life expectancy (years)	65	68	69
Fertility rate (births per woman)	5.5	4.0	3.8
Infant mortality rate (per 1,000 live births)	64	42	39
Under 5 mortality rate (per 1,000 children)	..	56	50
Child malnutrition (% of children under 5)	..	14	..
Urban population (% of total)	44	59	61
Rural population density (per km^2 arable land)	465	437	..
Illiteracy male (% of people 15 and above)	24	16	16
Illiteracy female (% of people 15 and above)	46	35	35
Net primary enrollment (% of relevant age group)	99	..	..
Net secondary enrollment (% of relevant age group)	..	48	..
Girls in primary school (% of enrollment)	49	49	49
Girls in secondary school (% of enrollment)	..	49	..
Environment			
Forests (1,000 sq. km.)	0	..	1
Deforestation (% change 1990-2000)			-9.3
Water use (% of total resources)	..	..	10.0
CO$_2$ emissions (metric tons per capita)	0.2	0.3	..
Access to improved water source (% of urban pop.)	..	..	64
Access to sanitation (% of urban population)	..	..	95
Energy use per capita (kg of oil equivalent)	..	..	..
Electricity use per capita (kWh)	..	..	..
Economy			
GDP ($ millions)	339	540	581
GDP growth (annual %)	0.7	8.0	8.0
GDP implicit price deflator (annual % growth)	2.3	4.0	4.3
Value added in agriculture (% of GDP)	14.4	11.6	12.0
Value added in industry (% of GDP)	21.4	17.0	16.4
Value added in services (% of GDP)	64.3	71.4	71.6
Exports of goods and services (% of GDP)	12.7	22.9	23.2
Imports of goods and services (% of GDP)	43.7	52.3	50.3
Gross domestic investment (% of GDP)	22.9	37.0	37.6
Central government revenues (% of GDP)	..	..	..
Overall budget deficit (% of GDP)	..	..	..
Money and quasi money (annual % growth)	14.6	2.8	14.9
Technology and infrastructure			
Telephone mainlines (per 1,000 people)	24	98	112
Cost of 3 min local call ($)	0.06	0.04	0.04
Personal computers (per 1,000 people)	..	..	..
Internet users (thousands)	..	2	5
Paved roads (% of total)	78	78	..
Aircraft departures (thousands)	7	11	12
Trade and finance			
Trade as share of PPP GDP (%)	14.1	14.3	..
Trade growth less GDP growth (average %, 1989-99)			2.9
High-technology exports (% of manufactured exports)	..	..	..
Net barter terms of trade (1995=100)	100	97	..
Foreign direct investment ($ millions)	0	9	15
Present value of debt ($ millions)			181
Total debt service ($ millions)	6	19	22
Short term debt ($ millions)	5	6	19
Aid per capita ($)	316	312	319

Population (thousands)	39	Population growth (%)	..
Surface area (1,000 sq km)	0.3	Population per sq km	150
GNI ($ millions)	..	GNI per capita ($)	..

	1990	1998	1999
People			
Life expectancy (years)	..	..	..
Fertility rate (births per woman)	..	..	..
Infant mortality rate (per 1,000 live births)	..	..	..
Under 5 mortality rate (per 1,000 children)	..	..	..
Child malnutrition (% of children under 5)	..	..	..
Urban population (% of total)	100	100	100
Rural population density (per km^2 arable land)	..	..	..
Illiteracy male (% of people 15 and above)	..	..	..
Illiteracy female (% of people 15 and above)	..	..	..
Net primary enrollment (% of relevant age group)	..	..	..
Net secondary enrollment (% of relevant age group)	..	..	..
Girls in primary school (% of enrollment)	..	..	..
Girls in secondary school (% of enrollment)	..	..	..
Environment			
Forests (1,000 sq. km.)	0	..	0
Deforestation (% change 1990-2000)			0.0
Water use (% of total resources)	..	..	..
CO_2 emissions (metric tons per capita)	..	..	..
Access to improved water source (% of urban pop.)	..	..	..
Access to sanitation (% of urban population)	..	..	..
Energy use per capita (kg of oil equivalent)	..	..	..
Electricity use per capita (kWh)	..	..	..
Economy			
GDP ($ millions)	..	1,012	..
GDP growth (annual %)	..	5.3	..
GDP implicit price deflator (annual % growth)	..	3.1	..
Value added in agriculture (% of GDP)	..	..	..
Value added in industry (% of GDP)	..	..	..
Value added in services (% of GDP)	..	..	..
Exports of goods and services (% of GDP)	..	..	..
Imports of goods and services (% of GDP)	..	..	..
Gross domestic investment (% of GDP)	..	..	..
Central government revenues (% of GDP)	..	..	..
Overall budget deficit (% of GDP)	..	..	..
Money and quasi money (annual % growth)	..	..	..
Technology and infrastructure			
Telephone mainlines (per 1,000 people)	470	654	..
Cost of 3 min local call ($)	..	0.10	..
Personal computers (per 1,000 people)	..	..	..
Internet users (thousands)	..	1	..
Paved roads (% of total)	..	..	..
Aircraft departures (thousands)	..	..	..
Trade and finance			
Trade as share of PPP GDP (%)	..	..	..
Trade growth less GDP growth (average %, 1989-99)			..
High-technology exports (% of manufactured exports)	..	..	..
Net barter terms of trade (1995=100)	..	..	..
Foreign direct investment ($ millions)	..	..	..
Present value of debt ($ millions)			..
Total debt service ($ millions)	..	..	..
Short term debt ($ millions)	..	..	..
Aid per capita ($)	..	..	77

CENTRAL AFRICAN REPUBLIC

Population (millions)	4	Population growth (%)	1.7
Surface area (1,000 sq km)	623	Population per sq km	6
GNI ($ millions)	1,035	GNI per capita ($)	290

	1990	1998	1999
People			
Life expectancy (years)	48	45	44
Fertility rate (births per woman)	5.5	4.9	4.7
Infant mortality rate (per 1,000 live births)	102	95	96
Under 5 mortality rate (per 1,000 children)	..	148	151
Child malnutrition (% of children under 5)	..	23	..
Urban population (% of total)	38	40	41
Rural population density (per km^2 arable land)	96	108	..
Illiteracy male (% of people 15 and above)	53	43	41
Illiteracy female (% of people 15 and above)	79	68	67
Net primary enrollment (% of relevant age group)	53	..	..
Net secondary enrollment (% of relevant age group)	..	..	..
Girls in primary school (% of enrollment)	39	..	..
Girls in secondary school (% of enrollment)	29	..	..
Environment			
Forests (1,000 sq. km.)	232	..	229
Deforestation (% change 1990-2000)			0.1
Water use (% of total resources)	..	..	0.0
CO_2 emissions (metric tons per capita)	0.1	0.1	..
Access to improved water source (% of urban pop.)	80	..	80
Access to sanitation (% of urban population)	43	..	43
Energy use per capita (kg of oil equivalent)	..	..	..
Electricity use per capita (kWh)	..	..	..
Economy			
GDP ($ millions)	1,488	1,049	1,053
GDP growth (annual %)	-2.1	4.7	3.4
GDP implicit price deflator (annual % growth)	2.3	1.7	1.3
Value added in agriculture (% of GDP)	47.6	52.6	55.1
Value added in industry (% of GDP)	19.7	18.8	19.6
Value added in services (% of GDP)	32.7	28.6	25.3
Exports of goods and services (% of GDP)	14.8	16.2	16.9
Imports of goods and services (% of GDP)	27.6	25.2	24.0
Gross domestic investment (% of GDP)	12.3	13.5	14.3
Central government revenues (% of GDP)	..	..	..
Overall budget deficit (% of GDP)	..	..	..
Money and quasi money (annual % growth)	-3.7	-16.1	11.1
Technology and infrastructure			
Telephone mainlines (per 1,000 people)	2	3	3
Cost of 3 min local call ($)	1.13	0.61	0.49
Personal computers (per 1,000 people)	..	1.0	1.4
Internet users (thousands)	..	0	1
Paved roads (% of total)	..	3	..
Aircraft departures (thousands)	4	2	2
Trade and finance			
Trade as share of PPP GDP (%)	8.8	11.8	12.0
Trade growth less GDP growth (average %, 1989-99)			..
High-technology exports (% of manufactured exports)	..	15	..
Net barter terms of trade (1995=100)	124	64	..
Foreign direct investment ($ millions)	1	5	13
Present value of debt ($ millions)			564
Total debt service ($ millions)	29	29	19
Short term debt ($ millions)	38	60	60
Aid per capita ($)	85	34	33

Sub-Saharan Africa   **Low income**

Population (millions)	7	Population growth (%)		2.7
Surface area (1,000 sq km)	1,284	Population per sq km		6
GNI ($ millions)	1,555	GNI per capita ($)		210

	1990	1998	1999
People			
Life expectancy (years)	46	..	49
Fertility rate (births per woman)	7.1	..	6.3
Infant mortality rate (per 1,000 live births)	118	..	101
Under 5 mortality rate (per 1,000 children)	209	..	189
Child malnutrition (% of children under 5)	..	..	..
Urban population (% of total)	21	23	23
Rural population density (per km² arable land)	139	159	..
Illiteracy male (% of people 15 and above)	63	51	50
Illiteracy female (% of people 15 and above)	81	69	68
Net primary enrollment (% of relevant age group)	..	..	..
Net secondary enrollment (% of relevant age group)	..	..	..
Girls in primary school (% of enrollment)	..	35	..
Girls in secondary school (% of enrollment)	..	..	..
Environment			
Forests (1,000 sq. km.)	135	..	..
Deforestation (% change 1990-2000)			..
Water use (% of total resources)	..	..	0.4
CO₂ emissions (metric tons per capita)	0.0	..	..
Access to improved water source (% of urban pop.)	..	..	..
Access to sanitation (% of urban population)	70	..	..
Energy use per capita (kg of oil equivalent)	..	..	..
Electricity use per capita (kWh)	..	..	..
Economy			
GDP ($ millions)	1,739	1,682	1,530
GDP growth (annual %)	-4.2	6.7	-0.7
GDP implicit price deflator (annual % growth)	8.0	5.7	-4.4
Value added in agriculture (% of GDP)	29.3	38.1	36.0
Value added in industry (% of GDP)	17.7	15.3	14.7
Value added in services (% of GDP)	53.0	46.6	49.3
Exports of goods and services (% of GDP)	13.5	18.6	17.0
Imports of goods and services (% of GDP)	29.0	30.3	30.4
Gross domestic investment (% of GDP)	15.9	16.0	10.3
Central government revenues (% of GDP)	6.7	..	..
Overall budget deficit (% of GDP)	-4.7	..	..
Money and quasi money (annual % growth)	-2.4	-7.7	-2.6
Technology and infrastructure			
Telephone mainlines (per 1,000 people)	1	1	1
Cost of 3 min local call ($)	0.36	0.16	..
Personal computers (per 1,000 people)	..	1.1	1.3
Internet users (thousands)	..	0	1
Paved roads (% of total)	1	..	..
Aircraft departures (thousands)	1	2	2
Trade and finance			
Trade as share of PPP GDP (%)	10.7	8.4	9.8
Trade growth less GDP growth (average %, 1989-99)			-1.9
High-technology exports (% of manufactured exports)	..	..	..
Net barter terms of trade (1995=100)	116	103	..
Foreign direct investment ($ millions)	0	16	15
Present value of debt ($ millions)			656
Total debt service ($ millions)	12	35	32
Short term debt ($ millions)	30	23	28
Aid per capita ($)	55	23	25

61

Channel Islands

Population (thousands)	149	Population growth (%)	0.1
Surface area (1,000 sq km)	..	Population per sq km	479
GNI ($ millions)	..	GNI per capita ($)	..

	1990	1998	1999
People			
Life expectancy (years)	77	78	79
Fertility rate (births per woman)	1.7	1.8	1.8
Infant mortality rate (per 1,000 live births)	7	6	6
Under 5 mortality rate (per 1,000 children)	..	..	..
Child malnutrition (% of children under 5)	..	..	..
Urban population (% of total)	30	30	30
Rural population density (per km^2 arable land)	..	..	..
Illiteracy male (% of people 15 and above)	..	..	..
Illiteracy female (% of people 15 and above)	..	..	..
Net primary enrollment (% of relevant age group)	..	..	..
Net secondary enrollment (% of relevant age group)	..	..	..
Girls in primary school (% of enrollment)	..	..	..
Girls in secondary school (% of enrollment)	..	..	..
Environment			
Forests (1,000 sq. km.)		..	..
Deforestation (% change 1990-2000)			..
Water use (% of total resources)		..	..
CO_2 emissions (metric tons per capita)		..	..
Access to improved water source (% of urban pop.)	..	..	100
Access to sanitation (% of urban population)	..	..	100
Energy use per capita (kg of oil equivalent)	..	..	..
Electricity use per capita (kWh)	..	..	..
Economy			
GDP ($ millions)	..	..	..
GDP growth (annual %)	..	..	..
GDP implicit price deflator (annual % growth)	..	..	..
Value added in agriculture (% of GDP)	..	..	..
Value added in industry (% of GDP)	..	..	..
Value added in services (% of GDP)	..	..	..
Exports of goods and services (% of GDP)	..	..	..
Imports of goods and services (% of GDP)	..	..	..
Gross domestic investment (% of GDP)	..	..	..
Central government revenues (% of GDP)	..	..	..
Overall budget deficit (% of GDP)	..	..	..
Money and quasi money (annual % growth)	..	..	..
Technology and infrastructure			
Telephone mainlines (per 1,000 people)	..	..	..
Cost of 3 min local call ($)	..	..	..
Personal computers (per 1,000 people)	..	..	..
Internet users (thousands)	..	..	..
Paved roads (% of total)	..	..	..
Aircraft departures (thousands)	..	..	..
Trade and finance			
Trade as share of PPP GDP (%)	..	..	..
Trade growth less GDP growth (average %, 1989-99)			..
High-technology exports (% of manufactured exports)	..	..	..
Net barter terms of trade (1995=100)	..	..	..
Foreign direct investment ($ millions)	..	..	..
Present value of debt ($ millions)			..
Total debt service ($ millions)	..	..	..
Short term debt ($ millions)	..	..	..
Aid per capita ($)	..	..	..

Latin America & Caribbean   **Upper middle income**

Population (millions)	15	Population growth (%)	1.3
Surface area (1,000 sq km)	757	Population per sq km	20
GNI ($ millions)	69,602	GNI per capita ($)	4,630

	1990	1998	1999
People			
Life expectancy (years)	74	75	76
Fertility rate (births per woman)	2.6	2.3	2.2
Infant mortality rate (per 1,000 live births)	16	10	10
Under 5 mortality rate (per 1,000 children)	20	13	12
Child malnutrition (% of children under 5)	..	1	1
Urban population (% of total)	83	85	85
Rural population density (per km^2 arable land)	78	111	..
Illiteracy male (% of people 15 and above)	6	4	4
Illiteracy female (% of people 15 and above)	6	5	5
Net primary enrollment (% of relevant age group)	88	89	..
Net secondary enrollment (% of relevant age group)	55	58	..
Girls in primary school (% of enrollment)	49	48	..
Girls in secondary school (% of enrollment)	51	51	..
Environment			
Forests (1,000 sq. km.)	157	..	155
Deforestation (% change 1990-2000)			0.1
Water use (% of total resources)	..	..	2.3
CO$_2$ emissions (metric tons per capita)	2.8	4.1	..
Access to improved water source (% of urban pop.)	98	..	99
Access to sanitation (% of urban population)	98	..	98
Energy use per capita (kg of oil equivalent)	1,075	1,594	..
Electricity use per capita (kWh)	1,178	2,082	..
Economy			
GDP ($ millions)	30,323	72,809	67,469
GDP growth (annual %)	3.7	3.4	-1.1
GDP implicit price deflator (annual % growth)	21.2	2.7	3.6
Value added in agriculture (% of GDP)	8.7	8.4	8.4
Value added in industry (% of GDP)	41.5	34.2	34.2
Value added in services (% of GDP)	49.8	57.4	57.4
Exports of goods and services (% of GDP)	34.6	26.9	29.1
Imports of goods and services (% of GDP)	31.4	31.0	27.3
Gross domestic investment (% of GDP)	25.1	26.5	21.1
Central government revenues (% of GDP)	20.7	23.1	22.6
Overall budget deficit (% of GDP)	0.8	0.4	-1.5
Money and quasi money (annual % growth)	23.5	9.6	14.8
Technology and infrastructure			
Telephone mainlines (per 1,000 people)	66	205	207
Cost of 3 min local call ($)	..	0.11	0.12
Personal computers (per 1,000 people)	11.5	48.2	66.6
Internet users (thousands)	5	250	700
Paved roads (% of total)	14	18	19
Aircraft departures (thousands)	40	109	93
Trade and finance			
Trade as share of PPP GDP (%)	24.6	26.1	23.7
Trade growth less GDP growth (average %, 1989-99)			3.5
High-technology exports (% of manufactured exports)	5	4	..
Net barter terms of trade (1995=100)	83	75	..
Foreign direct investment ($ millions)	590	4,638	9,221
Present value of debt ($ millions)			35,931
Total debt service ($ millions)	2,772	4,481	5,210
Short term debt ($ millions)	3,382	7,756	5,493
Aid per capita ($)	8	7	5

CHINA

Population (millions)	1,254	Population growth (%)	0.9
Surface area (1,000 sq km)	9,598	Population per sq km	134
GNI ($ millions)	979,894	GNI per capita ($)	780

	1990	1998	1999
People			
Life expectancy (years)	69	70	70
Fertility rate (births per woman)	2.1	1.9	1.9
Infant mortality rate (per 1,000 live births)	33	32	30
Under 5 mortality rate (per 1,000 children)	47	39	37
Child malnutrition (% of children under 5)	17	9	..
Urban population (% of total)	27	31	32
Rural population density (per km^2 arable land)	666	689	..
Illiteracy male (% of people 15 and above)	14	9	9
Illiteracy female (% of people 15 and above)	33	25	25
Net primary enrollment (% of relevant age group)	97	102	..
Net secondary enrollment (% of relevant age group)	..	..	..
Girls in primary school (% of enrollment)	46	48	48
Girls in secondary school (% of enrollment)	41	50	..
Environment			
Forests (1,000 sq. km.)	1,454	..	1,635
Deforestation (% change 1990-2000)			-1.2
Water use (% of total resources)	..	..	18.6
CO_2 emissions (metric tons per capita)	2.2	2.9	..
Access to improved water source (% of urban pop.)	99	93	94
Access to sanitation (% of urban population)	57	58	68
Energy use per capita (kg of oil equivalent)	754	830	..
Electricity use per capita (kWh)	471	746	..
Economy			
GDP ($ millions)	354,644	946,312	989,465
GDP growth (annual %)	4.0	7.8	7.1
GDP implicit price deflator (annual % growth)	5.5	-2.4	-2.3
Value added in agriculture (% of GDP)	27.0	18.6	17.6
Value added in industry (% of GDP)	41.6	49.3	49.3
Value added in services (% of GDP)	31.3	32.1	33.0
Exports of goods and services (% of GDP)	17.5	21.9	22.1
Imports of goods and services (% of GDP)	14.3	17.3	19.2
Gross domestic investment (% of GDP)	34.7	37.7	37.2
Central government revenues (% of GDP)	6.3	6.3	..
Overall budget deficit (% of GDP)	-1.9	-2.2	..
Money and quasi money (annual % growth)	28.9	14.9	14.7
Technology and infrastructure			
Telephone mainlines (per 1,000 people)	6	70	86
Cost of 3 min local call ($)	..	0.01	0.01
Personal computers (per 1,000 people)	0.4	8.9	12.2
Internet users (thousands)	..	2,100	8,900
Paved roads (% of total)	..	..	..
Aircraft departures (thousands)	196	522	548
Trade and finance			
Trade as share of PPP GDP (%)	7.3	7.8	8.0
Trade growth less GDP growth (average %, 1989-99)			-6.2
High-technology exports (% of manufactured exports)	7	16	17
Net barter terms of trade (1995=100)	101	109	..
Foreign direct investment ($ millions)	3,487	43,751	38,753
Present value of debt ($ millions)			134,51
Total debt service ($ millions)	7,057	18,435	20,655
Short term debt ($ millions)	9,317	27,932	17,682
Aid per capita ($)	2	2	2

64

Latin America & Caribbean		Lower middle income	
Population (millions)	42	Population growth (%)	1.8
Surface area (1,000 sq km)	1,139	Population per sq km	40
GNI ($ millions)	90,007	GNI per capita ($)	2,170

	1990	1998	1999
People			
Life expectancy (years)	69	70	70
Fertility rate (births per woman)	3.1	2.8	2.7
Infant mortality rate (per 1,000 live births)	30	24	23
Under 5 mortality rate (per 1,000 children)	40	30	28
Child malnutrition (% of children under 5)	10	8	..
Urban population (% of total)	70	73	73
Rural population density (per km^2 arable land)	356	529	..
Illiteracy male (% of people 15 and above)	11	9	9
Illiteracy female (% of people 15 and above)	12	9	9
Net primary enrollment (% of relevant age group)	69	85	..
Net secondary enrollment (% of relevant age group)	34	46	..
Girls in primary school (% of enrollment)	53	49	..
Girls in secondary school (% of enrollment)	54	50	..
Environment			
Forests (1,000 sq. km.)	515	..	496
Deforestation (% change 1990-2000)			0.4
Water use (% of total resources)	..	..	0.4
CO_2 emissions (metric tons per capita)	1.7	1.8	..
Access to improved water source (% of urban pop.)	95	..	98
Access to sanitation (% of urban population)	95	..	97
Energy use per capita (kg of oil equivalent)	715	753	..
Electricity use per capita (kWh)	768	866	..
Economy			
GDP ($ millions)	40,274	99,050	86,605
GDP growth (annual %)	4.0	0.5	-4.3
GDP implicit price deflator (annual % growth)	28.6	15.5	12.5
Value added in agriculture (% of GDP)	16.7	14.0	12.8
Value added in industry (% of GDP)	37.9	27.0	26.0
Value added in services (% of GDP)	45.4	59.0	61.2
Exports of goods and services (% of GDP)	20.6	15.0	17.8
Imports of goods and services (% of GDP)	14.8	20.9	19.5
Gross domestic investment (% of GDP)	18.5	19.5	13.0
Central government revenues (% of GDP)	12.6	11.7	12.3
Overall budget deficit (% of GDP)	3.9	-5.1	-7.0
Money and quasi money (annual % growth)	33.0	20.9	13.8
Technology and infrastructure			
Telephone mainlines (per 1,000 people)	75	161	160
Cost of 3 min local call ($)	0.02	0.01	0.04
Personal computers (per 1,000 people)	9.6	32.9	33.7
Internet users (thousands)	..	350	664
Paved roads (% of total)	12	14	14
Aircraft departures (thousands)	117	230	209
Trade and finance			
Trade as share of PPP GDP (%)	7.4	10.5	9.3
Trade growth less GDP growth (average %, 1989-99)			5.9
High-technology exports (% of manufactured exports)	5	9	8
Net barter terms of trade (1995=100)	95	105	..
Foreign direct investment ($ millions)	500	2,961	1,109
Present value of debt ($ millions)			33,695
Total debt service ($ millions)	3,889	4,553	6,611
Short term debt ($ millions)	1,438	6,232	3,965
Aid per capita ($)	3	4	7

COMOROS

Population (thousands)	544	Population growth (%)	2.5
Surface area (1,000 sq km)	2.2	Population per sq km	244
GNI ($ millions)	189	GNI per capita ($)	350

	1990	1998	1999
People			
Life expectancy (years)	56	60	61
Fertility rate (births per woman)	5.8	4.6	4.4
Infant mortality rate (per 1,000 live births)	84	65	61
Under 5 mortality rate (per 1,000 children)	120	93	86
Child malnutrition (% of children under 5)	19	26	..
Urban population (% of total)	28	32	33
Rural population density (per km^2 arable land)	399	462	..
Illiteracy male (% of people 15 and above)	39	35	34
Illiteracy female (% of people 15 and above)	54	48	48
Net primary enrollment (% of relevant age group)	..	52	..
Net secondary enrollment (% of relevant age group)	..	..	..
Girls in primary school (% of enrollment)	42	45	..
Girls in secondary school (% of enrollment)	..	..	..

	1990	1998	1999
Environment			
Forests (1,000 sq. km.)	0	..	0
Deforestation (% change 1990-2000)			4.0
Water use (% of total resources)	..	..	..
CO_2 emissions (metric tons per capita)	0.2	0.1	..
Access to improved water source (% of urban pop.)	97	..	98
Access to sanitation (% of urban population)	98	..	98
Energy use per capita (kg of oil equivalent)	..	..	..
Electricity use per capita (kWh)	..	..	..

	1990	1998	1999
Economy			
GDP ($ millions)	250	197	193
GDP growth (annual %)	5.1	-0.5	-1.4
GDP implicit price deflator (annual % growth)	2.2	3.5	3.5
Value added in agriculture (% of GDP)	41.4	38.7	39.4
Value added in industry (% of GDP)	8.3	12.8	13.1
Value added in services (% of GDP)	50.3	48.5	47.5
Exports of goods and services (% of GDP)	14.3	24.9	26.1
Imports of goods and services (% of GDP)	37.1	39.9	40.6
Gross domestic investment (% of GDP)	19.7	16.6	14.6
Central government revenues (% of GDP)	..	..	..
Overall budget deficit (% of GDP)	..	..	..
Money and quasi money (annual % growth)	3.9	-14.2	18.5

	1990	1998	1999
Technology and infrastructure			
Telephone mainlines (per 1,000 people)	8	9	10
Cost of 3 min local call ($)	0.26	0.16	0.16
Personal computers (per 1,000 people)	0.1	2.3	3.0
Internet users (thousands)	..	0	1
Paved roads (% of total)	69	77	..
Aircraft departures (thousands)	1	1	..

	1990	1998	1999
Trade and finance			
Trade as share of PPP GDP (%)	9.8	8.1	..
Trade growth less GDP growth (average %, 1989-99)			2.2
High-technology exports (% of manufactured exports)	..	..	..
Net barter terms of trade (1995=100)	170	77	..
Foreign direct investment ($ millions)	-1	2	1
Present value of debt ($ millions)			133
Total debt service ($ millions)	1	6	8
Short term debt ($ millions)	12	12	19
Aid per capita ($)	105	67	39

66

DEMOCRATIC REPUBLIC OF CONGO

Sub-Saharan Africa   **Low income**

Population (millions)	50	Population growth (%)	3.2
Surface area (1,000 sq km)	2,345	Population per sq km	22
GNI ($ millions)	..	GNI per capita ($)	..

	1990	1998	1999
People			
Life expectancy (years)	52	..	46
Fertility rate (births per woman)	6.7	..	6.2
Infant mortality rate (per 1,000 live births)	96	..	85
Under 5 mortality rate (per 1,000 children)	155	..	161
Child malnutrition (% of children under 5)	..	..	..
Urban population (% of total)	28	30	30
Rural population density (per km^2 arable land)	404	506	..
Illiteracy male (% of people 15 and above)	38	29	28
Illiteracy female (% of people 15 and above)	66	53	51
Net primary enrollment (% of relevant age group)	54	..	..
Net secondary enrollment (% of relevant age group)	..	..	..
Girls in primary school (% of enrollment)	..	..	..
Girls in secondary school (% of enrollment)	..	..	..
Environment			
Forests (1,000 sq. km.)	1,405	..	..
Deforestation (% change 1990-2000)			
Water use (% of total resources)	..	..	0.0
CO_2 emissions (metric tons per capita)	0.1	..	..
Access to improved water source (% of urban pop.)	..	..	..
Access to sanitation (% of urban population)	..	..	21
Energy use per capita (kg of oil equivalent)	317	284	..
Electricity use per capita (kWh)	122	110	..
Economy			
GDP ($ millions)	9,348	5,584	..
GDP growth (annual %)	-6.6	3.0	..
GDP implicit price deflator (annual % growth)	109.0	15.0	..
Value added in agriculture (% of GDP)	30.1	..	..
Value added in industry (% of GDP)	28.2	..	..
Value added in services (% of GDP)	41.6	..	..
Exports of goods and services (% of GDP)	29.5	..	..
Imports of goods and services (% of GDP)	29.2	..	..
Gross domestic investment (% of GDP)	9.1	8.1	..
Central government revenues (% of GDP)	10.1	..	..
Overall budget deficit (% of GDP)	-6.5	..	..
Money and quasi money (annual % growth)	195.4	..	..
Technology and infrastructure			
Telephone mainlines (per 1,000 people)	1	0	..
Cost of 3 min local call ($)	..	..	..
Personal computers (per 1,000 people)	..	..	..
Internet users (thousands)	..	0	1
Paved roads (% of total)	..	..	..
Aircraft departures (thousands)	5	..	..
Trade and finance			
Trade as share of PPP GDP (%)	3.7	2.4	..
Trade growth less GDP growth (average %, 1989-99)			5.6
High-technology exports (% of manufactured exports)	..	..	..
Net barter terms of trade (1995=100)	108	83	..
Foreign direct investment ($ millions)	-12	1	1
Present value of debt ($ millions)			11,159
Total debt service ($ millions)	348	19	21
Short term debt ($ millions)	743	3,565	3,306
Aid per capita ($)	24	3	3

REPUBLIC OF CONGO

Sub-Saharan Africa   Low income

Population (millions)	3	Population growth (%)	2.7
Surface area (1,000 sq km)	342	Population per sq km	8
GNI ($ millions)	1,571	GNI per capita ($)	550

	1990	1998	1999
People			
Life expectancy (years)	49	48	48
Fertility rate (births per woman)	6.3	6.1	5.9
Infant mortality rate (per 1,000 live births)	88	90	89
Under 5 mortality rate (per 1,000 children)	..	145	144
Child malnutrition (% of children under 5)	..	..	..
Urban population (% of total)	53	61	62
Rural population density (per km^2 arable land)	672	630	..
Illiteracy male (% of people 15 and above)	23	14	13
Illiteracy female (% of people 15 and above)	42	29	27
Net primary enrollment (% of relevant age group)	..	..	..
Net secondary enrollment (% of relevant age group)	..	..	..
Girls in primary school (% of enrollment)	47	48	..
Girls in secondary school (% of enrollment)	43	43	..
Environment			
Forests (1,000 sq. km.)	222	..	221
Deforestation (% change 1990-2000)			0.1
Water use (% of total resources)			0.0
CO$_2$ emissions (metric tons per capita)	0.9	0.1	..
Access to improved water source (% of urban pop.)	..	50	71
Access to sanitation (% of urban population)	..	15	14
Energy use per capita (kg of oil equivalent)	501	433	..
Electricity use per capita (kWh)	156	83	..
Economy			
GDP ($ millions)	2,799	1,949	2,217
GDP growth (annual %)	0.9	3.7	-3.0
GDP implicit price deflator (annual % growth)	-0.9	-18.2	22.4
Value added in agriculture (% of GDP)	12.9	11.6	10.4
Value added in industry (% of GDP)	40.6	50.2	49.1
Value added in services (% of GDP)	46.5	38.2	40.5
Exports of goods and services (% of GDP)	53.7	74.0	77.9
Imports of goods and services (% of GDP)	45.8	64.5	70.5
Gross domestic investment (% of GDP)	15.9	26.7	22.3
Central government revenues (% of GDP)	22.5	25.1	27.7
Overall budget deficit (% of GDP)	-14.1	-20.8	-3.6
Money and quasi money (annual % growth)	18.5	-12.8	19.9
Technology and infrastructure			
Telephone mainlines (per 1,000 people)	7	8	..
Cost of 3 min local call ($)	0.25	0.12	..
Personal computers (per 1,000 people)	..	3.2	3.5
Internet users (thousands)	..	0	1
Paved roads (% of total)	10	10	..
Aircraft departures (thousands)	4	9	6
Trade and finance			
Trade as share of PPP GDP (%)	96.0	78.7	104.5
Trade growth less GDP growth (average %, 1989-99)			3.8
High-technology exports (% of manufactured exports)	..	13	..
Net barter terms of trade (1995=100)	121	82	..
Foreign direct investment ($ millions)	0	4	5
Present value of debt ($ millions)			4,764
Total debt service ($ millions)	531	41	25
Short term debt ($ millions)	736	834	1,070
Aid per capita ($)	98	23	49

COSTA RICA

Population (millions)	4	Population growth (%)	1.8
Surface area (1,000 sq km)	51	Population per sq km	70
GNI ($ millions)	12,828	GNI per capita ($)	3,570

	1990	1998	1999
People			
Life expectancy (years)	75	77	77
Fertility rate (births per woman)	3.2	2.6	2.5
Infant mortality rate (per 1,000 live births)	15	13	12
Under 5 mortality rate (per 1,000 children)	16	15	14
Child malnutrition (% of children under 5)	3	5	..
Urban population (% of total)	46	47	48
Rural population density (per km^2 arable land)	624	824	..
Illiteracy male (% of people 15 and above)	6	5	5
Illiteracy female (% of people 15 and above)	6	5	5
Net primary enrollment (% of relevant age group)	86	89	..
Net secondary enrollment (% of relevant age group)	36	40	..
Girls in primary school (% of enrollment)	49	49	..
Girls in secondary school (% of enrollment)	50	51	..
Environment			
Forests (1,000 sq. km.)	21	..	20
Deforestation (% change 1990-2000)			0.8
Water use (% of total resources)	..	..	5.1
CO_2 emissions (metric tons per capita)	1.1	1.6	..
Access to improved water source (% of urban pop.)	85	..	98
Access to sanitation (% of urban population)	..	100	98
Energy use per capita (kg of oil equivalent)	676	789	..
Electricity use per capita (kWh)	1,111	1,450	..
Economy			
GDP ($ millions)	7,188	13,885	15,148
GDP growth (annual %)	3.6	8.0	8.0
GDP implicit price deflator (annual % growth)	18.6	11.9	12.6
Value added in agriculture (% of GDP)	17.9	12.7	10.6
Value added in industry (% of GDP)	29.1	30.6	36.5
Value added in services (% of GDP)	53.0	56.7	52.9
Exports of goods and services (% of GDP)	34.6	48.0	53.7
Imports of goods and services (% of GDP)	41.4	50.9	47.2
Gross domestic investment (% of GDP)	27.3	20.5	17.3
Central government revenues (% of GDP)	18.3	20.7	20.7
Overall budget deficit (% of GDP)	-2.5	-1.2	-1.6
Money and quasi money (annual % growth)	27.5	26.3	21.7
Technology and infrastructure			
Telephone mainlines (per 1,000 people)	101	193	204
Cost of 3 min local call ($)	0.06	0.02	0.02
Personal computers (per 1,000 people)	..	78.1	101.7
Internet users (thousands)	0	100	150
Paved roads (% of total)	15	21	22
Aircraft departures (thousands)	13	34	32
Trade and finance			
Trade as share of PPP GDP (%)	21.6	44.3	40.6
Trade growth less GDP growth (average %, 1989-99)			4.9
High-technology exports (% of manufactured exports)	..	..	..
Net barter terms of trade (1995=100)	72	104	..
Foreign direct investment ($ millions)	163	613	669
Present value of debt ($ millions)			4,070
Total debt service ($ millions)	501	541	544
Short term debt ($ millions)	377	690	780
Aid per capita ($)	76	8	-3

CÔTE D'IVOIRE

Sub-Saharan Africa   Low income

Population (millions)	16	Population growth (%)	2.6
Surface area (1,000 sq km)	322	Population per sq km	49
GNI ($ millions)	10,387	GNI per capita ($)	670

	1990	1998	1999
People			
Life expectancy (years)	50	47	46
Fertility rate (births per woman)	6.2	5.2	4.9
Infant mortality rate (per 1,000 live births)	95	112	111
Under 5 mortality rate (per 1,000 children)	150	181	180
Child malnutrition (% of children under 5)	..	24	..
Urban population (% of total)	40	45	46
Rural population density (per km^2 arable land)	290	281	..
Illiteracy male (% of people 15 and above)	56	47	46
Illiteracy female (% of people 15 and above)	77	64	63
Net primary enrollment (% of relevant age group)	47	55	..
Net secondary enrollment (% of relevant age group)	..	..	..
Girls in primary school (% of enrollment)	41	43	..
Girls in secondary school (% of enrollment)	..	..	..
Environment			
Forests (1,000 sq. km.)	98	..	71
Deforestation (% change 1990-2000)			3.1
Water use (% of total resources)	..	..	0.9
CO$_2$ emissions (metric tons per capita)	0.9	0.9	..
Access to improved water source (% of urban pop.)	89	..	90
Access to sanitation (% of urban population)	78	..	..
Energy use per capita (kg of oil equivalent)	..	..	..
Electricity use per capita (kWh)	..	..	..
Economy			
GDP ($ millions)	10,796	11,236	11,206
GDP growth (annual %)	-1.1	4.5	2.8
GDP implicit price deflator (annual % growth)	-4.5	2.7	1.3
Value added in agriculture (% of GDP)	32.5	27.6	26.0
Value added in industry (% of GDP)	23.2	25.4	26.4
Value added in services (% of GDP)	44.3	47.0	47.6
Exports of goods and services (% of GDP)	31.7	43.6	44.3
Imports of goods and services (% of GDP)	27.1	37.0	37.5
Gross domestic investment (% of GDP)	6.7	18.2	16.3
Central government revenues (% of GDP)	22.0	21.0	20.9
Overall budget deficit (% of GDP)	-2.9	-1.3	-0.2
Money and quasi money (annual % growth)	-2.6	6.0	-1.7
Technology and infrastructure			
Telephone mainlines (per 1,000 people)	6	12	15
Cost of 3 min local call ($)	0.11	0.06	0.07
Personal computers (per 1,000 people)	..	4.5	5.5
Internet users (thousands)	..	10	20
Paved roads (% of total)	9	10	..
Aircraft departures (thousands)	5	6	6
Trade and finance			
Trade as share of PPP GDP (%)	28.2	29.7	28.6
Trade growth less GDP growth (average %, 1989-99)			1.0
High-technology exports (% of manufactured exports)	..	2	..
Net barter terms of trade (1995=100)	82	97	..
Foreign direct investment ($ millions)	48	435	350
Present value of debt ($ millions)			12,163
Total debt service ($ millions)	1,262	1,384	1,449
Short term debt ($ millions)	3,597	1,576	1,256
Aid per capita ($)	58	53	29

CROATIA

Europe & Central Asia   **Upper middle income**

Population (millions)	4	Population growth (%)		-0.8
Surface area (1,000 sq km)	57	Population per sq km		80
GNI ($ millions)	20,222	GNI per capita ($)		4,530

	1990	1998	1999
People			
Life expectancy (years)	72	72	73
Fertility rate (births per woman)	1.6	1.5	1.5
Infant mortality rate (per 1,000 live births)	11	8	8
Under 5 mortality rate (per 1,000 children)	13	10	9
Child malnutrition (% of children under 5)	..	1	..
Urban population (% of total)	54	57	57
Rural population density (per km^2 arable land)	179	133	..
Illiteracy male (% of people 15 and above)	1	1	1
Illiteracy female (% of people 15 and above)	5	3	3
Net primary enrollment (% of relevant age group)	79	82	..
Net secondary enrollment (% of relevant age group)	63	66	..
Girls in primary school (% of enrollment)	49	49	..
Girls in secondary school (% of enrollment)	51	49	..
Environment			
Forests (1,000 sq. km.)	18	..	18
Deforestation (% change 1990-2000)			-0.1
Water use (% of total resources)	..	..	0.1
CO$_2$ emissions (metric tons per capita)	3.7	4.4	..
Access to improved water source (% of urban pop.)	..	75	..
Access to sanitation (% of urban population)	72	71	..
Energy use per capita (kg of oil equivalent)	1,404	1,808	..
Electricity use per capita (kWh)	1,974	2,463	..
Economy			
GDP ($ millions)	18,156	20,931	20,426
GDP growth (annual %)	-21.1	2.5	-0.3
GDP implicit price deflator (annual % growth)	99.3	9.0	4.0
Value added in agriculture (% of GDP)	10.3	8.9	8.6
Value added in industry (% of GDP)	33.8	32.4	32.0
Value added in services (% of GDP)	55.9	58.7	59.4
Exports of goods and services (% of GDP)	77.7	40.0	40.7
Imports of goods and services (% of GDP)	86.1	49.0	48.1
Gross domestic investment (% of GDP)	13.7	23.2	23.2
Central government revenues (% of GDP)	33.0	45.6	42.8
Overall budget deficit (% of GDP)	-4.6	0.6	-2.0
Money and quasi money (annual % growth)	..	13.0	-1.8
Technology and infrastructure			
Telephone mainlines (per 1,000 people)	172	348	365
Cost of 3 min local call ($)	0.03	0.03	..
Personal computers (per 1,000 people)	14.6	55.8	67.0
Internet users (thousands)	..	150	200
Paved roads (% of total)	..	..	..
Aircraft departures (thousands)	2	17	16
Trade and finance			
Trade as share of PPP GDP (%)	..	40.2	36.5
Trade growth less GDP growth (average %, 1989-99)			..
High-technology exports (% of manufactured exports)	..	8	8
Net barter terms of trade (1995=100)	..	..	..
Foreign direct investment ($ millions)	0	898	1,408
Present value of debt ($ millions)			9,372
Total debt service ($ millions)	..	1,785	1,713
Short term debt ($ millions)	..	649	692
Aid per capita ($)	..	9	11

71

CUBA

Population (millions)	11	Population growth (%)	0.5
Surface area (1,000 sq km)	111	Population per sq km	102
GNI ($ millions)	..	GNI per capita ($)	..

	1990	1998	1999
People			
Life expectancy (years)	75	76	76
Fertility rate (births per woman)	1.7	1.6	1.6
Infant mortality rate (per 1,000 live births)	11	7	7
Under 5 mortality rate (per 1,000 children)	13	9	8
Child malnutrition (% of children under 5)	..	..	..
Urban population (% of total)	74	75	75
Rural population density (per km^2 arable land)	86	77	..
Illiteracy male (% of people 15 and above)	5	4	3
Illiteracy female (% of people 15 and above)	5	4	4
Net primary enrollment (% of relevant age group)	92	101	..
Net secondary enrollment (% of relevant age group)	69	59	..
Girls in primary school (% of enrollment)	48	48	..
Girls in secondary school (% of enrollment)	52	52	..
Environment			
Forests (1,000 sq. km.)	21	..	23
Deforestation (% change 1990-2000)			-1.3
Water use (% of total resources)	..	..	13.7
CO_2 emissions (metric tons per capita)	3.1	2.3	..
Access to improved water source (% of urban pop.)	..	96	99
Access to sanitation (% of urban population)	..	71	96
Energy use per capita (kg of oil equivalent)	1,555	1,066	..
Electricity use per capita (kWh)	1,125	954	..
Economy			
GDP ($ millions)	..	..	..
GDP growth (annual %)	..	..	..
GDP implicit price deflator (annual % growth)	..	..	..
Value added in agriculture (% of GDP)	..	..	..
Value added in industry (% of GDP)	..	..	..
Value added in services (% of GDP)	..	..	..
Exports of goods and services (% of GDP)	..	..	..
Imports of goods and services (% of GDP)	..	..	..
Gross domestic investment (% of GDP)	..	..	..
Central government revenues (% of GDP)	..	..	..
Overall budget deficit (% of GDP)	..	..	..
Money and quasi money (annual % growth)	..	..	..
Technology and infrastructure			
Telephone mainlines (per 1,000 people)	31	35	39
Cost of 3 min local call ($)	0.00	0.00	0.09
Personal computers (per 1,000 people)	..	6.3	9.9
Internet users (thousands)	..	25	35
Paved roads (% of total)	51	49	..
Aircraft departures (thousands)	19	20	16
Trade and finance			
Trade as share of PPP GDP (%)	..	..	..
Trade growth less GDP growth (average %, 1989-99)			..
High-technology exports (% of manufactured exports)	..	..	..
Net barter terms of trade (1995=100)	96	102	..
Foreign direct investment ($ millions)	..	..	..
Present value of debt ($ millions)			..
Total debt service ($ millions)	..	..	..
Short term debt ($ millions)	..	..	..
Aid per capita ($)	5	7	5

CYPRUS

High income

Population (thousands)	760	Population growth (%)	0.9
Surface area (1,000 sq km)	9.3	Population per sq km	82
GNI ($ millions)	9,086	GNI per capita ($)	11,950

	1990	1998	1999
People			
Life expectancy (years)	77	78	78
Fertility rate (births per woman)	2.4	1.9	1.9
Infant mortality rate (per 1,000 live births)	11	7	7
Under 5 mortality rate (per 1,000 children)	12	10	9
Child malnutrition (% of children under 5)	..	..	..
Urban population (% of total)	51	56	56
Rural population density (per km^2 arable land)	312	334	..
Illiteracy male (% of people 15 and above)	2	1	1
Illiteracy female (% of people 15 and above)	9	5	5
Net primary enrollment (% of relevant age group)	101	96	..
Net secondary enrollment (% of relevant age group)	80	92	..
Girls in primary school (% of enrollment)	48	48	..
Girls in secondary school (% of enrollment)	49	49	..
Environment			
Forests (1,000 sq. km.)	1	..	1
Deforestation (% change 1990-2000)			0.0
Water use (% of total resources)	..	..	27.5
CO_2 emissions (metric tons per capita)	7.6	8.0	..
Access to improved water source (% of urban pop.)	100	100	100
Access to sanitation (% of urban population)	100	100	100
Energy use per capita (kg of oil equivalent)	2,256	2,942	..
Electricity use per capita (kWh)	2,630	3,468	..
Economy			
GDP ($ millions)	5,592	8,970	9,031
GDP growth (annual %)	7.4	4.5	4.5
GDP implicit price deflator (annual % growth)	5.4	2.3	1.0
Value added in agriculture (% of GDP)	6.9	5.1	..
Value added in industry (% of GDP)	25.9	23.2	..
Value added in services (% of GDP)	67.2	71.7	..
Exports of goods and services (% of GDP)	51.5	44.0	44.2
Imports of goods and services (% of GDP)	57.1	51.7	49.2
Gross domestic investment (% of GDP)	27.0	24.7	..
Central government revenues (% of GDP)	27.6	31.8	..
Overall budget deficit (% of GDP)	-5.3	-5.6	..
Money and quasi money (annual % growth)	16.8	8.3	15.0
Technology and infrastructure			
Telephone mainlines (per 1,000 people)	428	545	545
Cost of 3 min local call ($)	0.02	0.01	0.01
Personal computers (per 1,000 people)	8.7	121.1	167.1
Internet users (thousands)	0	68	88
Paved roads (% of total)	60	57	87
Aircraft departures (thousands)	8	12	12
Trade and finance			
Trade as share of PPP GDP (%)	40.3	35.1	31.9
Trade growth less GDP growth (average %, 1989-99)			..
High-technology exports (% of manufactured exports)	6	4	4
Net barter terms of trade (1995=100)	102	100	..
Foreign direct investment ($ millions)	..	..	..
Present value of debt ($ millions)			..
Total debt service ($ millions)	..	..	..
Short term debt ($ millions)	..	..	..
Aid per capita ($)	57	43	66

73

CZECH REPUBLIC

Europe & Central Asia   **Upper middle income**

Population (millions)	10	Population growth (%)		-0.2
Surface area (1,000 sq km)	79	Population per sq km		133
GNI ($ millions)	51,623	GNI per capita ($)		5,020

	1990	1998	1999
People			
Life expectancy (years)	72	75	75
Fertility rate (births per woman)	1.9	1.2	1.2
Infant mortality rate (per 1,000 live births)	11	5	5
Under 5 mortality rate (per 1,000 children)	12	6	5
Child malnutrition (% of children under 5)	1	..	..
Urban population (% of total)	75	75	75
Rural population density (per km^2 arable land)	..	84	..
Illiteracy male (% of people 15 and above)	..	..	..
Illiteracy female (% of people 15 and above)	..	..	..
Net primary enrollment (% of relevant age group)	..	87	..
Net secondary enrollment (% of relevant age group)	..	87	..
Girls in primary school (% of enrollment)	49	49	..
Girls in secondary school (% of enrollment)	48	50	..
Environment			
Forests (1,000 sq. km.)	26	..	26
Deforestation (% change 1990-2000)			0.0
Water use (% of total resources)	..	..	15.8
CO_2 emissions (metric tons per capita)	13.1	12.2	..
Access to improved water source (% of urban pop.)	..	..	..
Access to sanitation (% of urban population)	..	..	..
Energy use per capita (kg of oil equivalent)	4,573	3,986	..
Electricity use per capita (kWh)	4,649	4,747	..
Economy			
GDP ($ millions)	34,880	55,708	53,111
GDP growth (annual %)	-11.6	-2.2	-0.2
GDP implicit price deflator (annual % growth)	36.2	10.2	2.3
Value added in agriculture (% of GDP)	8.4	4.8	3.9
Value added in industry (% of GDP)	48.8	45.3	43.3
Value added in services (% of GDP)	42.8	49.9	52.8
Exports of goods and services (% of GDP)	45.2	60.7	63.6
Imports of goods and services (% of GDP)	42.6	62.2	65.2
Gross domestic investment (% of GDP)	25.2	29.7	28.4
Central government revenues (% of GDP)	..	33.1	34.1
Overall budget deficit (% of GDP)	..	-1.6	-1.6
Money and quasi money (annual % growth)	..	3.4	2.6
Technology and infrastructure			
Telephone mainlines (per 1,000 people)	158	364	371
Cost of 3 min local call ($)	0.05	0.07	0.15
Personal computers (per 1,000 people)	11.7	97.1	107.2
Internet users (thousands)	..	400	700
Paved roads (% of total)	100	100	100
Aircraft departures (thousands)	22	30	35
Trade and finance			
Trade as share of PPP GDP (%)	22.6	41.8	41.6
Trade growth less GDP growth (average %, 1989-99)			9.9
High-technology exports (% of manufactured exports)	..	9	9
Net barter terms of trade (1995=100)	..	..	..
Foreign direct investment ($ millions)	207	2,734	5,093
Present value of debt ($ millions)			22,481
Total debt service ($ millions)	1,035	5,353	3,589
Short term debt ($ millions)	2,400	7,615	7,265
Aid per capita ($)	1	43	31

Population (millions)	5	Population growth (%)	0.5
Surface area (1,000 sq km)	43	Population per sq km	126
GNI ($ millions)	170,685	GNI per capita ($)	32,050

	1990	1998	1999
People			
Life expectancy (years)	75	76	76
Fertility rate (births per woman)	1.7	1.8	1.8
Infant mortality rate (per 1,000 live births)	8	5	5
Under 5 mortality rate (per 1,000 children)	9	6	6
Child malnutrition (% of children under 5)	..	..	..
Urban population (% of total)	85	85	85
Rural population density (per km^2 arable land)	31	33	..
Illiteracy male (% of people 15 and above)	..	..	..
Illiteracy female (% of people 15 and above)	..	..	..
Net primary enrollment (% of relevant age group)	98	99	..
Net secondary enrollment (% of relevant age group)	87	88	..
Girls in primary school (% of enrollment)	49	49	..
Girls in secondary school (% of enrollment)	49	50	..
Environment			
Forests (1,000 sq. km.)	4	..	5
Deforestation (% change 1990-2000)			-0.2
Water use (% of total resources)			14.8
CO$_2$ emissions (metric tons per capita)	10.0	10.9	..
Access to improved water source (% of urban pop.)	..	..	100
Access to sanitation (% of urban population)	..	100	..
Energy use per capita (kg of oil equivalent)	3,557	3,925	..
Electricity use per capita (kWh)	5,650	6,033	..
Economy			
GDP ($ millions)	133,361	173,683	174,280
GDP growth (annual %)	1.0	2.5	1.7
GDP implicit price deflator (annual % growth)	3.7	2.1	2.7
Value added in agriculture (% of GDP)	3.8	2.5	2.4
Value added in industry (% of GDP)	22.8	21.8	21.3
Value added in services (% of GDP)	73.3	75.7	76.3
Exports of goods and services (% of GDP)	35.8	35.3	36.9
Imports of goods and services (% of GDP)	30.8	33.4	32.7
Gross domestic investment (% of GDP)	20.3	21.2	19.6
Central government revenues (% of GDP)	38.1	38.6	38.0
Overall budget deficit (% of GDP)	-0.7	1.7	0.5
Money and quasi money (annual % growth)	6.5	3.3	-0.9
Technology and infrastructure			
Telephone mainlines (per 1,000 people)	567	660	685
Cost of 3 min local call ($)	0.13	0.12	0.12
Personal computers (per 1,000 people)	114.8	377.4	414.0
Internet users (thousands)	10	1,000	1,500
Paved roads (% of total)	100	100	100
Aircraft departures (thousands)	91	114	110
Trade and finance			
Trade as share of PPP GDP (%)	69.7	70.5	67.8
Trade growth less GDP growth (average %, 1989-99)			1.6
High-technology exports (% of manufactured exports)	16	18	20
Net barter terms of trade (1995=100)	100	99	100
Foreign direct investment ($ millions)	..	..	..
Present value of debt ($ millions)			..
Total debt service ($ millions)	..	..	..
Short term debt ($ millions)	..	..	..
Aid per capita ($)	..	..	..

Middle East & North Africa   **Lower middle income**

Population (thousands)	648	Population growth (%)	1.4
Surface area (1,000 sq km)	23.2	Population per sq km	46
GNI ($ millions)	511	GNI per capita ($)	5,020

	1990	1998	1999
People			
Life expectancy (years)	48	50	47
Fertility rate (births per woman)	6.0	5.3	5.2
Infant mortality rate (per 1,000 live births)	118	106	109
Under 5 mortality rate (per 1,000 children)	..	175	177
Child malnutrition (% of children under 5)	23	18	..
Urban population (% of total)	80	83	83
Rural population density (per km^2 arable land)	..	..	..
Illiteracy male (% of people 15 and above)	33	26	25
Illiteracy female (% of people 15 and above)	60	49	47
Net primary enrollment (% of relevant age group)	32	32	..
Net secondary enrollment (% of relevant age group)	..	12	..
Girls in primary school (% of enrollment)	41	42	..
Girls in secondary school (% of enrollment)	40	41	..
Environment			
Forests (1,000 sq. km.)	0	..	0
Deforestation (% change 1990-2000)			0.0
Water use (% of total resources)			3.3
CO$_2$ emissions (metric tons per capita)	0.7	0.6	..
Access to improved water source (% of urban pop.)	..	..	100
Access to sanitation (% of urban population)	..	..	99
Energy use per capita (kg of oil equivalent)	..	..	..
Electricity use per capita (kWh)	..	..	..
Economy			
GDP ($ millions)	425	519	..
GDP growth (annual %)	-0.3	0.7	..
GDP implicit price deflator (annual % growth)	3.4	3.0	..
Value added in agriculture (% of GDP)	3.3	3.6	..
Value added in industry (% of GDP)	20.0	20.5	..
Value added in services (% of GDP)	76.6	75.8	..
Exports of goods and services (% of GDP)	54.6	41.3	..
Imports of goods and services (% of GDP)	79.2	57.0	..
Gross domestic investment (% of GDP)	14.4	9.5	..
Central government revenues (% of GDP)	28.4	..	..
Overall budget deficit (% of GDP)	-1.0	..	..
Money and quasi money (annual % growth)	3.6	-4.1	-3.8
Technology and infrastructure			
Telephone mainlines (per 1,000 people)	11	13	14
Cost of 3 min local call ($)	0.19	0.19	0.19
Personal computers (per 1,000 people)	1.9	8.8	9.5
Internet users (thousands)	..	1	1
Paved roads (% of total)	13	13	..
Aircraft departures (thousands)	4	..	..
Trade and finance			
Trade as share of PPP GDP (%)	..	..	..
Trade growth less GDP growth (average %, 1989-99)			..
High-technology exports (% of manufactured exports)	..	..	..
Net barter terms of trade (1995=100)	..	..	..
Foreign direct investment ($ millions)	0	6	5
Present value of debt ($ millions)			189
Total debt service ($ millions)	15	5	5
Short term debt ($ millions)	50	15	14
Aid per capita ($)	375	127	116

DOMINICA

Population (thousands)	73	Population growth (%)		0.0
Surface area (1,000 sq km)	0.8	Population per sq km		97
GNI ($ millions)	238	GNI per capita ($)		3,260

	1990	1998	1999
People			
Life expectancy (years)	73	76	76
Fertility rate (births per woman)	27	1.9	1.9
Infant mortality rate (per 1,000 live births)	18	16	14
Under 5 mortality rate (per 1,000 children)	23	19	18
Child malnutrition (% of children under 5)	..	..	..
Urban population (% of total)	68	70	71
Rural population density (per km^2 arable land)	467	722	..
Illiteracy male (% of people 15 and above)	..	..	..
Illiteracy female (% of people 15 and above)	..	..	..
Net primary enrollment (% of relevant age group)	..	..	..
Net secondary enrollment (% of relevant age group)	..	..	..
Girls in primary school (% of enrollment)	49	50	..
Girls in secondary school (% of enrollment)	..	..	..
Environment			
Forests (1,000 sq. km.)	1	..	0
Deforestation (% change 1990-2000)			0.8
Water use (% of total resources)	..	..	
CO_2 emissions (metric tons per capita)	0.8	1.1	..
Access to improved water source (% of urban pop.)	100	..	..
Access to sanitation (% of urban population)	..	..	..
Energy use per capita (kg of oil equivalent)	..	..	..
Electricity use per capita (kWh)	..	..	..
Economy			
GDP ($ millions)	166	260	267
GDP growth (annual %)	5.3	4.8	0.1
GDP implicit price deflator (annual % growth)	3.0	2.4	2.3
Value added in agriculture (% of GDP)	25.0	18.9	18.5
Value added in industry (% of GDP)	18.6	22.1	22.5
Value added in services (% of GDP)	56.4	59.0	59.0
Exports of goods and services (% of GDP)	54.5	56.4	57.8
Imports of goods and services (% of GDP)	80.5	60.6	67.2
Gross domestic investment (% of GDP)	40.8	30.0	29.1
Central government revenues (% of GDP)	..	..	..
Overall budget deficit (% of GDP)	..	..	..
Money and quasi money (annual % growth)	23.0	6.2	9.3
Technology and infrastructure			
Telephone mainlines (per 1,000 people)	164	265	279
Cost of 3 min local call ($)	0.10	..	..
Personal computers (per 1,000 people)	..	..	65.4
Internet users (thousands)	..	2	2
Paved roads (% of total)	46	50	..
Aircraft departures (thousands)	..	..	..
Trade and finance			
Trade as share of PPP GDP (%)	61.8	51.4	49.2
Trade growth less GDP growth (average %, 1989-99)			-0.6
High-technology exports (% of manufactured exports)	..	6	4
Net barter terms of trade (1995=100)	..	..	..
Foreign direct investment ($ millions)	13	11	13
Present value of debt ($ millions)			82
Total debt service ($ millions)	6	10	12
Short term debt ($ millions)	2	18	19
Aid per capita ($)	267	267	135

DOMINICAN REPUBLIC

Population (millions)	8	Population growth (%)	1.8
Surface area (1,000 sq km)	49	Population per sq km	174
GNI ($ millions)	16,130	GNI per capita ($)	1,920

	1990	1998	1999
People			
Life expectancy (years)	69	71	71
Fertility rate (births per woman)	3.4	3.0	2.8
Infant mortality rate (per 1,000 live births)	51	40	39
Under 5 mortality rate (per 1,000 children)	59	47	47
Child malnutrition (% of children under 5)	10	6	..
Urban population (% of total)	58	64	64
Rural population density (per km^2 arable land)	282	280	..
Illiteracy male (% of people 15 and above)	20	17	17
Illiteracy female (% of people 15 and above)	21	17	17
Net primary enrollment (% of relevant age group)	..	..	..
Net secondary enrollment (% of relevant age group)	..	22	..
Girls in primary school (% of enrollment)	..	49	..
Girls in secondary school (% of enrollment)	..	56	..
Environment			
Forests (1,000 sq. km.)	14	..	14
Deforestation (% change 1990-2000)			0.0
Water use (% of total resources)	..	..	39.7
CO_2 emissions (metric tons per capita)	1.4	1.7	..
Access to improved water source (% of urban pop.)	83	..	83
Access to sanitation (% of urban population)	66	..	75
Energy use per capita (kg of oil equivalent)	559	676	..
Electricity use per capita (kWh)	437	627	..
Economy			
GDP ($ millions)	7,074	15,858	17,398
GDP growth (annual %)	-5.8	7.3	8.3
GDP implicit price deflator (annual % growth)	51.1	4.9	6.4
Value added in agriculture (% of GDP)	13.4	11.5	11.3
Value added in industry (% of GDP)	31.4	33.6	34.3
Value added in services (% of GDP)	55.2	54.9	54.3
Exports of goods and services (% of GDP)	33.8	30.6	30.4
Imports of goods and services (% of GDP)	43.7	39.5	38.8
Gross domestic investment (% of GDP)	25.1	23.4	25.1
Central government revenues (% of GDP)	12.2	16.7	..
Overall budget deficit (% of GDP)	0.6	0.6	..
Money and quasi money (annual % growth)	42.5	16.6	23.7
Technology and infrastructure			
Telephone mainlines (per 1,000 people)	48	93	98
Cost of 3 min local call ($)	0.00	..	..
Personal computers (per 1,000 people)	..	..	..
Internet users (thousands)	..	20	25
Paved roads (% of total)	45	79	..
Aircraft departures (thousands)	10	1	0
Trade and finance			
Trade as share of PPP GDP (%)	21.5	30.0	29.0
Trade growth less GDP growth (average %, 1989-99)			-1.1
High-technology exports (% of manufactured exports)	..	0	..
Net barter terms of trade (1995=100)	94	105	..
Foreign direct investment ($ millions)	133	700	1,338
Present value of debt ($ millions)			4,568
Total debt service ($ millions)	232	375	377
Short term debt ($ millions)	782	866	1,051
Aid per capita ($)	14	15	23

78

| Latin America & Caribbean | | Lower middle income |

Population (millions)	12	Population growth (%)	1.9
Surface area (1,000 sq km)	284	Population per sq km	45
GNI ($ millions)	16,841	GNI per capita ($)	1,360

	1990	1998	1999
People			
Life expectancy (years)	67	69	69
Fertility rate (births per woman)	3.7	3.4	3.1
Infant mortality rate (per 1,000 live births)	45	30	28
Under 5 mortality rate (per 1,000 children)	51	39	35
Child malnutrition (% of children under 5)	..	..	..
Urban population (% of total)	55	63	64
Rural population density (per km² arable land)	287	284	..
Illiteracy male (% of people 15 and above)	10	8	7
Illiteracy female (% of people 15 and above)	15	11	11
Net primary enrollment (% of relevant age group)	..	97	..
Net secondary enrollment (% of relevant age group)	..	..	..
Girls in primary school (% of enrollment)	..	49	..
Girls in secondary school (% of enrollment)	50	50	..
Environment			
Forests (1,000 sq. km.)	119	..	106
Deforestation (% change 1990-2000)			1.2
Water use (% of total resources)			3.8
CO_2 emissions (metric tons per capita)	1.7	1.8	..
Access to improved water source (% of urban pop.)	75	82	81
Access to sanitation (% of urban population)	..	87	70
Energy use per capita (kg of oil equivalent)	639	737	..
Electricity use per capita (kWh)	467	625	..
Economy			
GDP ($ millions)	10,686	19,723	18,991
GDP growth (annual %)	3.0	0.4	-7.3
GDP implicit price deflator (annual % growth)	54.0	35.4	62.0
Value added in agriculture (% of GDP)	13.4	12.0	12.2
Value added in industry (% of GDP)	38.0	32.7	37.5
Value added in services (% of GDP)	48.6	55.2	50.4
Exports of goods and services (% of GDP)	32.7	25.3	37.1
Imports of goods and services (% of GDP)	27.4	32.0	25.8
Gross domestic investment (% of GDP)	17.5	24.7	12.9
Central government revenues (% of GDP)	18.2	15.7	..
Overall budget deficit (% of GDP)	3.7	0.0	..
Money and quasi money (annual % growth)	101.6	31.1	99.2
Technology and infrastructure			
Telephone mainlines (per 1,000 people)	48	81	91
Cost of 3 min local call ($)	0.00	0.01	0.01
Personal computers (per 1,000 people)	1.9	18.4	20.1
Internet users (thousands)	1	15	35
Paved roads (% of total)	13	19	19
Aircraft departures (thousands)	28	27	20
Trade and finance			
Trade as share of PPP GDP (%)	16.0	25.3	20.1
Trade growth less GDP growth (average %, 1989-99)			1.2
High-technology exports (% of manufactured exports)	0	4	6
Net barter terms of trade (1995=100)	141	100	..
Foreign direct investment ($ millions)	126	814	690
Present value of debt ($ millions)			13,483
Total debt service ($ millions)	1,084	1,706	1,645
Short term debt ($ millions)	1,814	2,272	1,247
Aid per capita ($)	16	14	12

79

ARAB REPUBLIC OF EGYPT

| Middle East & North Africa | | | Lower middle income |

Population (millions)	63	Population growth (%)	1.8
Surface area (1,000 sq km)	1,001	Population per sq km	63
GNI ($ millions)	86,544	GNI per capita ($)	1,380

	1990	1998	1999
People			
Life expectancy (years)	63	*66*	67
Fertility rate (births per woman)	4.0	*3.4*	3.3
Infant mortality rate (per 1,000 live births)	69	51	47
Under 5 mortality rate (per 1,000 children)	85	66	61
Child malnutrition (% of children under 5)	10	11	..
Urban population (% of total)	44	45	45
Rural population density (per km^2 arable land)	1,283	1,197	..
Illiteracy male (% of people 15 and above)	40	35	34
Illiteracy female (% of people 15 and above)	66	58	57
Net primary enrollment (% of relevant age group)	..	93	..
Net secondary enrollment (% of relevant age group)	..	68	..
Girls in primary school (% of enrollment)	*44*	46	..
Girls in secondary school (% of enrollment)	43	*45*	..

Environment			
Forests (1,000 sq. km.)	1	..	*1*
Deforestation (% change 1990-2000)			*-3.4*
Water use (% of total resources)	..	..	94.5
CO$_2$ emissions (metric tons per capita)	1.6	*2.0*	..
Access to improved water source (% of urban pop.)	97	..	*96*
Access to sanitation (% of urban population)	96	..	*98*
Energy use per capita (kg of oil equivalent)	608	679	..
Electricity use per capita (kWh)	690	861	..

Economy			
GDP ($ millions)	43,130	82,710	89,148
GDP growth (annual %)	5.7	5.6	6.0
GDP implicit price deflator (annual % growth)	18.4	3.6	1.7
Value added in agriculture (% of GDP)	19.4	17.5	17.4
Value added in industry (% of GDP)	28.7	32.3	31.5
Value added in services (% of GDP)	52.0	50.2	51.0
Exports of goods and services (% of GDP)	20.0	16.8	16.0
Imports of goods and services (% of GDP)	32.7	23.3	24.4
Gross domestic investment (% of GDP)	28.8	20.5	22.8
Central government revenues (% of GDP)	24.4	*28.4*	..
Overall budget deficit (% of GDP)	-5.7	*-2.0*	..
Money and quasi money (annual % growth)	28.7	10.8	5.7

Technology and infrastructure			
Telephone mainlines (per 1,000 people)	30	60	75
Cost of 3 min local call ($)	*0.01*	0.02	0.03
Personal computers (per 1,000 people)	..	9.1	12.0
Internet users (thousands)	..	100	200
Paved roads (% of total)	72	*78*	..
Aircraft departures (thousands)	20	41	44

Trade and finance			
Trade as share of PPP GDP (%)	8.9	9.8	9.1
Trade growth less GDP growth (average %, 1989-99)			-1.3
High-technology exports (% of manufactured exports)	..	0	0
Net barter terms of trade (1995=100)	86	84	..
Foreign direct investment ($ millions)	734	1,076	1,065
Present value of debt ($ millions)			24,402
Total debt service ($ millions)	3,052	1,810	1,733
Short term debt ($ millions)	4,452	4,260	4,294
Aid per capita ($)	104	32	25

Latin America & Caribbean			Lower middle income

Population (millions)	6	Population growth (%)	2.0
Surface area (1,000 sq km)	21	Population per sq km	297
GNI ($ millions)	11,806	GNI per capita ($)	1,920

	1990	1998	1999
People			
Life expectancy (years)	66	..	70
Fertility rate (births per woman)	3.8	..	3.2
Infant mortality rate (per 1,000 live births)	46	..	30
Under 5 mortality rate (per 1,000 children)	54	..	36
Child malnutrition (% of children under 5)	..	12	..
Urban population (% of total)	44	46	46
Rural population density (per km^2 arable land)	521	582	..
Illiteracy male (% of people 15 and above)	24	19	19
Illiteracy female (% of people 15 and above)	31	25	24
Net primary enrollment (% of relevant age group)	..	..	..
Net secondary enrollment (% of relevant age group)	..	..	..
Girls in primary school (% of enrollment)	..	..	..
Girls in secondary school (% of enrollment)	..	..	..
Environment			
Forests (1,000 sq. km.)	2	..	..
Deforestation (% change 1990-2000)			..
Water use (% of total resources)			4.1
CO_2 emissions (metric tons per capita)	0.6	..	..
Access to improved water source (% of urban pop.)	..	..	..
Access to sanitation (% of urban population)	..	..	..
Energy use per capita (kg of oil equivalent)	496	640	..
Electricity use per capita (kWh)	358	559	..
Economy			
GDP ($ millions)	4,807	11,989	12,467
GDP growth (annual %)	4.8	3.5	3.4
GDP implicit price deflator (annual % growth)	22.5	4.0	0.5
Value added in agriculture (% of GDP)	17.1	11.9	10.3
Value added in industry (% of GDP)	26.2	27.6	29.4
Value added in services (% of GDP)	56.6	60.5	60.3
Exports of goods and services (% of GDP)	18.6	22.6	24.8
Imports of goods and services (% of GDP)	31.2	35.5	36.9
Gross domestic investment (% of GDP)	13.9	17.5	16.3
Central government revenues (% of GDP)	..	15.1	15.0
Overall budget deficit (% of GDP)	..	-1.4	-2.2
Money and quasi money (annual % growth)	32.4	10.5	9.1
Technology and infrastructure			
Telephone mainlines (per 1,000 people)	24	80	76
Cost of 3 min local call ($)	..	0.05	0.06
Personal computers (per 1,000 people)	..	..	16.2
Internet users (thousands)	..	30	40
Paved roads (% of total)	14	..	..
Aircraft departures (thousands)	11	18	32
Trade and finance			
Trade as share of PPP GDP (%)	12.1	17.5	16.1
Trade growth less GDP growth (average %, 1989-99)			-5.1
High-technology exports (% of manufactured exports)	..	8	7
Net barter terms of trade (1995=100)	69	105	..
Foreign direct investment ($ millions)	2	1,104	231
Present value of debt ($ millions)			3,748
Total debt service ($ millions)	208	438	353
Short term debt ($ millions)	210	849	1,053
Aid per capita ($)	68	30	30

EQUATORIAL GUINEA

Population (thousands)	443	Population growth (%)	2.6
Surface area (1,000 sq km)	28.1	Population per sq km	16
GNI ($ millions)	516	GNI per capita ($)	1,170

	1990	1998	1999
People			
Life expectancy (years)	47	50	51
Fertility rate (births per woman)	5.9	5.5	5.3
Infant mortality rate (per 1,000 live births)	121	108	104
Under 5 mortality rate (per 1,000 children)	206	177	170
Child malnutrition (% of children under 5)	..	..	..
Urban population (% of total)	36	46	47
Rural population density (per km^2 arable land)	174	180	..
Illiteracy male (% of people 15 and above)	14	9	8
Illiteracy female (% of people 15 and above)	39	29	27
Net primary enrollment (% of relevant age group)	..	83	..
Net secondary enrollment (% of relevant age group)	..	..	..
Girls in primary school (% of enrollment)	..	49	..
Girls in secondary school (% of enrollment)	..	35	..
Environment			
Forests (1,000 sq. km.)	19	..	18
Deforestation (% change 1990-2000)			0.6
Water use (% of total resources)			0.0
CO$_2$ emissions (metric tons per capita)	0.3	1.5	..
Access to improved water source (% of urban pop.)	..	..	45
Access to sanitation (% of urban population)	..	61	60
Energy use per capita (kg of oil equivalent)	..	..	..
Electricity use per capita (kWh)	..	..	..
Economy			
GDP ($ millions)	132	456	696
GDP growth (annual %)	3.3	21.9	15.1
GDP implicit price deflator (annual % growth)	-2.5	-24.1	38.4
Value added in agriculture (% of GDP)	61.5	21.7	16.0
Value added in industry (% of GDP)	10.6	66.5	75.3
Value added in services (% of GDP)	27.8	11.8	8.6
Exports of goods and services (% of GDP)	32.2	101.7	102.3
Imports of goods and services (% of GDP)	69.6	173.5	85.9
Gross domestic investment (% of GDP)	17.4	91.6	41.4
Central government revenues (% of GDP)	..	..	..
Overall budget deficit (% of GDP)	..	..	..
Money and quasi money (annual % growth)	-52.0	15.6	68.7
Technology and infrastructure			
Telephone mainlines (per 1,000 people)	4	13	..
Cost of 3 min local call ($)	..	0.05	..
Personal computers (per 1,000 people)	..	2.3	2.3
Internet users (thousands)	..	0	1
Paved roads (% of total)	..	..	..
Aircraft departures (thousands)	0	0	0
Trade and finance			
Trade as share of PPP GDP (%)	33.1	6.3	..
Trade growth less GDP growth (average %, 1989-99)			18.2
High-technology exports (% of manufactured exports)	..	..	..
Net barter terms of trade (1995=100)	108	111	..
Foreign direct investment ($ millions)	11	24	120
Present value of debt ($ millions)			218
Total debt service ($ millions)	5	6	5
Short term debt ($ millions)	26	79	55
Aid per capita ($)	173	58	46

Sub-Saharan Africa		Low income

Population (millions)	4	Population growth (%)	2.8
Surface area (1,000 sq km)	118	Population per sq km	40
GNI ($ millions)	779	GNI per capita ($)	200

	1990	1998	1999
People			
Life expectancy (years)	49	51	50
Fertility rate (births per woman)	6.7	58	5.6
Infant mortality rate (per 1,000 live births)	81	62	60
Under 5 mortality rate (per 1,000 children)	140	110	105
Child malnutrition (% of children under 5)	..	44	..
Urban population (% of total)	16	18	18
Rural population density (per km^2 arable land)	..	638	..
Illiteracy male (% of people 15 and above)	42	34	33
Illiteracy female (% of people 15 and above)	72	62	61
Net primary enrollment (% of relevant age group)	..	30	..
Net secondary enrollment (% of relevant age group)	..	16	..
Girls in primary school (% of enrollment)	49	45	..
Girls in secondary school (% of enrollment)	46	42	..
Environment			
Forests (1,000 sq. km.)	16	..	16
Deforestation (% change 1990-2000)			0.3
Water use (% of total resources)	..	..	
CO$_2$ emissions (metric tons per capita)	..	..	..
Access to improved water source (% of urban pop.)	..	..	63
Access to sanitation (% of urban population)	..	..	66
Energy use per capita (kg of oil equivalent)	..	..	
Electricity use per capita (kWh)	..	..	..
Economy			
GDP ($ millions)	437	680	645
GDP growth (annual %)	..	3.9	0.8
GDP implicit price deflator (annual % growth)	..	2.7	8.2
Value added in agriculture (% of GDP)	28.7	16.1	17.1
Value added in industry (% of GDP)	19.2	27.4	29.2
Value added in services (% of GDP)	52.0	56.5	53.7
Exports of goods and services (% of GDP)	20.1	16.0	10.2
Imports of goods and services (% of GDP)	56.7	87.6	78.8
Gross domestic investment (% of GDP)	5.4	47.2	47.3
Central government revenues (% of GDP)	..	..	..
Overall budget deficit (% of GDP)	..	..	..
Money and quasi money (annual % growth)	..	..	..
Technology and infrastructure			
Telephone mainlines (per 1,000 people)	4	7	7
Cost of 3 min local call ($)	0.03	0.02	0.02
Personal computers (per 1,000 people)	..	..	..
Internet users (thousands)	..	0	1
Paved roads (% of total)	19	22	..
Aircraft departures (thousands)	..	..	..
Trade and finance			
Trade as share of PPP GDP (%)	..	..	..
Trade growth less GDP growth (average %, 1989-99)			3.9
High-technology exports (% of manufactured exports)	..	..	..
Net barter terms of trade (1995=100)	..	..	..
Foreign direct investment ($ millions)	0	0	0
Present value of debt ($ millions)			147
Total debt service ($ millions)	..	4	4
Short term debt ($ millions)	..	5	0
Aid per capita ($)	..	43	37

Population (millions)	1	Population growth (%)	-0.5
Surface area (1,000 sq km)	45	Population per sq km	34
GNI ($ millions)	4,906	GNI per capita ($)	3,400

	1990	1998	1999
People			
Life expectancy (years)	69	70	71
Fertility rate (births per woman)	2.0	1.2	1.2
Infant mortality rate (per 1,000 live births)	12	9	10
Under 5 mortality rate (per 1,000 children)	17	13	12
Child malnutrition (% of children under 5)	..	..	..
Urban population (% of total)	71	69	69
Rural population density (per km^2 arable land)	40	40	..
Illiteracy male (% of people 15 and above)	..	..	..
Illiteracy female (% of people 15 and above)	..	..	..
Net primary enrollment (% of relevant age group)	94	87	..
Net secondary enrollment (% of relevant age group)	82	83	..
Girls in primary school (% of enrollment)	48	48	..
Girls in secondary school (% of enrollment)	51	50	..
Environment			
Forests (1,000 sq. km.)	19	..	21
Deforestation (% change 1990-2000)			-0.6
Water use (% of total resources)			1.3
CO_2 emissions (metric tons per capita)	16.1	13.1	..
Access to improved water source (% of urban pop.)	..	..	..
Access to sanitation (% of urban population)	..	..	93
Energy use per capita (kg of oil equivalent)	3,972	3,335	..
Electricity use per capita (kWh)	3,720	3,531	..
Economy			
GDP ($ millions)	6,760	5,200	5,233
GDP growth (annual %)	-7.1	4.7	-1.1
GDP implicit price deflator (annual % growth)	33.7	8.9	3.9
Value added in agriculture (% of GDP)	16.6	6.4	5.8
Value added in industry (% of GDP)	49.7	28.1	25.7
Value added in services (% of GDP)	33.7	65.5	68.5
Exports of goods and services (% of GDP)	60.3	79.9	76.9
Imports of goods and services (% of GDP)	54.4	90.4	82.6
Gross domestic investment (% of GDP)	30.2	29.4	24.5
Central government revenues (% of GDP)	26.3	32.7	31.0
Overall budget deficit (% of GDP)	0.4	-0.1	-0.2
Money and quasi money (annual % growth)	71.1	6.6	24.7
Technology and infrastructure			
Telephone mainlines (per 1,000 people)	204	344	357
Cost of 3 min local call ($)	0.01	0.06	0.07
Personal computers (per 1,000 people)	..	113.8	135.2
Internet users (thousands)	1	150	200
Paved roads (% of total)	52	22	21
Aircraft departures (thousands)	6	11	11
Trade and finance			
Trade as share of PPP GDP (%)	..	67.5	58.5
Trade growth less GDP growth (average %, 1989-99)			13.1
High-technology exports (% of manufactured exports)	..	12	13
Net barter terms of trade (1995=100)	..	..	..
Foreign direct investment ($ millions)	0	581	305
Present value of debt ($ millions)			2,754
Total debt service ($ millions)	4	341	539
Short term debt ($ millions)	0	1,308	1,242
Aid per capita ($)	10	62	57

Sub-Saharan Africa			Low income

Population (millions)	63	Population growth (%)	2.4
Surface area (1,000 sq km)	1,104	Population per sq km	63
GNI ($ millions)	6,524	GNI per capita ($)	100

	1990	1998	1999
People			
Life expectancy (years)	45	43	42
Fertility rate (births per woman)	6.8	6.5	6.3
Infant mortality rate (per 1,000 live births)	124	107	104
Under 5 mortality rate (per 1,000 children)	190	175	180
Child malnutrition (% of children under 5)	48	..	..
Urban population (% of total)	13	17	17
Rural population density (per km^2 arable land)	..	513	..
Illiteracy male (% of people 15 and above)	64	58	57
Illiteracy female (% of people 15 and above)	80	70	68
Net primary enrollment (% of relevant age group)	30	32	..
Net secondary enrollment (% of relevant age group)	..	..	..
Girls in primary school (% of enrollment)	40	37	..
Girls in secondary school (% of enrollment)	43	41	..
Environment			
Forests (1,000 sq. km.)	50	..	46
Deforestation (% change 1990-2000)			0.8
Water use (% of total resources)	..	..	2.0
CO$_2$ emissions (metric tons per capita)	0.1	0.1	..
Access to improved water source (% of urban pop.)	77	..	77
Access to sanitation (% of urban population)	58	..	58
Energy use per capita (kg of oil equivalent)	297	284	..
Electricity use per capita (kWh)	18	22	..
Economy			
GDP ($ millions)	6,842	6,564	6,439
GDP growth (annual %)	2.5	-1.4	6.2
GDP implicit price deflator (annual % growth)	3.5	10.1	1.3
Value added in agriculture (% of GDP)	49.3	52.3	52.3
Value added in industry (% of GDP)	12.7	11.1	11.1
Value added in services (% of GDP)	38.0	36.5	36.5
Exports of goods and services (% of GDP)	7.8	15.8	13.9
Imports of goods and services (% of GDP)	12.4	27.7	29.2
Gross domestic investment (% of GDP)	11.8	17.2	18.1
Central government revenues (% of GDP)	17.4	..	..
Overall budget deficit (% of GDP)	-9.8	..	..
Money and quasi money (annual % growth)	18.5	-2.8	6.8
Technology and infrastructure			
Telephone mainlines (per 1,000 people)	3	3	3
Cost of 3 min local call ($)	0.09	0.02	0.03
Personal computers (per 1,000 people)	..	0.6	0.7
Internet users (thousands)	..	6	8
Paved roads (% of total)	15	14	13
Aircraft departures (thousands)	21	27	25
Trade and finance			
Trade as share of PPP GDP (%)	..	5.5	5.5
Trade growth less GDP growth (average %, 1989-99)			0.7
High-technology exports (% of manufactured exports)	..	0	..
Net barter terms of trade (1995=100)	90	89	..
Foreign direct investment ($ millions)	12	178	90
Present value of debt ($ millions)			3,529
Total debt service ($ millions)	236	119	159
Short term debt ($ millions)	145	626	96
Aid per capita ($)	20	11	10

FAEROE ISLANDS

Population (thousands)	44	Population growth (%)	1.4
Surface area (1,000 sq km)	1.4	Population per sq km	46
GNI ($ millions)	..	GNI per capita ($)	5,020

	1990	1998	1999
People			
Life expectancy (years)	..	..	..
Fertility rate (births per woman)	..	..	..
Infant mortality rate (per 1,000 live births)	..	..	..
Under 5 mortality rate (per 1,000 children)	..	..	..
Child malnutrition (% of children under 5)	..	..	..
Urban population (% of total)	33	37	38
Rural population density (per km^2 arable land)	..	..	..
Illiteracy male (% of people 15 and above)	..	..	..
Illiteracy female (% of people 15 and above)	..	..	..
Net primary enrollment (% of relevant age group)	..	..	..
Net secondary enrollment (% of relevant age group)	..	..	..
Girls in primary school (% of enrollment)	..	..	..
Girls in secondary school (% of enrollment)	..	..	..
Environment			
Forests (1,000 sq. km.)	..	..	..
Deforestation (% change 1990-2000)			..
Water use (% of total resources)	..	..	..
CO_2 emissions (metric tons per capita)	..	..	..
Access to improved water source (% of urban pop.)	..	..	..
Access to sanitation (% of urban population)	..	..	..
Energy use per capita (kg of oil equivalent)	..	..	..
Electricity use per capita (kWh)	..	..	..
Economy			
GDP ($ millions)	..	..	..
GDP growth (annual %)	..	..	..
GDP implicit price deflator (annual % growth)	..	..	..
Value added in agriculture (% of GDP)	..	..	..
Value added in industry (% of GDP)	..	..	..
Value added in services (% of GDP)	..	..	..
Exports of goods and services (% of GDP)	..	..	..
Imports of goods and services (% of GDP)	..	..	..
Gross domestic investment (% of GDP)	..	..	..
Central government revenues (% of GDP)	..	..	..
Overall budget deficit (% of GDP)	..	..	..
Money and quasi money (annual % growth)	..	..	..
Technology and infrastructure			
Telephone mainlines (per 1,000 people)	481	544	557
Cost of 3 min local call ($)	0.37	0.40	..
Personal computers (per 1,000 people)	..	67.1	..
Internet users (thousands)	..	2	3
Paved roads (% of total)	..	..	..
Aircraft departures (thousands)	..	..	..
Trade and finance			
Trade as share of PPP GDP (%)	..	..	..
Trade growth less GDP growth (average %, 1989-99)			..
High-technology exports (% of manufactured exports)	0	1	0
Net barter terms of trade (1995=100)	..	..	..
Foreign direct investment ($ millions)	..	..	..
Present value of debt ($ millions)			..
Total debt service ($ millions)	..	..	..
Short term debt ($ millions)	..	..	..
Aid per capita ($)	..	..	..

East Asia and Pacific   **Lower middle income**

Population (thousands)	801	Population growth (%)		1.3
Surface area (1,000 sq km)	18.3	Population per sq km		44
GNI ($ millions)	1,848	GNI per capita ($)		2,310

	1990	1998	1999
People			
Life expectancy (years)	71	73	73
Fertility rate (births per woman)	3.1	3.0	2.8
Infant mortality rate (per 1,000 live births)	25	20	18
Under 5 mortality rate (per 1,000 children)	31	25	22
Child malnutrition (% of children under 5)	..	8	..
Urban population (% of total)	42	48	49
Rural population density (per km^2 arable land)	269	206	..
Illiteracy male (% of people 15 and above)	8	6	5
Illiteracy female (% of people 15 and above)	15	10	10
Net primary enrollment (% of relevant age group)	101	..	..
Net secondary enrollment (% of relevant age group)	..	..	..
Girls in primary school (% of enrollment)	49	..	..
Girls in secondary school (% of enrollment)	48	..	..
Environment			
Forests (1,000 sq. km.)	8	..	8
Deforestation (% change 1990-2000)			0.2
Water use (% of total resources)	..	..	..
CO_2 emissions (metric tons per capita)	1.2	1.0	..
Access to improved water source (% of urban pop.)	..	..	43
Access to sanitation (% of urban population)	..	..	75
Energy use per capita (kg of oil equivalent)	..	..	..
Electricity use per capita (kWh)	..	..	..
Economy			
GDP ($ millions)	1,381	1,577	1,758
GDP growth (annual %)	2.6	-1.3	7.8
GDP implicit price deflator (annual % growth)	7.1	4.7	2.5
Value added in agriculture (% of GDP)	19.1	19.5	17.9
Value added in industry (% of GDP)	20.6	31.0	29.0
Value added in services (% of GDP)	60.3	49.5	53.1
Exports of goods and services (% of GDP)	63.6	66.0	68.3
Imports of goods and services (% of GDP)	66.0	64.7	63.1
Gross domestic investment (% of GDP)	17.5	12.0	12.7
Central government revenues (% of GDP)	25.9	24.7	..
Overall budget deficit (% of GDP)	-2.3	-4.9	..
Money and quasi money (annual % growth)	25.2	-0.3	14.2
Technology and infrastructure			
Telephone mainlines (per 1,000 people)	57	98	101
Cost of 3 min local call ($)	0.06	0.06	0.06
Personal computers (per 1,000 people)	..	..	49.6
Internet users (thousands)	..	5	8
Paved roads (% of total)	45	49	..
Aircraft departures (thousands)	24	75	67
Trade and finance			
Trade as share of PPP GDP (%)	48.7	38.1	..
Trade growth less GDP growth (average %, 1989-99)			-0.8
High-technology exports (% of manufactured exports)	12	..	..
Net barter terms of trade (1995=100)	86	87	..
Foreign direct investment ($ millions)	92	107	-33
Present value of debt ($ millions)			155
Total debt service ($ millions)	106	35	39
Short term debt ($ millions)	12	21	17
Aid per capita ($)	68	46	43

FINLAND

Population (millions)	5	Population growth (%)	0.3
Surface area (1,000 sq km)	338	Population per sq km	17
GNI ($ millions)	127,764	GNI per capita ($)	24,730

	1990	1998	1999
People			
Life expectancy (years)	75	77	77
Fertility rate (births per woman)	1.8	1.8	1.8
Infant mortality rate (per 1,000 live births)	6	4	4
Under 5 mortality rate (per 1,000 children)	7	5	5
Child malnutrition (% of children under 5)	..	..	..
Urban population (% of total)	61	66	67
Rural population density (per km^2 arable land)	85	81	..
Illiteracy male (% of people 15 and above)	..	..	..
Illiteracy female (% of people 15 and above)	..	..	..
Net primary enrollment (% of relevant age group)	99	98	..
Net secondary enrollment (% of relevant age group)	93	93	..
Girls in primary school (% of enrollment)	49	49	..
Girls in secondary school (% of enrollment)	53	51	..
Environment			
Forests (1,000 sq. km.)	219	..	219
Deforestation (% change 1990-2000)			0.0
Water use (% of total resources)	..	..	2.2
CO_2 emissions (metric tons per capita)	10.8	11.0	..
Access to improved water source (% of urban pop.)	100	100	100
Access to sanitation (% of urban population)	100	100	100
Energy use per capita (kg of oil equivalent)	5,779	6,493	..
Electricity use per capita (kWh)	11,822	14,129	..
Economy			
GDP ($ millions)	136,794	129,335	129,661
GDP growth (annual %)	0.0	5.5	4.0
GDP implicit price deflator (annual % growth)	5.4	3.1	0.7
Value added in agriculture (% of GDP)	5.8	3.3	3.2
Value added in industry (% of GDP)	29.2	28.8	28.4
Value added in services (% of GDP)	65.0	67.9	68.5
Exports of goods and services (% of GDP)	22.8	38.7	37.4
Imports of goods and services (% of GDP)	24.4	29.8	29.3
Gross domestic investment (% of GDP)	29.0	19.7	19.6
Central government revenues (% of GDP)	30.6	32.0	..
Overall budget deficit (% of GDP)	0.2	-0.3	..
Money and quasi money (annual % growth)	..	..	..
Technology and infrastructure			
Telephone mainlines (per 1,000 people)	534	551	557
Cost of 3 min local call ($)	0.16	0.12	0.13
Personal computers (per 1,000 people)	100.0	348.8	360.1
Internet users (thousands)	70	1,740	2,143
Paved roads (% of total)	61	64	65
Aircraft departures (thousands)	93	119	108
Trade and finance			
Trade as share of PPP GDP (%)	60.1	66.9	61.3
Trade growth less GDP growth (average %, 1989-99)			5.0
High-technology exports (% of manufactured exports)	8	22	24
Net barter terms of trade (1995=100)	102	97	..
Foreign direct investment ($ millions)	..	..	..
Present value of debt ($ millions)			..
Total debt service ($ millions)	..	..	..
Short term debt ($ millions)	..	..	..
Aid per capita ($)	..	..	..

88

Population (millions)	59	Population growth (%)		0.4
Surface area (1,000 sq km)	552	Population per sq km		107
GNI ($ millions)	1,453,211	GNI per capita ($)		24,170

	1990	1998	1999
People			
Life expectancy (years)	77	78	79
Fertility rate (births per woman)	1.8	1.8	1.8
Infant mortality rate (per 1,000 live births)	7	5	5
Under 5 mortality rate (per 1,000 children)	9	6	5
Child malnutrition (% of children under 5)	..	..	..
Urban population (% of total)	74	75	75
Rural population density (per km^2 arable land)	82	79	..
Illiteracy male (% of people 15 and above)	..	..	..
Illiteracy female (% of people 15 and above)	..	..	..
Net primary enrollment (% of relevant age group)	101	100	..
Net secondary enrollment (% of relevant age group)	86	95	..
Girls in primary school (% of enrollment)	48	49	..
Girls in secondary school (% of enrollment)	50	49	..
Environment			
Forests (1,000 sq. km.)	147	..	153
Deforestation (% change 1990-2000)			-0.4
Water use (% of total resources)			21.3
CO_2 emissions (metric tons per capita)	6.4	6.0	..
Access to improved water source (% of urban pop.)	..	100	..
Access to sanitation (% of urban population)	..	..	..
Energy use per capita (kg of oil equivalent)	4,012	4,378	..
Electricity use per capita (kWh)	5,321	6,287	..
Economy			
GDP ($ millions)	1,215,893	1,446,951	1,432,323
GDP growth (annual %)	2.6	3.1	2.9
GDP implicit price deflator (annual % growth)	2.9	0.9	0.4
Value added in agriculture (% of GDP)	3.4	2.8	..
Value added in industry (% of GDP)	26.5	23.3	..
Value added in services (% of GDP)	70.1	73.9	..
Exports of goods and services (% of GDP)	21.2	26.1	26.1
Imports of goods and services (% of GDP)	22.2	23.5	23.6
Gross domestic investment (% of GDP)	23.4	18.8	19.0
Central government revenues (% of GDP)	39.9	41.9	..
Overall budget deficit (% of GDP)	-2.1	-3.5	..
Money and quasi money (annual % growth)	..	..	..
Technology and infrastructure			
Telephone mainlines (per 1,000 people)	495	571	582
Cost of 3 min local call ($)	0.13	0.12	0.12
Personal computers (per 1,000 people)	70.5	189.3	221.8
Internet users (thousands)	80	3,500	5,370
Paved roads (% of total)	..	100	100
Aircraft departures (thousands)	442	695	747
Trade and finance			
Trade as share of PPP GDP (%)	44.1	46.5	44.0
Trade growth less GDP growth (average %, 1989-99)			3.6
High-technology exports (% of manufactured exports)	17	23	23
Net barter terms of trade (1995=100)	94	100	..
Foreign direct investment ($ millions)	..	..	..
Present value of debt ($ millions)			..
Total debt service ($ millions)	..	..	..
Short term debt ($ millions)	..	..	..
Aid per capita ($)	..	..	..

FRENCH POLYNESIA

High income

Population (thousands)	231	Population growth (%)		1.5
Surface area (1,000 sq km)	4.0	Population per sq km		63
GNI ($ millions)	3,908	GNI per capita ($)		16,930

	1990	1998	1999
People			
Life expectancy (years)	70	72	73
Fertility rate (births per woman)	3.3	2.8	2.7
Infant mortality rate (per 1,000 live births)	18	11	10
Under 5 mortality rate (per 1,000 children)	..	14	13
Child malnutrition (% of children under 5)	..	..	..
Urban population (% of total)	56	53	53
Rural population density (per km^2 arable land)	1,730	1,767	..
Illiteracy male (% of people 15 and above)	..	..	..
Illiteracy female (% of people 15 and above)	..	..	..
Net primary enrollment (% of relevant age group)	105	103	..
Net secondary enrollment (% of relevant age group)	62	..	..
Girls in primary school (% of enrollment)	48	48	..
Girls in secondary school (% of enrollment)	53	..	..
Environment			
Forests (1,000 sq. km.)	1	..	1
Deforestation (% change 1990-2000)			0.0
Water use (% of total resources)	..	..	..
CO$_2$ emissions (metric tons per capita)	3.1	2.5	..
Access to improved water source (% of urban pop.)	..	..	100
Access to sanitation (% of urban population)	..	..	99
Energy use per capita (kg of oil equivalent)	..	..	..
Electricity use per capita (kWh)	..	..	..
Economy			
GDP ($ millions)	3,181	4,053	3,796
GDP growth (annual %)	2.2	6.2	4.0
GDP implicit price deflator (annual % growth)	0.8	0.7	0.9
Value added in agriculture (% of GDP)	1.2	4.1	4.5
Value added in industry (% of GDP)	..	..	..
Value added in services (% of GDP)	..	..	..
Exports of goods and services (% of GDP)	1.3	4.1	5.0
Imports of goods and services (% of GDP)	28.0	28.7	24.2
Gross domestic investment (% of GDP)	..	..	..
Central government revenues (% of GDP)	..	..	..
Overall budget deficit (% of GDP)	..	..	..
Money and quasi money (annual % growth)	..	..	..
Technology and infrastructure			
Telephone mainlines (per 1,000 people)	194	232	226
Cost of 3 min local call ($)	0.30	0.33	0.29
Personal computers (per 1,000 people)	..	..	..
Internet users (thousands)	..	3	5
Paved roads (% of total)	..	..	..
Aircraft departures (thousands)	..	..	..
Trade and finance			
Trade as share of PPP GDP (%)	..	..	..
Trade growth less GDP growth (average %, 1989-99)			..
High-technology exports (% of manufactured exports)			..
Net barter terms of trade (1995=100)	..	..	..
Foreign direct investment ($ millions)	..	..	..
Present value of debt ($ millions)			..
Total debt service ($ millions)	..	..	..
Short term debt ($ millions)	..	..	..
Aid per capita ($)	1,318	1,629	1,523

Sub-Saharan Africa			Upper middle income
Population (millions)	1	Population growth (%)	2.3
Surface area (1,000 sq km)	268	Population per sq km	5
GNI ($ millions)	3,987	GNI per capita ($)	3,300

	1990	1998	1999
People			
Life expectancy (years)	52	52	53
Fertility rate (births per woman)	5.1	5.2	5.1
Infant mortality rate (per 1,000 live births)	96	87	84
Under 5 mortality rate (per 1,000 children)	164	136	133
Child malnutrition (% of children under 5)	..	..	
Urban population (% of total)	68	79	80
Rural population density (per km^2 arable land)	104	76	..
Illiteracy male (% of people 15 and above)	..	..	..
Illiteracy female (% of people 15 and above)	..	..	..
Net primary enrollment (% of relevant age group)	..	..	..
Net secondary enrollment (% of relevant age group)	..	..	..
Girls in primary school (% of enrollment)	50	50	..
Girls in secondary school (% of enrollment)	..	47	..
Environment			
Forests (1,000 sq. km.)	219	..	218
Deforestation (% change 1990-2000)			0.0
Water use (% of total resources)	..	..	0.0
CO_2 emissions (metric tons per capita)	7.0	3.0	..
Access to improved water source (% of urban pop.)	..	80	73
Access to sanitation (% of urban population)	..	..	25
Energy use per capita (kg of oil equivalent)	1,321	1,413	..
Electricity use per capita (kWh)	806	749	..
Economy			
GDP ($ millions)	5,952	4,619	4,352
GDP growth (annual %)	5.2	2.1	-6.2
GDP implicit price deflator (annual % growth)	15.4	-15.7	4.8
Value added in agriculture (% of GDP)	7.3	7.4	7.8
Value added in industry (% of GDP)	43.0	43.5	41.2
Value added in services (% of GDP)	49.7	49.1	51.1
Exports of goods and services (% of GDP)	46.0	45.9	45.1
Imports of goods and services (% of GDP)	30.9	44.2	38.3
Gross domestic investment (% of GDP)	21.7	37.3	28.0
Central government revenues (% of GDP)	23.0	..	..
Overall budget deficit (% of GDP)	3.2	..	..
Money and quasi money (annual % growth)	3.3	-1.8	-3.0
Technology and infrastructure			
Telephone mainlines (per 1,000 people)	22	33	32
Cost of 3 min local call ($)	0.23	0.15	..
Personal computers (per 1,000 people)	..	8.5	8.4
Internet users (thousands)	..	2	3
Paved roads (% of total)	8	8	..
Aircraft departures (thousands)	10	10	7
Trade and finance			
Trade as share of PPP GDP (%)	62.5	43.1	52.2
Trade growth less GDP growth (average %, 1989-99)			-1.4
High-technology exports (% of manufactured exports)	..	27	..
Net barter terms of trade (1995=100)	135	97	..
Foreign direct investment ($ millions)	74	211	200
Present value of debt ($ millions)			4,125
Total debt service ($ millions)	176	307	538
Short term debt ($ millions)	693	478	602
Aid per capita ($)	138	38	39

THE GAMBIA

Sub-Saharan Africa — Low income

Population (millions)	1	Population growth (%)	2.8
Surface area (1,000 sq km)	11	Population per sq km	125
GNI ($ millions)	415	GNI per capita ($)	330

	1990	1998	1999
People			
Life expectancy (years)	49	53	53
Fertility rate (births per woman)	5.9	5.7	5.5
Infant mortality rate (per 1,000 live births)	109	78	75
Under 5 mortality rate (per 1,000 children)	127	110	110
Child malnutrition (% of children under 5)	..	26	..
Urban population (% of total)	26	31	32
Rural population density (per km^2 arable land)	376	430	..
Illiteracy male (% of people 15 and above)	68	58	57
Illiteracy female (% of people 15 and above)	80	73	72
Net primary enrollment (% of relevant age group)	51	65	..
Net secondary enrollment (% of relevant age group)	18	..	..
Girls in primary school (% of enrollment)	41	44	45
Girls in secondary school (% of enrollment)	33	38	..
Environment			
Forests (1,000 sq. km.)	4	..	5
Deforestation (% change 1990-2000)			-1.0
Water use (% of total resources)	..	..	0.4
CO_2 emissions (metric tons per capita)	0.2	0.2	..
Access to improved water source (% of urban pop.)	..	..	80
Access to sanitation (% of urban population)	..	..	41
Energy use per capita (kg of oil equivalent)	..	..	..
Electricity use per capita (kWh)	..	..	..
Economy			
GDP ($ millions)	317	417	393
GDP growth (annual %)	3.6	4.9	6.4
GDP implicit price deflator (annual % growth)	12.0	1.1	-5.0
Value added in agriculture (% of GDP)	29.0	29.6	31.4
Value added in industry (% of GDP)	13.1	13.3	13.0
Value added in services (% of GDP)	57.9	57.1	55.7
Exports of goods and services (% of GDP)	59.9	51.0	50.5
Imports of goods and services (% of GDP)	71.6	66.6	66.6
Gross domestic investment (% of GDP)	22.3	18.4	17.8
Central government revenues (% of GDP)	19.5	..	..
Overall budget deficit (% of GDP)	-0.8	..	..
Money and quasi money (annual % growth)	8.4	10.2	12.1
Technology and infrastructure			
Telephone mainlines (per 1,000 people)	7	21	23
Cost of 3 min local call ($)	0.05	0.32	0.30
Personal computers (per 1,000 people)	..	3.3	7.9
Internet users (thousands)	..	3	3
Paved roads (% of total)	32	35	..
Aircraft departures (thousands)	..	..	..
Trade and finance			
Trade as share of PPP GDP (%)	17.3	14.9	..
Trade growth less GDP growth (average %, 1989-99)			-2.8
High-technology exports (% of manufactured exports)	..	19	..
Net barter terms of trade (1995=100)	102	101	..
Foreign direct investment ($ millions)	0	13	14
Present value of debt ($ millions)			258
Total debt service ($ millions)	38	27	21
Short term debt ($ millions)	16	15	22
Aid per capita ($)	108	31	26

GEORGIA

Europe & Central Asia		Low income	
Population (millions)	5	Population growth (%)	0.2
Surface area (1,000 sq km)	70	Population per sq km	78
GNI ($ millions)	3,362	GNI per capita ($)	620

	1990	1998	1999
People			
Life expectancy (years)	72	73	73
Fertility rate (births per woman)	2.2	1.3	1.3
Infant mortality rate (per 1,000 live births)	16	15	15
Under 5 mortality rate (per 1,000 children)	..	21	20
Child malnutrition (% of children under 5)	..	..	3
Urban population (% of total)	56	60	60
Rural population density (per km^2 arable land)	336	279	..
Illiteracy male (% of people 15 and above)	..	..	..
Illiteracy female (% of people 15 and above)	..	..	..
Net primary enrollment (% of relevant age group)	..	87	..
Net secondary enrollment (% of relevant age group)	..	74	..
Girls in primary school (% of enrollment)	49	48	..
Girls in secondary school (% of enrollment)	48	49	..
Environment			
Forests (1,000 sq. km.)	30	..	30
Deforestation (% change 1990-2000)			0.0
Water use (% of total resources)	..	..	5.5
CO_2 emissions (metric tons per capita)	2.8	0.8	..
Access to improved water source (% of urban pop.)	..	..	..
Access to sanitation (% of urban population)	..	..	..
Energy use per capita (kg of oil equivalent)	1,230	464	..
Electricity use per capita (kWh)	1,785	1,257	..
Economy			
GDP ($ millions)	..	3,451	2,737
GDP growth (annual %)	..	2.9	3.3
GDP implicit price deflator (annual % growth)	..	4.5	9.4
Value added in agriculture (% of GDP)	..	35.6	36.0
Value added in industry (% of GDP)	..	13.0	12.9
Value added in services (% of GDP)	..	51.5	51.1
Exports of goods and services (% of GDP)	..	20.9	27.0
Imports of goods and services (% of GDP)	..	41.6	46.0
Gross domestic investment (% of GDP)	..	17.2	16.8
Central government revenues (% of GDP)	..	12.2	12.3
Overall budget deficit (% of GDP)	..	-3.6	-4.6
Money and quasi money (annual % growth)	..	-1.1	21.1
Technology and infrastructure			
Telephone mainlines (per 1,000 people)	99	115	123
Cost of 3 min local call ($)	0.00	0.00	..
Personal computers (per 1,000 people)	..	..	..
Internet users (thousands)	..	5	20
Paved roads (% of total)	94	94	..
Aircraft departures (thousands)	..	3	3
Trade and finance			
Trade as share of PPP GDP (%)	..	8.5	6.3
Trade growth less GDP growth (average %, 1989-99)			..
High-technology exports (% of manufactured exports)	..	..	..
Net barter terms of trade (1995=100)	..	..	..
Foreign direct investment ($ millions)	0	265	82
Present value of debt ($ millions)			1,289
Total debt service ($ millions)	0	213	108
Short term debt ($ millions)	0	28	7
Aid per capita ($)	0	31	44

93

GERMANY

Population (millions)	82	Population growth (%)	0.1
Surface area (1,000 sq km)	357	Population per sq km	235
GNI ($ millions)	2,103,804	GNI per capita ($)	25,620

	1990	1998	1999
People			
Life expectancy (years)	75	77	77
Fertility rate (births per woman)	1.5	1.4	1.4
Infant mortality rate (per 1,000 live births)	7	5	5
Under 5 mortality rate (per 1,000 children)	9	6	5
Child malnutrition (% of children under 5)	..	..	..
Urban population (% of total)	85	87	87
Rural population density (per km² arable land)	98	89	..
Illiteracy male (% of people 15 and above)	..	..	..
Illiteracy female (% of people 15 and above)	..	..	..
Net primary enrollment (% of relevant age group)	84	86	..
Net secondary enrollment (% of relevant age group)	89	88	..
Girls in primary school (% of enrollment)	49	48	..
Girls in secondary school (% of enrollment)	48	48	..
Environment			
Forests (1,000 sq. km.)	107	..	107
Deforestation (% change 1990-2000)			0.0
Water use (% of total resources)	..	..	26.0
CO_2 emissions (metric tons per capita)	11.3	10.4	..
Access to improved water source (% of urban pop.)	100	..	..
Access to sanitation (% of urban population)	..	..	..
Energy use per capita (kg of oil equivalent)	4,478	4,199	..
Electricity use per capita (kWh)	5,729	5,681	..
Economy			
GDP ($ millions)	1,770,368	2,150,519	2,111,940
GDP growth (annual %)	2.2	2.2	1.5
GDP implicit price deflator (annual % growth)	5.0	1.0	1.0
Value added in agriculture (% of GDP)	1.3	1.2	1.1
Value added in industry (% of GDP)	33.1	29.0	28.4
Value added in services (% of GDP)	64.4	69.9	70.6
Exports of goods and services (% of GDP)	26.3	28.9	29.2
Imports of goods and services (% of GDP)	26.5	27.2	28.1
Gross domestic investment (% of GDP)	24.3	21.8	22.2
Central government revenues (% of GDP)	27.5	31.4	..
Overall budget deficit (% of GDP)	-2.1	-0.9	..
Money and quasi money (annual % growth)	..	..	..
Technology and infrastructure			
Telephone mainlines (per 1,000 people)	441	567	590
Cost of 3 min local call ($)	0.14	0.11	0.11
Personal computers (per 1,000 people)	89.9	279.3	297.0
Internet users (thousands)	200	8,100	14,400
Paved roads (% of total)	99	99	..
Aircraft departures (thousands)	344	672	710
Trade and finance			
Trade as share of PPP GDP (%)	51.9	53.9	52.0
Trade growth less GDP growth (average %, 1989-99)			3.4
High-technology exports (% of manufactured exports)	12	15	17
Net barter terms of trade (1995=100)	102	99	..
Foreign direct investment ($ millions)	..	..	..
Present value of debt ($ millions)			..
Total debt service ($ millions)	..	..	..
Short term debt ($ millions)	..	..	..
Aid per capita ($)	..	..	..

94

GHANA

Population (millions)	19	Population growth (%)	2.3
Surface area (1,000 sq km)	239	Population per sq km	83
GNI ($ millions)	7,451	GNI per capita ($)	400

	1990	1998	1999
People			
Life expectancy (years)	57	60	58
Fertility rate (births per woman)	5.5	4.5	4.3
Infant mortality rate (per 1,000 live births)	66	55	57
Under 5 mortality rate (per 1,000 children)	119	104	109
Child malnutrition (% of children under 5)	30	27	25
Urban population (% of total)	34	37	38
Rural population density (per km^2 arable land)	364	319	..
Illiteracy male (% of people 15 and above)	30	22	21
Illiteracy female (% of people 15 and above)	53	40	39
Net primary enrollment (% of relevant age group)	..	..	..
Net secondary enrollment (% of relevant age group)	..	..	..
Girls in primary school (% of enrollment)	45	46	..
Girls in secondary school (% of enrollment)	..	..	..
Environment			
Forests (1,000 sq. km.)	75	..	63
Deforestation (% change 1990-2000)			1.7
Water use (% of total resources)			0.6
CO_2 emissions (metric tons per capita)	0.3	0.3	..
Access to improved water source (% of urban pop.)	83	..	87
Access to sanitation (% of urban population)	59	..	62
Energy use per capita (kg of oil equivalent)	355	396	..
Electricity use per capita (kWh)	300	289	..
Economy			
GDP ($ millions)	5,886	7,474	7,774
GDP growth (annual %)	3.3	4.7	4.4
GDP implicit price deflator (annual % growth)	31.2	16.0	14.0
Value added in agriculture (% of GDP)	44.8	36.0	35.6
Value added in industry (% of GDP)	16.8	25.3	25.3
Value added in services (% of GDP)	38.4	38.7	39.1
Exports of goods and services (% of GDP)	16.9	33.9	33.5
Imports of goods and services (% of GDP)	25.9	46.7	50.5
Gross domestic investment (% of GDP)	14.4	23.6	23.2
Central government revenues (% of GDP)	12.5	17.0	..
Overall budget deficit (% of GDP)	0.2	-2.5	..
Money and quasi money (annual % growth)	13.3	26.1	16.2
Technology and infrastructure			
Telephone mainlines (per 1,000 people)	3	8	8
Cost of 3 min local call ($)	0.06	0.08	0.08
Personal computers (per 1,000 people)	0.0	2.1	2.5
Internet users (thousands)	..	6	20
Paved roads (% of total)	20	24	..
Aircraft departures (thousands)	13	4	5
Trade and finance			
Trade as share of PPP GDP (%)	10.0	13.1	15.1
Trade growth less GDP growth (average %, 1989-99)			5.7
High-technology exports (% of manufactured exports)	..	..	14
Net barter terms of trade (1995=100)	100	98	..
Foreign direct investment ($ millions)	15	56	17
Present value of debt ($ millions)			5,004
Total debt service ($ millions)	368	578	524
Short term debt ($ millions)	320	716	711
Aid per capita ($)	38	38	32

95

GREECE

Population (millions)	11	Population growth (%)	0.2
Surface area (1,000 sq km)	132	Population per sq km	82
GNI ($ millions)	127,648	GNI per capita ($)	12,110

	1990	1998	1999
People			
Life expectancy (years)	77	78	78
Fertility rate (births per woman)	1.4	1.3	1.3
Infant mortality rate (per 1,000 live births)	10	6	6
Under 5 mortality rate (per 1,000 children)	11	9	7
Child malnutrition (% of children under 5)	..	..	..
Urban population (% of total)	59	60	60
Rural population density (per km² arable land)	148	149	..
Illiteracy male (% of people 15 and above)	2	2	2
Illiteracy female (% of people 15 and above)	8	5	4
Net primary enrollment (% of relevant age group)	94	90	..
Net secondary enrollment (% of relevant age group)	83	87	..
Girls in primary school (% of enrollment)	48	48	..
Girls in secondary school (% of enrollment)	48	49	..
Environment			
Forests (1,000 sq. km.)	33	..	36
Deforestation (% change 1990-2000)			-0.9
Water use (% of total resources)			10.2
CO_2 emissions (metric tons per capita)	7.8	8.3	..
Access to improved water source (% of urban pop.)	..		..
Access to sanitation (% of urban population)	..	..	..
Energy use per capita (kg of oil equivalent)	2,171	2,565	..
Electricity use per capita (kWh)	2,802	3,739	..
Economy			
GDP ($ millions)	84,925	121,513	125,088
GDP growth (annual %)	0.0	3.7	3.4
GDP implicit price deflator (annual % growth)	20.6	4.9	3.0
Value added in agriculture (% of GDP)	9.7	7.4	..
Value added in industry (% of GDP)	25.5	20.4	..
Value added in services (% of GDP)	64.8	72.2	..
Exports of goods and services (% of GDP)	18.5	17.6	18.6
Imports of goods and services (% of GDP)	28.5	25.5	25.3
Gross domestic investment (% of GDP)	22.6	22.0	22.5
Central government revenues (% of GDP)	27.6	23.6	..
Overall budget deficit (% of GDP)	-22.7	-4.4	..
Money and quasi money (annual % growth)	14.3	6.7	16.7
Technology and infrastructure			
Telephone mainlines (per 1,000 people)	389	522	528
Cost of 3 min local call ($)	0.00	0.04	0.07
Personal computers (per 1,000 people)	17.2	51.9	60.2
Internet users (thousands)	5	350	750
Paved roads (% of total)	92	92	..
Aircraft departures (thousands)	80	91	91
Trade and finance			
Trade as share of PPP GDP (%)	24.4	25.8	25.5
Trade growth less GDP growth (average %, 1989-99)			2.9
High-technology exports (% of manufactured exports)	3	9	10
Net barter terms of trade (1995=100)	92	90	..
Foreign direct investment ($ millions)	..	..	..
Present value of debt ($ millions)			..
Total debt service ($ millions)	..	..	..
Short term debt ($ millions)	..	..	..
Aid per capita ($)	4	..	..

96

Population (thousands)	56	Population growth (%)	..
Surface area (1,000 sq km)	341.7	Population per sq km	0
GNI ($ millions)	..	GNI per capita ($)	..

	1990	1998	1999
People			
Life expectancy (years)	..	..	..
Fertility rate (births per woman)	..	..	..
Infant mortality rate (per 1,000 live births)	..	..	..
Under 5 mortality rate (per 1,000 children)	..	..	..
Child malnutrition (% of children under 5)	..	..	..
Urban population (% of total)	79	82	82
Rural population density (per km^2 arable land)	..	..	..
Illiteracy male (% of people 15 and above)	..	..	..
Illiteracy female (% of people 15 and above)	..	..	..
Net primary enrollment (% of relevant age group)	..	..	..
Net secondary enrollment (% of relevant age group)	..	..	..
Girls in primary school (% of enrollment)	..	..	..
Girls in secondary school (% of enrollment)	..	..	..
Environment			
Forests (1,000 sq. km.)	..	..	..
Deforestation (% change 1990-2000)			..
Water use (% of total resources)			..
CO_2 emissions (metric tons per capita)	..	..	..
Access to improved water source (% of urban pop.)	..	..	..
Access to sanitation (% of urban population)	..	..	..
Energy use per capita (kg of oil equivalent)	..	..	..
Electricity use per capita (kWh)	..	..	..
Economy			
GDP ($ millions)	..	*1,252*	..
GDP growth (annual %)	..	..	..
GDP implicit price deflator (annual % growth)	..	..	..
Value added in agriculture (% of GDP)	..	..	..
Value added in industry (% of GDP)	..	..	..
Value added in services (% of GDP)	..	..	..
Exports of goods and services (% of GDP)	..	..	..
Imports of goods and services (% of GDP)	..	..	..
Gross domestic investment (% of GDP)	..	..	..
Central government revenues (% of GDP)	..	..	..
Overall budget deficit (% of GDP)	..	..	..
Money and quasi money (annual % growth)	..	..	..
Technology and infrastructure			
Telephone mainlines (per 1,000 people)	299	445	457
Cost of 3 min local call ($)	0.48	0.32	0.30
Personal computers (per 1,000 people)	..	107.3	..
Internet users (thousands)	..	1	..
Paved roads (% of total)	..	..	..
Aircraft departures (thousands)	..	..	..
Trade and finance			
Trade as share of PPP GDP (%)	..	..	..
Trade growth less GDP growth (average %, 1989-99)			..
High-technology exports (% of manufactured exports)	11	12	11
Net barter terms of trade (1995=100)	..	..	..
Foreign direct investment ($ millions)	..	..	..
Present value of debt ($ millions)			..
Total debt service ($ millions)	..	..	..
Short term debt ($ millions)	..	..	..
Aid per capita ($)	..	..	..

97

GRENADA

Population (thousands)	97	Population growth (%)	0.8
Surface area (1,000 sq km)	0.3	Population per sq km	285
GNI ($ millions)	334	GNI per capita ($)	3,440

	1990	1998	1999
People			
Life expectancy (years)	..	72	72
Fertility rate (births per woman)	..	3.6	3.4
Infant mortality rate (per 1,000 live births)	..	14	13
Under 5 mortality rate (per 1,000 children)	37	20	18
Child malnutrition (% of children under 5)	..	..	..
Urban population (% of total)	34	37	37
Rural population density (per km^2 arable land)	3,079	3,027	..
Illiteracy male (% of people 15 and above)	..	..	..
Illiteracy female (% of people 15 and above)	..	..	..
Net primary enrollment (% of relevant age group)	..	..	..
Net secondary enrollment (% of relevant age group)	..	..	..
Girls in primary school (% of enrollment)	45	49	..
Girls in secondary school (% of enrollment)	53	..	..
Environment			
Forests (1,000 sq. km.)	0	..	0
Deforestation (% change 1990-2000)			0.0
Water use (% of total resources)			..
CO_2 emissions (metric tons per capita)	1.3	1.9	..
Access to improved water source (% of urban pop.)	..	..	97
Access to sanitation (% of urban population)	..	..	96
Energy use per capita (kg of oil equivalent)	..	..	..
Electricity use per capita (kWh)	..	..	..
Economy			
GDP ($ millions)	221	341	366
GDP growth (annual %)	5.2	6.8	8.2
GDP implicit price deflator (annual % growth)	-1.4	1.3	-0.7
Value added in agriculture (% of GDP)	13.4	7.9	8.1
Value added in industry (% of GDP)	18.0	21.5	22.2
Value added in services (% of GDP)	68.6	70.6	69.7
Exports of goods and services (% of GDP)	42.4	47.4	48.9
Imports of goods and services (% of GDP)	62.8	74.6	76.5
Gross domestic investment (% of GDP)	38.1	37.4	41.0
Central government revenues (% of GDP)	25.4	27.5	..
Overall budget deficit (% of GDP)	-1.9	2.3	..
Money and quasi money (annual % growth)	10.0	11.8	13.4
Technology and infrastructure			
Telephone mainlines (per 1,000 people)	177	298	315
Cost of 3 min local call ($)	0.00	0.00	0.00
Personal computers (per 1,000 people)	..	108.3	117.8
Internet users (thousands)	0	2	3
Paved roads (% of total)	55	61	..
Aircraft departures (thousands)	..	..	..
Trade and finance			
Trade as share of PPP GDP (%)	30.5	38.0	..
Trade growth less GDP growth (average %, 1989-99)			1.8
High-technology exports (% of manufactured exports)	..	3	0
Net barter terms of trade (1995=100)	..	..	..
Foreign direct investment ($ millions)	13	51	43
Present value of debt ($ millions)			127
Total debt service ($ millions)	3	9	9
Short term debt ($ millions)	13	70	29
Aid per capita ($)	147	64	106

98

GUAM

Population (thousands)	152	Population growth (%)	1.9
Surface area (1,000 sq km)	0.6	Population per sq km	276
GNI ($ millions)	..	GNI per capita ($)	..

	1990	1998	1999
People			
Life expectancy (years)	74	77	78
Fertility rate (births per woman)	3.3	4.1	3.9
Infant mortality rate (per 1,000 live births)	9	8	8
Under 5 mortality rate (per 1,000 children)	..	11	10
Child malnutrition (% of children under 5)	..	..	..
Urban population (% of total)	38	39	39
Rural population density (per km^2 arable land)	1,381	1,521	..
Illiteracy male (% of people 15 and above)	..	..	..
Illiteracy female (% of people 15 and above)	..	..	..
Net primary enrollment (% of relevant age group)	..	..	..
Net secondary enrollment (% of relevant age group)	..	..	..
Girls in primary school (% of enrollment)	..	..	..
Girls in secondary school (% of enrollment)	..	..	..
Environment			
Forests (1,000 sq. km.)	0	..	0
Deforestation (% change 1990-2000)			0.0
Water use (% of total resources)	..		..
CO_2 emissions (metric tons per capita)	16.9	27.9	..
Access to improved water source (% of urban pop.)	..	..	..
Access to sanitation (% of urban population)	..	..	..
Energy use per capita (kg of oil equivalent)	..	..	..
Electricity use per capita (kWh)	..	..	..
Economy			
GDP ($ millions)	..	..	..
GDP growth (annual %)	..	..	..
GDP implicit price deflator (annual % growth)	..	..	..
Value added in agriculture (% of GDP)	..	..	..
Value added in industry (% of GDP)	..	..	..
Value added in services (% of GDP)	..	..	..
Exports of goods and services (% of GDP)	..	..	..
Imports of goods and services (% of GDP)	..	..	..
Gross domestic investment (% of GDP)	..	..	..
Central government revenues (% of GDP)	..	..	..
Overall budget deficit (% of GDP)	..	..	..
Money and quasi money (annual % growth)	..	..	..
Technology and infrastructure			
Telephone mainlines (per 1,000 people)	293	466	..
Cost of 3 min local call ($)	0.00	0.00	0.00
Personal computers (per 1,000 people)	..	..	..
Internet users (thousands)	..	4	5
Paved roads (% of total)	..	..	..
Aircraft departures (thousands)	..	..	..
Trade and finance			
Trade as share of PPP GDP (%)	..	..	..
Trade growth less GDP growth (average %, 1989-99)			..
High-technology exports (% of manufactured exports)	..	..	..
Net barter terms of trade (1995=100)	..	..	..
Foreign direct investment ($ millions)	..	..	..
Present value of debt ($ millions)			..
Total debt service ($ millions)	..	..	..
Short term debt ($ millions)	..	..	..
Aid per capita ($)	..	..	..

GUATEMALA

Lower middle income

Population (millions)	11	Population growth (%)		2.6
Surface area (1,000 sq km)	109	Population per sq km		102
GNI ($ millions)	18,625	GNI per capita ($)		1,680

	1990	1998	1999
People			
Life expectancy (years)	61	64	65
Fertility rate (births per woman)	5.3	5.0	4.7
Infant mortality rate (per 1,000 live births)	56	43	40
Under 5 mortality rate (per 1,000 children)	68	57	52
Child malnutrition (% of children under 5)	..	27	24
Urban population (% of total)	38	39	39
Rural population density (per km² arable land)	417	482	..
Illiteracy male (% of people 15 and above)	31	25	24
Illiteracy female (% of people 15 and above)	47	40	40
Net primary enrollment (% of relevant age group)	..	73	..
Net secondary enrollment (% of relevant age group)	..	..	..
Girls in primary school (% of enrollment)	46	46	..
Girls in secondary school (% of enrollment)	..	47	..
Environment			
Forests (1,000 sq. km.)	34	..	29
Deforestation (% change 1990-2000)			1.7
Water use (% of total resources)			0.9
CO₂ emissions (metric tons per capita)	0.7	0.8	..
Access to improved water source (% of urban pop.)	88	..	97
Access to sanitation (% of urban population)	94	..	98
Energy use per capita (kg of oil equivalent)	501	579	..
Electricity use per capita (kWh)	226	322	..
Economy			
GDP ($ millions)	7,650	19,306	18,215
GDP growth (annual %)	3.1	5.0	3.6
GDP implicit price deflator (annual % growth)	40.5	9.5	5.2
Value added in agriculture (% of GDP)	25.9	23.4	23.1
Value added in industry (% of GDP)	19.8	20.0	20.2
Value added in services (% of GDP)	54.3	56.6	56.7
Exports of goods and services (% of GDP)	21.0	18.2	19.0
Imports of goods and services (% of GDP)	24.8	26.3	27.4
Gross domestic investment (% of GDP)	13.6	17.4	17.4
Central government revenues (% of GDP)	..	..	..
Overall budget deficit (% of GDP)	..	..	..
Money and quasi money (annual % growth)	25.8	19.4	12.5
Technology and infrastructure			
Telephone mainlines (per 1,000 people)	21	48	55
Cost of 3 min local call ($)	0.04	0.10	0.09
Personal computers (per 1,000 people)	..	8.3	9.9
Internet users (thousands)	..	50	65
Paved roads (% of total)	25	31	35
Aircraft departures (thousands)	3	10	7
Trade and finance			
Trade as share of PPP GDP (%)	11.3	18.8	16.6
Trade growth less GDP growth (average %, 1989-99)			3.7
High-technology exports (% of manufactured exports)	..	7	9
Net barter terms of trade (1995=100)	75	96	..
Foreign direct investment ($ millions)	48	673	155
Present value of debt ($ millions)			4,375
Total debt service ($ millions)	214	396	414
Short term debt ($ millions)	409	1,394	1,369
Aid per capita ($)	23	22	26

Population (millions)	7	Population growth (%)		2.3
Surface area (1,000 sq km)	246	Population per sq km		30
GNI ($ millions)	3,556	GNI per capita ($)		490

	1990	1998	1999
People			
Life expectancy (years)	44	46	46
Fertility rate (births per woman)	5.9	5.5	5.3
Infant mortality rate (per 1,000 live births)	121	98	96
Under 5 mortality rate (per 1,000 children)	215	177	167
Child malnutrition (% of children under 5)	..	..	..
Urban population (% of total)	26	31	32
Rural population density (per km^2 arable land)	587	550	..
Illiteracy male (% of people 15 and above)	..	..	..
Illiteracy female (% of people 15 and above)	..	..	..
Net primary enrollment (% of relevant age group)	26	42	..
Net secondary enrollment (% of relevant age group)	7	..	..
Girls in primary school (% of enrollment)	32	37	38
Girls in secondary school (% of enrollment)	24	26	..

	1990	1998	1999
Environment			
Forests (1,000 sq. km.)	73	..	69
Deforestation (% change 1990-2000)			0.5
Water use (% of total resources)			0.3
CO$_2$ emissions (metric tons per capita)	0.2	0.2	..
Access to improved water source (% of urban pop.)	72	..	72
Access to sanitation (% of urban population)	94	..	94
Energy use per capita (kg of oil equivalent)	..	..	..
Electricity use per capita (kWh)	..	..	..

	1990	1998	1999
Economy			
GDP ($ millions)	2,818	3,585	3,482
GDP growth (annual %)	4.4	4.5	3.3
GDP implicit price deflator (annual % growth)	23.9	2.4	5.5
Value added in agriculture (% of GDP)	23.8	23.7	23.9
Value added in industry (% of GDP)	33.3	37.5	37.4
Value added in services (% of GDP)	42.9	38.8	38.7
Exports of goods and services (% of GDP)	30.9	23.1	21.4
Imports of goods and services (% of GDP)	30.6	25.2	23.5
Gross domestic investment (% of GDP)	17.5	18.0	17.5
Central government revenues (% of GDP)	16.0	11.2	11.9
Overall budget deficit (% of GDP)	-3.3	-4.3	-2.4
Money and quasi money (annual % growth)	-17.4	6.4	-77.5

	1990	1998	1999
Technology and infrastructure			
Telephone mainlines (per 1,000 people)	2	5	6
Cost of 3 min local call ($)	0.09	0.09	0.10
Personal computers (per 1,000 people)	..	3.2	3.4
Internet users (thousands)	..	1	5
Paved roads (% of total)	15	17	..
Aircraft departures (thousands)	1	0	1

	1990	1998	1999
Trade and finance			
Trade as share of PPP GDP (%)	15.9	14.2	14.1
Trade growth less GDP growth (average %, 1989-99)			-1.8
High-technology exports (% of manufactured exports)	..	0	
Net barter terms of trade (1995=100)	143	89	..
Foreign direct investment ($ millions)	18	18	63
Present value of debt ($ millions)			2,415
Total debt service ($ millions)	169	159	132
Short term debt ($ millions)	172	293	334
Aid per capita ($)	51	51	33

GUINEA-BISSAU

Population (millions)	1	Population growth (%)		2.0
Surface area (1,000 sq km)	36	Population per sq km		42
GNI ($ millions)	194	GNI per capita ($)		160

	1990	1998	1999
People			
Life expectancy (years)	42	*44*	44
Fertility rate (births per woman)	6.0	*5.8*	5.5
Infant mortality rate (per 1,000 live births)	145	*130*	127
Under 5 mortality rate (per 1,000 children)	246	*220*	214
Child malnutrition (% of children under 5)	..	..	..
Urban population (% of total)	20	23	23
Rural population density (per km^2 arable land)	259	298	..
Illiteracy male (% of people 15 and above)	54	43	42
Illiteracy female (% of people 15 and above)	89	83	82
Net primary enrollment (% of relevant age group)	..	..	..
Net secondary enrollment (% of relevant age group)	..	..	..
Girls in primary school (% of enrollment)	*36*	*37*	..
Girls in secondary school (% of enrollment)	..	..	..
Environment			
Forests (1,000 sq. km.)	24	..	22
Deforestation (% change 1990-2000)			*0.9*
Water use (% of total resources)			0.1
CO$_2$ emissions (metric tons per capita)	0.2	*0.2*	..
Access to improved water source (% of urban pop.)	..	..	29
Access to sanitation (% of urban population)	..	..	*88*
Energy use per capita (kg of oil equivalent)	..	..	..
Electricity use per capita (kWh)	..	..	..
Economy			
GDP ($ millions)	244	206	218
GDP growth (annual %)	6.1	-28.1	7.8
GDP implicit price deflator (annual % growth)	30.2	7.6	2.8
Value added in agriculture (% of GDP)	60.8	62.4	62.3
Value added in industry (% of GDP)	18.6	12.7	11.8
Value added in services (% of GDP)	20.6	24.9	26.0
Exports of goods and services (% of GDP)	9.9	14.5	25.6
Imports of goods and services (% of GDP)	37.0	35.1	44.0
Gross domestic investment (% of GDP)	29.9	11.3	16.3
Central government revenues (% of GDP)	*11.1*	..	..
Overall budget deficit (% of GDP)	*-13.9*	..	..
Money and quasi money (annual % growth)	574.6	-11.1	21.5
Technology and infrastructure			
Telephone mainlines (per 1,000 people)	6	7	..
Cost of 3 min local call ($)	0.08	*0.14*	0.15
Personal computers (per 1,000 people)	..	..	..
Internet users (thousands)	..	0	2
Paved roads (% of total)	8	*10*	..
Aircraft departures (thousands)	1	1	0
Trade and finance			
Trade as share of PPP GDP (%)	12.7	12.3	17.9
Trade growth less GDP growth (average %, 1989-99)			-0.7
High-technology exports (% of manufactured exports)	..	..	..
Net barter terms of trade (1995=100)	143	*87*	..
Foreign direct investment ($ millions)	2	0	3
Present value of debt ($ millions)			709
Total debt service ($ millions)	8	8	10
Short term debt ($ millions)	57	76	82
Aid per capita ($)	132	82	44

GUYANA

Lower middle income

Population (thousands)	856	Population growth (%)	0.8
Surface area (1,000 sq km)	215.0	Population per sq km	4
GNI ($ millions)	651	GNI per capita ($)	760

	1990	1998	1999
People			
Life expectancy (years)	63	*64*	64
Fertility rate (births per woman)	2.6	*2.3*	2.3
Infant mortality rate (per 1,000 live births)	64	58	57
Under 5 mortality rate (per 1,000 children)	90	78	76
Child malnutrition (% of children under 5)	..	18	..
Urban population (% of total)	33	37	38
Rural population density (per km^2 arable land)	111	111	..
Illiteracy male (% of people 15 and above)	2	1	1
Illiteracy female (% of people 15 and above)	4	2	2
Net primary enrollment (% of relevant age group)	93	87	..
Net secondary enrollment (% of relevant age group)	71	66	..
Girls in primary school (% of enrollment)	*49*	*49*	..
Girls in secondary school (% of enrollment)	52	*51*	..
Environment			
Forests (1,000 sq. km.)	174	..	*169*
Deforestation (% change 1990-2000)			0.3
Water use (% of total resources)	..	..	0.6
CO_2 emissions (metric tons per capita)	1.4	*1.2*	..
Access to improved water source (% of urban pop.)	*90*	..	98
Access to sanitation (% of urban population)	82	..	97
Energy use per capita (kg of oil equivalent)	..	..	..
Electricity use per capita (kWh)	..	..	..
Economy			
GDP ($ millions)	397	718	679
GDP growth (annual %)	-3.0	-1.7	3.0
GDP implicit price deflator (annual % growth)	56.4	3.0	8.5
Value added in agriculture (% of GDP)	38.1	34.6	35.1
Value added in industry (% of GDP)	24.9	30.8	28.5
Value added in services (% of GDP)	37.0	34.6	36.4
Exports of goods and services (% of GDP)	62.7	96.0	98.9
Imports of goods and services (% of GDP)	79.9	108.0	107.2
Gross domestic investment (% of GDP)	31.1	28.8	24.5
Central government revenues (% of GDP)	..	..	..
Overall budget deficit (% of GDP)	..	..	..
Money and quasi money (annual % growth)	52.6	6.7	10.8
Technology and infrastructure			
Telephone mainlines (per 1,000 people)	20	70	75
Cost of 3 min local call ($)	0.01	*0.00*	0.00
Personal computers (per 1,000 people)	..	23.5	24.6
Internet users (thousands)	..	2	3
Paved roads (% of total)	7	7	..
Aircraft departures (thousands)	4	4	1
Trade and finance			
Trade as share of PPP GDP (%)	25.7	35.6	..
Trade growth less GDP growth (average %, 1989-99)			4.7
High-technology exports (% of manufactured exports)	..	..	..
Net barter terms of trade (1995=100)	105	96	..
Foreign direct investment ($ millions)	0	47	48
Present value of debt ($ millions)			867
Total debt service ($ millions)	295	136	105
Short term debt ($ millions)	75	137	144
Aid per capita ($)	212	109	31

103

HAITI

Population (millions)	8	Population growth (%)		2.0
Surface area (1,000 sq km)	28	Population per sq km		283
GNI ($ millions)	3,584	GNI per capita ($)		460

	1990	1998	1999
People			
Life expectancy (years)	53	54	53
Fertility rate (births per woman)	5.1	4.4	4.1
Infant mortality rate (per 1,000 live births)	85	71	70
Under 5 mortality rate (per 1,000 children)	131	125	118
Child malnutrition (% of children under 5)	27	28	..
Urban population (% of total)	30	34	35
Rural population density (per km^2 arable land)	822	895	..
Illiteracy male (% of people 15 and above)	57	50	49
Illiteracy female (% of people 15 and above)	63	54	53
Net primary enrollment (% of relevant age group)	22	..	..
Net secondary enrollment (% of relevant age group)	..	..	..
Girls in primary school (% of enrollment)	48	49	..
Girls in secondary school (% of enrollment)	..	..	..

	1990	1998	1999
Environment			
Forests (1,000 sq. km.)	2	..	1
Deforestation (% change 1990-2000)			5.7
Water use (% of total resources)	..	..	8.1
CO_2 emissions (metric tons per capita)	0.2	0.2	..
Access to improved water source (% of urban pop.)	55	..	49
Access to sanitation (% of urban population)	48	42	50
Energy use per capita (kg of oil equivalent)	245	271	..
Electricity use per capita (kWh)	61	33	..

	1990	1998	1999
Economy			
GDP ($ millions)	2,981	3,871	4,302
GDP growth (annual %)	4.2	3.1	2.2
GDP implicit price deflator (annual % growth)	13.9	12.7	9.6
Value added in agriculture (% of GDP)	33.3	30.4	29.4
Value added in industry (% of GDP)	21.8	20.1	22.2
Value added in services (% of GDP)	45.0	49.6	48.4
Exports of goods and services (% of GDP)	16.0	11.5	12.4
Imports of goods and services (% of GDP)	29.2	29.1	27.7
Gross domestic investment (% of GDP)	12.2	10.7	11.0
Central government revenues (% of GDP)	..	..	..
Overall budget deficit (% of GDP)	..	..	..
Money and quasi money (annual % growth)	2.5	9.7	23.0

	1990	1998	1999
Technology and infrastructure			
Telephone mainlines (per 1,000 people)	7	8	9
Cost of 3 min local call ($)	..	0.00	..
Personal computers (per 1,000 people)	..	..	..
Internet users (thousands)	..	2	6
Paved roads (% of total)	22	24	..
Aircraft departures (thousands)	1	..	..

	1990	1998	1999
Trade and finance			
Trade as share of PPP GDP (%)	4.4	8.8	10.7
Trade growth less GDP growth (average %, 1989-99)			-0.3
High-technology exports (% of manufactured exports)	14	4	..
Net barter terms of trade (1995=100)	116	105	..
Foreign direct investment ($ millions)	8	11	30
Present value of debt ($ millions)			724
Total debt service ($ millions)	33	51	59
Short term debt ($ millions)	101	30	96
Aid per capita ($)	26	53	34

HONDURAS

Latin America & Caribbean   **Lower middle income**

Population (millions)	6	Population growth (%)	2.7
Surface area (1,000 sq km)	112	Population per sq km	56
GNI ($ millions)	4,829	GNI per capita ($)	760

	1990	1998	1999
People			
Life expectancy (years)	67	69	70
Fertility rate (births per woman)	5.2	4.3	4.0
Infant mortality rate (per 1,000 live births)	50	36	34
Under 5 mortality rate (per 1,000 children)	65	48	46
Child malnutrition (% of children under 5)	18	25	..
Urban population (% of total)	42	51	52
Rural population density (per km^2 arable land)	176	179	..
Illiteracy male (% of people 15 and above)	31	27	26
Illiteracy female (% of people 15 and above)	32	27	26
Net primary enrollment (% of relevant age group)	89	90	..
Net secondary enrollment (% of relevant age group)	21	..	..
Girls in primary school (% of enrollment)	50	50	..
Girls in secondary school (% of enrollment)	55	..	..
Environment			
Forests (1,000 sq. km.)	60	..	54
Deforestation (% change 1990-2000)			1.0
Water use (% of total resources)	..	..	1.6
CO$_2$ emissions (metric tons per capita)	0.6	0.8	..
Access to improved water source (% of urban pop.)	90	..	97
Access to sanitation (% of urban population)	85	..	94
Energy use per capita (kg of oil equivalent)	495	542	..
Electricity use per capita (kWh)	369	446	..
Economy			
GDP ($ millions)	3,049	5,247	5,387
GDP growth (annual %)	0.1	2.9	-1.9
GDP implicit price deflator (annual % growth)	21.2	11.0	11.1
Value added in agriculture (% of GDP)	22.4	19.2	16.2
Value added in industry (% of GDP)	26.4	30.4	31.9
Value added in services (% of GDP)	51.2	50.4	51.9
Exports of goods and services (% of GDP)	36.4	47.2	42.9
Imports of goods and services (% of GDP)	39.8	53.3	56.7
Gross domestic investment (% of GDP)	22.9	30.8	32.9
Central government revenues (% of GDP)	..	..	..
Overall budget deficit (% of GDP)	..	..	..
Money and quasi money (annual % growth)	21.4	22.9	24.7
Technology and infrastructure			
Telephone mainlines (per 1,000 people)	17	40	44
Cost of 3 min local call ($)	0.01	0.06	0.06
Personal computers (per 1,000 people)	..	8.0	9.5
Internet users (thousands)	..	18	20
Paved roads (% of total)	21	20	20
Aircraft departures (thousands)	17	14	..
Trade and finance			
Trade as share of PPP GDP (%)	17.3	27.3	26.9
Trade growth less GDP growth (average %, 1989-99)			-0.6
High-technology exports (% of manufactured exports)	..	1	3
Net barter terms of trade (1995=100)	81	118	..
Foreign direct investment ($ millions)	44	84	230
Present value of debt ($ millions)			3,296
Total debt service ($ millions)	389	505	366
Short term debt ($ millions)	199	532	453
Aid per capita ($)	92	52	129

HONG KONG, CHINA

High income

Population (millions)	7	Population growth (%)	1.1
Surface area (1,000 sq km)	1	Population per sq km	..
GNI ($ millions)	165,122	GNI per capita ($)	24,570

	1990	1998	1999
People			
Life expectancy (years)	78	79	80
Fertility rate (births per woman)	1.3	1.0	1.0
Infant mortality rate (per 1,000 live births)	6	3	3
Under 5 mortality rate (per 1,000 children)	..	..	5
Child malnutrition (% of children under 5)	..	..	..
Urban population (% of total)	100	100	100
Rural population density (per km^2 arable land)	95	0	..
Illiteracy male (% of people 15 and above)	5	4	4
Illiteracy female (% of people 15 and above)	16	11	10
Net primary enrollment (% of relevant age group)	..	90	..
Net secondary enrollment (% of relevant age group)	..	69	..
Girls in primary school (% of enrollment)	..	..	..
Girls in secondary school (% of enrollment)	..	..	..
Environment			
Forests (1,000 sq. km.)	..	..	..
Deforestation (% change 1990-2000)			..
Water use (% of total resources)			..
CO_2 emissions (metric tons per capita)	4.7	3.7	..
Access to improved water source (% of urban pop.)	..	..	..
Access to sanitation (% of urban population)	..	..	..
Energy use per capita (kg of oil equivalent)	1,869	2,497	..
Electricity use per capita (kWh)	4,178	5,244	..
Economy			
GDP ($ millions)	74,784	162,938	158,943
GDP growth (annual %)	3.4	-5.1	2.9
GDP implicit price deflator (annual % growth)	7.5	0.5	-5.1
Value added in agriculture (% of GDP)	0.3	0.1	..
Value added in industry (% of GDP)	25.3	15.2	..
Value added in services (% of GDP)	74.5	84.7	..
Exports of goods and services (% of GDP)	134.3	129.0	133.3
Imports of goods and services (% of GDP)	125.8	128.0	127.9
Gross domestic investment (% of GDP)	27.4	29.1	25.2
Central government revenues (% of GDP)	..	..	..
Overall budget deficit (% of GDP)	..	..	..
Money and quasi money (annual % growth)	8.5	11.1	8.3
Technology and infrastructure			
Telephone mainlines (per 1,000 people)	450	561	576
Cost of 3 min local call ($)	0.00	0.00	0.00
Personal computers (per 1,000 people)	47.3	255.6	297.6
Internet users (thousands)	7	947	2,430
Paved roads (% of total)	100	100	..
Aircraft departures (thousands)	..	72	72
Trade and finance			
Trade as share of PPP GDP (%)	175.8	255.9	239.2
Trade growth less GDP growth (average %, 1989-99)			5.3
High-technology exports (% of manufactured exports)	..	21	21
Net barter terms of trade (1995=100)	101	103	..
Foreign direct investment ($ millions)	..	..	..
Present value of debt ($ millions)			..
Total debt service ($ millions)	..	..	..
Short term debt ($ millions)	..	..	..
Aid per capita ($)	7	1	1

Europe & Central Asia   **Upper middle income**

Population (millions)	10	Population growth (%)	-0.5
Surface area (1,000 sq km)	93	Population per sq km	109
GNI ($ millions)	46,751	GNI per capita ($)	4,640

	1990	1998	1999
People			
Life expectancy (years)	69	71	71
Fertility rate (births per woman)	1.8	1.3	1.3
Infant mortality rate (per 1,000 live births)	15	10	8
Under 5 mortality rate (per 1,000 children)	17	12	10
Child malnutrition (% of children under 5)	2	..	..
Urban population (% of total)	62	64	64
Rural population density (per km^2 arable land)	78	76	..
Illiteracy male (% of people 15 and above)	1	1	1
Illiteracy female (% of people 15 and above)	1	1	1
Net primary enrollment (% of relevant age group)	91	97	..
Net secondary enrollment (% of relevant age group)	75	86	..
Girls in primary school (% of enrollment)	49	48	..
Girls in secondary school (% of enrollment)	49	49	..
Environment			
Forests (1,000 sq. km.)	18	..	18
Deforestation (% change 1990-2000)			-0.4
Water use (% of total resources)	..	..	5.2
CO$_2$ emissions (metric tons per capita)	5.8	5.9	..
Access to improved water source (% of urban pop.)	100	..	100
Access to sanitation (% of urban population)	100	..	100
Energy use per capita (kg of oil equivalent)	2,746	2,497	..
Electricity use per capita (kWh)	3,048	2,888	..
Economy			
GDP ($ millions)	33,056	47,049	48,436
GDP growth (annual %)	-3.5	4.9	4.5
GDP implicit price deflator (annual % growth)	25.7	12.6	9.0
Value added in agriculture (% of GDP)	14.5	5.7	..
Value added in industry (% of GDP)	39.1	33.7	..
Value added in services (% of GDP)	46.4	60.6	..
Exports of goods and services (% of GDP)	31.1	50.6	52.6
Imports of goods and services (% of GDP)	28.5	52.7	55.0
Gross domestic investment (% of GDP)	25.4	29.7	28.8
Central government revenues (% of GDP)	52.9	36.5	38.4
Overall budget deficit (% of GDP)	0.8	-6.2	-3.6
Money and quasi money (annual % growth)	29.2	30.2	15.5
Technology and infrastructure			
Telephone mainlines (per 1,000 people)	96	336	371
Cost of 3 min local call ($)	0.07	0.12	0.13
Personal computers (per 1,000 people)	9.6	64.7	74.7
Internet users (thousands)	0	400	600
Paved roads (% of total)	50	43	43
Aircraft departures (thousands)	19	28	30
Trade and finance			
Trade as share of PPP GDP (%)	20.7	44.8	46.1
Trade growth less GDP growth (average %, 1989-99)			7.1
High-technology exports (% of manufactured exports)	..	21	23
Net barter terms of trade (1995=100)	100	..	..
Foreign direct investment ($ millions)	0	2,037	1,950
Present value of debt ($ millions)			28,046
Total debt service ($ millions)	4,224	7,305	7,527
Short term debt ($ millions)	2,940	4,780	3,543
Aid per capita ($)	6	24	25

ICELAND

Population (thousands)	278	Population growth (%)	1.3
Surface area (1,000 sq km)	103.0	Population per sq km	3
GNI ($ millions)	8,197	GNI per capita ($)	29,540

	1990	1998	1999
People			
Life expectancy (years)	78	79	79
Fertility rate (births per woman)	2.3	2.0	2.0
Infant mortality rate (per 1,000 live births)	6	3	3
Under 5 mortality rate (per 1,000 children)	..	7	5
Child malnutrition (% of children under 5)	..	..	..
Urban population (% of total)	91	92	92
Rural population density (per km^2 arable land)	342	359	..
Illiteracy male (% of people 15 and above)	..	..	..
Illiteracy female (% of people 15 and above)	..	..	..
Net primary enrollment (% of relevant age group)	..	98	..
Net secondary enrollment (% of relevant age group)	..	87	..
Girls in primary school (% of enrollment)	..	49	..
Girls in secondary school (% of enrollment)	48	49	..
Environment			
Forests (1,000 sq. km.)	0	..	0
Deforestation (% change 1990-2000)			-2.2
Water use (% of total resources)	..	..	0.1
CO_2 emissions (metric tons per capita)	8.1	7.9	..
Access to improved water source (% of urban pop.)	..	100	..
Access to sanitation (% of urban population)	..	100	..
Energy use per capita (kg of oil equivalent)	8,230	9,588	..
Electricity use per capita (kWh)	15,345	20,150	..
Economy			
GDP ($ millions)	6,245	8,268	8,815
GDP growth (annual %)	1.1	5.1	4.3
GDP implicit price deflator (annual % growth)	16.9	5.3	4.2
Value added in agriculture (% of GDP)	10.2	9.7	..
Value added in industry (% of GDP)	23.6	22.2	..
Value added in services (% of GDP)	66.3	68.1	..
Exports of goods and services (% of GDP)	34.3	34.7	33.9
Imports of goods and services (% of GDP)	33.0	39.2	38.1
Gross domestic investment (% of GDP)	18.1	21.9	19.9
Central government revenues (% of GDP)	29.6	29.9	..
Overall budget deficit (% of GDP)	-2.5	2.3	..
Money and quasi money (annual % growth)	14.1	15.2	-13.4
Technology and infrastructure			
Telephone mainlines (per 1,000 people)	510	648	677
Cost of 3 min local call ($)	0.05	0.11	0.11
Personal computers (per 1,000 people)	39.1	327.3	358.8
Internet users (thousands)	1	100	150
Paved roads (% of total)	20	27	28
Aircraft departures (thousands)	18	22	15
Trade and finance			
Trade as share of PPP GDP (%)	60.4	62.5	58.3
Trade growth less GDP growth (average %, 1989-99)			0.8
High-technology exports (% of manufactured exports)	10	20	17
Net barter terms of trade (1995=100)	99	..	..
Foreign direct investment ($ millions)	..	..	..
Present value of debt ($ millions)			..
Total debt service ($ millions)	..	..	..
Short term debt ($ millions)	..	..	..
Aid per capita ($)	..	..	..

108

INDIA

South Asia   **Low income**

Population (millions)	998	Population growth (%)	1.8
Surface area (1,000 sq km)	3,288	Population per sq km	336
GNI ($ millions)	441,834	GNI per capita ($)	440

	1990	1998	1999
People			
Life expectancy (years)	60	63	63
Fertility rate (births per woman)	3.8	3.3	3.1
Infant mortality rate (per 1,000 live births)	80	72	71
Under 5 mortality rate (per 1,000 children)	112	95	90
Child malnutrition (% of children under 5)	64	45	..
Urban population (% of total)	26	28	28
Rural population density (per km^2 arable land)	388	438	..
Illiteracy male (% of people 15 and above)	38	33	32
Illiteracy female (% of people 15 and above)	64	57	56
Net primary enrollment (% of relevant age group)	..	..	..
Net secondary enrollment (% of relevant age group)	..	..	..
Girls in primary school (% of enrollment)	41	44	..
Girls in secondary school (% of enrollment)	37	39	..
Environment			
Forests (1,000 sq. km.)	637	..	641
Deforestation (% change 1990-2000)			-0.1
Water use (% of total resources)			26.2
CO_2 emissions (metric tons per capita)	0.8	1.1	..
Access to improved water source (% of urban pop.)	92	..	92
Access to sanitation (% of urban population)	58	..	73
Energy use per capita (kg of oil equivalent)	424	486	..
Electricity use per capita (kWh)	254	384	..
Economy			
GDP ($ millions)	316,211	419,070	447,292
GDP growth (annual %)	5.7	6.8	6.5
GDP implicit price deflator (annual % growth)	10.9	8.9	3.3
Value added in agriculture (% of GDP)	31.4	29.1	27.7
Value added in industry (% of GDP)	27.6	25.7	26.3
Value added in services (% of GDP)	40.9	45.2	46.0
Exports of goods and services (% of GDP)	7.3	11.3	12.1
Imports of goods and services (% of GDP)	10.0	14.0	15.0
Gross domestic investment (% of GDP)	25.2	21.8	22.9
Central government revenues (% of GDP)	12.7	12.1	12.8
Overall budget deficit (% of GDP)	-7.7	-4.8	-4.2
Money and quasi money (annual % growth)	15.1	18.2	17.2
Technology and infrastructure			
Telephone mainlines (per 1,000 people)	6	22	27
Cost of 3 min local call ($)	0.04	0.01	0.01
Personal computers (per 1,000 people)	0.3	2.7	3.3
Internet users (thousands)	1	1,400	2,800
Paved roads (% of total)	47	57	..
Aircraft departures (thousands)	126	195	181
Trade and finance			
Trade as share of PPP GDP (%)	3.5	3.7	3.6
Trade growth less GDP growth (average %, 1989-99)			4.3
High-technology exports (% of manufactured exports)	4	6	..
Net barter terms of trade (1995=100)	79	104	..
Foreign direct investment ($ millions)	162	2,635	2,169
Present value of debt ($ millions)			70,451
Total debt service ($ millions)	8,191	12,094	10,109
Short term debt ($ millions)	8,544	4,329	4,043
Aid per capita ($)	2	2	1

INDONESIA

Population (millions)	207	Population growth (%)	1.6
Surface area (1,000 sq km)	1,905	Population per sq km	114
GNI ($ millions)	125,043	GNI per capita ($)	600

	1990	1998	1999
People			
Life expectancy (years)	62	65	66
Fertility rate (births per woman)	3.0	2.8	2.6
Infant mortality rate (per 1,000 live births)	60	44	42
Under 5 mortality rate (per 1,000 children)	83	56	52
Child malnutrition (% of children under 5)	..	34	..
Urban population (% of total)	31	39	40
Rural population density (per km^2 arable land)	611	695	..
Illiteracy male (% of people 15 and above)	13	9	9
Illiteracy female (% of people 15 and above)	27	20	19
Net primary enrollment (% of relevant age group)	98	95	..
Net secondary enrollment (% of relevant age group)	38	42	..
Girls in primary school (% of enrollment)	49	48	..
Girls in secondary school (% of enrollment)	45	46	..
Environment			
Forests (1,000 sq. km.)	1,181	..	1,050
Deforestation (% change 1990-2000)			1.2
Water use (% of total resources)	..	..	2.6
CO_2 emissions (metric tons per capita)	1.0	1.3	..
Access to improved water source (% of urban pop.)	90	..	91
Access to sanitation (% of urban population)	76	..	87
Energy use per capita (kg of oil equivalent)	555	604	..
Electricity use per capita (kWh)	156	320	..
Economy			
GDP ($ millions)	114,427	98,827	142,511
GDP growth (annual %)	9.0	-13.0	0.3
GDP implicit price deflator (annual % growth)	7.7	81.2	12.8
Value added in agriculture (% of GDP)	19.4	17.6	19.5
Value added in industry (% of GDP)	39.1	44.9	43.3
Value added in services (% of GDP)	41.5	37.5	37.3
Exports of goods and services (% of GDP)	25.3	51.2	34.9
Imports of goods and services (% of GDP)	23.7	41.7	26.9
Gross domestic investment (% of GDP)	30.7	27.1	23.7
Central government revenues (% of GDP)	18.8	16.1	18.3
Overall budget deficit (% of GDP)	0.4	-2.7	-1.1
Money and quasi money (annual % growth)	44.6	63.5	12.5
Technology and infrastructure			
Telephone mainlines (per 1,000 people)	6	27	29
Cost of 3 min local call ($)	0.05	0.01	0.02
Personal computers (per 1,000 people)	1.1	8.3	9.1
Internet users (thousands)	..	500	900
Paved roads (% of total)	46	46	..
Aircraft departures (thousands)	205	178	135
Trade and finance			
Trade as share of PPP GDP (%)	13.6	13.4	12.3
Trade growth less GDP growth (average %, 1989-99)			2.4
High-technology exports (% of manufactured exports)	2	10	10
Net barter terms of trade (1995=100)	102	95	..
Foreign direct investment ($ millions)	1,093	-356	-2,745
Present value of debt ($ millions)			149,74
Total debt service ($ millions)	9,946	18,302	17,848
Short term debt ($ millions)	11,135	20,113	20,029
Aid per capita ($)	10	6	11

ISLAMIC REPUBLIC OF IRAN

Middle East & North Africa   **Lower middle income**

Population (millions)	63	Population growth (%)		1.7
Surface area (1,000 sq km)	1,633	Population per sq km		39
GNI ($ millions)	113,729	GNI per capita ($)		1,810

	1990	1998	1999
People			
Life expectancy (years)	66	70	71
Fertility rate (births per woman)	4.7	2.8	2.7
Infant mortality rate (per 1,000 live births)	47	26	26
Under 5 mortality rate (per 1,000 children)	59	35	33
Child malnutrition (% of children under 5)	..	11	..
Urban population (% of total)	56	61	61
Rural population density (per km^2 arable land)	157	145	..
Illiteracy male (% of people 15 and above)	27	18	17
Illiteracy female (% of people 15 and above)	45	33	31
Net primary enrollment (% of relevant age group)	99	90	..
Net secondary enrollment (% of relevant age group)	48	71	..
Girls in primary school (% of enrollment)	46	47	47
Girls in secondary school (% of enrollment)	41	45	..
Environment			
Forests (1,000 sq. km.)	73	..	73
Deforestation (% change 1990-2000)			0.0
Water use (% of total resources)	..	..	54.5
CO$_2$ emissions (metric tons per capita)	4.0	4.9	..
Access to improved water source (% of urban pop.)	95	..	99
Access to sanitation (% of urban population)	86	..	86
Energy use per capita (kg of oil equivalent)	1,317	1,649	..
Electricity use per capita (kWh)	906	1,343	..
Economy			
GDP ($ millions)	120,404	112,772	110,791
GDP growth (annual %)	11.2	2.2	2.5
GDP implicit price deflator (annual % growth)	18.6	16.1	23.7
Value added in agriculture (% of GDP)	23.5	22.0	20.9
Value added in industry (% of GDP)	28.6	29.7	31.2
Value added in services (% of GDP)	47.9	48.2	47.9
Exports of goods and services (% of GDP)	22.0	15.3	21.2
Imports of goods and services (% of GDP)	23.5	17.5	16.5
Gross domestic investment (% of GDP)	28.6	23.9	18.2
Central government revenues (% of GDP)	18.1	18.7	24.5
Overall budget deficit (% of GDP)	-1.8	-5.7	-1.3
Money and quasi money (annual % growth)	18.0	20.4	21.5
Technology and infrastructure			
Telephone mainlines (per 1,000 people)	40	112	125
Cost of 3 min local call ($)	0.01	0.01	0.01
Personal computers (per 1,000 people)	..	45.6	52.4
Internet users (thousands)	..	65	100
Paved roads (% of total)	..	56	..
Aircraft departures (thousands)	40	88	76
Trade and finance			
Trade as share of PPP GDP (%)	15.4	7.6	8.4
Trade growth less GDP growth (average %, 1989-99)			-8.4
High-technology exports (% of manufactured exports)	..	0	1
Net barter terms of trade (1995=100)	170	110	..
Foreign direct investment ($ millions)	-362	24	85
Present value of debt ($ millions)			8,655
Total debt service ($ millions)	655	3,078	4,602
Short term debt ($ millions)	7,224	4,503	3,618
Aid per capita ($)	2	3	3

IRAQ

Lower middle income

Population (millions)	23	Population growth (%)		2.1
Surface area (1,000 sq km)	438	Population per sq km		52
GNI ($ millions)	..	GNI per capita ($)		..

	1990	1998	1999
People			
Life expectancy (years)	61	*58*	59
Fertility rate (births per woman)	5.9	*4.7*	4.4
Infant mortality rate (per 1,000 live births)	102	103	101
Under 5 mortality rate (per 1,000 children)	..	125	128
Child malnutrition (% of children under 5)	*12*	..	..
Urban population (% of total)	72	76	76
Rural population density (per km^2 arable land)	96	104	..
Illiteracy male (% of people 15 and above)	43	36	35
Illiteracy female (% of people 15 and above)	67	57	55
Net primary enrollment (% of relevant age group)	*79*	*76*	..
Net secondary enrollment (% of relevant age group)	*37*	..	..
Girls in primary school (% of enrollment)	*44*	*45*	..
Girls in secondary school (% of enrollment)	*38*	*38*	..
Environment			
Forests (1,000 sq. km.)	8	..	*8*
Deforestation (% change 1990-2000)			*0.0*
Water use (% of total resources)	..	..	121.6
CO_2 emissions (metric tons per capita)	3.0	*4.2*	..
Access to improved water source (% of urban pop.)	..	..	96
Access to sanitation (% of urban population)	..	..	93
Energy use per capita (kg of oil equivalent)	1,153	1,342	..
Electricity use per capita (kWh)	1,261	1,359	..
Economy			
GDP ($ millions)	48,657	..	..
GDP growth (annual %)	-30.7	..	..
GDP implicit price deflator (annual % growth)	45.0	..	..
Value added in agriculture (% of GDP)	..	..	..
Value added in industry (% of GDP)	..	..	..
Value added in services (% of GDP)	..	..	..
Exports of goods and services (% of GDP)	..	..	..
Imports of goods and services (% of GDP)	..	..	..
Gross domestic investment (% of GDP)	..	..	..
Central government revenues (% of GDP)	..	..	..
Overall budget deficit (% of GDP)	..	..	..
Money and quasi money (annual % growth)	..	..	..
Technology and infrastructure			
Telephone mainlines (per 1,000 people)	37	31	30
Cost of 3 min local call ($)	..	..	..
Personal computers (per 1,000 people)	..	..	..
Internet users (thousands)	..	..	..
Paved roads (% of total)	78	*86*	..
Aircraft departures (thousands)	8	0	0
Trade and finance			
Trade as share of PPP GDP (%)	..	..	..
Trade growth less GDP growth (average %, 1989-99)			..
High-technology exports (% of manufactured exports)	..	..	..
Net barter terms of trade (1995=100)	121	76	..
Foreign direct investment ($ millions)	..	..	..
Present value of debt ($ millions)			..
Total debt service ($ millions)	..	..	..
Short term debt ($ millions)	..	..	..
Aid per capita ($)	4	5	3

High income

Population (millions)	4	Population growth (%)	1.1
Surface area (1,000 sq km)	70	Population per sq km	54
GNI ($ millions)	80,559	GNI per capita ($)	21,470

	1990	1998	1999
People			
Life expectancy (years)	75	76	76
Fertility rate (births per woman)	2.1	1.9	1.9
Infant mortality rate (per 1,000 live births)	8	6	6
Under 5 mortality rate (per 1,000 children)	9	7	7
Child malnutrition (% of children under 5)	..	..	..
Urban population (% of total)	57	59	59
Rural population density (per km^2 arable land)	121	114	..
Illiteracy male (% of people 15 and above)	..	..	..
Illiteracy female (% of people 15 and above)	..	..	..
Net primary enrollment (% of relevant age group)	91	92	..
Net secondary enrollment (% of relevant age group)	80	86	..
Girls in primary school (% of enrollment)	49	49	..
Girls in secondary school (% of enrollment)	51	50	..
Environment			
Forests (1,000 sq. km.)	5	..	7
Deforestation (% change 1990-2000)			-3.0
Water use (% of total resources)			2.3
CO$_2$ emissions (metric tons per capita)	8.7	10.2	..
Access to improved water source (% of urban pop.)	..	..	..
Access to sanitation (% of urban population)	..	..	..
Energy use per capita (kg of oil equivalent)	2,984	3,570	..
Electricity use per capita (kWh)	3,385	4,760	..
Economy			
GDP ($ millions)	47,301	86,265	93,410
GDP growth (annual %)	8.5	8.6	9.8
GDP implicit price deflator (annual % growth)	-0.7	5.8	3.8
Value added in agriculture (% of GDP)	8.3	4.7	..
Value added in industry (% of GDP)	31.8	33.6	..
Value added in services (% of GDP)	59.7	61.7	..
Exports of goods and services (% of GDP)	57.0	86.8	87.6
Imports of goods and services (% of GDP)	52.4	75.4	73.8
Gross domestic investment (% of GDP)	21.0	23.4	23.3
Central government revenues (% of GDP)	33.6	31.9	..
Overall budget deficit (% of GDP)	-2.4	0.7	..
Money and quasi money (annual % growth)	..	..	..
Technology and infrastructure			
Telephone mainlines (per 1,000 people)	281	435	478
Cost of 3 min local call ($)	0.18	0.17	..
Personal computers (per 1,000 people)	85.7	271.7	404.9
Internet users (thousands)	2	300	679
Paved roads (% of total)	94	94	..
Aircraft departures (thousands)	80	123	133
Trade and finance			
Trade as share of PPP GDP (%)	99.5	129.0	120.1
Trade growth less GDP growth (average %, 1989-99)			6.7
High-technology exports (% of manufactured exports)	41	44	47
Net barter terms of trade (1995=100)	107	102	..
Foreign direct investment ($ millions)	..	..	..
Present value of debt ($ millions)			..
Total debt service ($ millions)	..	..	..
Short term debt ($ millions)	..	..	..
Aid per capita ($)	..	..	..

ISLE OF MAN

Europe & Central Asia   Upper middle income

Population (thousands)	76	Population growth (%)		..
Surface area (1,000 sq km)	..	Population per sq km		129
GNI ($ millions)	..	GNI per capita ($)		..

	1990	1998	1999
People			
Life expectancy (years)	..	..	..
Fertility rate (births per woman)	..	..	..
Infant mortality rate (per 1,000 live births)	..	..	..
Under 5 mortality rate (per 1,000 children)	..	..	..
Child malnutrition (% of children under 5)	..	..	..
Urban population (% of total)	74	76	76
Rural population density (per km² arable land)	..	..	..
Illiteracy male (% of people 15 and above)	..	..	..
Illiteracy female (% of people 15 and above)	..	..	..
Net primary enrollment (% of relevant age group)	..	..	..
Net secondary enrollment (% of relevant age group)	..	..	..
Girls in primary school (% of enrollment)	..	..	..
Girls in secondary school (% of enrollment)	..	..	..
Environment			
Forests (1,000 sq. km.)	..	..	..
Deforestation (% change 1990-2000)			..
Water use (% of total resources)			..
CO_2 emissions (metric tons per capita)	..	..	..
Access to improved water source (% of urban pop.)	..	..	..
Access to sanitation (% of urban population)	..	..	..
Energy use per capita (kg of oil equivalent)	..	..	..
Electricity use per capita (kWh)	..	..	..
Economy			
GDP ($ millions)	..	..	..
GDP growth (annual %)	..	..	..
GDP implicit price deflator (annual % growth)	..	..	..
Value added in agriculture (% of GDP)	..	..	..
Value added in industry (% of GDP)	..	..	..
Value added in services (% of GDP)	..	..	..
Exports of goods and services (% of GDP)	..	..	..
Imports of goods and services (% of GDP)	..	..	..
Gross domestic investment (% of GDP)	..	..	..
Central government revenues (% of GDP)	..	..	..
Overall budget deficit (% of GDP)	..	..	..
Money and quasi money (annual % growth)	..	..	..
Technology and infrastructure			
Telephone mainlines (per 1,000 people)	..	..	..
Cost of 3 min local call ($)	..	..	..
Personal computers (per 1,000 people)	..	..	..
Internet users (thousands)	..	..	..
Paved roads (% of total)	..	..	..
Aircraft departures (thousands)	..	..	..
Trade and finance			
Trade as share of PPP GDP (%)	..	..	..
Trade growth less GDP growth (average %, 1989-99)			..
High-technology exports (% of manufactured exports)	..	..	..
Net barter terms of trade (1995=100)	..	..	..
Foreign direct investment ($ millions)	..	..	..
Present value of debt ($ millions)			..
Total debt service ($ millions)	..	..	..
Short term debt ($ millions)	..	..	..
Aid per capita ($)	..	..	..

114

ISRAEL

Population (millions)	6	Population growth (%)	2.4
Surface area (1,000 sq km)	21	Population per sq km	296
GNI ($ millions)	99,574	GNI per capita ($)	16,310

	1990	1998	1999
People			
Life expectancy (years)	76	78	78
Fertility rate (births per woman)	2.8	3.0	2.9
Infant mortality rate (per 1,000 live births)	10	6	6
Under 5 mortality rate (per 1,000 children)	12	8	8
Child malnutrition (% of children under 5)	..	..	..
Urban population (% of total)	90	91	91
Rural population density (per km^2 arable land)	130	153	..
Illiteracy male (% of people 15 and above)	3	2	2
Illiteracy female (% of people 15 and above)	9	6	6
Net primary enrollment (% of relevant age group)	..	..	..
Net secondary enrollment (% of relevant age group)	..	..	..
Girls in primary school (% of enrollment)	49	49	..
Girls in secondary school (% of enrollment)	51	49	..
Environment			
Forests (1,000 sq. km.)	1	..	1
Deforestation (% change 1990-2000)			-4.9
Water use (% of total resources)	..	..	155.5
CO$_2$ emissions (metric tons per capita)	7.7	10.4	..
Access to improved water source (% of urban pop.)	..	100	..
Access to sanitation (% of urban population)	..	100	..
Energy use per capita (kg of oil equivalent)	2,596	3,165	..
Electricity use per capita (kWh)	3,902	5,475	..
Economy			
GDP ($ millions)	52,490	100,733	100,840
GDP growth (annual %)	6.8	2.6	2.2
GDP implicit price deflator (annual % growth)	15.9	6.6	6.7
Value added in agriculture (% of GDP)	..	..	..
Value added in industry (% of GDP)	..	..	..
Value added in services (% of GDP)	..	..	..
Exports of goods and services (% of GDP)	34.7	31.9	35.7
Imports of goods and services (% of GDP)	45.4	40.4	45.3
Gross domestic investment (% of GDP)	25.1	20.1	21.0
Central government revenues (% of GDP)	40.0	41.8	41.5
Overall budget deficit (% of GDP)	-5.3	-1.4	-2.1
Money and quasi money (annual % growth)	19.4	19.7	15.5
Technology and infrastructure			
Telephone mainlines (per 1,000 people)	343	471	471
Cost of 3 min local call ($)	0.07	0.06	0.05
Personal computers (per 1,000 people)	63.3	217.4	245.7
Internet users (thousands)	5	450	800
Paved roads (% of total)	100	100	100
Aircraft departures (thousands)	30	50	52
Trade and finance			
Trade as share of PPP GDP (%)	45.9	48.3	52.4
Trade growth less GDP growth (average %, 1989-99)			3.4
High-technology exports (% of manufactured exports)	11	20	19
Net barter terms of trade (1995=100)	97	107	112
Foreign direct investment ($ millions)	..	..	..
Present value of debt ($ millions)			..
Total debt service ($ millions)	..	..	..
Short term debt ($ millions)	..	..	..
Aid per capita ($)	294	179	148

ITALY

Population (millions)	58	Population growth (%)	0.1
Surface area (1,000 sq km)	301	Population per sq km	196
GNI ($ millions)	1,162,910	GNI per capita ($)	20,170

	1990	1998	1999
People			
Life expectancy (years)	77	78	78
Fertility rate (births per woman)	1.3	1.2	1.2
Infant mortality rate (per 1,000 live births)	8	6	5
Under 5 mortality rate (per 1,000 children)	10	7	6
Child malnutrition (% of children under 5)	..	..	
Urban population (% of total)	67	67	67
Rural population density (per km^2 arable land)	210	231	..
Illiteracy male (% of people 15 and above)	2	1	1
Illiteracy female (% of people 15 and above)	3	2	2
Net primary enrollment (% of relevant age group)	..	100	..
Net secondary enrollment (% of relevant age group)	..	..	..
Girls in primary school (% of enrollment)	49	48	..
Girls in secondary school (% of enrollment)	49	49	..
Environment			
Forests (1,000 sq. km.)	97	..	100
Deforestation (% change 1990-2000)			-0.3
Water use (% of total resources)	..	..	34.4
CO$_2$ emissions (metric tons per capita)	7.4	7.4	..
Access to improved water source (% of urban pop.)	..	..	..
Access to sanitation (% of urban population)	..	..	..
Energy use per capita (kg of oil equivalent)	2,703	2,916	..
Electricity use per capita (kWh)	3,784	4,431	..
Economy			
GDP ($ millions)	1,102,435	1,190,929	1,170,971
GDP growth (annual %)	2.0	1.5	1.4
GDP implicit price deflator (annual % growth)	8.2	2.7	1.5
Value added in agriculture (% of GDP)	3.2	2.8	2.8
Value added in industry (% of GDP)	30.8	26.7	26.2
Value added in services (% of GDP)	65.9	70.5	71.0
Exports of goods and services (% of GDP)	19.7	26.5	25.5
Imports of goods and services (% of GDP)	19.7	23.1	23.5
Gross domestic investment (% of GDP)	22.2	19.7	20.3
Central government revenues (% of GDP)	38.5	40.7	40.8
Overall budget deficit (% of GDP)	-10.2	-3.1	-1.6
Money and quasi money (annual % growth)	..	..	..
Technology and infrastructure			
Telephone mainlines (per 1,000 people)	388	453	462
Cost of 3 min local call ($)	0.11	0.10	0.13
Personal computers (per 1,000 people)	36.4	174.2	191.8
Internet users (thousands)	20	2,600	7,000
Paved roads (% of total)	100	100	..
Aircraft departures (thousands)	229	358	357
Trade and finance			
Trade as share of PPP GDP (%)	35.5	37.4	35.0
Trade growth less GDP growth (average %, 1989-99)			3.8
High-technology exports (% of manufactured exports)	8	8	8
Net barter terms of trade (1995=100)	98	109	..
Foreign direct investment ($ millions)	..	..	..
Present value of debt ($ millions)			..
Total debt service ($ millions)	..	..	..
Short term debt ($ millions)	..	..	..
Aid per capita ($)	..	..	..

JAMAICA

Population (millions)	3	Population growth (%) 0.9
Surface area (1,000 sq km)	11	Population per sq km 240
GNI ($ millions)	6,311	GNI per capita ($) 2,430

	1990	1998	1999
People			
Life expectancy (years)	73	75	75
Fertility rate (births per woman)	2.9	2.7	2.5
Infant mortality rate (per 1,000 live births)	25	22	20
Under 5 mortality rate (per 1,000 children)	32	26	24
Child malnutrition (% of children under 5)	5	4	..
Urban population (% of total)	52	55	56
Rural population density (per km^2 arable land)	980	664	..
Illiteracy male (% of people 15 and above)	22	18	18
Illiteracy female (% of people 15 and above)	14	10	10
Net primary enrollment (% of relevant age group)	96	..	..
Net secondary enrollment (% of relevant age group)	64	..	..
Girls in primary school (% of enrollment)	50	49	..
Girls in secondary school (% of enrollment)	49	..	..
Environment			
Forests (1,000 sq. km.)	4	..	3
Deforestation (% change 1990-2000)			1.5
Water use (% of total resources)	..	..	9.6
CO$_2$ emissions (metric tons per capita)	3.4	4.3	..
Access to improved water source (% of urban pop.)	..	92	81
Access to sanitation (% of urban population)	..	89	98
Energy use per capita (kg of oil equivalent)	1,264	1,575	..
Electricity use per capita (kWh)	686	2,252	..
Economy			
GDP ($ millions)	4,239	6,979	6,889
GDP growth (annual %)	5.5	-0.5	-0.4
GDP implicit price deflator (annual % growth)	23.7	6.6	7.9
Value added in agriculture (% of GDP)	6.5	7.2	6.6
Value added in industry (% of GDP)	43.2	31.5	32.1
Value added in services (% of GDP)	50.4	61.3	61.3
Exports of goods and services (% of GDP)	52.0	41.6	48.9
Imports of goods and services (% of GDP)	56.1	54.6	58.6
Gross domestic investment (% of GDP)	27.9	30.8	26.3
Central government revenues (% of GDP)	..	..	..
Overall budget deficit (% of GDP)	..	..	..
Money and quasi money (annual % growth)	21.5	7.7	12.2
Technology and infrastructure			
Telephone mainlines (per 1,000 people)	45	185	199
Cost of 3 min local call ($)	0.01	0.06	..
Personal computers (per 1,000 people)	..	39.4	43.0
Internet users (thousands)	..	50	60
Paved roads (% of total)	64	71	..
Aircraft departures (thousands)	21	13	21
Trade and finance			
Trade as share of PPP GDP (%)	35.9	47.5	40.2
Trade growth less GDP growth (average %, 1989-99)			0.4
High-technology exports (% of manufactured exports)	0	0	..
Net barter terms of trade (1995=100)	105	100	..
Foreign direct investment ($ millions)	138	369	524
Present value of debt ($ millions)			3,877
Total debt service ($ millions)	662	524	732
Short term debt ($ millions)	347	628	759
Aid per capita ($)	113	7	-9

117

JAPAN

Population (millions)	127	Population growth (%)	0.1
Surface area (1,000 sq km)	378	Population per sq km	336
GNI ($ millions)	4,054,545	GNI per capita ($)	32,030

	1990	1998	1999
People			
Life expectancy (years)	79	81	81
Fertility rate (births per woman)	1.5	1.4	1.4
Infant mortality rate (per 1,000 live births)	5	4	4
Under 5 mortality rate (per 1,000 children)	6	5	4
Child malnutrition (% of children under 5)	3	..	
Urban population (% of total)	77	79	79
Rural population density (per km^2 arable land)	586	599	..
Illiteracy male (% of people 15 and above)	..	..	
Illiteracy female (% of people 15 and above)	..	..	
Net primary enrollment (% of relevant age group)	100	103	..
Net secondary enrollment (% of relevant age group)	97	99	..
Girls in primary school (% of enrollment)	49	49	..
Girls in secondary school (% of enrollment)	49	49	..
Environment			
Forests (1,000 sq. km.)	240	..	241
Deforestation (% change 1990-2000)			0.0
Water use (% of total resources)	..	..	21.3
CO_2 emissions (metric tons per capita)	9.0	9.6	..
Access to improved water source (% of urban pop.)	..	..	..
Access to sanitation (% of urban population)	..	..	..
Energy use per capita (kg of oil equivalent)	3,552	4,035	..
Electricity use per capita (kWh)	6,125	7,322	..
Economy			
GDP ($ millions)	2,970,043	3,808,089	4,346,922
GDP growth (annual %)	5.1	-2.5	0.2
GDP implicit price deflator (annual % growth)	2.3	0.3	-0.9
Value added in agriculture (% of GDP)	2.5	1.7	..
Value added in industry (% of GDP)	41.2	36.0	..
Value added in services (% of GDP)	56.3	62.3	..
Exports of goods and services (% of GDP)	10.7	11.1	10.4
Imports of goods and services (% of GDP)	10.0	9.1	8.7
Gross domestic investment (% of GDP)	32.3	26.7	26.1
Central government revenues (% of GDP)	14.5	21.0	..
Overall budget deficit (% of GDP)	-1.6	-1.5	..
Money and quasi money (annual % growth)	8.2	4.1	3.4
Technology and infrastructure			
Telephone mainlines (per 1,000 people)	441	534	558
Cost of 3 min local call ($)	0.06	0.07	0.09
Personal computers (per 1,000 people)	59.7	238.1	286.9
Internet users (thousands)	50	16,900	27,060
Paved roads (% of total)	69	76	..
Aircraft departures (thousands)	476	637	662
Trade and finance			
Trade as share of PPP GDP (%)	21.3	21.7	23.2
Trade growth less GDP growth (average %, 1989-99)			2.9
High-technology exports (% of manufactured exports)	24	26	27
Net barter terms of trade (1995=100)	73	97	102
Foreign direct investment ($ millions)	..	..	..
Present value of debt ($ millions)			..
Total debt service ($ millions)	..	..	..
Short term debt ($ millions)	..	..	..
Aid per capita ($)	..	..	..

JORDAN

Middle East & North Africa　　　　**Lower middle income**

Population (millions)	5	Population growth (%)	3.1
Surface area (1,000 sq km)	89	Population per sq km	53
GNI ($ millions)	7,717	GNI per capita ($)	1,630

	1990	1998	1999
People			
Life expectancy (years)	68	71	71
Fertility rate (births per woman)	5.4	3.8	3.7
Infant mortality rate (per 1,000 live births)	30	28	26
Under 5 mortality rate (per 1,000 children)	34	34	31
Child malnutrition (% of children under 5)	6	5	..
Urban population (% of total)	68	73	74
Rural population density (per km^2 arable land)	350	485	..
Illiteracy male (% of people 15 and above)	10	6	6
Illiteracy female (% of people 15 and above)	28	17	17
Net primary enrollment (% of relevant age group)	66	68	..
Net secondary enrollment (% of relevant age group)	33	41	..
Girls in primary school (% of enrollment)	48	49	..
Girls in secondary school (% of enrollment)	47	50	..
Environment			
Forests (1,000 sq. km.)	1	..	1
Deforestation (% change 1990-2000)			0.0
Water use (% of total resources)	..	..	140.0
CO$_2$ emissions (metric tons per capita)	3.5	3.5	..
Access to improved water source (% of urban pop.)	99	..	100
Access to sanitation (% of urban population)	100	..	100
Energy use per capita (kg of oil equivalent)	1,104	1,063	..
Electricity use per capita (kWh)	959	1,205	..
Economy			
GDP ($ millions)	4,020	7,964	8,073
GDP growth (annual %)	1.0	2.9	3.1
GDP implicit price deflator (annual % growth)	11.4	5.6	-1.6
Value added in agriculture (% of GDP)	8.1	3.0	2.4
Value added in industry (% of GDP)	28.1	25.5	25.6
Value added in services (% of GDP)	63.8	71.5	72.0
Exports of goods and services (% of GDP)	61.9	44.6	43.6
Imports of goods and services (% of GDP)	92.7	63.9	61.8
Gross domestic investment (% of GDP)	31.9	21.7	20.8
Central government revenues (% of GDP)	26.2	25.2	26.7
Overall budget deficit (% of GDP)	-3.5	-5.8	-2.5
Money and quasi money (annual % growth)	8.3	6.3	15.5
Technology and infrastructure			
Telephone mainlines (per 1,000 people)	58	83	87
Cost of 3 min local call ($)	0.01	0.04	0.03
Personal computers (per 1,000 people)	..	12.6	13.9
Internet users (thousands)	..	61	120
Paved roads (% of total)	100	100	..
Aircraft departures (thousands)	14	15	16
Trade and finance			
Trade as share of PPP GDP (%)	34.2	32.2	29.4
Trade growth less GDP growth (average %, 1989-99)			-0.9
High-technology exports (% of manufactured exports)	2	2	..
Net barter terms of trade (1995=100)	85	108	..
Foreign direct investment ($ millions)	38	310	158
Present value of debt ($ millions)			8,232
Total debt service ($ millions)	625	896	649
Short term debt ($ millions)	1,040	594	875
Aid per capita ($)	280	89	91

KAZAKHSTAN

Europe & Central Asia   Lower middle income

Population (millions)	15	Population growth (%)	-1.0
Surface area (1,000 sq km)	2,717	Population per sq km	6
GNI ($ millions)	18,732	GNI per capita ($)	1,250

	1990	1998	1999
People			
Life expectancy (years)	68	64	65
Fertility rate (births per woman)	2.7	2.0	2.0
Infant mortality rate (per 1,000 live births)	26	22	22
Under 5 mortality rate (per 1,000 children)	34	29	28
Child malnutrition (% of children under 5)	..	8	..
Urban population (% of total)	57	56	56
Rural population density (per km^2 arable land)	20	22	..
Illiteracy male (% of people 15 and above)	..	..	..
Illiteracy female (% of people 15 and above)	..	..	..
Net primary enrollment (% of relevant age group)	..	..	..
Net secondary enrollment (% of relevant age group)	..	..	..
Girls in primary school (% of enrollment)	..	50	..
Girls in secondary school (% of enrollment)	..	51	..
Environment			
Forests (1,000 sq. km.)	98	..	121
Deforestation (% change 1990-2000)			-2.2
Water use (% of total resources)	..	..	30.7
CO_2 emissions (metric tons per capita)	15.8	8.0	..
Access to improved water source (% of urban pop.)	..	..	98
Access to sanitation (% of urban population)	..	..	100
Energy use per capita (kg of oil equivalent)	4,937	2,590	..
Electricity use per capita (kWh)	5,439	2,399	..
Economy			
GDP ($ millions)	40,304	21,979	15,842
GDP growth (annual %)	-4.6	-1.9	1.7
GDP implicit price deflator (annual % growth)	18.8	4.9	8.2
Value added in agriculture (% of GDP)	26.7	9.2	10.5
Value added in industry (% of GDP)	44.6	31.2	32.4
Value added in services (% of GDP)	28.7	59.6	57.1
Exports of goods and services (% of GDP)	74.0	30.6	45.2
Imports of goods and services (% of GDP)	75.3	35.1	40.1
Gross domestic investment (% of GDP)	31.5	17.3	17.6
Central government revenues (% of GDP)	..	15.3	11.0
Overall budget deficit (% of GDP)	..	-4.2	-4.1
Money and quasi money (annual % growth)	..	-14.1	84.4
Technology and infrastructure			
Telephone mainlines (per 1,000 people)	80	109	108
Cost of 3 min local call ($)	0.00	0.00	..
Personal computers (per 1,000 people)	..	..	..
Internet users (thousands)	..	20	70
Paved roads (% of total)	55	87	90
Aircraft departures (thousands)	..	20	18
Trade and finance			
Trade as share of PPP GDP (%)	..	14.0	12.5
Trade growth less GDP growth (average %, 1989-99)			8.3
High-technology exports (% of manufactured exports)	..	8	..
Net barter terms of trade (1995=100)	..	..	..
Foreign direct investment ($ millions)	100	1,151	1,587
Present value of debt ($ millions)			6,264
Total debt service ($ millions)	0	989	1,364
Short term debt ($ millions)	9	424	474
Aid per capita ($)	7	14	11

120

KENYA

Population (millions)	29	Population growth (%)		2.1
Surface area (1,000 sq km)	580	Population per sq km		52
GNI ($ millions)	10,696	GNI per capita ($)		360

	1990	1998	1999
People			
Life expectancy (years)	57	50	48
Fertility rate (births per woman)	5.6	4.7	4.5
Infant mortality rate (per 1,000 live births)	62	74	76
Under 5 mortality rate (per 1,000 children)	97	112	118
Child malnutrition (% of children under 5)	..	22	..
Urban population (% of total)	24	31	32
Rural population density (per km^2 arable land)	447	494	..
Illiteracy male (% of people 15 and above)	19	12	12
Illiteracy female (% of people 15 and above)	39	27	25
Net primary enrollment (% of relevant age group)	..	..	..
Net secondary enrollment (% of relevant age group)	..	..	..
Girls in primary school (% of enrollment)	49	49	..
Girls in secondary school (% of enrollment)	..	..	..
Environment			
Forests (1,000 sq. km.)	180	..	171
Deforestation (% change 1990-2000)			0.5
Water use (% of total resources)	..	..	6.8
CO$_2$ emissions (metric tons per capita)	0.3	0.3	..
Access to improved water source (% of urban pop.)	89	..	87
Access to sanitation (% of urban population)	94	..	96
Energy use per capita (kg of oil equivalent)	530	505	..
Electricity use per capita (kWh)	115	129	..
Economy			
GDP ($ millions)	8,533	11,465	10,638
GDP growth (annual %)	4.2	1.6	1.3
GDP implicit price deflator (annual % growth)	9.4	9.2	6.8
Value added in agriculture (% of GDP)	29.1	26.4	23.2
Value added in industry (% of GDP)	19.1	15.8	16.2
Value added in services (% of GDP)	51.7	57.8	60.5
Exports of goods and services (% of GDP)	25.9	24.9	24.4
Imports of goods and services (% of GDP)	31.2	32.6	31.1
Gross domestic investment (% of GDP)	19.7	14.6	13.5
Central government revenues (% of GDP)	22.4	27.2	..
Overall budget deficit (% of GDP)	-3.8	-0.9	..
Money and quasi money (annual % growth)	20.1	2.6	6.0
Technology and infrastructure			
Telephone mainlines (per 1,000 people)	8	10	10
Cost of 3 min local call ($)	..	0.05	0.05
Personal computers (per 1,000 people)	0.3	3.4	4.2
Internet users (thousands)	..	15	35
Paved roads (% of total)	13	14	..
Aircraft departures (thousands)	13	20	25
Trade and finance			
Trade as share of PPP GDP (%)	13.7	17.9	15.6
Trade growth less GDP growth (average %, 1989-99)			2.3
High-technology exports (% of manufactured exports)	4	4	4
Net barter terms of trade (1995=100)	68	106	..
Foreign direct investment ($ millions)	57	11	14
Present value of debt ($ millions)			5,183
Total debt service ($ millions)	791	612	716
Short term debt ($ millions)	934	858	826
Aid per capita ($)	50	16	10

KIRIBATI

Population (thousands)	88	Population growth (%)	2.8
Surface area (1,000 sq km)	0.7	Population per sq km	121
GNI ($ millions)	81	GNI per capita ($)	910

	1990	1998	1999
People			
Life expectancy (years)	57	60	61
Fertility rate (births per woman)	4.0	4.2	4.0
Infant mortality rate (per 1,000 live births)	65	60	56
Under 5 mortality rate (per 1,000 children)	..	..	72
Child malnutrition (% of children under 5)	..	..	..
Urban population (% of total)	35	38	39
Rural population density (per km^2 arable land)	..	..	..
Illiteracy male (% of people 15 and above)	..	..	..
Illiteracy female (% of people 15 and above)	..	..	..
Net primary enrollment (% of relevant age group)	..	..	..
Net secondary enrollment (% of relevant age group)	..	..	..
Girls in primary school (% of enrollment)	50	49	..
Girls in secondary school (% of enrollment)	49	54	..
Environment			
Forests (1,000 sq. km.)	0	..	0
Deforestation (% change 1990-2000)			0.0
Water use (% of total resources)	..	..	..
CO$_2$ emissions (metric tons per capita)	0.3	0.3	..
Access to improved water source (% of urban pop.)	..	..	82
Access to sanitation (% of urban population)	..	..	54
Energy use per capita (kg of oil equivalent)	..	..	..
Electricity use per capita (kWh)	..	..	..
Economy			
GDP ($ millions)	32	45	48
GDP growth (annual %)	-0.3	6.1	2.5
GDP implicit price deflator (annual % growth)	0.9	3.5	2.0
Value added in agriculture (% of GDP)	23.8	20.7	..
Value added in industry (% of GDP)	13.1	6.1	..
Value added in services (% of GDP)	63.1	73.2	..
Exports of goods and services (% of GDP)	10.3	..	..
Imports of goods and services (% of GDP)	130.0	..	..
Gross domestic investment (% of GDP)	82.3	..	..
Central government revenues (% of GDP)	..	..	..
Overall budget deficit (% of GDP)	..	..	..
Money and quasi money (annual % growth)	..	..	..
Technology and infrastructure			
Telephone mainlines (per 1,000 people)	17	34	43
Cost of 3 min local call ($)	..	0.11	..
Personal computers (per 1,000 people)	..	7.4	12.2
Internet users (thousands)	..	1	1
Paved roads (% of total)	..	..	..
Aircraft departures (thousands)	3	0	0
Trade and finance			
Trade as share of PPP GDP (%)	..	..	..
Trade growth less GDP growth (average %, 1989-99)			..
High-technology exports (% of manufactured exports)	..	..	..
Net barter terms of trade (1995=100)	..	..	..
Foreign direct investment ($ millions)	..	..	..
Present value of debt ($ millions)			..
Total debt service ($ millions)	..	..	..
Short term debt ($ millions)	..	..	..
Aid per capita ($)	280	201	236

DEMOCRATIC REPUBLIC OF KOREA

Population (millions)	23	Population growth (%)	1.0
Surface area (1,000 sq km)	121	Population per sq km	194
GNI ($ millions)	..	GNI per capita ($)	..

	1990	1998	1999
People			
Life expectancy (years)	66	..	60
Fertility rate (births per woman)	2.2	..	2.0
Infant mortality rate (per 1,000 live births)	45	..	58
Under 5 mortality rate (per 1,000 children)	35	..	93
Child malnutrition (% of children under 5)	..	32	..
Urban population (% of total)	58	60	60
Rural population density (per km^2 arable land)	501	548	..
Illiteracy male (% of people 15 and above)	..	..	..
Illiteracy female (% of people 15 and above)	..	..	..
Net primary enrollment (% of relevant age group)	..	..	..
Net secondary enrollment (% of relevant age group)	..	..	..
Girls in primary school (% of enrollment)	..	..	..
Girls in secondary school (% of enrollment)	..	..	..
Environment			
Forests (1,000 sq. km.)	82	..	..
Deforestation (% change 1990-2000)			..
Water use (% of total resources)	..	..	18.4
CO_2 emissions (metric tons per capita)	12.3	..	..
Access to improved water source (% of urban pop.)	..	..	..
Access to sanitation (% of urban population)	..	..	..
Energy use per capita (kg of oil equivalent)	..	..	..
Electricity use per capita (kWh)	..	..	..
Economy			
GDP ($ millions)	..	..	..
GDP growth (annual %)	..	..	..
GDP implicit price deflator (annual % growth)	..	..	..
Value added in agriculture (% of GDP)	..	..	..
Value added in industry (% of GDP)	..	..	..
Value added in services (% of GDP)	..	..	..
Exports of goods and services (% of GDP)	..	..	..
Imports of goods and services (% of GDP)	..	..	..
Gross domestic investment (% of GDP)	..	..	..
Central government revenues (% of GDP)	..	..	..
Overall budget deficit (% of GDP)	..	..	..
Money and quasi money (annual % growth)	..	..	..
Technology and infrastructure			
Telephone mainlines (per 1,000 people)	38	47	46
Cost of 3 min local call ($)	..	..	..
Personal computers (per 1,000 people)	..	..	..
Internet users (thousands)	..	..	..
Paved roads (% of total)	6	..	..
Aircraft departures (thousands)	6	1	1
Trade and finance			
Trade as share of PPP GDP (%)	..	..	..
Trade growth less GDP growth (average %, 1989-99)			..
High-technology exports (% of manufactured exports)	..	..	..
Net barter terms of trade (1995=100)	..	..	..
Foreign direct investment ($ millions)	..	..	..
Present value of debt ($ millions)			..
Total debt service ($ millions)	..	..	..
Short term debt ($ millions)	..	..	..
Aid per capita ($)	0	5	9

REPUBLIC OF KOREA

East Asia and Pacific   Upper middle income

Population (millions)	47	Population growth (%)		0.9
Surface area (1,000 sq km)	99	Population per sq km		475
GNI ($ millions)	397,910	GNI per capita ($)		8,490

	1990	1998	1999
People			
Life expectancy (years)	70	70	73
Fertility rate (births per woman)	1.8	1.8	1.6
Infant mortality rate (per 1,000 live births)	12	12	8
Under 5 mortality rate (per 1,000 children)	..	..	9
Child malnutrition (% of children under 5)	..	..	
Urban population (% of total)	74	74	81
Rural population density (per km^2 arable land)	575	575	..
Illiteracy male (% of people 15 and above)	2	2	1
Illiteracy female (% of people 15 and above)	7	7	4
Net primary enrollment (% of relevant age group)	104	104	..
Net secondary enrollment (% of relevant age group)	86	86	..
Girls in primary school (% of enrollment)	*49*	*49*	47
Girls in secondary school (% of enrollment)	48	48	..
Environment			
Forests (1,000 sq. km.)	63	63	*63*
Deforestation (% change 1990-2000)			*0.1*
Water use (% of total resources)	..	..	33.9
CO_2 emissions (metric tons per capita)	6.0	6.0	..
Access to improved water source (% of urban pop.)	..	..	97
Access to sanitation (% of urban population)	..	..	76
Energy use per capita (kg of oil equivalent)	2,132	2,132	..
Electricity use per capita (kWh)	2,202	2,202	..
Economy			
GDP ($ millions)	252,622	252,622	406,940
GDP growth (annual %)	9.5	9.5	10.7
GDP implicit price deflator (annual % growth)	9.9	9.9	-1.6
Value added in agriculture (% of GDP)	8.5	8.5	5.0
Value added in industry (% of GDP)	43.1	43.1	43.5
Value added in services (% of GDP)	48.4	48.4	51.5
Exports of goods and services (% of GDP)	29.1	29.1	42.1
Imports of goods and services (% of GDP)	30.3	30.3	35.3
Gross domestic investment (% of GDP)	37.7	37.7	26.8
Central government revenues (% of GDP)	17.9	17.9	..
Overall budget deficit (% of GDP)	-0.7	-0.7	..
Money and quasi money (annual % growth)	17.2	17.2	27.4
Technology and infrastructure			
Telephone mainlines (per 1,000 people)	310	310	438
Cost of 3 min local call ($)	0.03	0.03	0.04
Personal computers (per 1,000 people)	37.3	37.3	181.8
Internet users (thousands)	*20*	*20*	10,860
Paved roads (% of total)	72	72	..
Aircraft departures (thousands)	120	120	206
Trade and finance			
Trade as share of PPP GDP (%)	35.3	35.3	35.9
Trade growth less GDP growth (average %, 1989-99)			6.7
High-technology exports (% of manufactured exports)	18	18	32
Net barter terms of trade (1995=100)	98	98	..
Foreign direct investment ($ millions)	788	788	9,333
Present value of debt ($ millions)			124,34
Total debt service ($ millions)	8,274	8,274	43,020
Short term debt ($ millions)	10,800	10,800	34,743
Aid per capita ($)	1	1	-1

Population (millions)	2	Population growth (%)	3.1
Surface area (1,000 sq km)	18	Population per sq km	108
GNI ($ millions)	..	GNI per capita ($)	..

	1990	1998	1999
People			
Life expectancy (years)	75	76	77
Fertility rate (births per woman)	3.4	2.9	2.7
Infant mortality rate (per 1,000 live births)	14	12	11
Under 5 mortality rate (per 1,000 children)	16	14	13
Child malnutrition (% of children under 5)	..	2	..
Urban population (% of total)	96	97	97
Rural population density (per km^2 arable land)	2,231	821	..
Illiteracy male (% of people 15 and above)	20	17	16
Illiteracy female (% of people 15 and above)	27	22	21
Net primary enrollment (% of relevant age group)	45	62	..
Net secondary enrollment (% of relevant age group)	45	61	..
Girls in primary school (% of enrollment)	48	49	..
Girls in secondary school (% of enrollment)	49	49	..
Environment			
Forests (1,000 sq. km.)	0	..	0
Deforestation (% change 1990-2000)			-5.2
Water use (% of total resources)	..	..	
CO$_2$ emissions (metric tons per capita)	20.1	28.2	..
Access to improved water source (% of urban pop.)	100	100	..
Access to sanitation (% of urban population)	100	100	..
Energy use per capita (kg of oil equivalent)	3,959	7,823	..
Electricity use per capita (kWh)	7,303	13,800	..
Economy			
GDP ($ millions)	18,428	25,326	29,572
GDP growth (annual %)	25.9	-3.3	..
GDP implicit price deflator (annual % growth)	-1.7	21.4	..
Value added in agriculture (% of GDP)	0.6	0.4	..
Value added in industry (% of GDP)	52.3	53.5	..
Value added in services (% of GDP)	47.0	46.1	..
Exports of goods and services (% of GDP)	44.9	44.9	47.1
Imports of goods and services (% of GDP)	58.1	48.2	37.1
Gross domestic investment (% of GDP)	17.6	16.2	12.3
Central government revenues (% of GDP)	59.0	44.8	34.0
Overall budget deficit (% of GDP)	..	-5.7	-9.6
Money and quasi money (annual % growth)	0.7	-0.8	1.6
Technology and infrastructure			
Telephone mainlines (per 1,000 people)	247	236	240
Cost of 3 min local call ($)	0.00	0.00	0.00
Personal computers (per 1,000 people)	6.7	105.0	121.3
Internet users (thousands)	..	60	100
Paved roads (% of total)	73	81	..
Aircraft departures (thousands)	10	18	17
Trade and finance			
Trade as share of PPP GDP (%)	..	..	..
Trade growth less GDP growth (average %, 1989-99)			..
High-technology exports (% of manufactured exports)	3	0	1
Net barter terms of trade (1995=100)	95	77	..
Foreign direct investment ($ millions)	..	..	..
Present value of debt ($ millions)			..
Total debt service ($ millions)	..	..	..
Short term debt ($ millions)	..	..	..
Aid per capita ($)	3	3	4

KYRGYZ REPUBLIC

Europe & Central Asia — Low income

Population (millions)	5	Population growth (%)		1.4
Surface area (1,000 sq km)	199	Population per sq km		25
GNI ($ millions)	1,465	GNI per capita ($)		300

	1990	1998	1999
People			
Life expectancy (years)	68	67	67
Fertility rate (births per woman)	3.7	2.8	2.7
Infant mortality rate (per 1,000 live births)	30	26	26
Under 5 mortality rate (per 1,000 children)	41	41	38
Child malnutrition (% of children under 5)	..	11	..
Urban population (% of total)	37	34	34
Rural population density (per km^2 arable land)	229	235	..
Illiteracy male (% of people 15 and above)	..	..	..
Illiteracy female (% of people 15 and above)	..	..	..
Net primary enrollment (% of relevant age group)	..	95	..
Net secondary enrollment (% of relevant age group)	..	..	..
Girls in primary school (% of enrollment)	50	49	..
Girls in secondary school (% of enrollment)	50	51	..
Environment			
Forests (1,000 sq. km.)	8	..	10
Deforestation (% change 1990-2000)			-2.6
Water use (% of total resources)	..	..	21.7
CO$_2$ emissions (metric tons per capita)	2.6	1.4	..
Access to improved water source (% of urban pop.)	..	93	98
Access to sanitation (% of urban population)	83	..	100
Energy use per capita (kg of oil equivalent)	1,129	609	..
Electricity use per capita (kWh)	1,816	1,430	..
Economy			
GDP ($ millions)	..	1,646	1,251
GDP growth (annual %)	5.7	2.1	3.7
GDP implicit price deflator (annual % growth)	7.9	9.1	37.6
Value added in agriculture (% of GDP)	34.2	39.5	37.7
Value added in industry (% of GDP)	35.8	22.8	26.7
Value added in services (% of GDP)	30.0	37.7	35.6
Exports of goods and services (% of GDP)	29.2	36.5	42.2
Imports of goods and services (% of GDP)	49.6	58.0	57.0
Gross domestic investment (% of GDP)	24.2	15.4	18.0
Central government revenues (% of GDP)	..	17.8	13.3
Overall budget deficit (% of GDP)	..	-3.0	-2.5
Money and quasi money (annual % growth)	..	17.5	33.7
Technology and infrastructure			
Telephone mainlines (per 1,000 people)	72	76	76
Cost of 3 min local call ($)	0.00	..	..
Personal computers (per 1,000 people)	..	..	..
Internet users (thousands)	..	4	10
Paved roads (% of total)	90	91	..
Aircraft departures (thousands)	..	11	8
Trade and finance			
Trade as share of PPP GDP (%)	..	11.6	8.4
Trade growth less GDP growth (average %, 1989-99)			-0.6
High-technology exports (% of manufactured exports)	..	..	6
Net barter terms of trade (1995=100)	..	..	..
Foreign direct investment ($ millions)	0	109	36
Present value of debt ($ millions)			1,227
Total debt service ($ millions)	0	116	117
Short term debt ($ millions)	0	28	60
Aid per capita ($)	1	45	55

126

LAO PDR

Population (millions)	5	Population growth (%)	2.4
Surface area (1,000 sq km)	237	Population per sq km	22
GNI ($ millions)	1,476	GNI per capita ($)	290

	1990	1998	1999
People			
Life expectancy (years)	50	53	54
Fertility rate (births per woman)	6.3	5.6	5.4
Infant mortality rate (per 1,000 live births)	108	98	93
Under 5 mortality rate (per 1,000 children)	170	170	143
Child malnutrition (% of children under 5)	..	40	..
Urban population (% of total)	18	22	23
Rural population density (per km² arable land)	409	483	..
Illiteracy male (% of people 15 and above)	47	38	37
Illiteracy female (% of people 15 and above)	80	70	68
Net primary enrollment (% of relevant age group)	61	72	..
Net secondary enrollment (% of relevant age group)	15	22	..
Girls in primary school (% of enrollment)	43	45	..
Girls in secondary school (% of enrollment)	39	40	..
Environment			
Forests (1,000 sq. km.)	131	..	126
Deforestation (% change 1990-2000)			0.4
Water use (% of total resources)	..	..	0.4
CO_2 emissions (metric tons per capita)	0.1	0.1	..
Access to improved water source (% of urban pop.)	..	40	59
Access to sanitation (% of urban population)	..	70	84
Energy use per capita (kg of oil equivalent)	..	..	..
Electricity use per capita (kWh)	..	..	..
Economy			
GDP ($ millions)	865	1,261	1,432
GDP growth (annual %)	6.7	4.0	7.4
GDP implicit price deflator (annual % growth)	38.0	84.0	127.8
Value added in agriculture (% of GDP)	61.2	52.6	..
Value added in industry (% of GDP)	14.5	22.0	..
Value added in services (% of GDP)	24.3	25.4	..
Exports of goods and services (% of GDP)	11.3	37.0	..
Imports of goods and services (% of GDP)	24.5	48.5	..
Gross domestic investment (% of GDP)	13.5	24.9	..
Central government revenues (% of GDP)	..	..	..
Overall budget deficit (% of GDP)	..	..	..
Money and quasi money (annual % growth)	7.8	113.3	78.4
Technology and infrastructure			
Telephone mainlines (per 1,000 people)	2	6	7
Cost of 3 min local call ($)	0.28	..	..
Personal computers (per 1,000 people)	..	1.9	2.3
Internet users (thousands)	..	1	2
Paved roads (% of total)	24	14	..
Aircraft departures (thousands)	3	10	6
Trade and finance			
Trade as share of PPP GDP (%)	7.7	13.5	11.2
Trade growth less GDP growth (average %, 1989-99)			..
High-technology exports (% of manufactured exports)	..	..	..
Net barter terms of trade (1995=100)	..	..	..
Foreign direct investment ($ millions)	6	45	79
Present value of debt ($ millions)			1,387
Total debt service ($ millions)	9	31	37
Short term debt ($ millions)	2	1	3
Aid per capita ($)	37	57	58

LATVIA

Population (millions)	2	Population growth (%)		-0.7
Surface area (1,000 sq km)	65	Population per sq km		39
GNI ($ millions)	5,913	GNI per capita ($)		2,430

	1990	1998	1999
People			
Life expectancy (years)	69	70	70
Fertility rate (births per woman)	2.0	1.1	1.1
Infant mortality rate (per 1,000 live births)	14	15	14
Under 5 mortality rate (per 1,000 children)	18	19	18
Child malnutrition (% of children under 5)	..	..	..
Urban population (% of total)	70	69	69
Rural population density (per km^2 arable land)	..	41	..
Illiteracy male (% of people 15 and above)	0	0	0
Illiteracy female (% of people 15 and above)	0	0	0
Net primary enrollment (% of relevant age group)	..	..	..
Net secondary enrollment (% of relevant age group)	..	..	..
Girls in primary school (% of enrollment)	..	48	..
Girls in secondary school (% of enrollment)	49	..	..
Environment			
Forests (1,000 sq. km.)	28	..	..
Deforestation (% change 1990-2000)			..
Water use (% of total resources)	..	..	0.8
CO_2 emissions (metric tons per capita)	..	..	..
Access to improved water source (% of urban pop.)	..	..	..
Access to sanitation (% of urban population)	..	..	..
Energy use per capita (kg of oil equivalent)	..	1,746	..
Electricity use per capita (kWh)	..	1,879	..
Economy			
GDP ($ millions)	12,490	6,084	6,260
GDP growth (annual %)	-1.2	3.9	0.1
GDP implicit price deflator (annual % growth)	15.7	5.5	2.0
Value added in agriculture (% of GDP)	21.9	4.3	4.0
Value added in industry (% of GDP)	46.2	30.2	27.6
Value added in services (% of GDP)	31.9	65.4	68.4
Exports of goods and services (% of GDP)	47.7	51.3	46.7
Imports of goods and services (% of GDP)	49.0	64.8	57.6
Gross domestic investment (% of GDP)	40.1	27.6	26.3
Central government revenues (% of GDP)	..	34.7	33.7
Overall budget deficit (% of GDP)	..	0.2	-4.0
Money and quasi money (annual % growth)	..	6.7	8.3
Technology and infrastructure			
Telephone mainlines (per 1,000 people)	234	302	300
Cost of 3 min local call ($)	..	0.07	0.12
Personal computers (per 1,000 people)	..	61.0	82.0
Internet users (thousands)	..	80	105
Paved roads (% of total)	13	39	39
Aircraft departures (thousands)	..	10	9
Trade and finance			
Trade as share of PPP GDP (%)	..	34.1	30.7
Trade growth less GDP growth (average %, 1989-99)			5.9
High-technology exports (% of manufactured exports)	..	4	4
Net barter terms of trade (1995=100)	..	..	..
Foreign direct investment ($ millions)	0	357	348
Present value of debt ($ millions)			2,435
Total debt service ($ millions)	..	199	461
Short term debt ($ millions)	..	935	1,111
Aid per capita ($)	..	40	40

LEBANON

Population (millions)	4	Population growth (%)	1.4
Surface area (1,000 sq km)	10	Population per sq km	418
GNI ($ millions)	15,796	GNI per capita ($)	3,700

	1990	1998	1999
People			
Life expectancy (years)	68	70	70
Fertility rate (births per woman)	3.2	2.5	2.4
Infant mortality rate (per 1,000 live births)	36	28	26
Under 5 mortality rate (per 1,000 children)	40	32	32
Child malnutrition (% of children under 5)		3	..
Urban population (% of total)	84	89	89
Rural population density (per km^2 arable land)	314	262	..
Illiteracy male (% of people 15 and above)	12	9	8
Illiteracy female (% of people 15 and above)	27	21	20
Net primary enrollment (% of relevant age group)	..	76	..
Net secondary enrollment (% of relevant age group)	..	..	..
Girls in primary school (% of enrollment)	48	48	..
Girls in secondary school (% of enrollment)	..	52	..
Environment			
Forests (1,000 sq. km.)	0	..	0
Deforestation (% change 1990-2000)			0.3
Water use (% of total resources)	..	..	26.9
CO$_2$ emissions (metric tons per capita)	2.6	4.3	..
Access to improved water source (% of urban pop.)	..	100	100
Access to sanitation (% of urban population)	..	100	100
Energy use per capita (kg of oil equivalent)	635	1,256	..
Electricity use per capita (kWh)	369	1,820	..
Economy			
GDP ($ millions)	2,838	17,229	..
GDP growth (annual %)	26.5	5.0	..
GDP implicit price deflator (annual % growth)	15.5	8.0	..
Value added in agriculture (% of GDP)	..	12.4	..
Value added in industry (% of GDP)	..	26.5	..
Value added in services (% of GDP)	..	61.1	..
Exports of goods and services (% of GDP)	18.0	10.6	..
Imports of goods and services (% of GDP)	99.9	51.1	..
Gross domestic investment (% of GDP)	17.8	27.6	..
Central government revenues (% of GDP)	..	17.0	..
Overall budget deficit (% of GDP)	..	-15.1	..
Money and quasi money (annual % growth)	55.1	16.1	11.7
Technology and infrastructure			
Telephone mainlines (per 1,000 people)	118	194	201
Cost of 3 min local call ($)	0.03	0.06	0.07
Personal computers (per 1,000 people)	..	39.2	46.4
Internet users (thousands)	..	100	200
Paved roads (% of total)	95	95	..
Aircraft departures (thousands)	10	10	10
Trade and finance			
Trade as share of PPP GDP (%)	45.1	39.0	..
Trade growth less GDP growth (average %, 1989-99)			3.1
High-technology exports (% of manufactured exports)	..	..	..
Net barter terms of trade (1995=100)	105	117	..
Foreign direct investment ($ millions)	6	200	250
Present value of debt ($ millions)			8,541
Total debt service ($ millions)	99	528	1,010
Short term debt ($ millions)	1,421	1,961	2,202
Aid per capita ($)	71	57	45

129

LESOTHO

Population (millions)	2	Population growth (%)	2.3
Surface area (1,000 sq km)	30	Population per sq km	69
GNI ($ millions)	1,158	GNI per capita ($)	550

	1990	1998	1999
People			
Life expectancy (years)	58	48	45
Fertility rate (births per woman)	5.1	4.8	4.5
Infant mortality rate (per 1,000 live births)	102	93	92
Under 5 mortality rate (per 1,000 children)	148	137	141
Child malnutrition (% of children under 5)	16	16	..
Urban population (% of total)	20	26	27
Rural population density (per km^2 arable land)	434	466	..
Illiteracy male (% of people 15 and above)	35	29	28
Illiteracy female (% of people 15 and above)	11	7	7
Net primary enrollment (% of relevant age group)	73	70	..
Net secondary enrollment (% of relevant age group)	15	18	..
Girls in primary school (% of enrollment)	55	52	..
Girls in secondary school (% of enrollment)	60	59	..
Environment			
Forests (1,000 sq. km.)	0	..	0
Deforestation (% change 1990-2000)			0.0
Water use (% of total resources)	..	..	1.0
CO_2 emissions (metric tons per capita)	..	..	..
Access to improved water source (% of urban pop.)	..	..	98
Access to sanitation (% of urban population)	..	..	93
Energy use per capita (kg of oil equivalent)	..	..	..
Electricity use per capita (kWh)	..	..	..
Economy			
GDP ($ millions)	622	878	874
GDP growth (annual %)	6.2	-5.0	2.5
GDP implicit price deflator (annual % growth)	9.0	8.4	7.2
Value added in agriculture (% of GDP)	23.4	18.2	..
Value added in industry (% of GDP)	33.7	38.1	..
Value added in services (% of GDP)	42.9	43.7	..
Exports of goods and services (% of GDP)	16.6	27.2	..
Imports of goods and services (% of GDP)	121.1	108.8	..
Gross domestic investment (% of GDP)	53.2	47.0	..
Central government revenues (% of GDP)	39.0	44.6	..
Overall budget deficit (% of GDP)	-1.0	-3.7	..
Money and quasi money (annual % growth)	8.4	20.5	-5.1
Technology and infrastructure			
Telephone mainlines (per 1,000 people)	7	10	..
Cost of 3 min local call ($)	0.02	0.02	..
Personal computers (per 1,000 people)	..	..	..
Internet users (thousands)	..	0	1
Paved roads (% of total)	18	17	18
Aircraft departures (thousands)	5	2	0
Trade and finance			
Trade as share of PPP GDP (%)	39.5	29.6	28.4
Trade growth less GDP growth (average %, 1989-99)			0.3
High-technology exports (% of manufactured exports)	..	..	..
Net barter terms of trade (1995=100)	84	101	..
Foreign direct investment ($ millions)	17	265	163
Present value of debt ($ millions)			499
Total debt service ($ millions)	23	51	51
Short term debt ($ millions)	3	8	7
Aid per capita ($)	82	32	15

130

LIBERIA

Population (thousands)	3,044	Population growth (%)	2.7
Surface area (1,000 sq km)	111.4	Population per sq km	32
GNI ($ millions)	..	GNI per capita ($)	..

	1990	1998	1999
People			
Life expectancy (years)	45	47	47
Fertility rate (births per woman)	6.8	6.3	6.1
Infant mortality rate (per 1,000 live births)	168	116	113
Under 5 mortality rate (per 1,000 children)	..	194	188
Child malnutrition (% of children under 5)	..	..	..
Urban population (% of total)	42	44	44
Rural population density (per km^2 arable land)	831	877	..
Illiteracy male (% of people 15 and above)	45	33	31
Illiteracy female (% of people 15 and above)	77	66	63
Net primary enrollment (% of relevant age group)	..	..	..
Net secondary enrollment (% of relevant age group)	..	..	..
Girls in primary school (% of enrollment)	..	..	..
Girls in secondary school (% of enrollment)	..	..	..
Environment			
Forests (1,000 sq. km.)	42	..	35
Deforestation (% change 1990-2000)			2.0
Water use (% of total resources)	..	..	0.1
CO_2 emissions (metric tons per capita)	0.2	0.1	..
Access to improved water source (% of urban pop.)	50	58	..
Access to sanitation (% of urban population)	..	38	..
Energy use per capita (kg of oil equivalent)	..	..	..
Electricity use per capita (kWh)	..	..	..
Economy			
GDP ($ millions)	1,202	..	..
GDP growth (annual %)	..	..	..
GDP implicit price deflator (annual % growth)	..	..	..
Value added in agriculture (% of GDP)	..	..	..
Value added in industry (% of GDP)	..	..	..
Value added in services (% of GDP)	..	..	..
Exports of goods and services (% of GDP)	..	..	..
Imports of goods and services (% of GDP)	..	..	..
Gross domestic investment (% of GDP)	..	..	..
Central government revenues (% of GDP)	17.8	..	..
Overall budget deficit (% of GDP)	-7.7	..	..
Money and quasi money (annual % growth)	19.6	106.0	11.6
Technology and infrastructure			
Telephone mainlines (per 1,000 people)	4	2	..
Cost of 3 min local call ($)	..	..	..
Personal computers (per 1,000 people)	..	..	..
Internet users (thousands)	..	0	0
Paved roads (% of total)	6	6	..
Aircraft departures (thousands)	2	..	..
Trade and finance			
Trade as share of PPP GDP (%)	..	..	..
Trade growth less GDP growth (average %, 1989-99)			..
High-technology exports (% of manufactured exports)	..	..	..
Net barter terms of trade (1995=100)	112	97	..
Foreign direct investment ($ millions)	0	16	10
Present value of debt ($ millions)			1,996
Total debt service ($ millions)	3	1	3
Short term debt ($ millions)	411	694	706
Aid per capita ($)	46	25	31

131

LIBYA

Population (millions)	5	Population growth (%)	2.2
Surface area (1,000 sq km)	1,760	Population per sq km	3
GNI ($ millions)	..	GNI per capita ($)	..

	1990	1998	1999
People			
Life expectancy (years)	68	70	71
Fertility rate (births per woman)	5.0	3.8	3.6
Infant mortality rate (per 1,000 live births)	33	24	22
Under 5 mortality rate (per 1,000 children)	42	30	28
Child malnutrition (% of children under 5)	..	5	..
Urban population (% of total)	82	87	87
Rural population density (per km^2 arable land)	45	39	..
Illiteracy male (% of people 15 and above)	17	10	10
Illiteracy female (% of people 15 and above)	49	35	33
Net primary enrollment (% of relevant age group)	97	..	..
Net secondary enrollment (% of relevant age group)	..	..	..
Girls in primary school (% of enrollment)	48	49	..
Girls in secondary school (% of enrollment)	..	..	..
Environment			
Forests (1,000 sq. km.)	3	..	4
Deforestation (% change 1990-2000)			-1.4
Water use (% of total resources)	..	..	486.3
CO$_2$ emissions (metric tons per capita)	8.9	8.4	..
Access to improved water source (% of urban pop.)	72	..	72
Access to sanitation (% of urban population)	97	..	97
Energy use per capita (kg of oil equivalent)	2,613	2,343	..
Electricity use per capita (kWh)	3,804	3,677	..
Economy			
GDP ($ millions)	21,864	..	..
GDP growth (annual %)	0.6	..	..
GDP implicit price deflator (annual % growth)	7.6	..	..
Value added in agriculture (% of GDP)	..	..	..
Value added in industry (% of GDP)	..	..	..
Value added in services (% of GDP)	..	..	..
Exports of goods and services (% of GDP)	..	..	..
Imports of goods and services (% of GDP)	..	..	..
Gross domestic investment (% of GDP)	..	..	..
Central government revenues (% of GDP)	..	..	..
Overall budget deficit (% of GDP)	..	..	..
Money and quasi money (annual % growth)	19.0	3.8	7.4
Technology and infrastructure			
Telephone mainlines (per 1,000 people)	48	91	101
Cost of 3 min local call ($)	0.04	0.02	0.03
Personal computers (per 1,000 people)	..	..	..
Internet users (thousands)	..	..	7
Paved roads (% of total)	52	57	..
Aircraft departures (thousands)	18	6	6
Trade and finance			
Trade as share of PPP GDP (%)	..	..	..
Trade growth less GDP growth (average %, 1989-99)			..
High-technology exports (% of manufactured exports)	..	..	..
Net barter terms of trade (1995=100)	145	101	..
Foreign direct investment ($ millions)	..	..	..
Present value of debt ($ millions)			..
Total debt service ($ millions)	..	..	..
Short term debt ($ millions)	..	..	..
Aid per capita ($)	4	1	1

Population (thousands)	32	Population growth (%)		..
Surface area (1,000 sq km)	0.2	Population per sq km		200
GNI ($ millions)	..	GNI per capita ($)		..

	1990	1998	1999
People			
Life expectancy (years)	..	..	..
Fertility rate (births per woman)	..	..	..
Infant mortality rate (per 1,000 live births)	..	..	..
Under 5 mortality rate (per 1,000 children)	..	..	..
Child malnutrition (% of children under 5)	..	..	..
Urban population (% of total)	20	22	22
Rural population density (per km^2 arable land)	..	..	..
Illiteracy male (% of people 15 and above)	..	..	..
Illiteracy female (% of people 15 and above)	..	..	..
Net primary enrollment (% of relevant age group)	..	..	..
Net secondary enrollment (% of relevant age group)	..	..	..
Girls in primary school (% of enrollment)	..	..	..
Girls in secondary school (% of enrollment)	..	..	..
Environment			
Forests (1,000 sq. km.)	0	..	0
Deforestation (% change 1990-2000)			-1.6
Water use (% of total resources)	..	..	..
CO_2 emissions (metric tons per capita)	..	..	..
Access to improved water source (% of urban pop.)	..	..	..
Access to sanitation (% of urban population)	..	..	..
Energy use per capita (kg of oil equivalent)	..	..	..
Electricity use per capita (kWh)	..	..	..
Economy			
GDP ($ millions)	..	..	..
GDP growth (annual %)	..	..	..
GDP implicit price deflator (annual % growth)	..	..	..
Value added in agriculture (% of GDP)	..	..	..
Value added in industry (% of GDP)	..	..	..
Value added in services (% of GDP)	..	..	..
Exports of goods and services (% of GDP)	..	..	..
Imports of goods and services (% of GDP)	..	..	..
Gross domestic investment (% of GDP)	..	..	..
Central government revenues (% of GDP)	..	..	..
Overall budget deficit (% of GDP)	..	..	..
Money and quasi money (annual % growth)	..	..	..
Technology and infrastructure			
Telephone mainlines (per 1,000 people)	572	618	609
Cost of 3 min local call ($)	..	0.13	..
Personal computers (per 1,000 people)	..	..	..
Internet users (thousands)	..	..	..
Paved roads (% of total)	..	..	..
Aircraft departures (thousands)	..	..	..
Trade and finance			
Trade as share of PPP GDP (%)	..	..	..
Trade growth less GDP growth (average %, 1989-99)			..
High-technology exports (% of manufactured exports)	..	..	..
Net barter terms of trade (1995=100)	..	..	..
Foreign direct investment ($ millions)	..	..	..
Present value of debt ($ millions)			..
Total debt service ($ millions)	..	..	..
Short term debt ($ millions)	..	..	..
Aid per capita ($)	..	..	..

LITHUANIA

Population (millions)	4	Population growth (%)	-0.1
Surface area (1,000 sq km)	65	Population per sq km	57
GNI ($ millions)	9,751	GNI per capita ($)	2,640

	1990	1998	1999
People			
Life expectancy (years)	71	72	72
Fertility rate (births per woman)	2.0	1.4	1.4
Infant mortality rate (per 1,000 live births)	10	9	9
Under 5 mortality rate (per 1,000 children)	14	12	12
Child malnutrition (% of children under 5)	..	..	..
Urban population (% of total)	68	68	68
Rural population density (per km^2 arable land)	..	40	..
Illiteracy male (% of people 15 and above)	1	0	0
Illiteracy female (% of people 15 and above)	1	1	1
Net primary enrollment (% of relevant age group)	..	..	..
Net secondary enrollment (% of relevant age group)	..	..	..
Girls in primary school (% of enrollment)	..	48	..
Girls in secondary school (% of enrollment)	..	..	..
Environment			
Forests (1,000 sq. km.)	19	..	..
Deforestation (% change 1990-2000)			..
Water use (% of total resources)	..	..	1.0
CO_2 emissions (metric tons per capita)	..	..	..
Access to improved water source (% of urban pop.)	..	..	..
Access to sanitation (% of urban population)	..	..	..
Energy use per capita (kg of oil equivalent)	..	2,524	..
Electricity use per capita (kWh)	..	1,909	..
Economy			
GDP ($ millions)	13,254	10,747	10,634
GDP growth (annual %)	9.5	5.1	-4.2
GDP implicit price deflator (annual % growth)	..	6.7	3.3
Value added in agriculture (% of GDP)	27.1	10.4	8.8
Value added in industry (% of GDP)	30.9	32.9	31.8
Value added in services (% of GDP)	42.1	56.6	59.5
Exports of goods and services (% of GDP)	52.1	47.2	39.9
Imports of goods and services (% of GDP)	60.7	59.1	50.2
Gross domestic investment (% of GDP)	32.6	24.4	22.9
Central government revenues (% of GDP)	..	26.7	26.0
Overall budget deficit (% of GDP)	..	-0.4	-7.1
Money and quasi money (annual % growth)	..	14.5	7.7
Technology and infrastructure			
Telephone mainlines (per 1,000 people)	212	300	312
Cost of 3 min local call ($)	..	0.05	0.06
Personal computers (per 1,000 people)	..	54.1	59.5
Internet users (thousands)	..	70	103
Paved roads (% of total)	82	91	91
Aircraft departures (thousands)	..	10	11
Trade and finance			
Trade as share of PPP GDP (%)	..	37.7	31.8
Trade growth less GDP growth (average %, 1989-99)			4.2
High-technology exports (% of manufactured exports)	..	3	12
Net barter terms of trade (1995=100)	..	..	..
Foreign direct investment ($ millions)	0	926	487
Present value of debt ($ millions)			3,483
Total debt service ($ millions)	..	334	276
Short term debt ($ millions)	..	371	548
Aid per capita ($)	..	34	35

LUXEMBOURG

Population (thousands)	432	Population growth (%)	1.3
Surface area (1,000 sq km)	..	Population per sq km	166
GNI ($ millions)	18,545	GNI per capita ($)	42,930

	1990	1998	1999
People			
Life expectancy (years)	75	76	77
Fertility rate (births per woman)	1.6	1.7	1.7
Infant mortality rate (per 1,000 live births)	7	5	5
Under 5 mortality rate (per 1,000 children)	9	7	5
Child malnutrition (% of children under 5)	..	..	..
Urban population (% of total)	86	91	91
Rural population density (per km^2 arable land)	..	..	..
Illiteracy male (% of people 15 and above)	..	..	..
Illiteracy female (% of people 15 and above)	..	..	..
Net primary enrollment (% of relevant age group)	..	..	..
Net secondary enrollment (% of relevant age group)	..	68	..
Girls in primary school (% of enrollment)	51	..	..
Girls in secondary school (% of enrollment)	49	50	..
Environment			
Forests (1,000 sq. km.)	..	..	..
Deforestation (% change 1990-2000)			
Water use (% of total resources)	..	..	3.8
CO_2 emissions (metric tons per capita)	26.7	19.6	..
Access to improved water source (% of urban pop.)	..	..	..
Access to sanitation (% of urban population)	..	..	..
Energy use per capita (kg of oil equivalent)	9,351	7,775	..
Electricity use per capita (kWh)	10,806	12,400	..
Economy			
GDP ($ millions)	10,929	18,340	19,328
GDP growth (annual %)	2.2	5.0	7.5
GDP implicit price deflator (annual % growth)	3.4	1.5	2.3
Value added in agriculture (% of GDP)	1.8	0.7	0.7
Value added in industry (% of GDP)	29.1	20.6	18.4
Value added in services (% of GDP)	69.1	78.7	80.9
Exports of goods and services (% of GDP)	113.3	113.7	113.4
Imports of goods and services (% of GDP)	108.9	95.1	97.3
Gross domestic investment (% of GDP)	21.5	19.5	..
Central government revenues (% of GDP)	41.0	41.9	..
Overall budget deficit (% of GDP)	4.6	2.0	..
Money and quasi money (annual % growth)	..	..	..
Technology and infrastructure			
Telephone mainlines (per 1,000 people)	481	692	724
Cost of 3 min local call ($)	0.14	0.11	0.11
Personal computers (per 1,000 people)	..	389.2	396.3
Internet users (thousands)	1	50	75
Paved roads (% of total)	99	100	100
Aircraft departures (thousands)	12	25	30
Trade and finance			
Trade as share of PPP GDP (%)	..	..	100.9
Trade growth less GDP growth (average %, 1989-99)			-0.2
High-technology exports (% of manufactured exports)	..	..	..
Net barter terms of trade (1995=100)	..	..	..
Foreign direct investment ($ millions)	..	..	..
Present value of debt ($ millions)			..
Total debt service ($ millions)	..	..	..
Short term debt ($ millions)	..	..	..
Aid per capita ($)	..	..	..

135

MACOA, CHINA

Population (millions)	434	Population growth (%)	1.9
Surface area (1,000 sq km)	0.0	Population per sq km	..
GNI ($ millions)	6,161	GNI per capita ($)	14,200

	1990	1998	1999
People			
Life expectancy (years)	76	78	78
Fertility rate (births per woman)	1.8	1.4	1.4
Infant mortality rate (per 1,000 live births)	10	6	6
Under 5 mortality rate (per 1,000 children)	..	..	..
Child malnutrition (% of children under 5)	..	..	..
Urban population (% of total)	99	99	99
Rural population density (per km^2 arable land)	..	..	..
Illiteracy male (% of people 15 and above)	..	..	..
Illiteracy female (% of people 15 and above)	..	..	..
Net primary enrollment (% of relevant age group)	81	..	..
Net secondary enrollment (% of relevant age group)	53	..	..
Girls in primary school (% of enrollment)	48	48	..
Girls in secondary school (% of enrollment)	52	..	..
Environment			
Forests (1,000 sq. km.)	..	..	..
Deforestation (% change 1990-2000)			..
Water use (% of total resources)			..
CO_2 emissions (metric tons per capita)	2.8	3.5	..
Access to improved water source (% of urban pop.)	..	..	..
Access to sanitation (% of urban population)	..	..	..
Energy use per capita (kg of oil equivalent)	..	..	..
Electricity use per capita (kWh)	..	..	..
Economy			
GDP ($ millions)	3,301	6,447	6,113
GDP growth (annual %)	9.8	-4.6	-2.9
GDP implicit price deflator (annual % growth)	9.1	-2.6	-2.4
Value added in agriculture (% of GDP)	..	..	..
Value added in industry (% of GDP)	..	16.1	..
Value added in services (% of GDP)	..	83.9	..
Exports of goods and services (% of GDP)	96.5	76.6	79.4
Imports of goods and services (% of GDP)	68.1	46.6	51.6
Gross domestic investment (% of GDP)	22.8	18.5	17.4
Central government revenues (% of GDP)	..	..	..
Overall budget deficit (% of GDP)	..	..	..
Money and quasi money (annual % growth)	..	..	..
Technology and infrastructure			
Telephone mainlines (per 1,000 people)	255	404	408
Cost of 3 min local call ($)	0.00	0.00	0.00
Personal computers (per 1,000 people)	..	..	137.3
Internet users (thousands)	..	30	40
Paved roads (% of total)	100	100	100
Aircraft departures (thousands)	..	..	..
Trade and finance			
Trade as share of PPP GDP (%)	62.1	55.0	57.0
Trade growth less GDP growth (average %, 1989-99)			-0.5
High-technology exports (% of manufactured exports)	2	1	1
Net barter terms of trade (1995=100)	..	..	..
Foreign direct investment ($ millions)	..	..	..
Present value of debt ($ millions)			..
Total debt service ($ millions)	..	..	..
Short term debt ($ millions)	..	..	..
Aid per capita ($)	1	1	1

MACEDONIA, FYR

Population (millions)	2	Population growth (%)		0.5
Surface area (1,000 sq km)	26	Population per sq km		79
GNI ($ millions)	3,348	GNI per capita ($)		1,660

	1990	1998	1999
People			
Life expectancy (years)	72	..	73
Fertility rate (births per woman)	2.1	..	1.8
Infant mortality rate (per 1,000 live births)	32	16	16
Under 5 mortality rate (per 1,000 children)	33	18	17
Child malnutrition (% of children under 5)	..	..	6
Urban population (% of total)	58	61	62
Rural population density (per km^2 arable land)	..	133	..
Illiteracy male (% of people 15 and above)	..	..	..
Illiteracy female (% of people 15 and above)	..	..	..
Net primary enrollment (% of relevant age group)	94	..	..
Net secondary enrollment (% of relevant age group)	..	..	..
Girls in primary school (% of enrollment)	..	..	..
Girls in secondary school (% of enrollment)	..	..	..
Environment			
Forests (1,000 sq. km.)	9	..	..
Deforestation (% change 1990-2000)			..
Water use (% of total resources)	..	..	..
CO_2 emissions (metric tons per capita)	..	..	..
Access to improved water source (% of urban pop.)	..	..	..
Access to sanitation (% of urban population)	..	..	..
Energy use per capita (kg of oil equivalent)	..	..	..
Electricity use per capita (kWh)	..	..	..
Economy			
GDP ($ millions)	..	3,449	3,452
GDP growth (annual %)	..	2.9	2.7
GDP implicit price deflator (annual % growth)	..	0.2	-0.3
Value added in agriculture (% of GDP)	8.5	12.2	11.6
Value added in industry (% of GDP)	46.7	35.0	35.2
Value added in services (% of GDP)	44.9	52.8	53.2
Exports of goods and services (% of GDP)	25.9	43.5	41.5
Imports of goods and services (% of GDP)	36.0	57.8	55.7
Gross domestic investment (% of GDP)	19.0	23.0	21.4
Central government revenues (% of GDP)	..	..	..
Overall budget deficit (% of GDP)	..	..	..
Money and quasi money (annual % growth)	..	13.0	32.0
Technology and infrastructure			
Telephone mainlines (per 1,000 people)	148	219	234
Cost of 3 min local call ($)	..	0.01	0.01
Personal computers (per 1,000 people)	..	..	..
Internet users (thousands)	..	20	30
Paved roads (% of total)	59	..	..
Aircraft departures (thousands)	..	5	6
Trade and finance			
Trade as share of PPP GDP (%)	..	35.9	33.1
Trade growth less GDP growth (average %, 1989-99)			0.8
High-technology exports (% of manufactured exports)	..	2	..
Net barter terms of trade (1995=100)	..	..	..
Foreign direct investment ($ millions)	..	118	30
Present value of debt ($ millions)			1,265
Total debt service ($ millions)	..	158	458
Short term debt ($ millions)	..	157	68
Aid per capita ($)	..	46	135

MADAGASCAR

Sub-Saharan Africa   Low income

Population (millions)	15	Population growth (%)	3.1
Surface area (1,000 sq km)	587	Population per sq km	26
GNI ($ millions)	3,712	GNI per capita ($)	250

	1990	1998	1999
People			
Life expectancy (years)	53	53	54
Fertility rate (births per woman)	6.2	5.8	5.6
Infant mortality rate (per 1,000 live births)	103	94	90
Under 5 mortality rate (per 1,000 children)	170	158	149
Child malnutrition (% of children under 5)	41	40	..
Urban population (% of total)	24	28	29
Rural population density (per km^2 arable land)	356	408	..
Illiteracy male (% of people 15 and above)	34	28	27
Illiteracy female (% of people 15 and above)	50	42	41
Net primary enrollment (% of relevant age group)	70	61	..
Net secondary enrollment (% of relevant age group)	..	..	..
Girls in primary school (% of enrollment)	49	49	..
Girls in secondary school (% of enrollment)	..	49	..
Environment			
Forests (1,000 sq. km.)	129	..	117
Deforestation (% change 1990-2000)			0.9
Water use (% of total resources)	..	..	5.8
CO_2 emissions (metric tons per capita)	0.1	0.1	..
Access to improved water source (% of urban pop.)	85	..	85
Access to sanitation (% of urban population)	70	..	70
Energy use per capita (kg of oil equivalent)	..	..	..
Electricity use per capita (kWh)	..	..	..
Economy			
GDP ($ millions)	3,081	3,739	3,721
GDP growth (annual %)	3.1	3.9	4.7
GDP implicit price deflator (annual % growth)	11.5	8.4	9.8
Value added in agriculture (% of GDP)	32.3	30.6	30.0
Value added in industry (% of GDP)	14.3	13.6	13.8
Value added in services (% of GDP)	53.4	55.8	56.2
Exports of goods and services (% of GDP)	16.6	21.4	24.8
Imports of goods and services (% of GDP)	27.3	29.3	32.7
Gross domestic investment (% of GDP)	17.0	12.5	12.9
Central government revenues (% of GDP)	11.7	8.7	..
Overall budget deficit (% of GDP)	-0.9	-1.3	..
Money and quasi money (annual % growth)	4.5	6.2	19.2
Technology and infrastructure			
Telephone mainlines (per 1,000 people)	2	3	3
Cost of 3 min local call ($)	0.07	0.09	0.08
Personal computers (per 1,000 people)	..	1.6	1.9
Internet users (thousands)	..	3	8
Paved roads (% of total)	15	12	..
Aircraft departures (thousands)	17	8	19
Trade and finance			
Trade as share of PPP GDP (%)	9.3	6.7	..
Trade growth less GDP growth (average %, 1989-99)			2.7
High-technology exports (% of manufactured exports)	8	18	3
Net barter terms of trade (1995=100)	99	125	..
Foreign direct investment ($ millions)	22	17	58
Present value of debt ($ millions)			2,943
Total debt service ($ millions)	223	125	166
Short term debt ($ millions)	226	230	324
Aid per capita ($)	34	34	24

Sub-Saharan Africa   **Low income**

Population (millions)	11	Population growth (%)	2.4
Surface area (1,000 sq km)	118	Population per sq km	115
GNI ($ millions)	1,961	GNI per capita ($)	180

	1990	1998	1999
People			
Life expectancy (years)	45	43	39
Fertility rate (births per woman)	7.0	6.4	6.3
Infant mortality rate (per 1,000 live births)	135	133	132
Under 5 mortality rate (per 1,000 children)	230	224	227
Child malnutrition (% of children under 5)	28	30	..
Urban population (% of total)	13	22	24
Rural population density (per km^2 arable land)	406	437	..
Illiteracy male (% of people 15 and above)	31	27	26
Illiteracy female (% of people 15 and above)	64	56	55
Net primary enrollment (% of relevant age group)	50	103	..
Net secondary enrollment (% of relevant age group)	..	..	..
Girls in primary school (% of enrollment)	45	47	..
Girls in secondary school (% of enrollment)	19	18	..
Environment			
Forests (1,000 sq. km.)	33	..	26
Deforestation (% change 1990-2000)			2.4
Water use (% of total resources)	..	..	5.1
CO$_2$ emissions (metric tons per capita)	0.1	0.1	..
Access to improved water source (% of urban pop.)	90	..	95
Access to sanitation (% of urban population)	96	..	96
Energy use per capita (kg of oil equivalent)	..	..	..
Electricity use per capita (kWh)	..	..	..
Economy			
GDP ($ millions)	1,803	1,737	1,810
GDP growth (annual %)	5.7	2.0	4.0
GDP implicit price deflator (annual % growth)	10.9	27.0	42.2
Value added in agriculture (% of GDP)	45.0	35.9	37.6
Value added in industry (% of GDP)	28.9	17.8	17.8
Value added in services (% of GDP)	26.1	46.4	44.6
Exports of goods and services (% of GDP)	24.8	33.3	27.1
Imports of goods and services (% of GDP)	34.9	40.7	42.5
Gross domestic investment (% of GDP)	19.7	13.5	14.8
Central government revenues (% of GDP)	20.7	..	..
Overall budget deficit (% of GDP)	-1.7	..	..
Money and quasi money (annual % growth)	11.1	60.0	26.5
Technology and infrastructure			
Telephone mainlines (per 1,000 people)	3	4	4
Cost of 3 min local call ($)	0.03	0.01	0.03
Personal computers (per 1,000 people)	..	0.8	0.9
Internet users (thousands)	..	2	10
Paved roads (% of total)	22	19	..
Aircraft departures (thousands)	4	4	4
Trade and finance			
Trade as share of PPP GDP (%)	24.7	19.5	16.6
Trade growth less GDP growth (average %, 1989-99)			-1.7
High-technology exports (% of manufactured exports)	0	..	..
Net barter terms of trade (1995=100)	116	109	..
Foreign direct investment ($ millions)	0	70	60
Present value of debt ($ millions)			1,482
Total debt service ($ millions)	133	84	69
Short term debt ($ millions)	58	32	67
Aid per capita ($)	59	41	41

MALAYSIA

Population (millions)	23	Population growth (%)	2.4
Surface area (1,000 sq km)	330	Population per sq km	69
GNI ($ millions)	76,944	GNI per capita ($)	3,390

	1990	1998	1999
People			
Life expectancy (years)	71	72	72
Fertility rate (births per woman)	3.8	3.2	3.0
Infant mortality rate (per 1,000 live births)	16	8	8
Under 5 mortality rate (per 1,000 children)	21	14	10
Child malnutrition (% of children under 5)	25	20	..
Urban population (% of total)	50	56	57
Rural population density (per km^2 arable land)	537	537	..
Illiteracy male (% of people 15 and above)	13	9	9
Illiteracy female (% of people 15 and above)	25	18	17
Net primary enrollment (% of relevant age group)	..	102	..
Net secondary enrollment (% of relevant age group)	..	..	..
Girls in primary school (% of enrollment)	49	49	..
Girls in secondary school (% of enrollment)	51	51	..
Environment			
Forests (1,000 sq. km.)	217	..	193
Deforestation (% change 1990-2000)			1.2
Water use (% of total resources)	..	..	2.2
CO$_2$ emissions (metric tons per capita)	3.2	6.3	..
Access to improved water source (% of urban pop.)	100	100	..
Access to sanitation (% of urban population)	..	100	..
Energy use per capita (kg of oil equivalent)	1,234	1,967	..
Electricity use per capita (kWh)	1,095	2,554	..
Economy			
GDP ($ millions)	44,024	72,488	79,039
GDP growth (annual %)	9.0	-7.4	5.8
GDP implicit price deflator (annual % growth)	3.8	9.0	-0.2
Value added in agriculture (% of GDP)	15.2	13.3	10.7
Value added in industry (% of GDP)	42.2	43.6	46.0
Value added in services (% of GDP)	42.6	43.2	43.4
Exports of goods and services (% of GDP)	74.5	115.2	121.7
Imports of goods and services (% of GDP)	72.4	93.3	96.6
Gross domestic investment (% of GDP)	32.4	26.6	22.3
Central government revenues (% of GDP)	26.4	23.1	..
Overall budget deficit (% of GDP)	-2.0	2.9	..
Money and quasi money (annual % growth)	10.6	-1.4	16.9
Technology and infrastructure			
Telephone mainlines (per 1,000 people)	89	202	203
Cost of 3 min local call ($)	0.04	0.02	0.02
Personal computers (per 1,000 people)	8.4	59.9	68.7
Internet users (thousands)	0	800	1,500
Paved roads (% of total)	70	75	76
Aircraft departures (thousands)	131	173	165
Trade and finance			
Trade as share of PPP GDP (%)	67.7	77.5	80.2
Trade growth less GDP growth (average %, 1989-99)			4.8
High-technology exports (% of manufactured exports)	38	55	59
Net barter terms of trade (1995=100)	102	99	..
Foreign direct investment ($ millions)	2,333	2,163	1,553
Present value of debt ($ millions)			47,054
Total debt service ($ millions)	4,333	6,275	4,695
Short term debt ($ millions)	1,906	8,656	7,550
Aid per capita ($)	26	9	6

140

MALDIVES

South Asia   **Lower middle income**

Population (thousands)	269	Population growth (%)	2.5
Surface area (1,000 sq km)	0.3	Population per sq km	898
GNI ($ millions)	322	GNI per capita ($)	1,200

	1990	1998	1999
People			
Life expectancy (years)	62	67	68
Fertility rate (births per woman)	5.7	4.5	4.3
Infant mortality rate (per 1,000 live births)	60	32	29
Under 5 mortality rate (per 1,000 children)	84	39	35
Child malnutrition (% of children under 5)	..	45	..
Urban population (% of total)	26	26	26
Rural population density (per km^2 arable land)	15,783	19,447	..
Illiteracy male (% of people 15 and above)	6	4	4
Illiteracy female (% of people 15 and above)	6	4	4
Net primary enrollment (% of relevant age group)	..	..	..
Net secondary enrollment (% of relevant age group)	..	..	..
Girls in primary school (% of enrollment)	49	48	..
Girls in secondary school (% of enrollment)	..	50	..
Environment			
Forests (1,000 sq. km.)	0	..	0
Deforestation (% change 1990-2000)			0.0
Water use (% of total resources)	..	..	
CO_2 emissions (metric tons per capita)	0.7	1.2	..
Access to improved water source (% of urban pop.)	91	98	100
Access to sanitation (% of urban population)	..	95	100
Energy use per capita (kg of oil equivalent)	..	..	..
Electricity use per capita (kWh)	..	..	..
Economy			
GDP ($ millions)	146	368	..
GDP growth (annual %)	16.3	6.8	..
GDP implicit price deflator (annual % growth)	4.4	0.8	..
Value added in agriculture (% of GDP)	21.9	16.4	..
Value added in industry (% of GDP)	..	..	..
Value added in services (% of GDP)	..	..	..
Exports of goods and services (% of GDP)	36.1	..	..
Imports of goods and services (% of GDP)	94.4	..	..
Gross domestic investment (% of GDP)	..	..	..
Central government revenues (% of GDP)	33.0	40.7	..
Overall budget deficit (% of GDP)	-12.3	-2.8	..
Money and quasi money (annual % growth)	18.7	22.8	3.6
Technology and infrastructure			
Telephone mainlines (per 1,000 people)	29	72	80
Cost of 3 min local call ($)	0.04	0.06	0.06
Personal computers (per 1,000 people)	..	16.3	18.0
Internet users (thousands)	0	2	3
Paved roads (% of total)	..	..	..
Aircraft departures (thousands)	1	6	5
Trade and finance			
Trade as share of PPP GDP (%)	31.4	37.0	..
Trade growth less GDP growth (average %, 1989-99)			..
High-technology exports (% of manufactured exports)	..	..	..
Net barter terms of trade (1995=100)	..	..	..
Foreign direct investment ($ millions)	6	12	12
Present value of debt ($ millions)			147
Total debt service ($ millions)	9	16	18
Short term debt ($ millions)	14	10	25
Aid per capita ($)	99	95	114

MALI

Population (millions)	11	Population growth (%)	2.4
Surface area (1,000 sq km)	1,240	Population per sq km	9
GNI ($ millions)	2,577	GNI per capita ($)	240

	1990	1998	1999
People			
Life expectancy (years)	45	44	43
Fertility rate (births per woman)	6.9	6.6	6.4
Infant mortality rate (per 1,000 live births)	136	118	120
Under 5 mortality rate (per 1,000 children)	268	235	223
Child malnutrition (% of children under 5)	..	27	..
Urban population (% of total)	24	29	29
Rural population density (per km^2 arable land)	314	160	..
Illiteracy male (% of people 15 and above)	67	54	53
Illiteracy female (% of people 15 and above)	81	69	67
Net primary enrollment (% of relevant age group)	21	31	..
Net secondary enrollment (% of relevant age group)	5	..	..
Girls in primary school (% of enrollment)	37	41	..
Girls in secondary school (% of enrollment)	33	33	..
Environment			
Forests (1,000 sq. km.)	142	..	132
Deforestation (% change 1990-2000)			0.7
Water use (% of total resources)	..	..	1.4
CO$_2$ emissions (metric tons per capita)	0.1	0.0	..
Access to improved water source (% of urban pop.)	65	..	74
Access to sanitation (% of urban population)	95	..	93
Energy use per capita (kg of oil equivalent)	..	..	..
Electricity use per capita (kWh)	..	..	..
Economy			
GDP ($ millions)	2,421	2,597	2,570
GDP growth (annual %)	-1.9	3.4	5.5
GDP implicit price deflator (annual % growth)	4.9	2.5	-2.0
Value added in agriculture (% of GDP)	45.5	46.5	46.5
Value added in industry (% of GDP)	15.9	17.3	16.7
Value added in services (% of GDP)	38.6	36.2	36.8
Exports of goods and services (% of GDP)	17.1	24.5	24.9
Imports of goods and services (% of GDP)	33.7	34.2	36.0
Gross domestic investment (% of GDP)	23.0	20.9	21.2
Central government revenues (% of GDP)	19.7	..	..
Overall budget deficit (% of GDP)	-4.8	..	..
Money and quasi money (annual % growth)	-4.9	4.2	1.0
Technology and infrastructure			
Telephone mainlines (per 1,000 people)	1	3	..
Cost of 3 min local call ($)	0.25	0.14	..
Personal computers (per 1,000 people)	..	0.8	1.0
Internet users (thousands)	..	1	10
Paved roads (% of total)	11	12	..
Aircraft departures (thousands)	1	2	2
Trade and finance			
Trade as share of PPP GDP (%)	19.8	17.7	16.1
Trade growth less GDP growth (average %, 1989-99)			1.9
High-technology exports (% of manufactured exports)	..	..	..
Net barter terms of trade (1995=100)	122	99	..
Foreign direct investment ($ millions)	-7	17	19
Present value of debt ($ millions)			1,429
Total debt service ($ millions)	68	82	106
Short term debt ($ millions)	62	188	192
Aid per capita ($)	57	34	33

Middle East & North Africa		Upper middle income

Population (thousands)	379	Population growth (%)	0.5
Surface area (1,000 sq km)	0.3	Population per sq km	1,184
GNI ($ millions)	3,492	GNI per capita ($)	9,210

	1990	1998	1999
People			
Life expectancy (years)	75	77	77
Fertility rate (births per woman)	2.0	1.8	1.8
Infant mortality rate (per 1,000 live births)	9	5	5
Under 5 mortality rate (per 1,000 children)	14	9	7
Child malnutrition (% of children under 5)	..	..	..
Urban population (% of total)	88	90	90
Rural population density (per km^2 arable land)	366	376	..
Illiteracy male (% of people 15 and above)	12	9	9
Illiteracy female (% of people 15 and above)	11	8	8
Net primary enrollment (% of relevant age group)	99	100	..
Net secondary enrollment (% of relevant age group)	80	79	..
Girls in primary school (% of enrollment)	48	49	..
Girls in secondary school (% of enrollment)	47	48	..
Environment			
Forests (1,000 sq. km.)	..	..	0
Deforestation (% change 1990-2000)			..
Water use (% of total resources)	..	..	30.0
CO_2 emissions (metric tons per capita)	4.7	4.7	..
Access to improved water source (% of urban pop.)	100	100	100
Access to sanitation (% of urban population)	100	..	100
Energy use per capita (kg of oil equivalent)	2,186	2,517	..
Electricity use per capita (kWh)	2,569	3,719	..
Economy			
GDP ($ millions)	2,312	3,471	..
GDP growth (annual %)	6.3	4.1	..
GDP implicit price deflator (annual % growth)	3.2	0.5	..
Value added in agriculture (% of GDP)	3.5	3.2	..
Value added in industry (% of GDP)	38.8	34.9	..
Value added in services (% of GDP)	57.7	62.0	..
Exports of goods and services (% of GDP)	85.2	88.5	..
Imports of goods and services (% of GDP)	98.9	93.9	..
Gross domestic investment (% of GDP)	33.4	23.0	..
Central government revenues (% of GDP)	38.2	34.2	..
Overall budget deficit (% of GDP)	-5.2	-9.8	..
Money and quasi money (annual % growth)	11.2	7.9	9.8
Technology and infrastructure			
Telephone mainlines (per 1,000 people)	360	499	512
Cost of 3 min local call ($)	0.03	0.12	0.12
Personal computers (per 1,000 people)	14.0	156.3	181.3
Internet users (thousands)	..	9	15
Paved roads (% of total)	..	95	..
Aircraft departures (thousands)	7	13	14
Trade and finance			
Trade as share of PPP GDP (%)	98.6	78.7	..
Trade growth less GDP growth (average %, 1989-99)			..
High-technology exports (% of manufactured exports)	45	60	62
Net barter terms of trade (1995=100)	123	..	..
Foreign direct investment ($ millions)	46	0	0
Present value of debt ($ millions)			0
Total debt service ($ millions)	46	562	801
Short term debt ($ millions)	476	1,165	1,410
Aid per capita ($)	10	58	66

143

MARSHALL ISLANDS

East Asia and Pacific — Lower middle income

Population (thousands)	51	Population growth (%)		..
Surface area (1,000 sq km)	..	Population per sq km		255
GNI ($ millions)	99	GNI per capita ($)		1,950

	1990	1998	1999
People			
Life expectancy (years)	..	..	..
Fertility rate (births per woman)	..	..	..
Infant mortality rate (per 1,000 live births)	..	..	..
Under 5 mortality rate (per 1,000 children)	..	..	..
Child malnutrition (% of children under 5)	..	..	..
Urban population (% of total)	66	71	71
Rural population density (per km^2 arable land)	..	..	..
Illiteracy male (% of people 15 and above)	..	..	..
Illiteracy female (% of people 15 and above)	..	..	..
Net primary enrollment (% of relevant age group)	..	..	..
Net secondary enrollment (% of relevant age group)	..	..	..
Girls in primary school (% of enrollment)	..	..	..
Girls in secondary school (% of enrollment)	..	..	..
Environment			
Forests (1,000 sq. km.)	..	..	..
Deforestation (% change 1990-2000)			..
Water use (% of total resources)	..	..	..
CO_2 emissions (metric tons per capita)	..	..	..
Access to improved water source (% of urban pop.)	..	..	..
Access to sanitation (% of urban population)	..	..	..
Energy use per capita (kg of oil equivalent)	..	..	..
Electricity use per capita (kWh)	..	..	..
Economy			
GDP ($ millions)	69	96	97
GDP growth (annual %)	3.2	-5.0	0.5
GDP implicit price deflator (annual % growth)	0.7	4.0	1.0
Value added in agriculture (% of GDP)	..	..	..
Value added in industry (% of GDP)	..	..	..
Value added in services (% of GDP)	..	..	..
Exports of goods and services (% of GDP)	..	..	..
Imports of goods and services (% of GDP)	..	..	..
Gross domestic investment (% of GDP)	..	..	..
Central government revenues (% of GDP)	..	..	..
Overall budget deficit (% of GDP)	..	..	..
Money and quasi money (annual % growth)	..	..	..
Technology and infrastructure			
Telephone mainlines (per 1,000 people)	11	62	..
Cost of 3 min local call ($)	0.00	0.00	..
Personal computers (per 1,000 people)	0.1	..	48.2
Internet users (thousands)	0	..	1
Paved roads (% of total)	..	..	..
Aircraft departures (thousands)	3	4	2
Trade and finance			
Trade as share of PPP GDP (%)	..	..	..
Trade growth less GDP growth (average %, 1989-99)			..
High-technology exports (% of manufactured exports)	..	..	..
Net barter terms of trade (1995=100)	..	..	..
Foreign direct investment ($ millions)	..	..	..
Present value of debt ($ millions)			..
Total debt service ($ millions)	..	..	..
Short term debt ($ millions)	..	..	..
Aid per capita ($)	..	..	1,233

144

Sub-Saharan Africa   **Low income**

Population (millions)	3	Population growth (%)	2.7
Surface area (1,000 sq km)	1,026	Population per sq km	3
GNI ($ millions)	1,001	GNI per capita ($)	390

	1990	1998	1999
People			
Life expectancy (years)	51	53	54
Fertility rate (births per woman)	6.0	5.5	5.3
Infant mortality rate (per 1,000 live births)	105	92	88
Under 5 mortality rate (per 1,000 children)	..	149	142
Child malnutrition (% of children under 5)	48	23	..
Urban population (% of total)	44	55	56
Rural population density (per km² arable land)	286	233	..
Illiteracy male (% of people 15 and above)	53	48	48
Illiteracy female (% of people 15 and above)	74	69	69
Net primary enrollment (% of relevant age group)	..	57	..
Net secondary enrollment (% of relevant age group)	..	..	..
Girls in primary school (% of enrollment)	42	48	48
Girls in secondary school (% of enrollment)	32	34	..
Environment			
Forests (1,000 sq. km.)	4	..	3
Deforestation (% change 1990-2000)			2.7
Water use (% of total resources)	..	..	143.0
CO₂ emissions (metric tons per capita)	1.3	1.2	..
Access to improved water source (% of urban pop.)	34	..	34
Access to sanitation (% of urban population)	44	..	44
Energy use per capita (kg of oil equivalent)	..	..	..
Electricity use per capita (kWh)	..	..	..
Economy			
GDP ($ millions)	1,020	1,002	958
GDP growth (annual %)	-1.8	3.7	4.1
GDP implicit price deflator (annual % growth)	2.6	9.4	2.1
Value added in agriculture (% of GDP)	29.6	24.4	25.2
Value added in industry (% of GDP)	28.8	31.2	29.3
Value added in services (% of GDP)	41.6	44.4	45.5
Exports of goods and services (% of GDP)	45.6	39.8	38.6
Imports of goods and services (% of GDP)	60.7	53.8	49.2
Gross domestic investment (% of GDP)	20.0	19.0	17.8
Central government revenues (% of GDP)	..	..	..
Overall budget deficit (% of GDP)	..	..	..
Money and quasi money (annual % growth)	11.5	4.1	2.1
Technology and infrastructure			
Telephone mainlines (per 1,000 people)	3	6	6
Cost of 3 min local call ($)	0.16	0.09	0.09
Personal computers (per 1,000 people)	..	5.9	27.2
Internet users (thousands)	..	1	13
Paved roads (% of total)	11	11	..
Aircraft departures (thousands)	4	5	4
Trade and finance			
Trade as share of PPP GDP (%)	36.3	19.4	18.8
Trade growth less GDP growth (average %, 1989-99)			-2.9
High-technology exports (% of manufactured exports)	..	..	..
Net barter terms of trade (1995=100)	96	99	..
Foreign direct investment ($ millions)	7	0	2
Present value of debt ($ millions)			1,567
Total debt service ($ millions)	146	110	106
Short term debt ($ millions)	238	265	283
Aid per capita ($)	117	68	84

MAURITIUS

Population (millions)	1	Population growth (%)	1.3
Surface area (1,000 sq km)	2	Population per sq km	579
GNI ($ millions)	4,157	GNI per capita ($)	3,540

	1990	1998	1999
People			
Life expectancy (years)	70	70	71
Fertility rate (births per woman)	2.2	2.0	2.0
Infant mortality rate (per 1,000 live births)	20	19	19
Under 5 mortality rate (per 1,000 children)	25	23	23
Child malnutrition (% of children under 5)	..	15	..
Urban population (% of total)	41	41	41
Rural population density (per km^2 arable land)	629	684	..
Illiteracy male (% of people 15 and above)	15	13	12
Illiteracy female (% of people 15 and above)	25	20	19
Net primary enrollment (% of relevant age group)	95	98	..
Net secondary enrollment (% of relevant age group)	..	..	..
Girls in primary school (% of enrollment)	49	49	..
Girls in secondary school (% of enrollment)	50	50	..
Environment			
Forests (1,000 sq. km.)	0	..	0
Deforestation (% change 1990-2000)			0.6
Water use (% of total resources)	..	..	16.4
CO$_2$ emissions (metric tons per capita)	1.1	1.5	..
Access to improved water source (% of urban pop.)	100	..	100
Access to sanitation (% of urban population)	100	..	100
Energy use per capita (kg of oil equivalent)	..	..	..
Electricity use per capita (kWh)	..	..	..
Economy			
GDP ($ millions)	2,642	4,073	4,244
GDP growth (annual %)	7.2	5.6	3.4
GDP implicit price deflator (annual % growth)	10.1	7.7	5.8
Value added in agriculture (% of GDP)	12.1	8.7	6.2
Value added in industry (% of GDP)	32.2	32.0	32.5
Value added in services (% of GDP)	55.7	59.3	61.2
Exports of goods and services (% of GDP)	65.2	67.2	63.8
Imports of goods and services (% of GDP)	72.5	68.1	68.9
Gross domestic investment (% of GDP)	30.9	24.4	27.7
Central government revenues (% of GDP)	22.6	20.8	21.6
Overall budget deficit (% of GDP)	-0.4	0.9	-1.5
Money and quasi money (annual % growth)	21.2	11.2	15.2
Technology and infrastructure			
Telephone mainlines (per 1,000 people)	52	214	224
Cost of 3 min local call ($)	0.06	0.04	0.04
Personal computers (per 1,000 people)	3.8	87.0	95.7
Internet users (thousands)	..	30	55
Paved roads (% of total)	93	96	96
Aircraft departures (thousands)	8	11	11
Trade and finance			
Trade as share of PPP GDP (%)	47.2	36.7	34.4
Trade growth less GDP growth (average %, 1989-99)			0.3
High-technology exports (% of manufactured exports)	1	1	1
Net barter terms of trade (1995=100)	108	101	..
Foreign direct investment ($ millions)	41	12	49
Present value of debt ($ millions)			2,562
Total debt service ($ millions)	156	312	262
Short term debt ($ millions)	52	573	573
Aid per capita ($)	84	34	35

146

Sub-Saharan Africa		Upper middle income

Population (thousands)	140	Population growth (%)	..
Surface area (1,000 sq km)	..	Population per sq km	350
GNI ($ millions)	..	GNI per capita ($)	..

	1990	1998	1999
People			
Life expectancy (years)	..	..	..
Fertility rate (births per woman)	..	..	..
Infant mortality rate (per 1,000 live births)	..	..	..
Under 5 mortality rate (per 1,000 children)	..	..	..
Child malnutrition (% of children under 5)	..	..	..
Urban population (% of total)	..	..	..
Rural population density (per km^2 arable land)	..	..	..
Illiteracy male (% of people 15 and above)	..	..	..
Illiteracy female (% of people 15 and above)	..	..	..
Net primary enrollment (% of relevant age group)	..	..	..
Net secondary enrollment (% of relevant age group)	..	..	..
Girls in primary school (% of enrollment)	..	..	..
Girls in secondary school (% of enrollment)	..	..	..
Environment			
Forests (1,000 sq. km.)	..		..
Deforestation (% change 1990-2000)			..
Water use (% of total resources)			..
CO_2 emissions (metric tons per capita)	..	..	..
Access to improved water source (% of urban pop.)	..	..	..
Access to sanitation (% of urban population)	..	..	..
Energy use per capita (kg of oil equivalent)	..	..	..
Electricity use per capita (kWh)	..	..	..
Economy			
GDP ($ millions)	..	..	..
GDP growth (annual %)	..	..	..
GDP implicit price deflator (annual % growth)	..	..	..
Value added in agriculture (% of GDP)	..	..	..
Value added in industry (% of GDP)	..	..	..
Value added in services (% of GDP)	..	..	..
Exports of goods and services (% of GDP)	..	..	..
Imports of goods and services (% of GDP)	..	..	..
Gross domestic investment (% of GDP)	..	..	..
Central government revenues (% of GDP)	..	..	..
Overall budget deficit (% of GDP)	..	..	..
Money and quasi money (annual % growth)	..	..	..
Technology and infrastructure			
Telephone mainlines (per 1,000 people)	31	95	73
Cost of 3 min local call ($)	..	..	0.10
Personal computers (per 1,000 people)	..	..	..
Internet users (thousands)	..	..	..
Paved roads (% of total)	..	..	..
Aircraft departures (thousands)	..	..	..
Trade and finance			
Trade as share of PPP GDP (%)	..	..	..
Trade growth less GDP growth (average %, 1989-99)			..
High-technology exports (% of manufactured exports)	..	..	..
Net barter terms of trade (1995=100)	..	..	..
Foreign direct investment ($ millions)	..	..	..
Present value of debt ($ millions)			..
Total debt service ($ millions)	..	..	..
Short term debt ($ millions)	..	..	..
Aid per capita ($)	..	..	798

147

MEXICO

Population (millions)	97	Population growth (%)	1.4
Surface area (1,000 sq km)	1,958	Population per sq km	51
GNI ($ millions)	428,877	GNI per capita ($)	4,440

	1990	1998	1999
People			
Life expectancy (years)	70	72	72
Fertility rate (births per woman)	3.3	2.9	2.8
Infant mortality rate (per 1,000 live births)	36	31	29
Under 5 mortality rate (per 1,000 children)	46	38	36
Child malnutrition (% of children under 5)	14	17	8
Urban population (% of total)	73	74	74
Rural population density (per km^2 arable land)	95	98	..
Illiteracy male (% of people 15 and above)	10	7	7
Illiteracy female (% of people 15 and above)	15	11	11
Net primary enrollment (% of relevant age group)	100	101	..
Net secondary enrollment (% of relevant age group)	45	51	..
Girls in primary school (% of enrollment)	49	49	..
Girls in secondary school (% of enrollment)	50	50	..
Environment			
Forests (1,000 sq. km.)	615	..	552
Deforestation (% change 1990-2000)			1.1
Water use (% of total resources)	..	..	17.0
CO_2 emissions (metric tons per capita)	3.7	4.0	..
Access to improved water source (% of urban pop.)	92	91	94
Access to sanitation (% of urban population)	85	81	87
Energy use per capita (kg of oil equivalent)	1,492	1,552	..
Electricity use per capita (kWh)	1,204	1,513	..
Economy			
GDP ($ millions)	262,710	416,117	483,737
GDP growth (annual %)	5.1	4.9	3.5
GDP implicit price deflator (annual % growth)	28.1	15.4	16.2
Value added in agriculture (% of GDP)	7.8	5.2	5.0
Value added in industry (% of GDP)	28.4	28.5	28.2
Value added in services (% of GDP)	63.7	66.3	66.8
Exports of goods and services (% of GDP)	18.6	30.8	30.8
Imports of goods and services (% of GDP)	19.7	32.8	32.0
Gross domestic investment (% of GDP)	23.1	24.3	23.2
Central government revenues (% of GDP)	15.3	13.0	..
Overall budget deficit (% of GDP)	-2.5	-1.4	..
Money and quasi money (annual % growth)	81.9	19.7	11.8
Technology and infrastructure			
Telephone mainlines (per 1,000 people)	65	104	112
Cost of 3 min local call ($)	0.10	0.13	0.14
Personal computers (per 1,000 people)	8.2	36.5	44.2
Internet users (thousands)	5	1,310	1,822
Paved roads (% of total)	35	34	..
Aircraft departures (thousands)	177	314	310
Trade and finance			
Trade as share of PPP GDP (%)	15.8	32.6	35.6
Trade growth less GDP growth (average %, 1989-99)			9.8
High-technology exports (% of manufactured exports)	8	19	21
Net barter terms of trade (1995=100)	113	99	..
Foreign direct investment ($ millions)	2,634	11,312	11,786
Present value of debt ($ millions)			171,96
Total debt service ($ millions)	11,313	27,990	39,954
Short term debt ($ millions)	16,082	26,321	24,062
Aid per capita ($)	2	0	0

FEDERATED STATES OF MICRONESIA

East Asia and Pacific	Lower middle income

Population (thousands)	116	Population growth (%)	2.2
Surface area (1,000 sq km)	..	Population per sq km	166
GNI ($ millions)	212	GNI per capita ($)	1,830

	1990	1998	1999
People			
Life expectancy (years)	63	67	68
Fertility rate (births per woman)	4.8	4.0	3.8
Infant mortality rate (per 1,000 live births)	39	30	27
Under 5 mortality rate (per 1,000 children)	..	36	33
Child malnutrition (% of children under 5)	..	..	..
Urban population (% of total)	26	28	28
Rural population density (per km^2 arable land)	..	..	..
Illiteracy male (% of people 15 and above)	..	..	..
Illiteracy female (% of people 15 and above)	..	..	..
Net primary enrollment (% of relevant age group)	..	..	..
Net secondary enrollment (% of relevant age group)	..	..	..
Girls in primary school (% of enrollment)	..	..	..
Girls in secondary school (% of enrollment)	..	..	..
Environment			
Forests (1,000 sq. km.)	..	..	..
Deforestation (% change 1990-2000)			..
Water use (% of total resources)	..	..	..
CO_2 emissions (metric tons per capita)	..	..	..
Access to improved water source (% of urban pop.)	..	100	..
Access to sanitation (% of urban population)	..	100	..
Energy use per capita (kg of oil equivalent)	..	..	..
Electricity use per capita (kWh)	..	..	..
Economy			
GDP ($ millions)	155	213	220
GDP growth (annual %)	-2.6	-0.6	0.2
GDP implicit price deflator (annual % growth)	3.5	0.5	3.0
Value added in agriculture (% of GDP)	..	..	..
Value added in industry (% of GDP)	..	..	..
Value added in services (% of GDP)	..	..	..
Exports of goods and services (% of GDP)	..	..	..
Imports of goods and services (% of GDP)	..	..	..
Gross domestic investment (% of GDP)	..	..	..
Central government revenues (% of GDP)	..	..	..
Overall budget deficit (% of GDP)	..	..	..
Money and quasi money (annual % growth)	..	0.7	3.4
Technology and infrastructure			
Telephone mainlines (per 1,000 people)	25	80	..
Cost of 3 min local call ($)	0.00	0.00	..
Personal computers (per 1,000 people)	..	..	..
Internet users (thousands)	..	1	2
Paved roads (% of total)	16	18	..
Aircraft departures (thousands)	..	..	..
Trade and finance			
Trade as share of PPP GDP (%)	..	..	..
Trade growth less GDP growth (average %, 1989-99)			..
High-technology exports (% of manufactured exports)	..	..	..
Net barter terms of trade (1995=100)	..	..	..
Foreign direct investment ($ millions)	..	..	..
Present value of debt ($ millions)			..
Total debt service ($ millions)	..	..	..
Short term debt ($ millions)	..	..	..
Aid per capita ($)	5	705	930

149

MOLDOVA

Population (millions)	4	Population growth (%)	-0.4
Surface area (1,000 sq km)	34	Population per sq km	130
GNI ($ millions)	1,481	GNI per capita ($)	410

	1990	1998	1999
People			
Life expectancy (years)	68	67	67
Fertility rate (births per woman)	2.4	1.7	1.7
Infant mortality rate (per 1,000 live births)	19	18	17
Under 5 mortality rate (per 1,000 children)	25	22	22
Child malnutrition (% of children under 5)	..	..	..
Urban population (% of total)	47	46	46
Rural population density (per km^2 arable land)	..	129	..
Illiteracy male (% of people 15 and above)	1	1	1
Illiteracy female (% of people 15 and above)	4	2	2
Net primary enrollment (% of relevant age group)	..	..	..
Net secondary enrollment (% of relevant age group)	..	..	..
Girls in primary school (% of enrollment)	..	..	..
Girls in secondary school (% of enrollment)	52	..	..
Environment			
Forests (1,000 sq. km.)	3	..	..
Deforestation (% change 1990-2000)			..
Water use (% of total resources)	..	..	25.3
CO_2 emissions (metric tons per capita)	..	..	..
Access to improved water source (% of urban pop.)	..	..	..
Access to sanitation (% of urban population)	..	..	..
Energy use per capita (kg of oil equivalent)	..	943	..
Electricity use per capita (kWh)	..	688	..
Economy			
GDP ($ millions)	10,583	1,699	1,160
GDP growth (annual %)	-2.4	-6.5	-4.4
GDP implicit price deflator (annual % growth)	..	9.4	39.9
Value added in agriculture (% of GDP)	..	30.5	25.1
Value added in industry (% of GDP)	..	23.5	21.6
Value added in services (% of GDP)	..	46.1	53.3
Exports of goods and services (% of GDP)	..	44.9	50.0
Imports of goods and services (% of GDP)	..	72.7	64.8
Gross domestic investment (% of GDP)	..	25.9	22.1
Central government revenues (% of GDP)	..	30.8	25.1
Overall budget deficit (% of GDP)	..	-3.2	-3.4
Money and quasi money (annual % growth)	..	-8.3	42.9
Technology and infrastructure			
Telephone mainlines (per 1,000 people)	106	150	127
Cost of 3 min local call ($)	..	0.02	0.02
Personal computers (per 1,000 people)	..	6.4	8.0
Internet users (thousands)	..	11	25
Paved roads (% of total)	87	87	87
Aircraft departures (thousands)	..	3	1
Trade and finance			
Trade as share of PPP GDP (%)	..	18.4	11.9
Trade growth less GDP growth (average %, 1989-99)			11.3
High-technology exports (% of manufactured exports)	..	7	4
Net barter terms of trade (1995=100)	..	..	..
Foreign direct investment ($ millions)	0	86	34
Present value of debt ($ millions)			886
Total debt service ($ millions)	..	187	175
Short term debt ($ millions)	..	32	33
Aid per capita ($)	..	8	24

MONACO

Population (thousands)	32	Population growth (%)		..
Surface area (1,000 sq km)	..	Population per sq km		16,410
GNI ($ millions)	..	GNI per capita ($)		..

	1990	1998	1999
People			
Life expectancy (years)	..	..	..
Fertility rate (births per woman)	..	..	..
Infant mortality rate (per 1,000 live births)	..	..	..
Under 5 mortality rate (per 1,000 children)	..	..	..
Child malnutrition (% of children under 5)		..	..
Urban population (% of total)	100	100	100
Rural population density (per km^2 arable land)	..	..	..
Illiteracy male (% of people 15 and above)	..	..	..
Illiteracy female (% of people 15 and above)	..	..	..
Net primary enrollment (% of relevant age group)	..	..	..
Net secondary enrollment (% of relevant age group)	..	..	..
Girls in primary school (% of enrollment)	*51*	*47*	..
Girls in secondary school (% of enrollment)	49	*49*	..
Environment			
Forests (1,000 sq. km.)	..	..	..
Deforestation (% change 1990-2000)			..
Water use (% of total resources)	..	..	..
CO$_2$ emissions (metric tons per capita)	..	..	..
Access to improved water source (% of urban pop.)	..	*100*	*100*
Access to sanitation (% of urban population)	..	*100*	*100*
Energy use per capita (kg of oil equivalent)	..	..	..
Electricity use per capita (kWh)	..	..	..
Economy			
GDP ($ millions)	..	..	..
GDP growth (annual %)	..	..	..
GDP implicit price deflator (annual % growth)	..	..	..
Value added in agriculture (% of GDP)	..	..	..
Value added in industry (% of GDP)	..	..	..
Value added in services (% of GDP)	..	..	..
Exports of goods and services (% of GDP)	..	..	..
Imports of goods and services (% of GDP)	..	..	..
Gross domestic investment (% of GDP)	..	..	..
Central government revenues (% of GDP)	..	..	..
Overall budget deficit (% of GDP)	..	..	..
Money and quasi money (annual % growth)	..	..	..
Technology and infrastructure			
Telephone mainlines (per 1,000 people)	..	..	..
Cost of 3 min local call ($)	..	..	..
Personal computers (per 1,000 people)	..	..	..
Internet users (thousands)	..	..	..
Paved roads (% of total)	100	*100*	..
Aircraft departures (thousands)	13	27	29
Trade and finance			
Trade as share of PPP GDP (%)	..	..	..
Trade growth less GDP growth (average %, 1989-99)			..
High-technology exports (% of manufactured exports)	..	..	..
Net barter terms of trade (1995=100)	..	..	..
Foreign direct investment ($ millions)	..	..	..
Present value of debt ($ millions)			..
Total debt service ($ millions)	..	..	..
Short term debt ($ millions)	..	..	..
Aid per capita ($)	..	..	..

151

MONGOLIA

Population (millions)	2	Population growth (%)	0.9
Surface area (1,000 sq km)	1,567	Population per sq km	2
GNI ($ millions)	927	GNI per capita ($)	390

	1990	1998	1999
People			
Life expectancy (years)	63	..	67
Fertility rate (births per woman)	4.0	..	2.7
Infant mortality rate (per 1,000 live births)	73	..	58
Under 5 mortality rate (per 1,000 children)	102	..	73
Child malnutrition (% of children under 5)	..	..	13
Urban population (% of total)	58	62	63
Rural population density (per km^2 arable land)	65	67	..
Illiteracy male (% of people 15 and above)	35	28	27
Illiteracy female (% of people 15 and above)	59	49	48
Net primary enrollment (% of relevant age group)	..	..	..
Net secondary enrollment (% of relevant age group)	..	..	..
Girls in primary school (% of enrollment)	..	50	..
Girls in secondary school (% of enrollment)	53	..	..
Environment			
Forests (1,000 sq. km.)	112	..	..
Deforestation (% change 1990-2000)			..
Water use (% of total resources)	..	..	1.2
CO_2 emissions (metric tons per capita)	4.8	..	..
Access to improved water source (% of urban pop.)	..	..	..
Access to sanitation (% of urban population)	..	..	..
Energy use per capita (kg of oil equivalent)	..	..	..
Electricity use per capita (kWh)	..	..	..
Economy			
GDP ($ millions)	..	1,042	916
GDP growth (annual %)	-2.5	3.5	3.0
GDP implicit price deflator (annual % growth)	0.0	11.5	3.8
Value added in agriculture (% of GDP)	15.2	32.8	31.6
Value added in industry (% of GDP)	40.6	27.6	29.6
Value added in services (% of GDP)	44.2	39.6	38.8
Exports of goods and services (% of GDP)	21.4	49.6	..
Imports of goods and services (% of GDP)	42.4	55.4	..
Gross domestic investment (% of GDP)	34.3	25.8	26.1
Central government revenues (% of GDP)	..	21.0	22.1
Overall budget deficit (% of GDP)	..	-10.8	-10.4
Money and quasi money (annual % growth)	..	-1.7	31.6
Technology and infrastructure			
Telephone mainlines (per 1,000 people)	32	41	39
Cost of 3 min local call ($)	..	0.01	0.02
Personal computers (per 1,000 people)	..	7.2	9.2
Internet users (thousands)	..	3	6
Paved roads (% of total)	10	3	4
Aircraft departures (thousands)	..	3	2
Trade and finance			
Trade as share of PPP GDP (%)	41.5	22.1	18.7
Trade growth less GDP growth (average %, 1989-99)			..
High-technology exports (% of manufactured exports)	..	..	..
Net barter terms of trade (1995=100)	..	..	..
Foreign direct investment ($ millions)	0	19	30
Present value of debt ($ millions)			507
Total debt service ($ millions)	..	35	26
Short term debt ($ millions)	..	31	23
Aid per capita ($)	6	86	92

Middle East & North Africa   **Lower middle income**

Population (millions)	28	Population growth (%)	1.7
Surface area (1,000 sq km)	447	Population per sq km	63
GNI ($ millions)	33,715	GNI per capita ($)	1,190

	1990	1998	1999
People			
Life expectancy (years)	63	67	67
Fertility rate (births per woman)	4.0	3.1	2.9
Infant mortality rate (per 1,000 live births)	64	51	48
Under 5 mortality rate (per 1,000 children)	83	67	62
Child malnutrition (% of children under 5)	10	..	..
Urban population (% of total)	48	55	55
Rural population density (per km^2 arable land)	143	140	..
Illiteracy male (% of people 15 and above)	47	40	39
Illiteracy female (% of people 15 and above)	75	66	65
Net primary enrollment (% of relevant age group)	58	74	..
Net secondary enrollment (% of relevant age group)	..	..	..
Girls in primary school (% of enrollment)	40	43	..
Girls in secondary school (% of enrollment)	41	43	..
Environment			
Forests (1,000 sq. km.)	30	..	30
Deforestation (% change 1990-2000)			0.0
Water use (% of total resources)	..	..	36.8
CO$_2$ emissions (metric tons per capita)	1.1	1.3	..
Access to improved water source (% of urban pop.)	94	..	100
Access to sanitation (% of urban population)	95	..	100
Energy use per capita (kg of oil equivalent)	280	336	..
Electricity use per capita (kWh)	340	443	..
Economy			
GDP ($ millions)	25,821	35,668	34,998
GDP growth (annual %)	4.0	6.8	-0.7
GDP implicit price deflator (annual % growth)	5.5	0.7	0.9
Value added in agriculture (% of GDP)	17.7	17.0	14.8
Value added in industry (% of GDP)	32.4	31.9	32.7
Value added in services (% of GDP)	49.9	51.1	52.6
Exports of goods and services (% of GDP)	26.5	28.0	30.1
Imports of goods and services (% of GDP)	32.4	32.0	34.2
Gross domestic investment (% of GDP)	25.3	22.5	24.2
Central government revenues (% of GDP)	26.6	29.1	..
Overall budget deficit (% of GDP)	-2.2	-4.4	..
Money and quasi money (annual % growth)	21.5	6.0	10.2
Technology and infrastructure			
Telephone mainlines (per 1,000 people)	16	50	53
Cost of 3 min local call ($)	0.08	0.08	0.08
Personal computers (per 1,000 people)	..	7.2	10.8
Internet users (thousands)	..	40	50
Paved roads (% of total)	49	52	56
Aircraft departures (thousands)	27	40	44
Trade and finance			
Trade as share of PPP GDP (%)	15.9	18.3	18.6
Trade growth less GDP growth (average %, 1989-99)			2.0
High-technology exports (% of manufactured exports)	..	..	..
Net barter terms of trade (1995=100)	101	103	..
Foreign direct investment ($ millions)	165	12	3
Present value of debt ($ millions)			17,205
Total debt service ($ millions)	1,794	2,795	3,096
Short term debt ($ millions)	407	116	183
Aid per capita ($)	44	19	24

MOZAMBIQUE

Sub-Saharan Africa   Low income

Population (millions)	17	Population growth (%)	1.9
Surface area (1,000 sq km)	802	Population per sq km	22
GNI ($ millions)	3,804	GNI per capita ($)	220

	1990	1998	1999
People			
Life expectancy (years)	43	45	43
Fertility rate (births per woman)	6.3	5.3	5.2
Infant mortality rate (per 1,000 live births)	150	135	131
Under 5 mortality rate (per 1,000 children)	238	201	203
Child malnutrition (% of children under 5)	..	26	..
Urban population (% of total)	27	38	39
Rural population density (per km^2 arable land)	338	339	..
Illiteracy male (% of people 15 and above)	51	42	41
Illiteracy female (% of people 15 and above)	82	73	72
Net primary enrollment (% of relevant age group)	47	40	..
Net secondary enrollment (% of relevant age group)	7	6	..
Girls in primary school (% of enrollment)	43	42	..
Girls in secondary school (% of enrollment)	36	39	..
Environment			
Forests (1,000 sq. km.)	312	..	306
Deforestation (% change 1990-2000)			0.2
Water use (% of total resources)	..	..	0.3
CO$_2$ emissions (metric tons per capita)	0.1	0.1	..
Access to improved water source (% of urban pop.)	50	..	86
Access to sanitation (% of urban population)	..	53	69
Energy use per capita (kg of oil equivalent)	509	405	..
Electricity use per capita (kWh)	35	54	..
Economy			
GDP ($ millions)	2,512	3,910	3,979
GDP growth (annual %)	1.0	11.9	7.3
GDP implicit price deflator (annual % growth)	34.1	2.3	2.0
Value added in agriculture (% of GDP)	37.1	34.1	33.0
Value added in industry (% of GDP)	18.4	20.7	25.2
Value added in services (% of GDP)	44.5	45.3	41.8
Exports of goods and services (% of GDP)	8.2	10.5	11.7
Imports of goods and services (% of GDP)	36.1	26.8	37.6
Gross domestic investment (% of GDP)	15.6	23.5	32.6
Central government revenues (% of GDP)	..	..	..
Overall budget deficit (% of GDP)	..	..	..
Money and quasi money (annual % growth)	37.2	17.9	31.8
Technology and infrastructure			
Telephone mainlines (per 1,000 people)	3	4	4
Cost of 3 min local call ($)	0.05	0.04	0.09
Personal computers (per 1,000 people)	..	2.1	2.6
Internet users (thousands)	..	4	15
Paved roads (% of total)	17	19	..
Aircraft departures (thousands)	6	5	6
Trade and finance			
Trade as share of PPP GDP (%)	13.1	8.3	8.7
Trade growth less GDP growth (average %, 1989-99)			-1.9
High-technology exports (% of manufactured exports)	..	..	..
Net barter terms of trade (1995=100)	161	104	..
Foreign direct investment ($ millions)	9	213	384
Present value of debt ($ millions)			1,042
Total debt service ($ millions)	79	104	125
Short term debt ($ millions)	345	365	388
Aid per capita ($)	71	61	7

154

MYANMAR

Population (millions)	45	Population growth (%)	1.3
Surface area (1,000 sq km)	677	Population per sq km	68
GNI ($ millions)	..	GNI per capita ($)	..

	1990	1998	1999
People			
Life expectancy (years)	57	..	60
Fertility rate (births per woman)	3.8	..	3.1
Infant mortality rate (per 1,000 live births)	94	..	77
Under 5 mortality rate (per 1,000 children)	130	..	120
Child malnutrition (% of children under 5)	32	..	..
Urban population (% of total)	25	27	27
Rural population density (per km^2 arable land)	319	340	..
Illiteracy male (% of people 15 and above)	13	11	11
Illiteracy female (% of people 15 and above)	26	21	20
Net primary enrollment (% of relevant age group)	..	..	..
Net secondary enrollment (% of relevant age group)	..	..	..
Girls in primary school (% of enrollment)	..	..	..
Girls in secondary school (% of enrollment)	49	..	..
Environment			
Forests (1,000 sq. km.)	396	..	..
Deforestation (% change 1990-2000)			
Water use (% of total resources)	..	..	0.4
CO$_2$ emissions (metric tons per capita)	0.1	..	..
Access to improved water source (% of urban pop.)	88	..	..
Access to sanitation (% of urban population)	65	..	..
Energy use per capita (kg of oil equivalent)	271	307	..
Electricity use per capita (kWh)	43	64	..
Economy			
GDP ($ millions)	..	..	..
GDP growth (annual %)	2.8	5.0	..
GDP implicit price deflator (annual % growth)	18.5	38.2	..
Value added in agriculture (% of GDP)	57.3	59.1	59.9
Value added in industry (% of GDP)	10.5	9.9	8.9
Value added in services (% of GDP)	32.2	31.1	31.2
Exports of goods and services (% of GDP)	2.6	0.4	..
Imports of goods and services (% of GDP)	4.8	1.0	..
Gross domestic investment (% of GDP)	13.4	10.8	..
Central government revenues (% of GDP)	10.6	7.2	..
Overall budget deficit (% of GDP)	-5.1	-0.4	..
Money and quasi money (annual % growth)	37.7	34.2	29.7
Technology and infrastructure			
Telephone mainlines (per 1,000 people)	2	5	6
Cost of 3 min local call ($)	..	0.15	0.48
Personal computers (per 1,000 people)	..	..	1.1
Internet users (thousands)	..	..	1
Paved roads (% of total)	11	..	..
Aircraft departures (thousands)	14	11	11
Trade and finance			
Trade as share of PPP GDP (%)	..	..	..
Trade growth less GDP growth (average %, 1989-99)			..
High-technology exports (% of manufactured exports)	..	..	
Net barter terms of trade (1995=100)	94	99	..
Foreign direct investment ($ millions)	161	315	216
Present value of debt ($ millions)			4,490
Total debt service ($ millions)	60	93	97
Short term debt ($ millions)	229	594	666
Aid per capita ($)	4	1	2

155

NAMIBIA

Population (millions)	2	Population growth (%)	2.3
Surface area (1,000 sq km)	824	Population per sq km	2
GNI ($ millions)	3,211	GNI per capita ($)	1,890

	1990	1998	1999
People			
Life expectancy (years)	58	56	50
Fertility rate (births per woman)	5.4	4.9	4.7
Infant mortality rate (per 1,000 live births)	64	65	63
Under 5 mortality rate (per 1,000 children)	84	101	108
Child malnutrition (% of children under 5)	26	..	..
Urban population (% of total)	27	30	30
Rural population density (per km^2 arable land)	150	143	..
Illiteracy male (% of people 15 and above)	23	18	18
Illiteracy female (% of people 15 and above)	28	20	20
Net primary enrollment (% of relevant age group)	89	91	..
Net secondary enrollment (% of relevant age group)	31	36	..
Girls in primary school (% of enrollment)	52	50	..
Girls in secondary school (% of enrollment)	56	53	..
Environment			
Forests (1,000 sq. km.)	88	..	80
Deforestation (% change 1990-2000)			0.9
Water use (% of total resources)	..	..	0.5
CO_2 emissions (metric tons per capita)	..	..	..
Access to improved water source (% of urban pop.)	98	..	100
Access to sanitation (% of urban population)	84	..	96
Energy use per capita (kg of oil equivalent)	..	..	..
Electricity use per capita (kWh)	..	..	..
Economy			
GDP ($ millions)	2,340	3,044	3,075
GDP growth (annual %)	2.0	2.4	3.1
GDP implicit price deflator (annual % growth)	4.3	10.3	8.3
Value added in agriculture (% of GDP)	11.8	12.3	12.8
Value added in industry (% of GDP)	38.3	33.8	32.6
Value added in services (% of GDP)	49.9	54.0	54.5
Exports of goods and services (% of GDP)	52.1	52.7	52.7
Imports of goods and services (% of GDP)	67.7	62.7	63.5
Gross domestic investment (% of GDP)	33.8	19.9	20.1
Central government revenues (% of GDP)	31.5	34.5	..
Overall budget deficit (% of GDP)	-1.2	-4.7	..
Money and quasi money (annual % growth)	30.3	11.3	18.4
Technology and infrastructure			
Telephone mainlines (per 1,000 people)	39	64	64
Cost of 3 min local call ($)	0.05	0.05	0.05
Personal computers (per 1,000 people)	..	24.1	29.5
Internet users (thousands)	..	5	6
Paved roads (% of total)	11	8	..
Aircraft departures (thousands)	8	8	8
Trade and finance			
Trade as share of PPP GDP (%)	38.4	35.5	36.0
Trade growth less GDP growth (average %, 1989-99)			-0.2
High-technology exports (% of manufactured exports)	..	..	..
Net barter terms of trade (1995=100)	..	..	..
Foreign direct investment ($ millions)	..	..	..
Present value of debt ($ millions)			..
Total debt service ($ millions)	..	..	..
Short term debt ($ millions)	..	..	..
Aid per capita ($)	90	108	104

NEPAL

Population (millions)	23	Population growth (%)		2.3
Surface area (1,000 sq km)	147	Population per sq km		164
GNI ($ millions)	5,173	GNI per capita ($)		220

	1990	1998	1999
People			
Life expectancy (years)	54	57	58
Fertility rate (births per woman)	5.3	4.4	4.3
Infant mortality rate (per 1,000 live births)	101	79	75
Under 5 mortality rate (per 1,000 children)	138	117	109
Child malnutrition (% of children under 5)	..	47	..
Urban population (% of total)	9	11	12
Rural population density (per km^2 arable land)	748	700	..
Illiteracy male (% of people 15 and above)	53	43	42
Illiteracy female (% of people 15 and above)	86	78	77
Net primary enrollment (% of relevant age group)	64	..	..
Net secondary enrollment (% of relevant age group)	23	..	..
Girls in primary school (% of enrollment)	36	41	..
Girls in secondary school (% of enrollment)	29	37	..
Environment			
Forests (1,000 sq. km.)	47	..	39
Deforestation (% change 1990-2000)			1.8
Water use (% of total resources)	..	..	13.8
CO$_2$ emissions (metric tons per capita)	0.0	0.1	..
Access to improved water source (% of urban pop.)	96	..	85
Access to sanitation (% of urban population)	68	34	75
Energy use per capita (kg of oil equivalent)	324	343	..
Electricity use per capita (kWh)	32	47	..
Economy			
GDP ($ millions)	3,628	4,852	4,995
GDP growth (annual %)	4.6	3.0	3.9
GDP implicit price deflator (annual % growth)	10.7	4.2	8.6
Value added in agriculture (% of GDP)	51.6	39.9	41.7
Value added in industry (% of GDP)	16.2	22.5	21.3
Value added in services (% of GDP)	32.1	37.6	36.9
Exports of goods and services (% of GDP)	10.5	22.8	23.0
Imports of goods and services (% of GDP)	21.1	33.9	30.0
Gross domestic investment (% of GDP)	18.4	24.8	20.2
Central government revenues (% of GDP)	8.5	10.5	10.3
Overall budget deficit (% of GDP)	-6.8	-4.6	-3.9
Money and quasi money (annual % growth)	18.5	24.0	21.6
Technology and infrastructure			
Telephone mainlines (per 1,000 people)	3	10	11
Cost of 3 min local call ($)	0.04	0.01	0.01
Personal computers (per 1,000 people)	..	2.3	2.7
Internet users (thousands)	0	15	35
Paved roads (% of total)	38	42	..
Aircraft departures (thousands)	26	17	12
Trade and finance			
Trade as share of PPP GDP (%)	5.4	6.2	6.8
Trade growth less GDP growth (average %, 1989-99)			7.4
High-technology exports (% of manufactured exports)	..	..	..
Net barter terms of trade (1995=100)	..	..	..
Foreign direct investment ($ millions)	6	12	4
Present value of debt ($ millions)			1,654
Total debt service ($ millions)	70	88	107
Short term debt ($ millions)	24	31	43
Aid per capita ($)	23	18	15

NETHERLANDS

Population (millions)	16	Population growth (%)	0.7
Surface area (1,000 sq km)	41	Population per sq km	466
GNI ($ millions)	397,384	GNI per capita ($)	25,140

	1990	1998	1999
People			
Life expectancy (years)	77	78	78
Fertility rate (births per woman)	1.6	1.6	1.6
Infant mortality rate (per 1,000 live births)	7	5	5
Under 5 mortality rate (per 1,000 children)	8	7	5
Child malnutrition (% of children under 5)	..	..	
Urban population (% of total)	89	89	89
Rural population density (per km^2 arable land)	192	186	..
Illiteracy male (% of people 15 and above)	..	..	..
Illiteracy female (% of people 15 and above)	..	..	..
Net primary enrollment (% of relevant age group)	95	100	..
Net secondary enrollment (% of relevant age group)	84	91	..
Girls in primary school (% of enrollment)	50	48	..
Girls in secondary school (% of enrollment)	47	48	..
Environment			
Forests (1,000 sq. km.)	4	..	4
Deforestation (% change 1990-2000)			-0.3
Water use (% of total resources)	..	..	8.6
CO_2 emissions (metric tons per capita)	10.2	10.5	..
Access to improved water source (% of urban pop.)	100	100	100
Access to sanitation (% of urban population)	100	100	100
Energy use per capita (kg of oil equivalent)	4,454	4,740	..
Electricity use per capita (kWh)	4,917	5,908	..
Economy			
GDP ($ millions)	295,961	391,263	393,692
GDP growth (annual %)	4.1	3.7	3.6
GDP implicit price deflator (annual % growth)	2.3	1.9	1.3
Value added in agriculture (% of GDP)	4.3	2.8	2.6
Value added in industry (% of GDP)	27.8	24.5	23.7
Value added in services (% of GDP)	67.9	72.6	73.6
Exports of goods and services (% of GDP)	58.3	60.9	60.6
Imports of goods and services (% of GDP)	54.7	55.3	55.8
Gross domestic investment (% of GDP)	24.3	21.9	22.0
Central government revenues (% of GDP)	45.1	44.1	..
Overall budget deficit (% of GDP)	-4.3	-1.6	..
Money and quasi money (annual % growth)	..	..	..
Technology and infrastructure			
Telephone mainlines (per 1,000 people)	464	593	607
Cost of 3 min local call ($)	0.15	0.14	0.14
Personal computers (per 1,000 people)	93.3	324.8	359.9
Internet users (thousands)	80	1,600	3,000
Paved roads (% of total)	88	90	90
Aircraft departures (thousands)	115	190	224
Trade and finance			
Trade as share of PPP GDP (%)	98.7	107.4	101.4
Trade growth less GDP growth (average %, 1989-99)			2.3
High-technology exports (% of manufactured exports)	17	30	33
Net barter terms of trade (1995=100)	98	..	..
Foreign direct investment ($ millions)	..	..	..
Present value of debt ($ millions)			..
Total debt service ($ millions)	..	..	..
Short term debt ($ millions)	..	..	..
Aid per capita ($)	..	..	..

NETHERLANDS ANTILLES

High income

Population (thousands)	215	Population growth (%)	1.1
Surface area (1,000 sq km)	0.8	Population per sq km	268
GNI ($ millions)	..	GNI per capita ($)	..

	1990	1998	1999
People			
Life expectancy (years)	74	75	76
Fertility rate (births per woman)	2.3	2.2	2.2
Infant mortality rate (per 1,000 live births)	8	14	13
Under 5 mortality rate (per 1,000 children)	..	17	16
Child malnutrition (% of children under 5)	..	..	..
Urban population (% of total)	68	70	70
Rural population density (per km^2 arable land)	751	799	..
Illiteracy male (% of people 15 and above)	4	4	4
Illiteracy female (% of people 15 and above)	4	4	4
Net primary enrollment (% of relevant age group)	..	..	..
Net secondary enrollment (% of relevant age group)	..	..	..
Girls in primary school (% of enrollment)	..	..	..
Girls in secondary school (% of enrollment)	..	..	..
Environment			
Forests (1,000 sq. km.)	0	..	..
Deforestation (% change 1990-2000)			..
Water use (% of total resources)	..	..	..
CO$_2$ emissions (metric tons per capita)	4.7	32.2	..
Access to improved water source (% of urban pop.)	..	..	..
Access to sanitation (% of urban population)	..	..	..
Energy use per capita (kg of oil equivalent)	10,870	8,153	..
Electricity use per capita (kWh)	3,182	4,117	..
Economy			
GDP ($ millions)	..	..	..
GDP growth (annual %)	..	..	..
GDP implicit price deflator (annual % growth)	..	..	..
Value added in agriculture (% of GDP)	..	..	..
Value added in industry (% of GDP)	..	..	..
Value added in services (% of GDP)	..	..	..
Exports of goods and services (% of GDP)	..	..	..
Imports of goods and services (% of GDP)	..	..	..
Gross domestic investment (% of GDP)	..	..	..
Central government revenues (% of GDP)	..	..	..
Overall budget deficit (% of GDP)	..	..	..
Money and quasi money (annual % growth)	10.1	4.0	5.6
Technology and infrastructure			
Telephone mainlines (per 1,000 people)	247	366	..
Cost of 3 min local call ($)	..	..	..
Personal computers (per 1,000 people)	..	..	..
Internet users (thousands)	..	1	2
Paved roads (% of total)	..	..	..
Aircraft departures (thousands)	..	..	..
Trade and finance			
Trade as share of PPP GDP (%)	..	..	..
Trade growth less GDP growth (average %, 1989-99)			..
High-technology exports (% of manufactured exports)	..	..	..
Net barter terms of trade (1995=100)	109	117	..
Foreign direct investment ($ millions)	..	..	..
Present value of debt ($ millions)			..
Total debt service ($ millions)	..	..	..
Short term debt ($ millions)	..	..	..
Aid per capita ($)	307	607	591

NEW CALEDONIA

South Asia   Low income

Population (thousands)	209	Population growth (%)		1.9
Surface area (1,000 sq km)	18.6	Population per sq km		11
GNI ($ millions)	3,169	GNI per capita ($)		15,160

	1990	1998	1999
People			
Life expectancy (years)	71	73	73
Fertility rate (births per woman)	2.9	2.7	2.6
Infant mortality rate (per 1,000 live births)	13	7	7
Under 5 mortality rate (per 1,000 children)	..	14	12
Child malnutrition (% of children under 5)	..	..	..
Urban population (% of total)	62	74	75
Rural population density (per km^2 arable land)	922	760	..
Illiteracy male (% of people 15 and above)	..	..	..
Illiteracy female (% of people 15 and above)	..	..	..
Net primary enrollment (% of relevant age group)	97	..	..
Net secondary enrollment (% of relevant age group)	69	..	..
Girls in primary school (% of enrollment)	48	..	..
Girls in secondary school (% of enrollment)	52	..	..
Environment			
Forests (1,000 sq. km.)	4	..	4
Deforestation (% change 1990-2000)			0.0
Water use (% of total resources)	..	..	
CO_2 emissions (metric tons per capita)	9.8	8.9	..
Access to improved water source (% of urban pop.)	..	..	..
Access to sanitation (% of urban population)	..	..	..
Energy use per capita (kg of oil equivalent)	..	..	..
Electricity use per capita (kWh)	..	..	..
Economy			
GDP ($ millions)	2,529	3,391	3,056
GDP growth (annual %)	3.6	-3.2	0.9
GDP implicit price deflator (annual % growth)	-4.6	0.2	0.1
Value added in agriculture (% of GDP)	3.6	3.7	..
Value added in industry (% of GDP)	23.3	19.6	..
Value added in services (% of GDP)	73.1	76.7	..
Exports of goods and services (% of GDP)	18.5	12.0	13.1
Imports of goods and services (% of GDP)	34.7	29.4	33.0
Gross domestic investment (% of GDP)	31.4	..	..
Central government revenues (% of GDP)	..	..	..
Overall budget deficit (% of GDP)	..	..	..
Money and quasi money (annual % growth)	..	..	..
Technology and infrastructure			
Telephone mainlines (per 1,000 people)	169	239	241
Cost of 3 min local call ($)	0.31	0.36	0.32
Personal computers (per 1,000 people)	..	..	..
Internet users (thousands)	..	4	5
Paved roads (% of total)	..	..	..
Aircraft departures (thousands)	..	..	..
Trade and finance			
Trade as share of PPP GDP (%)	40.0	31.7	..
Trade growth less GDP growth (average %, 1989-99)			..
High-technology exports (% of manufactured exports)	..	..	..
Net barter terms of trade (1995=100)	..	..	..
Foreign direct investment ($ millions)	..	..	..
Present value of debt ($ millions)			..
Total debt service ($ millions)	..	..	..
Short term debt ($ millions)	..	..	..
Aid per capita ($)	1,800	1,651	1,505

NEW ZEALAND

Population (millions)	4	Population growth (%)	0.5
Surface area (1,000 sq km)	271	Population per sq km	14
GNI ($ millions)	53,299	GNI per capita ($)	13,990

	1990	1998	1999
People			
Life expectancy (years)	75	77	77
Fertility rate (births per woman)	2.2	2.0	2.0
Infant mortality rate (per 1,000 live births)	8	5	5
Under 5 mortality rate (per 1,000 children)	11	7	6
Child malnutrition (% of children under 5)	..	..	..
Urban population (% of total)	85	86	86
Rural population density (per km^2 arable land)	21	35	..
Illiteracy male (% of people 15 and above)	..	..	..
Illiteracy female (% of people 15 and above)	..	..	..
Net primary enrollment (% of relevant age group)	101	100	..
Net secondary enrollment (% of relevant age group)	85	90	..
Girls in primary school (% of enrollment)	48	49	..
Girls in secondary school (% of enrollment)	49	50	..
Environment			
Forests (1,000 sq. km.)	76	..	79
Deforestation (% change 1990-2000)			-0.5
Water use (% of total resources)	..	..	0.6
CO_2 emissions (metric tons per capita)	7.0	8.4	..
Access to improved water source (% of urban pop.)	100	..	100
Access to sanitation (% of urban population)	100	..	..
Energy use per capita (kg of oil equivalent)	4,118	4,525	..
Electricity use per capita (kWh)	8,087	8,215	..
Economy			
GDP ($ millions)	43,103	52,944	54,651
GDP growth (annual %)	-0.6	0.0	4.4
GDP implicit price deflator (annual % growth)	2.7	0.9	0.0
Value added in agriculture (% of GDP)	6.8	7.2	..
Value added in industry (% of GDP)	25.9	25.5	..
Value added in services (% of GDP)	67.2	67.3	..
Exports of goods and services (% of GDP)	27.6	30.7	..
Imports of goods and services (% of GDP)	26.9	30.0	..
Gross domestic investment (% of GDP)	18.9	19.0	..
Central government revenues (% of GDP)	42.7	34.2	32.3
Overall budget deficit (% of GDP)	4.0	0.5	2.0
Money and quasi money (annual % growth)	12.5	1.8	5.0
Technology and infrastructure			
Telephone mainlines (per 1,000 people)	434	490	496
Cost of 3 min local call ($)	0.00	0.00	0.00
Personal computers (per 1,000 people)	96.8	288.7	328.0
Internet users (thousands)	10	600	700
Paved roads (% of total)	57	61	62
Aircraft departures (thousands)	128	236	228
Trade and finance			
Trade as share of PPP GDP (%)	38.8	35.9	36.7
Trade growth less GDP growth (average %, 1989-99)			3.1
High-technology exports (% of manufactured exports)	4	12	15
Net barter terms of trade (1995=100)	103	98	98
Foreign direct investment ($ millions)	..	..	..
Present value of debt ($ millions)			..
Total debt service ($ millions)	..	..	..
Short term debt ($ millions)	..	..	..
Aid per capita ($)	..	..	..

161

NICARAGUA

Latin America & Caribbean		Low income

Population (millions)	5	Population growth (%)	2.6
Surface area (1,000 sq km)	130	Population per sq km	41
GNI ($ millions)	2,012	GNI per capita ($)	410

	1990	1998	1999
People			
Life expectancy (years)	64	..	69
Fertility rate (births per woman)	4.8	..	3.6
Infant mortality rate (per 1,000 live births)	51	..	34
Under 5 mortality rate (per 1,000 children)	63	..	43
Child malnutrition (% of children under 5)	..	12	..
Urban population (% of total)	53	55	56
Rural population density (per km^2 arable land)	91	87	..
Illiteracy male (% of people 15 and above)	36	34	33
Illiteracy female (% of people 15 and above)	34	31	30
Net primary enrollment (% of relevant age group)	72	..	..
Net secondary enrollment (% of relevant age group)	..	..	..
Girls in primary school (% of enrollment)	51	50	..
Girls in secondary school (% of enrollment)	..	..	..
Environment			
Forests (1,000 sq. km.)	45	..	..
Deforestation (% change 1990-2000)			
Water use (% of total resources)	..	..	0.7
CO_2 emissions (metric tons per capita)	0.8	..	..
Access to improved water source (% of urban pop.)	93	..	..
Access to sanitation (% of urban population)	97	..	..
Energy use per capita (kg of oil equivalent)	569	553	..
Electricity use per capita (kWh)	284	281	..
Economy			
GDP ($ millions)	1,009	2,126	2,268
GDP growth (annual %)	-0.1	4.1	7.0
GDP implicit price deflator (annual % growth)	5,018.1	13.0	11.2
Value added in agriculture (% of GDP)	31.1	33.0	31.6
Value added in industry (% of GDP)	21.3	21.6	22.8
Value added in services (% of GDP)	47.6	45.4	45.7
Exports of goods and services (% of GDP)	24.9	35.8	33.6
Imports of goods and services (% of GDP)	46.3	77.9	88.7
Gross domestic investment (% of GDP)	19.3	33.1	43.0
Central government revenues (% of GDP)	33.5	..	..
Overall budget deficit (% of GDP)	-35.6	..	..
Money and quasi money (annual % growth)	7,677.8	32.2	18.8
Technology and infrastructure			
Telephone mainlines (per 1,000 people)	13	30	30
Cost of 3 min local call ($)	7.14	0.03	0.09
Personal computers (per 1,000 people)	..	7.5	8.1
Internet users (thousands)	..	15	20
Paved roads (% of total)	11	..	..
Aircraft departures (thousands)	4	1	1
Trade and finance			
Trade as share of PPP GDP (%)	14.2	19.7	21.3
Trade growth less GDP growth (average %, 1989-99)			-2.8
High-technology exports (% of manufactured exports)	..	5	6
Net barter terms of trade (1995=100)	119	102	..
Foreign direct investment ($ millions)	0	184	300
Present value of debt ($ millions)			5,541
Total debt service ($ millions)	16	253	187
Short term debt ($ millions)	2,427	754	926
Aid per capita ($)	87	119	137

Population (millions)	10	Population growth (%)	10
Surface area (1,000 sq km)	1,267	Population per sq km	1,267
GNI ($ millions)	1,974	GNI per capita ($)	1,974

	1990	1998	1999
People			
Life expectancy (years)	45	*46*	46
Fertility rate (births per woman)	7.4	*7.4*	7.3
Infant mortality rate (per 1,000 live births)	150	*120*	116
Under 5 mortality rate (per 1,000 children)	335	*260*	252
Child malnutrition (% of children under 5)	*43*	50	..
Urban population (% of total)	16	20	20
Rural population density (per km^2 arable land)	180	163	..
Illiteracy male (% of people 15 and above)	82	78	77
Illiteracy female (% of people 15 and above)	95	93	92
Net primary enrollment (% of relevant age group)	25	*25*	..
Net secondary enrollment (% of relevant age group)	6	*6*	..
Girls in primary school (% of enrollment)	*36*	39	..
Girls in secondary school (% of enrollment)	29	*37*	..
Environment			
Forests (1,000 sq. km.)	19	..	*13*
Deforestation (% change 1990-2000)			*3.7*
Water use (% of total resources)	..	..	1.5
CO_2 emissions (metric tons per capita)	0.1	*0.1*	..
Access to improved water source (% of urban pop.)	65	..	*70*
Access to sanitation (% of urban population)	71	79	*79*
Energy use per capita (kg of oil equivalent)	..	..	..
Electricity use per capita (kWh)	..	..	..
Economy			
GDP ($ millions)	2,481	2,077	2,018
GDP growth (annual %)	-1.3	10.4	-0.6
GDP implicit price deflator (annual % growth)	-1.6	3.0	2.0
Value added in agriculture (% of GDP)	35.3	42.6	40.7
Value added in industry (% of GDP)	16.2	16.7	17.2
Value added in services (% of GDP)	48.6	40.7	42.1
Exports of goods and services (% of GDP)	15.0	17.8	16.0
Imports of goods and services (% of GDP)	22.0	26.3	22.4
Gross domestic investment (% of GDP)	8.1	11.3	10.2
Central government revenues (% of GDP)	..	..	..
Overall budget deficit (% of GDP)	..	..	..
Money and quasi money (annual % growth)	-4.1	-18.5	15.4
Technology and infrastructure			
Telephone mainlines (per 1,000 people)	1	2	..
Cost of 3 min local call ($)	0.24	*0.15*	..
Personal computers (per 1,000 people)	..	0.3	0.4
Internet users (thousands)	..	0	3
Paved roads (% of total)	29	*8*	..
Aircraft departures (thousands)	1	2	2
Trade and finance			
Trade as share of PPP GDP (%)	11.7	9.1	8.5
Trade growth less GDP growth (average %, 1989-99)			-2.8
High-technology exports (% of manufactured exports)	..	5	..
Net barter terms of trade (1995=100)	90	100	..
Foreign direct investment ($ millions)	-1	9	15
Present value of debt ($ millions)			1,089
Total debt service ($ millions)	99	62	51
Short term debt ($ millions)	154	63	80
Aid per capita ($)	51	29	18

NIGERIA

Population (millions)	124	Population growth (%)	2.5
Surface area (1,000 sq km)	924	Population per sq km	136
GNI ($ millions)	31,600	GNI per capita ($)	260

	1990	1998	1999
People			
Life expectancy (years)	49	50	47
Fertility rate (births per woman)	6.0	5.3	5.2
Infant mortality rate (per 1,000 live births)	86	81	83
Under 5 mortality rate (per 1,000 children)	136	147	151
Child malnutrition (% of children under 5)	35	39	..
Urban population (% of total)	35	42	43
Rural population density (per km^2 arable land)	212	248	..
Illiteracy male (% of people 15 and above)	41	30	29
Illiteracy female (% of people 15 and above)	62	48	46
Net primary enrollment (% of relevant age group)	..	..	..
Net secondary enrollment (% of relevant age group)	..	..	..
Girls in primary school (% of enrollment)	43	45	..
Girls in secondary school (% of enrollment)	43	46	..
Environment			
Forests (1,000 sq. km.)	175	..	135
Deforestation (% change 1990-2000)			2.6
Water use (% of total resources)			1.4
CO_2 emissions (metric tons per capita)	0.9	0.7	..
Access to improved water source (% of urban pop.)	78	..	81
Access to sanitation (% of urban population)	77	..	85
Energy use per capita (kg of oil equivalent)	737	716	..
Electricity use per capita (kWh)	77	85	..
Economy			
GDP ($ millions)	28,472	32,249	35,045
GDP growth (annual %)	8.2	1.8	1.0
GDP implicit price deflator (annual % growth)	7.2	-5.2	12.9
Value added in agriculture (% of GDP)	32.7	39.0	42.1
Value added in industry (% of GDP)	41.4	33.3	..
Value added in services (% of GDP)	25.9	27.6	..
Exports of goods and services (% of GDP)	43.4	33.2	36.5
Imports of goods and services (% of GDP)	28.8	38.1	42.3
Gross domestic investment (% of GDP)	14.7	28.3	24.2
Central government revenues (% of GDP)	..	..	..
Overall budget deficit (% of GDP)	..	..	..
Money and quasi money (annual % growth)	32.7	23.2	31.7
Technology and infrastructure			
Telephone mainlines (per 1,000 people)	3	4	..
Cost of 3 min local call ($)	0.11	0.26	..
Personal computers (per 1,000 people)	..	6.1	6.4
Internet users (thousands)	..	30	100
Paved roads (% of total)	30	31	..
Aircraft departures (thousands)	17	8	8
Trade and finance			
Trade as share of PPP GDP (%)	26.2	19.4	20.5
Trade growth less GDP growth (average %, 1989-99)			2.1
High-technology exports (% of manufactured exports)	..	0	13
Net barter terms of trade (1995=100)	162	87	..
Foreign direct investment ($ millions)	588	1,051	1,005
Present value of debt ($ millions)			28,557
Total debt service ($ millions)	3,336	1,320	924
Short term debt ($ millions)	1,504	6,575	6,685
Aid per capita ($)	3	2	1

NORTHERN MARIANA ISLANDS

High income

Population (thousands)	69	Population growth (%)		..
Surface area (1,000 sq km)	..	Population per sq km		143
GNI ($ millions)	..	GNI per capita ($)		..

	1990	1998	1999
People			
Life expectancy (years)	..	..	..
Fertility rate (births per woman)	..	..	..
Infant mortality rate (per 1,000 live births)	..	..	..
Under 5 mortality rate (per 1,000 children)	..	..	..
Child malnutrition (% of children under 5)	..	..	..
Urban population (% of total)	53	53	53
Rural population density (per km^2 arable land)	..	..	..
Illiteracy male (% of people 15 and above)	..	..	..
Illiteracy female (% of people 15 and above)	..	..	..
Net primary enrollment (% of relevant age group)	..	..	..
Net secondary enrollment (% of relevant age group)	..	..	..
Girls in primary school (% of enrollment)	..	..	..
Girls in secondary school (% of enrollment)	..	..	..
Environment			
Forests (1,000 sq. km.)	0	..	0
Deforestation (% change 1990-2000)			0.0
Water use (% of total resources)	..	..	..
CO$_2$ emissions (metric tons per capita)	..	..	..
Access to improved water source (% of urban pop.)	..	..	..
Access to sanitation (% of urban population)	..	..	..
Energy use per capita (kg of oil equivalent)	..	..	..
Electricity use per capita (kWh)	..	..	..
Economy			
GDP ($ millions)	..	..	..
GDP growth (annual %)	..	..	..
GDP implicit price deflator (annual % growth)	..	..	..
Value added in agriculture (% of GDP)	..	..	..
Value added in industry (% of GDP)	..	..	..
Value added in services (% of GDP)	..	..	..
Exports of goods and services (% of GDP)	..	..	..
Imports of goods and services (% of GDP)	..	..	..
Gross domestic investment (% of GDP)	..	..	..
Central government revenues (% of GDP)	..	..	..
Overall budget deficit (% of GDP)	..	..	..
Money and quasi money (annual % growth)	..	..	..
Technology and infrastructure			
Telephone mainlines (per 1,000 people)	287	404	470
Cost of 3 min local call ($)	..	..	..
Personal computers (per 1,000 people)	..	..	..
Internet users (thousands)	..	..	..
Paved roads (% of total)	..	..	..
Aircraft departures (thousands)	..	..	..
Trade and finance			
Trade as share of PPP GDP (%)	..	..	..
Trade growth less GDP growth (average %, 1989-99)			..
High-technology exports (% of manufactured exports)	..	..	..
Net barter terms of trade (1995=100)	..	..	..
Foreign direct investment ($ millions)	..	..	..
Present value of debt ($ millions)			..
Total debt service ($ millions)	..	..	..
Short term debt ($ millions)	..	..	..
Aid per capita ($)	..	..	2

165

NORWAY

Population (millions)	4	Population growth (%)	0.6
Surface area (1,000 sq km)	324	Population per sq km	15
GNI ($ millions)	149,280	GNI per capita ($)	33,470

	1990	1998	1999
People			
Life expectancy (years)	77	78	78
Fertility rate (births per woman)	1.9	1.8	1.8
Infant mortality rate (per 1,000 live births)	7	4	4
Under 5 mortality rate (per 1,000 children)	9	6	4
Child malnutrition (% of children under 5)	..	..	
Urban population (% of total)	72	75	75
Rural population density (per km^2 arable land)	137	123	..
Illiteracy male (% of people 15 and above)	..	..	..
Illiteracy female (% of people 15 and above)	..	..	..
Net primary enrollment (% of relevant age group)	100	100	..
Net secondary enrollment (% of relevant age group)	88	97	..
Girls in primary school (% of enrollment)	49	49	..
Girls in secondary school (% of enrollment)	50	49	..
Environment			
Forests (1,000 sq. km.)	86	..	89
Deforestation (% change 1990-2000)			-0.4
Water use (% of total resources)	..	..	0.5
CO_2 emissions (metric tons per capita)	11.4	15.6	..
Access to improved water source (% of urban pop.)	100	100	100
Access to sanitation (% of urban population)	100	100	..
Energy use per capita (kg of oil equivalent)	5,064	5,736	..
Electricity use per capita (kWh)	22,824	24,607	..
Economy			
GDP ($ millions)	115,453	147,029	152,943
GDP growth (annual %)	2.0	2.0	0.9
GDP implicit price deflator (annual % growth)	3.9	-0.8	6.6
Value added in agriculture (% of GDP)	3.2	2.1	1.9
Value added in industry (% of GDP)	31.2	28.7	30.8
Value added in services (% of GDP)	65.6	69.1	67.3
Exports of goods and services (% of GDP)	40.6	37.2	39.0
Imports of goods and services (% of GDP)	34.1	36.7	33.0
Gross domestic investment (% of GDP)	23.3	28.3	24.3
Central government revenues (% of GDP)	42.5	41.9	..
Overall budget deficit (% of GDP)	0.5	-1.6	..
Money and quasi money (annual % growth)	5.6	15.5	1.7
Technology and infrastructure			
Telephone mainlines (per 1,000 people)	503	660	709
Cost of 3 min local call ($)	0.16	0.09	0.08
Personal computers (per 1,000 people)	145.5	404.5	446.6
Internet users (thousands)	60	1,600	2,000
Paved roads (% of total)	69	75	76
Aircraft departures (thousands)	234	304	335
Trade and finance			
Trade as share of PPP GDP (%)	73.7	61.7	62.2
Trade growth less GDP growth (average %, 1989-99)			1.6
High-technology exports (% of manufactured exports)	12	16	17
Net barter terms of trade (1995=100)	112	98	111
Foreign direct investment ($ millions)	..	..	..
Present value of debt ($ millions)			..
Total debt service ($ millions)	..	..	..
Short term debt ($ millions)	..	..	..
Aid per capita ($)	..	..	..

166

OMAN

Upper middle income

Population (millions)	2	Population growth (%)	2.0
Surface area (1,000 sq km)	212	Population per sq km	11
GNI ($ millions)	..	GNI per capita ($)	..

	1990	1998	1999
People			
Life expectancy (years)	69	73	73
Fertility rate (births per woman)	7.4	4.8	4.5
Infant mortality rate (per 1,000 live births)	22	18	17
Under 5 mortality rate (per 1,000 children)	30	25	24
Child malnutrition (% of children under 5)	24	23	..
Urban population (% of total)	62	81	82
Rural population density (per km^2 arable land)	3,854	2,785	..
Illiteracy male (% of people 15 and above)	33	22	21
Illiteracy female (% of people 15 and above)	62	43	40
Net primary enrollment (% of relevant age group)	70	69	..
Net secondary enrollment (% of relevant age group)	49	..	..
Girls in primary school (% of enrollment)	47	48	48
Girls in secondary school (% of enrollment)	44	49	..
Environment			
Forests (1,000 sq. km.)	0	..	0
Deforestation (% change 1990-2000)			0.0
Water use (% of total resources)	..	..	120.0
CO$_2$ emissions (metric tons per capita)	7.4	8.2	..
Access to improved water source (% of urban pop.)	41	..	41
Access to sanitation (% of urban population)	98	..	98
Energy use per capita (kg of oil equivalent)	2,669	3,165	..
Electricity use per capita (kWh)	2,284	2,828	..
Economy			
GDP ($ millions)	10,535	14,962	..
GDP growth (annual %)	7.5	3.2	..
GDP implicit price deflator (annual % growth)	16.6	3.7	..
Value added in agriculture (% of GDP)	3.3	..	..
Value added in industry (% of GDP)	57.7	..	..
Value added in services (% of GDP)	39.0	..	..
Exports of goods and services (% of GDP)	52.7	49.5	..
Imports of goods and services (% of GDP)	30.6	39.7	..
Gross domestic investment (% of GDP)	13.1	16.9	..
Central government revenues (% of GDP)	39.0	24.8	..
Overall budget deficit (% of GDP)	-0.8	-6.6	..
Money and quasi money (annual % growth)	10.0	4.8	6.4
Technology and infrastructure			
Telephone mainlines (per 1,000 people)	60	92	90
Cost of 3 min local call ($)	0.06	0.07	..
Personal computers (per 1,000 people)	1.7	21.0	26.4
Internet users (thousands)	..	20	50
Paved roads (% of total)	21	30	..
Aircraft departures (thousands)	12	16	22
Trade and finance			
Trade as share of PPP GDP (%)	..	..	..
Trade growth less GDP growth (average %, 1989-99)			..
High-technology exports (% of manufactured exports)	15	9	10
Net barter terms of trade (1995=100)	158	97	..
Foreign direct investment ($ millions)	141	106	60
Present value of debt ($ millions)			3,527
Total debt service ($ millions)	739	629	720
Short term debt ($ millions)	335	1,398	1,835
Aid per capita ($)	38	18	17

PAKISTAN

South Asia   Low income

Population (millions)	135	Population growth (%)	2.4
Surface area (1,000 sq km)	796	Population per sq km	175
GNI ($ millions)	62,915	GNI per capita ($)	470

	1990	1998	1999
People			
Life expectancy (years)	59	62	63
Fertility rate (births per woman)	5.8	5.0	4.8
Infant mortality rate (per 1,000 live births)	111	95	90
Under 5 mortality rate (per 1,000 children)	138	136	126
Child malnutrition (% of children under 5)	40	38	..
Urban population (% of total)	32	36	36
Rural population density (per km^2 arable land)	359	394	..
Illiteracy male (% of people 15 and above)	50	42	41
Illiteracy female (% of people 15 and above)	79	71	70
Net primary enrollment (% of relevant age group)	..	..	..
Net secondary enrollment (% of relevant age group)	..	..	..
Girls in primary school (% of enrollment)	32	39	..
Girls in secondary school (% of enrollment)	31	..	..
Environment			
Forests (1,000 sq. km.)	28	..	25
Deforestation (% change 1990-2000)			1.1
Water use (% of total resources)	..	..	61.0
CO_2 emissions (metric tons per capita)	0.7	0.8	..
Access to improved water source (% of urban pop.)	96	..	96
Access to sanitation (% of urban population)	78	..	94
Energy use per capita (kg of oil equivalent)	401	440	..
Electricity use per capita (kWh)	267	337	..
Economy			
GDP ($ millions)	40,010	62,228	58,154
GDP growth (annual %)	4.5	2.5	4.0
GDP implicit price deflator (annual % growth)	6.5	7.5	4.7
Value added in agriculture (% of GDP)	26.0	27.3	27.2
Value added in industry (% of GDP)	25.2	23.8	23.5
Value added in services (% of GDP)	48.8	48.9	49.4
Exports of goods and services (% of GDP)	15.5	16.2	15.2
Imports of goods and services (% of GDP)	23.4	20.7	20.1
Gross domestic investment (% of GDP)	18.9	17.7	15.0
Central government revenues (% of GDP)	19.1	16.2	17.2
Overall budget deficit (% of GDP)	-5.4	-6.4	-3.9
Money and quasi money (annual % growth)	11.6	7.9	4.3
Technology and infrastructure			
Telephone mainlines (per 1,000 people)	8	21	22
Cost of 3 min local call ($)	0.04	0.03	0.02
Personal computers (per 1,000 people)	1.3	4.3	4.3
Internet users (thousands)	..	62	80
Paved roads (% of total)	54	43	43
Aircraft departures (thousands)	66	69	65
Trade and finance			
Trade as share of PPP GDP (%)	8.9	7.7	8.0
Trade growth less GDP growth (average %, 1989-99)			-0.8
High-technology exports (% of manufactured exports)	0	0	0
Net barter terms of trade (1995=100)	91	114	..
Foreign direct investment ($ millions)	244	507	530
Present value of debt ($ millions)			25,136
Total debt service ($ millions)	1,902	2,300	2,828
Short term debt ($ millions)	3,185	2,160	1,830
Aid per capita ($)	10	8	5

168

PALAU

Population (thousands)	19	Population growth (%)	..
Surface area (1,000 sq km)	0.5	Population per sq km	41
GNI ($ millions)	..	GNI per capita ($)	..

	1990	1998	1999
People			
Life expectancy (years)	..	..	..
Fertility rate (births per woman)	..	..	..
Infant mortality rate (per 1,000 live births)	..	..	..
Under 5 mortality rate (per 1,000 children)	..	..	..
Child malnutrition (% of children under 5)	..	..	..
Urban population (% of total)	70	72	72
Rural population density (per km^2 arable land)	..	..	..
Illiteracy male (% of people 15 and above)	..	..	..
Illiteracy female (% of people 15 and above)	..	..	..
Net primary enrollment (% of relevant age group)	..	..	..
Net secondary enrollment (% of relevant age group)	..	..	..
Girls in primary school (% of enrollment)	..	..	..
Girls in secondary school (% of enrollment)	..	..	..
Environment			
Forests (1,000 sq. km.)	0	..	0
Deforestation (% change 1990-2000)			0.0
Water use (% of total resources)		..	..
CO_2 emissions (metric tons per capita)		..	..
Access to improved water source (% of urban pop.)		..	100
Access to sanitation (% of urban population)		..	100
Energy use per capita (kg of oil equivalent)		..	..
Electricity use per capita (kWh)		..	..
Economy			
GDP ($ millions)	77	129	133
GDP growth (annual %)	-6.4	-5.2	..
GDP implicit price deflator (annual % growth)	5.0	4.0	..
Value added in agriculture (% of GDP)	25.9	4.7	..
Value added in industry (% of GDP)	12.6	8.3	..
Value added in services (% of GDP)	68.9	86.9	..
Exports of goods and services (% of GDP)	..	..	..
Imports of goods and services (% of GDP)	..	..	..
Gross domestic investment (% of GDP)	..	..	..
Central government revenues (% of GDP)	..	..	..
Overall budget deficit (% of GDP)	..	..	..
Money and quasi money (annual % growth)	..	..	..
Technology and infrastructure			
Telephone mainlines (per 1,000 people)	..	..	..
Cost of 3 min local call ($)	..	..	..
Personal computers (per 1,000 people)	..	..	..
Internet users (thousands)	..	..	..
Paved roads (% of total)	..	..	..
Aircraft departures (thousands)	..	..	..
Trade and finance			
Trade as share of PPP GDP (%)	..	..	..
Trade growth less GDP growth (average %, 1989-99)			..
High-technology exports (% of manufactured exports)	..	..	..
Net barter terms of trade (1995=100)	..	..	..
Foreign direct investment ($ millions)	..	..	..
Present value of debt ($ millions)			..
Total debt service ($ millions)	..	..	..
Short term debt ($ millions)	..	..	..
Aid per capita ($)	..	..	1,513

169

PANAMA

Latin America & Caribbean **Upper middle income**

Population (millions)	3	Population growth (%)	1.7
Surface area (1,000 sq km)	76	Population per sq km	38
GNI ($ millions)	8,657	GNI per capita ($)	3,080

	1990	1998	1999
People			
Life expectancy (years)	72	74	74
Fertility rate (births per woman)	3.0	2.6	2.5
Infant mortality rate (per 1,000 live births)	26	21	20
Under 5 mortality rate (per 1,000 children)	..	26	25
Child malnutrition (% of children under 5)	6	..	..
Urban population (% of total)	54	56	56
Rural population density (per km² arable land)	222	244	..
Illiteracy male (% of people 15 and above)	10	8	8
Illiteracy female (% of people 15 and above)	12	9	9
Net primary enrollment (% of relevant age group)	91	..	..
Net secondary enrollment (% of relevant age group)	51	..	..
Girls in primary school (% of enrollment)	48	..	..
Girls in secondary school (% of enrollment)	51	..	..
Environment			
Forests (1,000 sq. km.)	34	..	29
Deforestation (% change 1990-2000)			1.6
Water use (% of total resources)	..	..	1.1
CO_2 emissions (metric tons per capita)	1.4	2.9	..
Access to improved water source (% of urban pop.)	100	99	88
Access to sanitation (% of urban population)	100	99	99
Energy use per capita (kg of oil equivalent)	640	862	..
Electricity use per capita (kWh)	883	1,211	..
Economy			
GDP ($ millions)	5,313	9,345	9,557
GDP growth (annual %)	8.1	4.4	3.0
GDP implicit price deflator (annual % growth)	0.6	3.4	-0.7
Value added in agriculture (% of GDP)	9.5	7.1	6.8
Value added in industry (% of GDP)	14.6	16.5	16.9
Value added in services (% of GDP)	75.9	76.5	76.3
Exports of goods and services (% of GDP)	38.4	32.8	32.9
Imports of goods and services (% of GDP)	33.8	41.8	41.4
Gross domestic investment (% of GDP)	16.8	32.1	32.5
Central government revenues (% of GDP)	25.6	24.9	..
Overall budget deficit (% of GDP)	3.0	-0.7	..
Money and quasi money (annual % growth)	36.6	13.0	8.5
Technology and infrastructure			
Telephone mainlines (per 1,000 people)	93	151	164
Cost of 3 min local call ($)	0.00	0.00	..
Personal computers (per 1,000 people)	..	27.1	32.0
Internet users (thousands)	..	30	45
Paved roads (% of total)	32	28	35
Aircraft departures (thousands)	5	22	21
Trade and finance			
Trade as share of PPP GDP (%)	20.1	24.9	26.3
Trade growth less GDP growth (average %, 1989-99)			-1.3
High-technology exports (% of manufactured exports)	..	2	1
Net barter terms of trade (1995=100)	69	109	..
Foreign direct investment ($ millions)	132	1,206	22
Present value of debt ($ millions)			6,852
Total debt service ($ millions)	345	729	741
Short term debt ($ millions)	2,418	462	443
Aid per capita ($)	41	8	5

East Asia and Pacific   **Lower middle income**

Population (millions)	5	Population growth (%)		2.2
Surface area (1,000 sq km)	463	Population per sq km		10
GNI ($ millions)	3,834	GNI per capita ($)		810

	1990	1998	1999
People			
Life expectancy (years)	55	..	58
Fertility rate (births per woman)	5.6	..	4.2
Infant mortality rate (per 1,000 live births)	83	..	58
Under 5 mortality rate (per 1,000 children)	..	..	77
Child malnutrition (% of children under 5)	..	..	..
Urban population (% of total)	15	17	17
Rural population density (per km^2 arable land)	9,323	6,379	..
Illiteracy male (% of people 15 and above)	34	29	29
Illiteracy female (% of people 15 and above)	52	45	44
Net primary enrollment (% of relevant age group)	..	..	..
Net secondary enrollment (% of relevant age group)	..	..	..
Girls in primary school (% of enrollment)	44	..	..
Girls in secondary school (% of enrollment)	38	..	..
Environment			
Forests (1,000 sq. km.)	317	..	..
Deforestation (% change 1990-2000)			
Water use (% of total resources)	..	..	0.0
CO_2 emissions (metric tons per capita)	0.6	..	..
Access to improved water source (% of urban pop.)	88	..	..
Access to sanitation (% of urban population)	92	..	..
Energy use per capita (kg of oil equivalent)	..	..	..
Electricity use per capita (kWh)	..	..	..
Economy			
GDP ($ millions)	3,221	3,821	3,586
GDP growth (annual %)	-3.0	-3.8	3.2
GDP implicit price deflator (annual % growth)	4.1	15.7	12.2
Value added in agriculture (% of GDP)	29.0	30.9	29.6
Value added in industry (% of GDP)	30.4	35.9	46.1
Value added in services (% of GDP)	40.6	33.2	24.4
Exports of goods and services (% of GDP)	40.6	50.1	44.9
Imports of goods and services (% of GDP)	48.9	45.5	41.9
Gross domestic investment (% of GDP)	24.4	17.7	17.8
Central government revenues (% of GDP)	25.3	21.4	19.2
Overall budget deficit (% of GDP)	-3.5	-1.7	-2.7
Money and quasi money (annual % growth)	4.3	2.5	9.2
Technology and infrastructure			
Telephone mainlines (per 1,000 people)	8	13	13
Cost of 3 min local call ($)	0.16	..	..
Personal computers (per 1,000 people)	..	..	..
Internet users (thousands)	..	..	2
Paved roads (% of total)	3	..	..
Aircraft departures (thousands)	62	25	24
Trade and finance			
Trade as share of PPP GDP (%)	37.6	28.4	27.5
Trade growth less GDP growth (average %, 1989-99)			-4.9
High-technology exports (% of manufactured exports)	..	..	..
Net barter terms of trade (1995=100)	..	..	..
Foreign direct investment ($ millions)	155	110	297
Present value of debt ($ millions)			2,627
Total debt service ($ millions)	553	182	211
Short term debt ($ millions)	72	157	98
Aid per capita ($)	107	78	46

171

PARAGUAY

Population (millions)	5	Population growth (%)		2.6
Surface area (1,000 sq km)	407	Population per sq km		13
GNI ($ millions)	8,374	GNI per capita ($)		1,560

	1990	1998	1999
People			
Life expectancy (years)	68	..	70
Fertility rate (births per woman)	4.6	..	4.0
Infant mortality rate (per 1,000 live births)	31	..	24
Under 5 mortality rate (per 1,000 children)	37	..	27
Child malnutrition (% of children under 5)	4	..	..
Urban population (% of total)	49	55	55
Rural population density (per km^2 arable land)	103	108	..
Illiteracy male (% of people 15 and above)	8	6	6
Illiteracy female (% of people 15 and above)	12	9	8
Net primary enrollment (% of relevant age group)	93	..	..
Net secondary enrollment (% of relevant age group)	26	..	..
Girls in primary school (% of enrollment)	48	..	..
Girls in secondary school (% of enrollment)	50	..	..
Environment			
Forests (1,000 sq. km.)	246	..	..
Deforestation (% change 1990-2000)			..
Water use (% of total resources)	..	..	0.5
CO_2 emissions (metric tons per capita)	0.6	..	..
Access to improved water source (% of urban pop.)	80	..	..
Access to sanitation (% of urban population)	92	..	..
Energy use per capita (kg of oil equivalent)	733	819	..
Electricity use per capita (kWh)	470	756	..
Economy			
GDP ($ millions)	5,265	8,598	7,741
GDP growth (annual %)	3.1	-0.4	-0.8
GDP implicit price deflator (annual % growth)	36.3	12.4	3.9
Value added in agriculture (% of GDP)	27.8	24.3	29.1
Value added in industry (% of GDP)	25.2	27.0	26.2
Value added in services (% of GDP)	47.0	48.8	44.6
Exports of goods and services (% of GDP)	33.2	28.2	23.0
Imports of goods and services (% of GDP)	39.5	45.1	36.7
Gross domestic investment (% of GDP)	22.9	22.9	23.0
Central government revenues (% of GDP)	12.3	..	..
Overall budget deficit (% of GDP)	2.9	..	..
Money and quasi money (annual % growth)	52.5	9.0	11.7
Technology and infrastructure			
Telephone mainlines (per 1,000 people)	27	55	55
Cost of 3 min local call ($)	0.07	..	0.05
Personal computers (per 1,000 people)	..	9.6	11.2
Internet users (thousands)	..	10	20
Paved roads (% of total)	9	..	..
Aircraft departures (thousands)	6	4	8
Trade and finance			
Trade as share of PPP GDP (%)	13.9	18.2	12.8
Trade growth less GDP growth (average %, 1989-99)			-2.5
High-technology exports (% of manufactured exports)	0	4	3
Net barter terms of trade (1995=100)	87	113	..
Foreign direct investment ($ millions)	76	196	72
Present value of debt ($ millions)			2,400
Total debt service ($ millions)	325	219	233
Short term debt ($ millions)	373	669	751
Aid per capita ($)	13	15	14

Latin America & Caribbean   **Lower middle income**

Population (millions)	25	Population growth (%)	1.7
Surface area (1,000 sq km)	1,285	Population per sq km	20
GNI ($ millions)	53,705	GNI per capita ($)	2,130

	1990	1998	1999
People			
Life expectancy (years)	66	..	69
Fertility rate (births per woman)	3.7	..	3.1
Infant mortality rate (per 1,000 live births)	54	..	39
Under 5 mortality rate (per 1,000 children)	75	..	48
Child malnutrition (% of children under 5)	..	..	..
Urban population (% of total)	69	72	72
Rural population density (per km^2 arable land)	192	189	..
Illiteracy male (% of people 15 and above)	8	6	6
Illiteracy female (% of people 15 and above)	21	16	15
Net primary enrollment (% of relevant age group)	..	..	..
Net secondary enrollment (% of relevant age group)	..	..	..
Girls in primary school (% of enrollment)	..	49	..
Girls in secondary school (% of enrollment)	..	48	
Environment			
Forests (1,000 sq. km.)	679	..	..
Deforestation (% change 1990-2000)			..
Water use (% of total resources)	..	..	1.1
CO_2 emissions (metric tons per capita)	1.1	..	..
Access to improved water source (% of urban pop.)	84	..	..
Access to sanitation (% of urban population)	81	..	..
Energy use per capita (kg of oil equivalent)	517	581	..
Electricity use per capita (kWh)	491	642	..
Economy			
GDP ($ millions)	26,294	57,006	51,933
GDP growth (annual %)	-5.1	-0.4	1.4
GDP implicit price deflator (annual % growth)	6,837.0	6.8	3.8
Value added in agriculture (% of GDP)	7.3	7.1	7.2
Value added in industry (% of GDP)	38.2	36.8	37.5
Value added in services (% of GDP)	54.6	56.1	55.3
Exports of goods and services (% of GDP)	15.8	13.2	14.7
Imports of goods and services (% of GDP)	13.8	18.6	17.0
Gross domestic investment (% of GDP)	16.5	24.2	22.0
Central government revenues (% of GDP)	12.5	17.6	16.5
Overall budget deficit (% of GDP)	-8.1	-0.1	-2.1
Money and quasi money (annual % growth)	6,384.9	17.3	14.5
Technology and infrastructure			
Telephone mainlines (per 1,000 people)	26	63	67
Cost of 3 min local call ($)	..	0.07	..
Personal computers (per 1,000 people)	..	30.2	35.7
Internet users (thousands)	..	200	400
Paved roads (% of total)	10	13	..
Aircraft departures (thousands)	22	45	37
Trade and finance			
Trade as share of PPP GDP (%)	9.5	13.9	12.2
Trade growth less GDP growth (average %, 1989-99)			-4.4
High-technology exports (% of manufactured exports)	..	4	5
Net barter terms of trade (1995=100)	93	90	..
Foreign direct investment ($ millions)	41	1,905	1,969
Present value of debt ($ millions)			31,898
Total debt service ($ millions)	476	2,451	2,940
Short term debt ($ millions)	5,350	7,398	6,355
Aid per capita ($)	19	20	18

PHILIPPINES

East Asia and Pacific		Lower middle income	
Population (millions)	74	Population growth (%)	1.9
Surface area (1,000 sq km)	300	Population per sq km	249
GNI ($ millions)	77,967	GNI per capita ($)	1,050

	1990	1998	1999
People			
Life expectancy (years)	65	..	69
Fertility rate (births per woman)	4.1	..	3.5
Infant mortality rate (per 1,000 live births)	37	..	31
Under 5 mortality rate (per 1,000 children)	62	..	41
Child malnutrition (% of children under 5)	34	..	..
Urban population (% of total)	49	57	58
Rural population density (per km^2 arable land)	567	573	..
Illiteracy male (% of people 15 and above)	7	5	5
Illiteracy female (% of people 15 and above)	8	5	5
Net primary enrollment (% of relevant age group)	..	..	..
Net secondary enrollment (% of relevant age group)	..	..	..
Girls in primary school (% of enrollment)	..	..	..
Girls in secondary school (% of enrollment)	..	..	..
Environment			
Forests (1,000 sq. km.)	67	..	..
Deforestation (% change 1990-2000)			..
Water use (% of total resources)	..	..	11.6
CO_2 emissions (metric tons per capita)	0.8	..	..
Access to improved water source (% of urban pop.)	94	..	..
Access to sanitation (% of urban population)	85	..	..
Energy use per capita (kg of oil equivalent)	466	526	..
Electricity use per capita (kWh)	344	451	..
Economy			
GDP ($ millions)	44,331	65,535	76,559
GDP growth (annual %)	3.0	-0.8	3.2
GDP implicit price deflator (annual % growth)	13.0	11.3	8.2
Value added in agriculture (% of GDP)	21.9	17.4	17.7
Value added in industry (% of GDP)	34.5	31.3	30.3
Value added in services (% of GDP)	43.6	51.3	52.0
Exports of goods and services (% of GDP)	27.5	51.9	51.2
Imports of goods and services (% of GDP)	33.3	58.5	50.2
Gross domestic investment (% of GDP)	24.2	20.2	18.6
Central government revenues (% of GDP)	16.6	17.2	16.0
Overall budget deficit (% of GDP)	-3.5	-1.9	-3.7
Money and quasi money (annual % growth)	22.5	8.1	16.8
Technology and infrastructure			
Telephone mainlines (per 1,000 people)	10	34	39
Cost of 3 min local call ($)	0.00	0.00	0.00
Personal computers (per 1,000 people)	3.5	15.1	16.9
Internet users (thousands)	..	150	500
Paved roads (% of total)	..	20	..
Aircraft departures (thousands)	70	30	36
Trade and finance			
Trade as share of PPP GDP (%)	10.3	22.6	24.5
Trade growth less GDP growth (average %, 1989-99)			-3.0
High-technology exports (% of manufactured exports)	..	72	59
Net barter terms of trade (1995=100)	90	103	..
Foreign direct investment ($ millions)	530	2,287	573
Present value of debt ($ millions)			51,898
Total debt service ($ millions)	3,590	5,202	6,732
Short term debt ($ millions)	4,427	7,185	5,745
Aid per capita ($)	21	8	9

Europe & Central Asia — **Upper middle income**

Population (millions)	39	Population growth (%)	0.0
Surface area (1,000 sq km)	323	Population per sq km	127
GNI ($ millions)	157,429	GNI per capita ($)	4,070

	1990	1998	1999
People			
Life expectancy (years)	71	73	73
Fertility rate (births per woman)	2.0	1.4	1.4
Infant mortality rate (per 1,000 live births)	19	10	9
Under 5 mortality rate (per 1,000 children)	22	11	10
Child malnutrition (% of children under 5)	..		..
Urban population (% of total)	62	65	65
Rural population density (per km^2 arable land)	101	97	..
Illiteracy male (% of people 15 and above)	0	0	0
Illiteracy female (% of people 15 and above)	1	0	0
Net primary enrollment (% of relevant age group)	97	95	..
Net secondary enrollment (% of relevant age group)	76	85	..
Girls in primary school (% of enrollment)	49	48	..
Girls in secondary school (% of enrollment)	50	49	..
Environment			
Forests (1,000 sq. km.)	92	..	93
Deforestation (% change 1990-2000)			-0.1
Water use (% of total resources)	..	..	19.2
CO$_2$ emissions (metric tons per capita)	9.3	9.2	..
Access to improved water source (% of urban pop.)	89	..	..
Access to sanitation (% of urban population)	..	..	..
Energy use per capita (kg of oil equivalent)	2,626	2,494	..
Electricity use per capita (kWh)	2,525	2,458	..
Economy			
GDP ($ millions)	61,197	158,160	155,166
GDP growth (annual %)	-7.0	4.8	4.1
GDP implicit price deflator (annual % growth)	57.8	11.8	6.8
Value added in agriculture (% of GDP)	8.0	4.2	3.4
Value added in industry (% of GDP)	48.3	31.8	31.2
Value added in services (% of GDP)	43.7	64.0	65.3
Exports of goods and services (% of GDP)	27.6	28.2	26.1
Imports of goods and services (% of GDP)	20.7	33.4	32.5
Gross domestic investment (% of GDP)	24.7	26.2	26.4
Central government revenues (% of GDP)	37.0	35.6	32.7
Overall budget deficit (% of GDP)	-2.3	-1.0	-0.9
Money and quasi money (annual % growth)	160.1	25.2	19.4
Technology and infrastructure			
Telephone mainlines (per 1,000 people)	86	228	263
Cost of 3 min local call ($)	0.01	0.06	0.07
Personal computers (per 1,000 people)	7.9	49.1	62.0
Internet users (thousands)	2	1,580	2,100
Paved roads (% of total)	62	66	66
Aircraft departures (thousands)	29	41	44
Trade and finance			
Trade as share of PPP GDP (%)	11.5	24.4	22.4
Trade growth less GDP growth (average %, 1989-99)			10.9
High-technology exports (% of manufactured exports)	..	3	3
Net barter terms of trade (1995=100)	91	99	100
Foreign direct investment ($ millions)	89	6,365	7,270
Present value of debt ($ millions)			51,180
Total debt service ($ millions)	966	4,534	8,374
Short term debt ($ millions)	9,595	6,191	5,943
Aid per capita ($)	35	23	25

PORTUGAL

Population (millions)	10	Population growth (%)	0.2
Surface area (1,000 sq km)	92	Population per sq km	109
GNI ($ millions)	110,175	GNI per capita ($)	11,030

	1990	1998	1999
People			
Life expectancy (years)	74	75	75
Fertility rate (births per woman)	1.4	1.5	1.5
Infant mortality rate (per 1,000 live births)	11	8	6
Under 5 mortality rate (per 1,000 children)	15	8	6
Child malnutrition (% of children under 5)	..	..	
Urban population (% of total)	47	61	63
Rural population density (per km^2 arable land)	222	206	..
Illiteracy male (% of people 15 and above)	9	6	6
Illiteracy female (% of people 15 and above)	16	11	11
Net primary enrollment (% of relevant age group)	102	104	..
Net secondary enrollment (% of relevant age group)	70	78	..
Girls in primary school (% of enrollment)	48	48	..
Girls in secondary school (% of enrollment)	53	51	..
Environment			
Forests (1,000 sq. km.)	31	..	37
Deforestation (% change 1990-2000)			-1.7
Water use (% of total resources)	..	..	10.1
CO$_2$ emissions (metric tons per capita)	4.6	5.4	..
Access to improved water source (% of urban pop.)	..	..	..
Access to sanitation (% of urban population)	..	..	..
Energy use per capita (kg of oil equivalent)	1,659	2,192	..
Electricity use per capita (kWh)	2,379	3,395	..
Economy			
GDP ($ millions)	70,936	110,872	113,716
GDP growth (annual %)	4.4	3.5	3.0
GDP implicit price deflator (annual % growth)	12.8	4.0	4.0
Value added in agriculture (% of GDP)	7.8	3.5	..
Value added in industry (% of GDP)	28.7	27.1	..
Value added in services (% of GDP)	63.5	69.3	..
Exports of goods and services (% of GDP)	33.2	31.0	..
Imports of goods and services (% of GDP)	39.7	40.0	..
Gross domestic investment (% of GDP)	27.0	25.3	..
Central government revenues (% of GDP)	31.8	35.0	..
Overall budget deficit (% of GDP)	-4.4	-1.2	..
Money and quasi money (annual % growth)	..	..	..
Technology and infrastructure			
Telephone mainlines (per 1,000 people)	243	413	423
Cost of 3 min local call ($)	0.05	0.09	0.10
Personal computers (per 1,000 people)	26.5	81.3	93.0
Internet users (thousands)	10	500	700
Paved roads (% of total)	..	86	..
Aircraft departures (thousands)	45	111	104
Trade and finance			
Trade as share of PPP GDP (%)	37.5	41.3	38.9
Trade growth less GDP growth (average %, 1989-99)			3.9
High-technology exports (% of manufactured exports)	4	4	5
Net barter terms of trade (1995=100)	100	..	..
Foreign direct investment ($ millions)	..	..	..
Present value of debt ($ millions)			..
Total debt service ($ millions)	..	..	..
Short term debt ($ millions)	..	..	..
Aid per capita ($)	..	..	..

176

PUERTO RICO

Upper middle income

Population (millions)	4	Population growth (%)	0.8
Surface area (1,000 sq km)	9	Population per sq km	439
GNI ($ millions)	..	GNI per capita ($)	..

	1990	1998	1999
People			
Life expectancy (years)	75	75	76
Fertility rate (births per woman)	2.2	1.9	1.9
Infant mortality rate (per 1,000 live births)	14	10	10
Under 5 mortality rate (per 1,000 children)	..	..	..
Child malnutrition (% of children under 5)	..	..	..
Urban population (% of total)	71	74	75
Rural population density (per km² arable land)	1,562	2,990	..
Illiteracy male (% of people 15 and above)	9	7	7
Illiteracy female (% of people 15 and above)	9	7	6
Net primary enrollment (% of relevant age group)	..	..	..
Net secondary enrollment (% of relevant age group)	..	..	..
Girls in primary school (% of enrollment)	..	..	..
Girls in secondary school (% of enrollment)	..	..	..
Environment			
Forests (1,000 sq. km.)	2	..	2
Deforestation (% change 1990-2000)			0.2
Water use (% of total resources)	..	..	
CO_2 emissions (metric tons per capita)	3.5	4.5	..
Access to improved water source (% of urban pop.)	..	..	..
Access to sanitation (% of urban population)	..	..	..
Energy use per capita (kg of oil equivalent)	..	..	..
Electricity use per capita (kWh)	..	..	..
Economy			
GDP ($ millions)	30,604	47,624	..
GDP growth (annual %)	3.8	3.2	..
GDP implicit price deflator (annual % growth)	4.3	1.9	..
Value added in agriculture (% of GDP)	1.4	1.1	..
Value added in industry (% of GDP)	42.0	41.7	..
Value added in services (% of GDP)	56.6	57.1	..
Exports of goods and services (% of GDP)	71.7	..	..
Imports of goods and services (% of GDP)	70.2	..	..
Gross domestic investment (% of GDP)	17.0	17.1	..
Central government revenues (% of GDP)	..	..	..
Overall budget deficit (% of GDP)	..	..	..
Money and quasi money (annual % growth)	..	..	..
Technology and infrastructure			
Telephone mainlines (per 1,000 people)	279	327	333
Cost of 3 min local call ($)	0.13	0.13	..
Personal computers (per 1,000 people)	..	..	..
Internet users (thousands)	..	100	200
Paved roads (% of total)	100	100	..
Aircraft departures (thousands)	..	..	..
Trade and finance			
Trade as share of PPP GDP (%)	..	..	..
Trade growth less GDP growth (average %, 1989-99)			..
High-technology exports (% of manufactured exports)	..	..	..
Net barter terms of trade (1995=100)	..	..	..
Foreign direct investment ($ millions)	..	..	..
Present value of debt ($ millions)			..
Total debt service ($ millions)	..	..	..
Short term debt ($ millions)	..	..	..
Aid per capita ($)	..	..	..

QATAR

Population (thousands)	565	Population growth (%)	3.4
Surface area (1,000 sq km)	11.0	Population per sq km	51
GNI ($ millions)	..	GNI per capita ($)	..

	1990	1998	1999
People			
Life expectancy (years)	72	74	75
Fertility rate (births per woman)	4.3	2.8	2.7
Infant mortality rate (per 1,000 live births)	21	18	16
Under 5 mortality rate (per 1,000 children)	36	25	22
Child malnutrition (% of children under 5)	..	6	..
Urban population (% of total)	90	92	92
Rural population density (per km^2 arable land)	490	310	..
Illiteracy male (% of people 15 and above)	23	20	20
Illiteracy female (% of people 15 and above)	24	18	17
Net primary enrollment (% of relevant age group)	87	80	..
Net secondary enrollment (% of relevant age group)	67	69	..
Girls in primary school (% of enrollment)	48	47	..
Girls in secondary school (% of enrollment)	50	49	..
Environment			
Forests (1,000 sq. km.)	0	..	0
Deforestation (% change 1990-2000)			..
Water use (% of total resources)	..	..	290.0
CO_2 emissions (metric tons per capita)	28.4	72.9	..
Access to improved water source (% of urban pop.)	100	100	..
Access to sanitation (% of urban population)	100	100	..
Energy use per capita (kg of oil equivalent)	13,267	27,734	..
Electricity use per capita (kWh)	9,419	13,912	..
Economy			
GDP ($ millions)	7,360	9,243	..
GDP growth (annual %)	..	..	..
GDP implicit price deflator (annual % growth)	..	..	..
Value added in agriculture (% of GDP)	..	..	..
Value added in industry (% of GDP)	..	..	..
Value added in services (% of GDP)	..	..	..
Exports of goods and services (% of GDP)	..	..	..
Imports of goods and services (% of GDP)	..	..	..
Gross domestic investment (% of GDP)	..	..	..
Central government revenues (% of GDP)	..	..	..
Overall budget deficit (% of GDP)	..	..	..
Money and quasi money (annual % growth)	-4.6	8.0	11.4
Technology and infrastructure			
Telephone mainlines (per 1,000 people)	190	260	263
Cost of 3 min local call ($)	..	..	0.00
Personal computers (per 1,000 people)	..	120.9	135.8
Internet users (thousands)	..	20	24
Paved roads (% of total)	86	90	..
Aircraft departures (thousands)	11	12	13
Trade and finance			
Trade as share of PPP GDP (%)	..	..	..
Trade growth less GDP growth (average %, 1989-99)			..
High-technology exports (% of manufactured exports)	..	..	..
Net barter terms of trade (1995=100)	146	94	..
Foreign direct investment ($ millions)	..	..	..
Present value of debt ($ millions)			..
Total debt service ($ millions)	..	..	..
Short term debt ($ millions)	..	..	..
Aid per capita ($)	3	2	9

178

Europe & Central Asia — **Lower middle income**

Population (millions)	22	Population growth (%)	-0.2
Surface area (1,000 sq km)	238	Population per sq km	97
GNI ($ millions)	33,034	GNI per capita ($)	1,470

	1990	1998	1999
People			
Life expectancy (years)	70	69	69
Fertility rate (births per woman)	1.8	1.3	1.3
Infant mortality rate (per 1,000 live births)	27	21	20
Under 5 mortality rate (per 1,000 children)	36	25	24
Child malnutrition (% of children under 5)	..	..	..
Urban population (% of total)	54	56	56
Rural population density (per km^2 arable land)	114	107	..
Illiteracy male (% of people 15 and above)	1	1	1
Illiteracy female (% of people 15 and above)	5	3	3
Net primary enrollment (% of relevant age group)	..	..	..
Net secondary enrollment (% of relevant age group)	..	..	..
Girls in primary school (% of enrollment)	..	49	..
Girls in secondary school (% of enrollment)	49	..	..
Environment			
Forests (1,000 sq. km.)	63	..	..
Deforestation (% change 1990-2000)			..
Water use (% of total resources)	..		..
CO_2 emissions (metric tons per capita)	6.9	..	..
Access to improved water source (% of urban pop.)	..	..	..
Access to sanitation (% of urban population)	..	..	..
Energy use per capita (kg of oil equivalent)	2,634	1,760	..
Electricity use per capita (kWh)	2,337	1,626	..
Economy			
GDP ($ millions)	38,299	41,490	34,027
GDP growth (annual %)	-5.7	-4.9	-3.2
GDP implicit price deflator (annual % growth)	13.7	55.0	46.4
Value added in agriculture (% of GDP)	20.3	15.0	15.5
Value added in industry (% of GDP)	50.0	36.6	31.0
Value added in services (% of GDP)	29.8	48.3	53.5
Exports of goods and services (% of GDP)	16.7	23.7	30.1
Imports of goods and services (% of GDP)	26.2	31.8	34.3
Gross domestic investment (% of GDP)	30.2	21.4	19.9
Central government revenues (% of GDP)	34.7	..	..
Overall budget deficit (% of GDP)	0.9	..	..
Money and quasi money (annual % growth)	26.4	48.9	44.9
Technology and infrastructure			
Telephone mainlines (per 1,000 people)	102	160	167
Cost of 3 min local call ($)	0.04	0.08	0.09
Personal computers (per 1,000 people)	2.2	21.3	26.8
Internet users (thousands)	..	500	600
Paved roads (% of total)	..	68	69
Aircraft departures (thousands)	22	17	18
Trade and finance			
Trade as share of PPP GDP (%)	8.7	14.7	13.9
Trade growth less GDP growth (average %, 1989-99)			1.5
High-technology exports (% of manufactured exports)	3	2	4
Net barter terms of trade (1995=100)	..	..	..
Foreign direct investment ($ millions)	0	2,031	1,041
Present value of debt ($ millions)			9,061
Total debt service ($ millions)	18	2,303	3,138
Short term debt ($ millions)	910	1,149	940
Aid per capita ($)	10	16	17

179

RUSSIAN FEDERATION

Lower middle income

Population (millions)	146	Population growth (%)	-0.4
Surface area (1,000 sq km)	17,075	Population per sq km	9
GNI ($ millions)	328,995	GNI per capita ($)	2,250

	1990	1998	1999
People			
Life expectancy (years)	69	67	66
Fertility rate (births per woman)	1.9	1.2	1.3
Infant mortality rate (per 1,000 live births)	17	16	16
Under 5 mortality rate (per 1,000 children)	21	20	20
Child malnutrition (% of children under 5)	..	..	..
Urban population (% of total)	74	77	77
Rural population density (per km^2 arable land)	..	27	..
Illiteracy male (% of people 15 and above)	0	0	0
Illiteracy female (% of people 15 and above)	1	1	1
Net primary enrollment (% of relevant age group)	..	..	..
Net secondary enrollment (% of relevant age group)	..	..	..
Girls in primary school (% of enrollment)	..	..	..
Girls in secondary school (% of enrollment)	..	..	..
Environment			
Forests (1,000 sq. km.)	8,500	..	..
Deforestation (% change 1990-2000)			
Water use (% of total resources)	..	..	1.7
CO_2 emissions (metric tons per capita)	..	..	..
Access to improved water source (% of urban pop.)	..	..	..
Access to sanitation (% of urban population)	..	..	..
Energy use per capita (kg of oil equivalent)	..	3,963	..
Electricity use per capita (kWh)	..	3,937	..
Economy			
GDP ($ millions)	579,068	277,829	401,442
GDP growth (annual %)	-3.0	-4.9	3.2
GDP implicit price deflator (annual % growth)	15.9	14.4	63.4
Value added in agriculture (% of GDP)	16.6	5.4	6.6
Value added in industry (% of GDP)	48.4	36.4	37.7
Value added in services (% of GDP)	35.0	58.2	55.7
Exports of goods and services (% of GDP)	18.2	31.4	46.0
Imports of goods and services (% of GDP)	17.9	26.6	28.5
Gross domestic investment (% of GDP)	30.1	15.7	15.5
Central government revenues (% of GDP)	..	19.0	22.6
Overall budget deficit (% of GDP)	..	-5.3	-0.5
Money and quasi money (annual % growth)	..	37.5	56.7
Technology and infrastructure			
Telephone mainlines (per 1,000 people)	140	199	210
Cost of 3 min local call ($)	..	..	0.02
Personal computers (per 1,000 people)	3.4	34.7	37.4
Internet users (thousands)	..	1,200	2,700
Paved roads (% of total)	74	..	..
Aircraft departures (thousands)	..	348	321
Trade and finance			
Trade as share of PPP GDP (%)	..	13.1	10.6
Trade growth less GDP growth (average %, 1989-99)			6.2
High-technology exports (% of manufactured exports)	..	12	16
Net barter terms of trade (1995=100)	..	..	..
Foreign direct investment ($ millions)	0	2,764	3,309
Present value of debt ($ millions)			130,88
Total debt service ($ millions)	11,746	10,901	11,487
Short term debt ($ millions)	11,800	14,979	15,745
Aid per capita ($)	2	7	12

RWANDA

| Sub-Saharan Africa | | | Low income |

Population (millions)	8	Population growth (%)	2.5
Surface area (1,000 sq km)	26	Population per sq km	337
GNI ($ millions)	2,041	GNI per capita ($)	250

	1990	1998	1999
People			
Life expectancy (years)	40	40	40
Fertility rate (births per woman)	6.7	6.2	6.0
Infant mortality rate (per 1,000 live births)	132	124	123
Under 5 mortality rate (per 1,000 children)	..	202	203
Child malnutrition (% of children under 5)	29	27	..
Urban population (% of total)	5	6	6
Rural population density (per km^2 arable land)	748	929	..
Illiteracy male (% of people 15 and above)	37	29	27
Illiteracy female (% of people 15 and above)	56	43	41
Net primary enrollment (% of relevant age group)	66	..	..
Net secondary enrollment (% of relevant age group)	7	..	..
Girls in primary school (% of enrollment)	50	..	..
Girls in secondary school (% of enrollment)	43	..	..
Environment			
Forests (1,000 sq. km.)	5	..	3
Deforestation (% change 1990-2000)			3.9
Water use (% of total resources)	..	..	12.2
CO_2 emissions (metric tons per capita)	0.1	0.1	..
Access to improved water source (% of urban pop.)	..	..	60
Access to sanitation (% of urban population)	..	..	12
Energy use per capita (kg of oil equivalent)	..	..	..
Electricity use per capita (kWh)	..	..	..
Economy			
GDP ($ millions)	2,584	2,024	1,956
GDP growth (annual %)	-2.4	9.5	6.1
GDP implicit price deflator (annual % growth)	13.5	2.6	-2.6
Value added in agriculture (% of GDP)	33.2	47.4	45.7
Value added in industry (% of GDP)	25.1	21.2	20.5
Value added in services (% of GDP)	41.7	31.4	33.8
Exports of goods and services (% of GDP)	5.6	5.4	5.6
Imports of goods and services (% of GDP)	14.1	22.9	21.1
Gross domestic investment (% of GDP)	14.6	15.7	14.3
Central government revenues (% of GDP)	10.8	10.5	..
Overall budget deficit (% of GDP)	-5.3	-6.9	..
Money and quasi money (annual % growth)	5.6	3.5	7.9
Technology and infrastructure			
Telephone mainlines (per 1,000 people)	2	2	2
Cost of 3 min local call ($)	..	0.04	0.04
Personal computers (per 1,000 people)	..	..	..
Internet users (thousands)	..	1	5
Paved roads (% of total)	9	9	..
Aircraft departures (thousands)	1	1	..
Trade and finance			
Trade as share of PPP GDP (%)	6.0	5.1	4.6
Trade growth less GDP growth (average %, 1989-99)			4.5
High-technology exports (% of manufactured exports)	..	..	..
Net barter terms of trade (1995=100)	50	134	..
Foreign direct investment ($ millions)	8	7	2
Present value of debt ($ millions)			696
Total debt service ($ millions)	21	21	31
Short term debt ($ millions)	47	50	54
Aid per capita ($)	42	43	45

181

SAMOA

Population (thousands)	169	Population growth (%)	0.5
Surface area (1,000 sq km)	2.8	Population per sq km	60
GNI ($ millions)	181	GNI per capita ($)	1,070

	1990	1998	1999
People			
Life expectancy (years)	66	..	69
Fertility rate (births per woman)	4.8	4.5	4.4
Infant mortality rate (per 1,000 live births)	27	25	23
Under 5 mortality rate (per 1,000 children)	..	..	..
Child malnutrition (% of children under 5)	..	..	..
Urban population (% of total)	21	21	21
Rural population density (per km^2 arable land)	230	240	..
Illiteracy male (% of people 15 and above)	22	19	19
Illiteracy female (% of people 15 and above)	26	22	21
Net primary enrollment (% of relevant age group)	..	..	..
Net secondary enrollment (% of relevant age group)	..	..	..
Girls in primary school (% of enrollment)	49	..	..
Girls in secondary school (% of enrollment)	51	..	..
Environment			
Forests (1,000 sq. km.)	1	..	..
Deforestation (% change 1990-2000)			..
Water use (% of total resources)			..
CO_2 emissions (metric tons per capita)	0.8	..	..
Access to improved water source (% of urban pop.)	..	..	..
Access to sanitation (% of urban population)	..	..	..
Energy use per capita (kg of oil equivalent)	..	..	..
Electricity use per capita (kWh)	..	..	..
Economy			
GDP ($ millions)	146	175	177
GDP growth (annual %)	-4.4	1.3	1.0
GDP implicit price deflator (annual % growth)	11.9	4.0	2.0
Value added in agriculture (% of GDP)	43.4	..	..
Value added in industry (% of GDP)	19.2	..	..
Value added in services (% of GDP)	37.4	..	..
Exports of goods and services (% of GDP)	30.6	..	..
Imports of goods and services (% of GDP)	65.1	..	..
Gross domestic investment (% of GDP)	34.4	..	..
Central government revenues (% of GDP)	..	..	..
Overall budget deficit (% of GDP)	..	..	..
Money and quasi money (annual % growth)	19.3	2.2	12.5
Technology and infrastructure			
Telephone mainlines (per 1,000 people)	26	49	..
Cost of 3 min local call ($)	0.04	0.04	..
Personal computers (per 1,000 people)	..	5.2	5.6
Internet users (thousands)	..	0	1
Paved roads (% of total)	..	..	..
Aircraft departures (thousands)	..	5	4
Trade and finance			
Trade as share of PPP GDP (%)	17.7	16.8	19.8
Trade growth less GDP growth (average %, 1989-99)			..
High-technology exports (% of manufactured exports)	..	..	..
Net barter terms of trade (1995=100)	109	102	..
Foreign direct investment ($ millions)	7	3	2
Present value of debt ($ millions)			120
Total debt service ($ millions)	6	5	7
Short term debt ($ millions)	0	26	36
Aid per capita ($)	297	217	136

Population (thousands)	26	Population growth (%)	..
Surface area (1,000 sq km)	0.1	Population per sq km	433
GNI ($ millions)	..	GNI per capita ($)	..

	1990	1998	1999
People			
Life expectancy (years)	..	..	..
Fertility rate (births per woman)	..	..	..
Infant mortality rate (per 1,000 live births)	..	..	..
Under 5 mortality rate (per 1,000 children)	..	..	..
Child malnutrition (% of children under 5)	..	..	..
Urban population (% of total)	90	89	89
Rural population density (per km^2 arable land)	..	..	..
Illiteracy male (% of people 15 and above)	..	..	..
Illiteracy female (% of people 15 and above)	..	..	..
Net primary enrollment (% of relevant age group)	..	..	..
Net secondary enrollment (% of relevant age group)	..	..	
Girls in primary school (% of enrollment)	47	48	..
Girls in secondary school (% of enrollment)	52	48	..
Environment			
Forests (1,000 sq. km.)			..
Deforestation (% change 1990-2000)			..
Water use (% of total resources)	..		..
CO_2 emissions (metric tons per capita)	..	..	..
Access to improved water source (% of urban pop.)	..	..	..
Access to sanitation (% of urban population)	..	..	..
Energy use per capita (kg of oil equivalent)	..	..	..
Electricity use per capita (kWh)	..	..	..
Economy			
GDP ($ millions)	..	..	..
GDP growth (annual %)	..	..	..
GDP implicit price deflator (annual % growth)	..	..	..
Value added in agriculture (% of GDP)	..	..	..
Value added in industry (% of GDP)	..	..	..
Value added in services (% of GDP)	..	..	..
Exports of goods and services (% of GDP)	..	..	..
Imports of goods and services (% of GDP)	..	..	..
Gross domestic investment (% of GDP)	..	..	..
Central government revenues (% of GDP)	..	..	..
Overall budget deficit (% of GDP)	..	..	..
Money and quasi money (annual % growth)	..	..	..
Technology and infrastructure			
Telephone mainlines (per 1,000 people)	..	689	..
Cost of 3 min local call ($)	..	..	..
Personal computers (per 1,000 people)	..	..	..
Internet users (thousands)	..	..	..
Paved roads (% of total)	..	..	..
Aircraft departures (thousands)	..	..	..
Trade and finance			
Trade as share of PPP GDP (%)	..	..	..
Trade growth less GDP growth (average %, 1989-99)			..
High-technology exports (% of manufactured exports)	..	..	..
Net barter terms of trade (1995=100)	..	..	..
Foreign direct investment ($ millions)	..	..	..
Present value of debt ($ millions)			..
Total debt service ($ millions)	..	..	..
Short term debt ($ millions)	..	..	..
Aid per capita ($)	..	..	..

183

SÃO TOMÉ AND PRINCIPE

Sub-Saharan Africa   Low income

Population (thousands)	145	Population growth (%)	2.3
Surface area (1,000 sq km)	1	Population per sq km	151
GNI ($ millions)	40	GNI per capita ($)	270

	1990	1998	1999
People			
Life expectancy (years)	62	..	65
Fertility rate (births per woman)	5.1	..	4.5
Infant mortality rate (per 1,000 live births)	61	..	47
Under 5 mortality rate (per 1,000 children)	90	..	66
Child malnutrition (% of children under 5)	..	..	..
Urban population (% of total)	39	45	46
Rural population density (per km^2 arable land)	3,513	3,892	..
Illiteracy male (% of people 15 and above)	..	..	..
Illiteracy female (% of people 15 and above)	..	..	..
Net primary enrollment (% of relevant age group)	..	..	..
Net secondary enrollment (% of relevant age group)	..	..	..
Girls in primary school (% of enrollment)	..	..	..
Girls in secondary school (% of enrollment)	..	..	..
Environment			
Forests (1,000 sq. km.)	0	..	..
Deforestation (% change 1990-2000)			..
Water use (% of total resources)			..
CO$_2$ emissions (metric tons per capita)	0.6	..	..
Access to improved water source (% of urban pop.)	..	..	..
Access to sanitation (% of urban population)	..	..	..
Energy use per capita (kg of oil equivalent)	..	..	..
Electricity use per capita (kWh)	..	..	..
Economy			
GDP ($ millions)	58	41	47
GDP growth (annual %)	1.8	2.5	2.5
GDP implicit price deflator (annual % growth)	41.2	37.1	16.0
Value added in agriculture (% of GDP)	27.6	21.3	20.6
Value added in industry (% of GDP)	17.9	16.7	17.0
Value added in services (% of GDP)	54.5	62.0	62.5
Exports of goods and services (% of GDP)	14.5	29.7	35.0
Imports of goods and services (% of GDP)	72.5	72.5	84.3
Gross domestic investment (% of GDP)	15.6	35.8	40.0
Central government revenues (% of GDP)	..	..	..
Overall budget deficit (% of GDP)	..	..	..
Money and quasi money (annual % growth)	..	2.8	-2.2
Technology and infrastructure			
Telephone mainlines (per 1,000 people)	19	30	31
Cost of 3 min local call ($)	..	0.00	0.00
Personal computers (per 1,000 people)	..	..	..
Internet users (thousands)	..	0	1
Paved roads (% of total)	62	..	..
Aircraft departures (thousands)	1	1	1
Trade and finance			
Trade as share of PPP GDP (%)	..	..	..
Trade growth less GDP growth (average %, 1989-99)			-1.7
High-technology exports (% of manufactured exports)	..	..	..
Net barter terms of trade (1995=100)	170	85	..
Foreign direct investment ($ millions)	0	0	0
Present value of debt ($ millions)			190
Total debt service ($ millions)	3	4	4
Short term debt ($ millions)	16	12	21
Aid per capita ($)	475	199	189

Middle East & North Africa   **Upper middle income**

Population (millions)	20	Population growth (%)	20
Surface area (1,000 sq km)	2,150	Population per sq km	2,150
GNI ($ millions)	139,365	GNI per capita ($)	139,365

	1990	1998	1999
People			
Life expectancy (years)	69	72	72
Fertility rate (births per woman)	6.6	5.7	5.5
Infant mortality rate (per 1,000 live births)	32	20	19
Under 5 mortality rate (per 1,000 children)	45	26	25
Child malnutrition (% of children under 5)	..	..	..
Urban population (% of total)	79	85	85
Rural population density (per km^2 arable land)	100	82	..
Illiteracy male (% of people 15 and above)	22	17	17
Illiteracy female (% of people 15 and above)	49	36	34
Net primary enrollment (% of relevant age group)	59	61	..
Net secondary enrollment (% of relevant age group)	31	43	..
Girls in primary school (% of enrollment)	46	48	..
Girls in secondary school (% of enrollment)	44	44	..
Environment			
Forests (1,000 sq. km.)	15	..	15
Deforestation (% change 1990-2000)			0.0
Water use (% of total resources)	..	..	708.3
CO$_2$ emissions (metric tons per capita)	11.6	14.3	..
Access to improved water source (% of urban pop.)	..	..	100
Access to sanitation (% of urban population)	100	..	100
Energy use per capita (kg of oil equivalent)	4,004	5,244	..
Electricity use per capita (kWh)	3,181	4,692	..
Economy			
GDP ($ millions)	104,670	128,377	139,383
GDP growth (annual %)	8.6	1.6	0.4
GDP implicit price deflator (annual % growth)	16.1	-13.7	8.1
Value added in agriculture (% of GDP)	6.4	7.1	..
Value added in industry (% of GDP)	50.3	47.8	..
Value added in services (% of GDP)	43.3	45.2	..
Exports of goods and services (% of GDP)	46.2	35.5	39.8
Imports of goods and services (% of GDP)	36.1	30.7	27.9
Gross domestic investment (% of GDP)	19.5	17.1	19.3
Central government revenues (% of GDP)	..	..	..
Overall budget deficit (% of GDP)	..	..	..
Money and quasi money (annual % growth)	4.6	3.6	6.8
Technology and infrastructure			
Telephone mainlines (per 1,000 people)	77	107	129
Cost of 3 min local call ($)	0.01	0.01	0.02
Personal computers (per 1,000 people)	23.8	49.5	57.4
Internet users (thousands)	..	20	300
Paved roads (% of total)	41	30	..
Aircraft departures (thousands)	93	101	107
Trade and finance			
Trade as share of PPP GDP (%)	45.9	32.7	36.0
Trade growth less GDP growth (average %, 1989-99)			..
High-technology exports (% of manufactured exports)	..	0	..
Net barter terms of trade (1995=100)	168	88	..
Foreign direct investment ($ millions)	..	..	..
Present value of debt ($ millions)			..
Total debt service ($ millions)	..	..	..
Short term debt ($ millions)	..	..	..
Aid per capita ($)	3	1	1

SENEGAL

Population (millions)	9	Population growth (%)	2.7
Surface area (1,000 sq km)	196.7	Population per sq km	48
GNI ($ millions)	4,685	GNI per capita ($)	500

	1990	1998	1999
People			
Life expectancy (years)	50	52	52
Fertility rate (births per woman)	6.2	5.6	5.4
Infant mortality rate (per 1,000 live births)	74	70	67
Under 5 mortality rate (per 1,000 children)	139	130	124
Child malnutrition (% of children under 5)	22	22	..
Urban population (% of total)	40	46	47
Rural population density (per km^2 arable land)	189	219	..
Illiteracy male (% of people 15 and above)	62	55	54
Illiteracy female (% of people 15 and above)	81	74	73
Net primary enrollment (% of relevant age group)	48	60	..
Net secondary enrollment (% of relevant age group)	13	..	..
Girls in primary school (% of enrollment)	42	45	45
Girls in secondary school (% of enrollment)	35	38	..
Environment			
Forests (1,000 sq. km.)	67	..	62
Deforestation (% change 1990-2000)			0.7
Water use (% of total resources)	..	..	3.8
CO$_2$ emissions (metric tons per capita)	0.4	0.4	..
Access to improved water source (% of urban pop.)	90	..	92
Access to sanitation (% of urban population)	86	83	94
Energy use per capita (kg of oil equivalent)	306	312	..
Electricity use per capita (kWh)	95	111	..
Economy			
GDP ($ millions)	5,698	4,666	4,752
GDP growth (annual %)	3.9	5.7	5.1
GDP implicit price deflator (annual % growth)	1.2	1.9	1.1
Value added in agriculture (% of GDP)	19.9	17.4	18.0
Value added in industry (% of GDP)	18.7	24.2	25.5
Value added in services (% of GDP)	61.4	58.4	56.4
Exports of goods and services (% of GDP)	25.4	33.0	32.7
Imports of goods and services (% of GDP)	30.3	38.7	39.1
Gross domestic investment (% of GDP)	13.8	18.6	19.0
Central government revenues (% of GDP)	..	..	..
Overall budget deficit (% of GDP)	..	..	..
Money and quasi money (annual % growth)	-4.8	8.5	13.1
Technology and infrastructure			
Telephone mainlines (per 1,000 people)	6	16	18
Cost of 3 min local call ($)	0.18	0.12	0.12
Personal computers (per 1,000 people)	2.5	13.3	15.1
Internet users (thousands)	..	8	30
Paved roads (% of total)	27	29	..
Aircraft departures (thousands)	4	2	2
Trade and finance			
Trade as share of PPP GDP (%)	22.4	19.5	19.3
Trade growth less GDP growth (average %, 1989-99)			-1.6
High-technology exports (% of manufactured exports)	..	6	13
Net barter terms of trade (1995=100)	116	108	..
Foreign direct investment ($ millions)	57	71	60
Present value of debt ($ millions)			2,495
Total debt service ($ millions)	325	321	237
Short term debt ($ millions)	421	273	308
Aid per capita ($)	112	55	58

SEYCHELLES

Sub-Saharan Africa		Upper middle income	
Population (thousands)	80	Population growth (%)	1.5
Surface area (1,000 sq km)	0	Population per sq km	178
GNI ($ millions)	520	GNI per capita ($)	6,500

	1990	1998	1999
People			
Life expectancy (years)	70	71	72
Fertility rate (births per woman)	2.8	2.1	2.1
Infant mortality rate (per 1,000 live births)	17	9	9
Under 5 mortality rate (per 1,000 children)	21	18	15
Child malnutrition (% of children under 5)	6	6	..
Urban population (% of total)	54	62	63
Rural population density (per km^2 arable land)	3,255	3,003	..
Illiteracy male (% of people 15 and above)	..	..	..
Illiteracy female (% of people 15 and above)	..	..	..
Net primary enrollment (% of relevant age group)	..	..	..
Net secondary enrollment (% of relevant age group)	..	..	..
Girls in primary school (% of enrollment)	49	49	..
Girls in secondary school (% of enrollment)	49	49	..

Environment			
Forests (1,000 sq. km.)	0	..	0
Deforestation (% change 1990-2000)			0.0
Water use (% of total resources)	..	..	
CO_2 emissions (metric tons per capita)	1.6	2.6	..
Access to improved water source (% of urban pop.)	..	99	
Access to sanitation (% of urban population)	..	..	..
Energy use per capita (kg of oil equivalent)	..	..	..
Electricity use per capita (kWh)	..	..	..

Economy			
GDP ($ millions)	369	535	545
GDP growth (annual %)	9.0	2.0	1.5
GDP implicit price deflator (annual % growth)	3.6	2.0	2.0
Value added in agriculture (% of GDP)	4.8	4.1	4.1
Value added in industry (% of GDP)	16.3	23.6	23.9
Value added in services (% of GDP)	78.9	72.4	72.0
Exports of goods and services (% of GDP)	62.5	70.2	70.9
Imports of goods and services (% of GDP)	66.7	87.4	88.5
Gross domestic investment (% of GDP)	24.6	37.5	37.5
Central government revenues (% of GDP)	51.8	50.4	..
Overall budget deficit (% of GDP)	3.3	1.4	..
Money and quasi money (annual % growth)	14.5	20.2	21.7

Technology and infrastructure			
Telephone mainlines (per 1,000 people)	124	248	..
Cost of 3 min local call ($)	0.14	0.16	..
Personal computers (per 1,000 people)	..	124.2	130.5
Internet users (thousands)	..	2	5
Paved roads (% of total)	57	63	..
Aircraft departures (thousands)	16	19	19

Trade and finance			
Trade as share of PPP GDP (%)	..	..	..
Trade growth less GDP growth (average %, 1989-99)			3.3
High-technology exports (% of manufactured exports)	..	..	..
Net barter terms of trade (1995=100)	72	107	..
Foreign direct investment ($ millions)	20	55	60
Present value of debt ($ millions)			154
Total debt service ($ millions)	22	21	26
Short term debt ($ millions)	46	42	40
Aid per capita ($)	513	303	161

SIERRA LEONE

Population (millions)	5	Population growth (%)		1.9
Surface area (1,000 sq km)	72	Population per sq km		69
GNI ($ millions)	653	GNI per capita ($)		130

	1990	1998	1999
People			
Life expectancy (years)	35	*37*	37
Fertility rate (births per woman)	6.5	*6.1*	5.9
Infant mortality rate (per 1,000 live births)	189	*170*	168
Under 5 mortality rate (per 1,000 children)	323	*286*	283
Child malnutrition (% of children under 5)	29	..	..
Urban population (% of total)	30	35	36
Rural population density (per km² arable land)	576	649	..
Illiteracy male (% of people 15 and above)	..	..	..
Illiteracy female (% of people 15 and above)	..	..	..
Net primary enrollment (% of relevant age group)	..	..	..
Net secondary enrollment (% of relevant age group)	..	..	..
Girls in primary school (% of enrollment)	*41*	..	..
Girls in secondary school (% of enrollment)	37	..	..
Environment			
Forests (1,000 sq. km.)	14	..	11
Deforestation (% change 1990-2000)			2.9
Water use (% of total resources)			0.2
CO$_2$ emissions (metric tons per capita)	0.1	*0.1*	..
Access to improved water source (% of urban pop.)	..	..	23
Access to sanitation (% of urban population)	..	..	23
Energy use per capita (kg of oil equivalent)	..	..	..
Electricity use per capita (kWh)	..	..	..
Economy			
GDP ($ millions)	897	672	669
GDP growth (annual %)	4.8	-0.8	-8.1
GDP implicit price deflator (annual % growth)	83.4	27.0	25.0
Value added in agriculture (% of GDP)	47.0	43.7	42.6
Value added in industry (% of GDP)	20.4	23.6	26.7
Value added in services (% of GDP)	32.6	32.7	30.7
Exports of goods and services (% of GDP)	24.0	14.1	13.9
Imports of goods and services (% of GDP)	25.1	21.3	20.2
Gross domestic investment (% of GDP)	9.4	5.3	0.3
Central government revenues (% of GDP)	4.0	*10.2*	..
Overall budget deficit (% of GDP)	-1.8	*-5.8*	..
Money and quasi money (annual % growth)	74.0	11.3	37.8
Technology and infrastructure			
Telephone mainlines (per 1,000 people)	3	4	..
Cost of 3 min local call ($)	0.12	0.03	0.03
Personal computers (per 1,000 people)	..	..	..
Internet users (thousands)	..	1	2
Paved roads (% of total)	11	*8*	..
Aircraft departures (thousands)	1	0	0
Trade and finance			
Trade as share of PPP GDP (%)	8.0	4.3	..
Trade growth less GDP growth (average %, 1989-99)			-4.3
High-technology exports (% of manufactured exports)	..	..	..
Net barter terms of trade (1995=100)	120	99	..
Foreign direct investment ($ millions)	32	5	1
Present value of debt ($ millions)			888
Total debt service ($ millions)	21	20	22
Short term debt ($ millions)	439	108	117
Aid per capita ($)	15	22	15

SINGAPORE

Population (millions)	4	Population growth (%)	1.7
Surface area (1,000 sq km)	1	Population per sq km	6,384
GNI ($ millions)	95,429	GNI per capita ($)	24,150

	1990	1998	1999
People			
Life expectancy (years)	74	77	78
Fertility rate (births per woman)	1.9	1.5	1.5
Infant mortality rate (per 1,000 live births)	7	4	3
Under 5 mortality rate (per 1,000 children)	8	6	4
Child malnutrition (% of children under 5)	..	..	..
Urban population (% of total)	100	100	100
Rural population density (per km^2 arable land)	0	0	..
Illiteracy male (% of people 15 and above)	6	4	4
Illiteracy female (% of people 15 and above)	17	12	12
Net primary enrollment (% of relevant age group)	97	93	..
Net secondary enrollment (% of relevant age group)	..	..	..
Girls in primary school (% of enrollment)	47	48	..
Girls in secondary school (% of enrollment)	47	47	..
Environment			
Forests (1,000 sq. km.)	0	..	0
Deforestation (% change 1990-2000)			0.0
Water use (% of total resources)	..	..	
CO_2 emissions (metric tons per capita)	14.2	21.9	..
Access to improved water source (% of urban pop.)	100	..	100
Access to sanitation (% of urban population)	100	..	100
Energy use per capita (kg of oil equivalent)	4,429	6,285	..
Electricity use per capita (kWh)	4,298	6,771	..
Economy			
GDP ($ millions)	36,638	82,773	84,945
GDP growth (annual %)	9.0	0.4	5.4
GDP implicit price deflator (annual % growth)	4.7	-1.8	-1.3
Value added in agriculture (% of GDP)	0.3	0.2	0.2
Value added in industry (% of GDP)	34.8	35.4	35.8
Value added in services (% of GDP)	64.9	64.5	64.1
Exports of goods and services (% of GDP)	202.0	170.5	..
Imports of goods and services (% of GDP)	195.0	156.8	..
Gross domestic investment (% of GDP)	36.7	32.8	32.8
Central government revenues (% of GDP)	32.6	31.1	..
Overall budget deficit (% of GDP)	10.8	3.4	..
Money and quasi money (annual % growth)	20.0	30.2	8.5
Technology and infrastructure			
Telephone mainlines (per 1,000 people)	349	460	482
Cost of 3 min local call ($)	0.00	0.02	0.02
Personal computers (per 1,000 people)	66.2	374.7	436.6
Internet users (thousands)	5	750	950
Paved roads (% of total)	97	97	100
Aircraft departures (thousands)	31	62	68
Trade and finance			
Trade as share of PPP GDP (%)	290.4	276.2	275.1
Trade growth less GDP growth (average %, 1989-99)			..
High-technology exports (% of manufactured exports)	40	59	61
Net barter terms of trade (1995=100)	111	100	..
Foreign direct investment ($ millions)	..	..	..
Present value of debt ($ millions)			..
Total debt service ($ millions)	..	..	..
Short term debt ($ millions)	..	..	..
Aid per capita ($)	-1	0	0

189

SLOVAK REPUBLIC

Europe & Central Asia   Upper middle income

Population (millions)	5	Population growth (%)		0.1
Surface area (1,000 sq km)	49	Population per sq km		112
GNI ($ millions)	20,318	GNI per capita ($)		3,770

	1990	1998	1999
People			
Life expectancy (years)	71	73	73
Fertility rate (births per woman)	2.1	1.4	1.4
Infant mortality rate (per 1,000 live births)	12	9	8
Under 5 mortality rate (per 1,000 children)	14	10	10
Child malnutrition (% of children under 5)	..	..	..
Urban population (% of total)	57	57	57
Rural population density (per km^2 arable land)	..	157	..
Illiteracy male (% of people 15 and above)	..	..	..
Illiteracy female (% of people 15 and above)	..	..	..
Net primary enrollment (% of relevant age group)	..	..	..
Net secondary enrollment (% of relevant age group)	..	..	..
Girls in primary school (% of enrollment)	..	49	..
Girls in secondary school (% of enrollment)	..	..	..
Environment			
Forests (1,000 sq. km.)	20	..	20
Deforestation (% change 1990-2000)			-0.3
Water use (% of total resources)	..	..	1.7
CO$_2$ emissions (metric tons per capita)	8.1	7.1	..
Access to improved water source (% of urban pop.)	..	..	100
Access to sanitation (% of urban population)	..	..	100
Energy use per capita (kg of oil equivalent)	4,044	3,136	..
Electricity use per capita (kWh)	4,432	3,899	..
Economy			
GDP ($ millions)	15,485	21,308	19,712
GDP growth (annual %)	-2.7	4.1	1.9
GDP implicit price deflator (annual % growth)	6.9	5.1	6.6
Value added in agriculture (% of GDP)	7.4	4.2	4.1
Value added in industry (% of GDP)	59.1	31.9	31.6
Value added in services (% of GDP)	33.5	63.9	64.3
Exports of goods and services (% of GDP)	26.5	61.2	61.5
Imports of goods and services (% of GDP)	35.5	72.2	66.9
Gross domestic investment (% of GDP)	33.2	36.1	31.9
Central government revenues (% of GDP)	..	34.8	37.0
Overall budget deficit (% of GDP)	..	-4.2	-3.3
Money and quasi money (annual % growth)	..	4.9	11.6
Technology and infrastructure			
Telephone mainlines (per 1,000 people)	135	286	307
Cost of 3 min local call ($)	0.03	0.11	0.12
Personal computers (per 1,000 people)	..	87.4	109.3
Internet users (thousands)	..	500	600
Paved roads (% of total)	99	87	87
Aircraft departures (thousands)	..	5	6
Trade and finance			
Trade as share of PPP GDP (%)	..	43.6	37.6
Trade growth less GDP growth (average %, 1989-99)			10.7
High-technology exports (% of manufactured exports)	..	4	5
Net barter terms of trade (1995=100)	..	..	..
Foreign direct investment ($ millions)	0	562	354
Present value of debt ($ millions)			8,475
Total debt service ($ millions)	318	2,040	1,716
Short term debt ($ millions)	503	1,981	1,577
Aid per capita ($)	1	29	59

Population (millions)	2	Population growth (%)	0.1
Surface area (1,000 sq km)	20.3	Population per sq km	99
GNI ($ millions)	19,862	GNI per capita ($)	10,000

	1990	1998	1999
People			
Life expectancy (years)	73	75	75
Fertility rate (births per woman)	1.5	1.2	1.2
Infant mortality rate (per 1,000 live births)	8	5	5
Under 5 mortality rate (per 1,000 children)	10	7	6
Child malnutrition (% of children under 5)	..	..	..
Urban population (% of total)	50	50	50
Rural population density (per km² arable land)	405	427	..
Illiteracy male (% of people 15 and above)	0	0	0
Illiteracy female (% of people 15 and above)	1	0	0
Net primary enrollment (% of relevant age group)	..	95	..
Net secondary enrollment (% of relevant age group)	..	..	..
Girls in primary school (% of enrollment)	..	49	..
Girls in secondary school (% of enrollment)	50	50	..
Environment			
Forests (1,000 sq. km.)	11	..	11
Deforestation (% change 1990-2000)			-0.2
Water use (% of total resources)	..	..	2.7
CO_2 emissions (metric tons per capita)	6.1	7.8	..
Access to improved water source (% of urban pop.)	100	100	100
Access to sanitation (% of urban population)	100	100	..
Energy use per capita (kg of oil equivalent)	2,476	3,354	..
Electricity use per capita (kWh)	4,371	5,096	..
Economy			
GDP ($ millions)	12,673	19,586	20,011
GDP growth (annual %)	-8.9	3.8	4.9
GDP implicit price deflator (annual % growth)	208.0	7.8	6.6
Value added in agriculture (% of GDP)	5.5	4.2	3.7
Value added in industry (% of GDP)	45.6	38.5	38.4
Value added in services (% of GDP)	48.9	57.3	57.8
Exports of goods and services (% of GDP)	83.5	56.6	52.7
Imports of goods and services (% of GDP)	74.2	58.1	56.7
Gross domestic investment (% of GDP)	17.1	25.6	27.9
Central government revenues (% of GDP)	39.8	39.1	39.8
Overall budget deficit (% of GDP)	0.3	-0.8	-0.7
Money and quasi money (annual % growth)	123.0	19.5	15.1
Technology and infrastructure			
Telephone mainlines (per 1,000 people)	211	364	378
Cost of 3 min local call ($)	0.01	0.03	..
Personal computers (per 1,000 people)	32.5	211.1	251.4
Internet users (thousands)	..	200	250
Paved roads (% of total)	72	91	91
Aircraft departures (thousands)	4	10	11
Trade and finance			
Trade as share of PPP GDP (%)	..	64.8	58.5
Trade growth less GDP growth (average %, 1989-99)			0.0
High-technology exports (% of manufactured exports)	..	5	4
Net barter terms of trade (1995=100)	..	..	..
Foreign direct investment ($ millions)	..	..	..
Present value of debt ($ millions)			..
Total debt service ($ millions)	..	..	..
Short term debt ($ millions)	..	..	..
Aid per capita ($)	..	20	16

191

SOLOMON ISLANDS

East Asia and Pacific — Low income

Population (thousands)	429	Population growth (%)		3.0
Surface area (1,000 sq km)	28.9	Population per sq km		15
GNI ($ millions)	320	GNI per capita ($)		750

	1990	1998	1999
People			
Life expectancy (years)	69	..	71
Fertility rate (births per woman)	5.6	..	4.6
Infant mortality rate (per 1,000 live births)	29	..	21
Under 5 mortality rate (per 1,000 children)	36	..	26
Child malnutrition (% of children under 5)	..		
Urban population (% of total)	15	19	19
Rural population density (per km^2 arable land)	685	807	..
Illiteracy male (% of people 15 and above)	..	..	..
Illiteracy female (% of people 15 and above)	..	..	..
Net primary enrollment (% of relevant age group)	..	..	..
Net secondary enrollment (% of relevant age group)	..	..	..
Girls in primary school (% of enrollment)	44	..	..
Girls in secondary school (% of enrollment)	37	..	..
Environment			
Forests (1,000 sq. km.)	26	..	..
Deforestation (% change 1990-2000)			
Water use (% of total resources)	..		
CO_2 emissions (metric tons per capita)	0.5	..	..
Access to improved water source (% of urban pop.)	..	..	..
Access to sanitation (% of urban population)	..	..	..
Energy use per capita (kg of oil equivalent)	..	..	..
Electricity use per capita (kWh)	..	..	..
Economy			
GDP ($ millions)	211	301	304
GDP growth (annual %)	1.8	0.4	-0.5
GDP implicit price deflator (annual % growth)	0.1	4.0	2.2
Value added in agriculture (% of GDP)	..	..	..
Value added in industry (% of GDP)	..	..	..
Value added in services (% of GDP)	..	..	..
Exports of goods and services (% of GDP)	46.8	..	..
Imports of goods and services (% of GDP)	72.8	..	..
Gross domestic investment (% of GDP)	29.0	..	..
Central government revenues (% of GDP)	23.0	..	..
Overall budget deficit (% of GDP)	..	..	..
Money and quasi money (annual % growth)	9.8	2.5	7.0
Technology and infrastructure			
Telephone mainlines (per 1,000 people)	14	19	19
Cost of 3 min local call ($)	0.11	0.09	0.09
Personal computers (per 1,000 people)	..	..	41.9
Internet users (thousands)	..	2	2
Paved roads (% of total)	2	..	..
Aircraft departures (thousands)	11	11	13
Trade and finance			
Trade as share of PPP GDP (%)	28.1	33.7	..
Trade growth less GDP growth (average %, 1989-99)			..
High-technology exports (% of manufactured exports)	..	..	..
Net barter terms of trade (1995=100)	..	..	..
Foreign direct investment ($ millions)	10	9	10
Present value of debt ($ millions)			96
Total debt service ($ millions)	12	12	11
Short term debt ($ millions)	17	3	5
Aid per capita ($)	141	102	93

Population (millions)	9	Population growth (%)	3.4
Surface area (1,000 sq km)	638	Population per sq km	15
GNI ($ millions)	..	GNI per capita ($)	..

	1990	1998	1999
People			
Life expectancy (years)	42	47	48
Fertility rate (births per woman)	7.3	7.3	7.1
Infant mortality rate (per 1,000 live births)	152	122	121
Under 5 mortality rate (per 1,000 children)	215	205	203
Child malnutrition (% of children under 5)	..	..	..
Urban population (% of total)	24	27	27
Rural population density (per km^2 arable land)	577	639	..
Illiteracy male (% of people 15 and above)	..	..	..
Illiteracy female (% of people 15 and above)	..	..	..
Net primary enrollment (% of relevant age group)	..	..	..
Net secondary enrollment (% of relevant age group)	..	..	..
Girls in primary school (% of enrollment)	..	..	..
Girls in secondary school (% of enrollment)	..	..	..
Environment			
Forests (1,000 sq. km.)	83	..	75
Deforestation (% change 1990-2000)			1.0
Water use (% of total resources)	..	..	5.2
CO_2 emissions (metric tons per capita)	0.0	0.0	..
Access to improved water source (% of urban pop.)	..	..	..
Access to sanitation (% of urban population)	..	..	..
Energy use per capita (kg of oil equivalent)	..	..	..
Electricity use per capita (kWh)	..	..	..
Economy			
GDP ($ millions)	917	..	..
GDP growth (annual %)	-1.5	..	..
GDP implicit price deflator (annual % growth)	215.5	..	..
Value added in agriculture (% of GDP)	65.5	..	..
Value added in industry (% of GDP)	..	..	..
Value added in services (% of GDP)	..	..	..
Exports of goods and services (% of GDP)	9.8	..	..
Imports of goods and services (% of GDP)	37.7	..	..
Gross domestic investment (% of GDP)	15.5	..	..
Central government revenues (% of GDP)	..	..	..
Overall budget deficit (% of GDP)	..	..	..
Money and quasi money (annual % growth)	..	..	..
Technology and infrastructure			
Telephone mainlines (per 1,000 people)	2	2	..
Cost of 3 min local call ($)	..	..	..
Personal computers (per 1,000 people)	..	..	..
Internet users (thousands)	..	0	0
Paved roads (% of total)	11	12	..
Aircraft departures (thousands)	2	..	..
Trade and finance			
Trade as share of PPP GDP (%)	..	..	..
Trade growth less GDP growth (average %, 1989-99)			..
High-technology exports (% of manufactured exports)	..	..	..
Net barter terms of trade (1995=100)	99	108	..
Foreign direct investment ($ millions)	6	0	0
Present value of debt ($ millions)			2,320
Total debt service ($ millions)	11	0	1
Short term debt ($ millions)	285	591	593
Aid per capita ($)	63	9	12

SOUTH AFRICA

Sub-Saharan Africa   **Upper middle income**

Population (millions)	42	Population growth (%)	1.7
Surface area (1,000 sq km)	1,221	Population per sq km	34
GNI ($ millions)	133,569	GNI per capita ($)	3,170

	1990	1998	1999
People			
Life expectancy (years)	62	..	48
Fertility rate (births per woman)	3.3	..	2.9
Infant mortality rate (per 1,000 live births)	55	..	62
Under 5 mortality rate (per 1,000 children)	73	..	76
Child malnutrition (% of children under 5)	..	..	..
Urban population (% of total)	49	50	50
Rural population density (per km^2 arable land)	134	140	..
Illiteracy male (% of people 15 and above)	18	15	14
Illiteracy female (% of people 15 and above)	20	16	16
Net primary enrollment (% of relevant age group)	..	..	..
Net secondary enrollment (% of relevant age group)	..	..	..
Girls in primary school (% of enrollment)	50	..	..
Girls in secondary school (% of enrollment)	54	..	..
Environment			
Forests (1,000 sq. km.)	90	..	..
Deforestation (% change 1990-2000)			..
Water use (% of total resources)	..	..	26.6
CO_2 emissions (metric tons per capita)	8.4	..	..
Access to improved water source (% of urban pop.)	..	..	..
Access to sanitation (% of urban population)	..	..	..
Energy use per capita (kg of oil equivalent)	2,592	2,681	..
Electricity use per capita (kWh)	3,676	3,832	..
Economy			
GDP ($ millions)	111,997	133,962	131,127
GDP growth (annual %)	-0.3	0.6	1.2
GDP implicit price deflator (annual % growth)	15.5	7.6	6.9
Value added in agriculture (% of GDP)	4.6	3.8	3.8
Value added in industry (% of GDP)	40.1	32.0	32.4
Value added in services (% of GDP)	55.3	64.2	63.7
Exports of goods and services (% of GDP)	24.4	25.7	25.4
Imports of goods and services (% of GDP)	18.6	24.4	22.9
Gross domestic investment (% of GDP)	11.8	16.2	15.7
Central government revenues (% of GDP)	26.3	27.4	28.3
Overall budget deficit (% of GDP)	-4.1	-2.6	-1.3
Money and quasi money (annual % growth)	11.4	13.7	10.9
Technology and infrastructure			
Telephone mainlines (per 1,000 people)	87	125	125
Cost of 3 min local call ($)	..	0.06	0.08
Personal computers (per 1,000 people)	6.6	51.6	54.7
Internet users (thousands)	..	1,270	1,820
Paved roads (% of total)	30	12	..
Aircraft departures (thousands)	84	93	101
Trade and finance			
Trade as share of PPP GDP (%)	14.3	15.3	14.2
Trade growth less GDP growth (average %, 1989-99)			-1.6
High-technology exports (% of manufactured exports)	..	9	8
Net barter terms of trade (1995=100)	98	100	..
Foreign direct investment ($ millions)	-89	550	1,376
Present value of debt ($ millions)			24,168
Total debt service ($ millions)	..	4,378	4,839
Short term debt ($ millions)	..	11,444	13,780
Aid per capita ($)	..	12	13

Population (millions)	39	Population growth (%)	0.1
Surface area (1,000 sq km)	506	Population per sq km	79
GNI ($ millions)	583,082	GNI per capita ($)	14,800

	1990	1998	1999
People			
Life expectancy (years)	77	78	78
Fertility rate (births per woman)	1.3	1.1	1.2
Infant mortality rate (per 1,000 live births)	8	6	5
Under 5 mortality rate (per 1,000 children)	9	7	6
Child malnutrition (% of children under 5)	..		..
Urban population (% of total)	75	77	77
Rural population density (per km^2 arable land)	62	63	..
Illiteracy male (% of people 15 and above)	2	2	2
Illiteracy female (% of people 15 and above)	5	4	3
Net primary enrollment (% of relevant age group)	103	105	..
Net secondary enrollment (% of relevant age group)	..	..	..
Girls in primary school (% of enrollment)	48	48	..
Girls in secondary school (% of enrollment)	50	50	..
Environment			
Forests (1,000 sq. km.)	135	..	144
Deforestation (% change 1990-2000)			-0.6
Water use (% of total resources)	..	..	31.7
CO_2 emissions (metric tons per capita)	5.8	6.6	..
Access to improved water source (% of urban pop.)	..	..	..
Access to sanitation (% of urban population)	..	..	..
Energy use per capita (kg of oil equivalent)	2,332	2,865	..
Electricity use per capita (kWh)	3,239	4,195	..
Economy			
GDP ($ millions)	513,665	582,137	595,927
GDP growth (annual %)	3.7	4.0	3.7
GDP implicit price deflator (annual % growth)	7.3	2.3	3.1
Value added in agriculture (% of GDP)	..	4.0	3.8
Value added in industry (% of GDP)	..	27.9	27.6
Value added in services (% of GDP)	..	68.1	68.7
Exports of goods and services (% of GDP)	16.1	27.1	27.6
Imports of goods and services (% of GDP)	19.5	26.8	28.4
Gross domestic investment (% of GDP)	26.9	23.1	24.2
Central government revenues (% of GDP)	29.3	28.9	..
Overall budget deficit (% of GDP)	-3.1	-2.9	..
Money and quasi money (annual % growth)	..	..	..
Technology and infrastructure			
Telephone mainlines (per 1,000 people)	316	414	410
Cost of 3 min local call ($)	0.04	0.10	0.09
Personal computers (per 1,000 people)	27.6	109.1	119.4
Internet users (thousands)	10	2,750	4,652
Paved roads (% of total)	74	99	99
Aircraft departures (thousands)	245	388	414
Trade and finance			
Trade as share of PPP GDP (%)	28.6	36.0	35.8
Trade growth less GDP growth (average %, 1989-99)			6.9
High-technology exports (% of manufactured exports)	7	7	8
Net barter terms of trade (1995=100)	96	103	102
Foreign direct investment ($ millions)	..	..	..
Present value of debt ($ millions)			..
Total debt service ($ millions)	..	..	..
Short term debt ($ millions)	..	..	..
Aid per capita ($)	..	..	..

SRI LANKA

Population (millions)	19	Population growth (%)	1.1
Surface area (1,000 sq km)	65.6	Population per sq km	294
GNI ($ millions)	15,578	GNI per capita ($)	820

	1990	1998	1999
People			
Life expectancy (years)	71	73	73
Fertility rate (births per woman)	2.5	2.2	2.1
Infant mortality rate (per 1,000 live births)	19	16	15
Under 5 mortality rate (per 1,000 children)	23	19	19
Child malnutrition (% of children under 5)	..	33	..
Urban population (% of total)	21	23	23
Rural population density (per km^2 arable land)	1,528	1,664	..
Illiteracy male (% of people 15 and above)	7	6	6
Illiteracy female (% of people 15 and above)	15	12	11
Net primary enrollment (% of relevant age group)	..	..	..
Net secondary enrollment (% of relevant age group)	..	..	..
Girls in primary school (% of enrollment)	48	48	..
Girls in secondary school (% of enrollment)	51	51	..
Environment			
Forests (1,000 sq. km.)	23	..	19
Deforestation (% change 1990-2000)			1.6
Water use (% of total resources)	..	..	19.5
CO_2 emissions (metric tons per capita)	0.2	0.4	..
Access to improved water source (% of urban pop.)	90	..	91
Access to sanitation (% of urban population)	93	..	91
Energy use per capita (kg of oil equivalent)	325	389	..
Electricity use per capita (kWh)	153	244	..
Economy			
GDP ($ millions)	8,032	15,401	15,958
GDP growth (annual %)	6.4	4.7	4.3
GDP implicit price deflator (annual % growth)	20.1	9.2	4.6
Value added in agriculture (% of GDP)	26.3	21.1	20.7
Value added in industry (% of GDP)	26.0	27.5	27.3
Value added in services (% of GDP)	47.7	51.4	52.1
Exports of goods and services (% of GDP)	30.2	36.2	35.3
Imports of goods and services (% of GDP)	38.1	42.2	42.6
Gross domestic investment (% of GDP)	22.2	25.1	27.1
Central government revenues (% of GDP)	21.1	17.2	17.6
Overall budget deficit (% of GDP)	-7.8	-8.0	-6.8
Money and quasi money (annual % growth)	21.1	9.6	12.4
Technology and infrastructure			
Telephone mainlines (per 1,000 people)	7	28	36
Cost of 3 min local call ($)	0.02	0.03	0.05
Personal computers (per 1,000 people)	0.2	4.9	5.6
Internet users (thousands)	..	55	65
Paved roads (% of total)	32	95	..
Aircraft departures (thousands)	8	9	10
Trade and finance			
Trade as share of PPP GDP (%)	13.5	18.3	16.9
Trade growth less GDP growth (average %, 1989-99)			2.7
High-technology exports (% of manufactured exports)	1	1	3
Net barter terms of trade (1995=100)	83	122	..
Foreign direct investment ($ millions)	43	193	177
Present value of debt ($ millions)			7,062
Total debt service ($ millions)	383	443	535
Short term debt ($ millions)	405	435	946
Aid per capita ($)	43	26	13

196

Latin America & Caribbean   **Upper middle income**

Population (thousands)	41	Population growth (%)		0.1
Surface area (1,000 sq km)	0.4	Population per sq km		114
GNI ($ millions)	259	GNI per capita ($)		6,330

	1990	1998	1999
People			
Life expectancy (years)	67	70	71
Fertility rate (births per woman)	2.7	2.4	2.3
Infant mortality rate (per 1,000 live births)	26	22	20
Under 5 mortality rate (per 1,000 children)	..	..	..
Child malnutrition (% of children under 5)	..	..	..
Urban population (% of total)	35	34	34
Rural population density (per km^2 arable land)	344	449	..
Illiteracy male (% of people 15 and above)	..	..	..
Illiteracy female (% of people 15 and above)	..	..	..
Net primary enrollment (% of relevant age group)	..	..	..
Net secondary enrollment (% of relevant age group)	..	..	..
Girls in primary school (% of enrollment)	48	49	..
Girls in secondary school (% of enrollment)	51	..	..
Environment			
Forests (1,000 sq. km.)	0	..	0
Deforestation (% change 1990-2000)			0.0
Water use (% of total resources)	..	..	
CO_2 emissions (metric tons per capita)	1.6	2.5	..
Access to improved water source (% of urban pop.)	..	..	..
Access to sanitation (% of urban population)	..	..	..
Energy use per capita (kg of oil equivalent)	..	..	..
Electricity use per capita (kWh)	..	..	..
Economy			
GDP ($ millions)	159	287	301
GDP growth (annual %)	2.3	1.1	2.8
GDP implicit price deflator (annual % growth)	8.7	3.3	1.8
Value added in agriculture (% of GDP)	6.5	4.2	3.7
Value added in industry (% of GDP)	28.9	24.4	25.7
Value added in services (% of GDP)	64.6	71.4	70.7
Exports of goods and services (% of GDP)	51.7	53.8	48.3
Imports of goods and services (% of GDP)	83.1	69.9	69.8
Gross domestic investment (% of GDP)	55.4	43.0	37.4
Central government revenues (% of GDP)	28.6	30.4	..
Overall budget deficit (% of GDP)	0.0	1.1	..
Money and quasi money (annual % growth)	7.7	11.1	3.8
Technology and infrastructure			
Telephone mainlines (per 1,000 people)	237	471	518
Cost of 3 min local call ($)	..	0.02	..
Personal computers (per 1,000 people)	..	128.2	154.6
Internet users (thousands)	..	2	2
Paved roads (% of total)	39	43	..
Aircraft departures (thousands)	..	..	..
Trade and finance			
Trade as share of PPP GDP (%)	54.2	43.6	..
Trade growth less GDP growth (average %, 1989-99)			-1.5
High-technology exports (% of manufactured exports)	..	1	..
Net barter terms of trade (1995=100)	..	..	..
Foreign direct investment ($ millions)	49	34	77
Present value of debt ($ millions)			109
Total debt service ($ millions)	3	11	17
Short term debt ($ millions)	1	2	2
Aid per capita ($)	187	161	114

St. Lucia

Latin America & Caribbean | **Upper middle income**

Population (thousands)	154	Population growth (%)	1.5
Surface area (1,000 sq km)	0.6	Population per sq km	253
GNI ($ millions)	590	GNI per capita ($)	3,820

	1990	1998	1999
People			
Life expectancy (years)	71	71	72
Fertility rate (births per woman)	3.3	2.5	2.4
Infant mortality rate (per 1,000 live births)	19	17	16
Under 5 mortality rate (per 1,000 children)	24	21	19
Child malnutrition (% of children under 5)	..	..	..
Urban population (% of total)	37	38	38
Rural population density (per km^2 arable land)	1,684	3,163	..
Illiteracy male (% of people 15 and above)	..	..	..
Illiteracy female (% of people 15 and above)	..	..	..
Net primary enrollment (% of relevant age group)	..	..	..
Net secondary enrollment (% of relevant age group)	..	..	..
Girls in primary school (% of enrollment)	*49*	*49*	..
Girls in secondary school (% of enrollment)	59	*56*	..
Environment			
Forests (1,000 sq. km.)	0	..	*0*
Deforestation (% change 1990-2000)			*4.3*
Water use (% of total resources)	..	..	
CO$_2$ emissions (metric tons per capita)	1.2	*1.3*	..
Access to improved water source (% of urban pop.)	..	..	..
Access to sanitation (% of urban population)	..	..	..
Energy use per capita (kg of oil equivalent)	..	..	..
Electricity use per capita (kWh)	..	..	..
Economy			
GDP ($ millions)	397	623	652
GDP growth (annual %)	23.5	2.9	3.1
GDP implicit price deflator (annual % growth)	3.2	4.1	1.5
Value added in agriculture (% of GDP)	14.5	9.5	8.4
Value added in industry (% of GDP)	18.1	19.8	20.6
Value added in services (% of GDP)	67.3	70.7	71.1
Exports of goods and services (% of GDP)	72.6	63.9	57.9
Imports of goods and services (% of GDP)	84.2	68.1	68.3
Gross domestic investment (% of GDP)	25.8	23.9	26.4
Central government revenues (% of GDP)	24.7	..	..
Overall budget deficit (% of GDP)	-0.1	..	..
Money and quasi money (annual % growth)	12.5	10.7	9.0
Technology and infrastructure			
Telephone mainlines (per 1,000 people)	127	266	..
Cost of 3 min local call ($)	..	*0.30*	..
Personal computers (per 1,000 people)	..	131.6	138.2
Internet users (thousands)	..	2	3
Paved roads (% of total)	5	*5*	..
Aircraft departures (thousands)	..	..	..
Trade and finance			
Trade as share of PPP GDP (%)	67.8	47.3	..
Trade growth less GDP growth (average %, 1989-99)			-2.7
High-technology exports (% of manufactured exports)	..	6	..
Net barter terms of trade (1995=100)	..	..	..
Foreign direct investment ($ millions)	45	84	87
Present value of debt ($ millions)			161
Total debt service ($ millions)	6	16	19
Short term debt ($ millions)	7	57	55
Aid per capita ($)	90	40	166

Latin America & Caribbean — **Lower middle income**

Population (thousands)	114	Population growth (%)	0.8
Surface area (1,000 sq km)	0	Population per sq km	293
GNI ($ millions)	301	GNI per capita ($)	2,640

	1990	1998	1999
People			
Life expectancy (years)	70	..	73
Fertility rate (births per woman)	2.6	..	2.2
Infant mortality rate (per 1,000 live births)	21	22	20
Under 5 mortality rate (per 1,000 children)	26	..	19
Child malnutrition (% of children under 5)	..	..	..
Urban population (% of total)	41	52	53
Rural population density (per km^2 arable land)	1,590	1,355	..
Illiteracy male (% of people 15 and above)	..	..	..
Illiteracy female (% of people 15 and above)	..	..	..
Net primary enrollment (% of relevant age group)	..	..	..
Net secondary enrollment (% of relevant age group)	..	..	..
Girls in primary school (% of enrollment)	..	..	..
Girls in secondary school (% of enrollment)	55	..	..
Environment			
Forests (1,000 sq. km.)	0	..	..
Deforestation (% change 1990-2000)			..
Water use (% of total resources)	..	..	..
CO$_2$ emissions (metric tons per capita)	0.8	..	..
Access to improved water source (% of urban pop.)	..	..	..
Access to sanitation (% of urban population)	..	..	..
Energy use per capita (kg of oil equivalent)	..	..	..
Electricity use per capita (kWh)	..	..	..
Economy			
GDP ($ millions)	198	316	329
GDP growth (annual %)	5.0	5.7	4.0
GDP implicit price deflator (annual % growth)	6.4	1.9	-0.1
Value added in agriculture (% of GDP)	21.2	10.8	10.4
Value added in industry (% of GDP)	22.9	26.9	25.8
Value added in services (% of GDP)	55.9	62.3	63.8
Exports of goods and services (% of GDP)	65.8	50.2	52.0
Imports of goods and services (% of GDP)	76.8	71.3	70.8
Gross domestic investment (% of GDP)	29.7	31.8	32.6
Central government revenues (% of GDP)	25.6	30.5	30.5
Overall budget deficit (% of GDP)	-2.4	-3.3	-5.9
Money and quasi money (annual % growth)	14.0	15.4	16.5
Technology and infrastructure			
Telephone mainlines (per 1,000 people)	124	188	209
Cost of 3 min local call ($)	0.09	0.09	0.09
Personal computers (per 1,000 people)	..	89.3	97.3
Internet users (thousands)	..	2	3
Paved roads (% of total)	28	..	..
Aircraft departures (thousands)	..	..	..
Trade and finance			
Trade as share of PPP GDP (%)	56.1	43.3	41.3
Trade growth less GDP growth (average %, 1989-99)			-3.3
High-technology exports (% of manufactured exports)	..	..	..
Net barter terms of trade (1995=100)	..	..	..
Foreign direct investment ($ millions)	8	28	25
Present value of debt ($ millions)			148
Total debt service ($ millions)	4	12	14
Short term debt ($ millions)	2	28	32
Aid per capita ($)	140	181	143

SUDAN

Population (millions)	29	Population growth (%)		2.3
Surface area (1,000 sq km)	2,505.8	Population per sq km		12
GNI ($ millions)	9,435	GNI per capita ($)		330

	1990	1998	1999
People			
Life expectancy (years)	51	55	56
Fertility rate (births per woman)	5.2	4.6	4.5
Infant mortality rate (per 1,000 live births)	85	71	67
Under 5 mortality rate (per 1,000 children)	125	115	109
Child malnutrition (% of children under 5)	..	34	
Urban population (% of total)	27	34	35
Rural population density (per km^2 arable land)	136	112	..
Illiteracy male (% of people 15 and above)	39	32	31
Illiteracy female (% of people 15 and above)	68	57	55
Net primary enrollment (% of relevant age group)	..	..	..
Net secondary enrollment (% of relevant age group)	..	..	..
Girls in primary school (% of enrollment)	43	45	..
Girls in secondary school (% of enrollment)	43	47	..
Environment			
Forests (1,000 sq. km.)	712	..	616
Deforestation (% change 1990-2000)			1.4
Water use (% of total resources)	..	..	11.6
CO_2 emissions (metric tons per capita)	0.1	0.1	..
Access to improved water source (% of urban pop.)	86	..	86
Access to sanitation (% of urban population)	87	..	87
Energy use per capita (kg of oil equivalent)	442	526	..
Electricity use per capita (kWh)	52	47	..
Economy			
GDP ($ millions)	13,167	10,018	9,718
GDP growth (annual %)	-0.4	6.1	5.2
GDP implicit price deflator (annual % growth)	62.4	17.1	16.0
Value added in agriculture (% of GDP)	..	39.8	..
Value added in industry (% of GDP)	..	18.4	..
Value added in services (% of GDP)	..	41.8	..
Exports of goods and services (% of GDP)	..	..	..
Imports of goods and services (% of GDP)	..	..	..
Gross domestic investment (% of GDP)	..	..	..
Central government revenues (% of GDP)	..	..	..
Overall budget deficit (% of GDP)	..	..	..
Money and quasi money (annual % growth)	48.8	29.9	23.5
Technology and infrastructure			
Telephone mainlines (per 1,000 people)	3	6	9
Cost of 3 min local call ($)	0.11	0.02	0.02
Personal computers (per 1,000 people)	..	1.9	2.9
Internet users (thousands)	..	2	5
Paved roads (% of total)	34	36	..
Aircraft departures (thousands)	9	4	7
Trade and finance			
Trade as share of PPP GDP (%)	..	..	..
Trade growth less GDP growth (average %, 1989-99)			..
High-technology exports (% of manufactured exports)	..	0	..
Net barter terms of trade (1995=100)	123	93	..
Foreign direct investment ($ millions)	0	371	371
Present value of debt ($ millions)			15,126
Total debt service ($ millions)	50	61	57
Short term debt ($ millions)	4,155	6,349	6,069
Aid per capita ($)	34	7	8

Latin America & Caribbean   **Lower middle income**

Population (thousands)	413	Population growth (%)	0.3
Surface area (1,000 sq km)	163.3	Population per sq km	3
GNI ($ millions)	..	GNI per capita ($)	..

	1990	1998	1999
People			
Life expectancy (years)	69	..	70
Fertility rate (births per woman)	2.6	..	24
Infant mortality rate (per 1,000 live births)	34	..	27
Under 5 mortality rate (per 1,000 children)	38	..	34
Child malnutrition (% of children under 5)	..	..	..
Urban population (% of total)	66	73	73
Rural population density (per km^2 arable land)	243	198	..
Illiteracy male (% of people 15 and above)	..	..	..
Illiteracy female (% of people 15 and above)	..	..	..
Net primary enrollment (% of relevant age group)	..	..	..
Net secondary enrollment (% of relevant age group)	..	..	..
Girls in primary school (% of enrollment)	..	..	..
Girls in secondary school (% of enrollment)	53	..	..
Environment			
Forests (1,000 sq. km.)	141	..	..
Deforestation (% change 1990-2000)			..
Water use (% of total resources)	..	..	0.2
CO$_2$ emissions (metric tons per capita)	4.6	..	..
Access to improved water source (% of urban pop.)	..	..	..
Access to sanitation (% of urban population)	..	..	..
Energy use per capita (kg of oil equivalent)	..	..	..
Electricity use per capita (kWh)	..	..	..
Economy			
GDP ($ millions)	317	808	..
GDP growth (annual %)	0.1	3.9	-1.0
GDP implicit price deflator (annual % growth)	13.7	27.2	180.1
Value added in agriculture (% of GDP)	11.2	6.3	..
Value added in industry (% of GDP)	27.3	21.1	..
Value added in services (% of GDP)	61.5	72.6	..
Exports of goods and services (% of GDP)	28.2	20.8	..
Imports of goods and services (% of GDP)	27.4	24.8	..
Gross domestic investment (% of GDP)	21.4	12.7	11.9
Central government revenues (% of GDP)	..	..	..
Overall budget deficit (% of GDP)	..	..	..
Money and quasi money (annual % growth)	4.3	37.8	37.2
Technology and infrastructure			
Telephone mainlines (per 1,000 people)	92	163	171
Cost of 3 min local call ($)	0.06	0.01	0.06
Personal computers (per 1,000 people)	..	..	..
Internet users (thousands)		7	10
Paved roads (% of total)	24	..	..
Aircraft departures (thousands)	2	6	6
Trade and finance			
Trade as share of PPP GDP (%)	90.2	57.6	..
Trade growth less GDP growth (average %, 1989-99)			-3.3
High-technology exports (% of manufactured exports)	..	1	..
Net barter terms of trade (1995=100)	113	104	..
Foreign direct investment ($ millions)	..	..	..
Present value of debt ($ millions)			..
Total debt service ($ millions)	..	..	..
Short term debt ($ millions)	..	..	..
Aid per capita ($)	153	143	87

SWAZILAND

Sub-Saharan Africa   **Lower middle income**

Population (millions)	1	Population growth (%)	2.9
Surface area (1,000 sq km)	17	Population per sq km	59
GNI ($ millions)	1,379	GNI per capita ($)	1,350

	1990	1998	1999
People			
Life expectancy (years)	57	..	46
Fertility rate (births per woman)	5.3	..	4.5
Infant mortality rate (per 1,000 live births)	79	..	64
Under 5 mortality rate (per 1,000 children)	115	..	113
Child malnutrition (% of children under 5)	..	..	..
Urban population (% of total)	24	26	26
Rural population density (per km^2 arable land)	326	437	..
Illiteracy male (% of people 15 and above)	26	21	20
Illiteracy female (% of people 15 and above)	30	23	22
Net primary enrollment (% of relevant age group)	88	..	..
Net secondary enrollment (% of relevant age group)	..	..	..
Girls in primary school (% of enrollment)	50	49	..
Girls in secondary school (% of enrollment)	..	50	..
Environment			
Forests (1,000 sq. km.)	5	..	..
Deforestation (% change 1990-2000)			..
Water use (% of total resources)	..	..	14.7
CO$_2$ emissions (metric tons per capita)	0.6	..	..
Access to improved water source (% of urban pop.)	..	..	..
Access to sanitation (% of urban population)	..	..	..
Energy use per capita (kg of oil equivalent)	..	..	..
Electricity use per capita (kWh)	..	..	..
Economy			
GDP ($ millions)	860	1,221	1,223
GDP growth (annual %)	8.9	2.0	2.0
GDP implicit price deflator (annual % growth)	7.6	8.5	9.5
Value added in agriculture (% of GDP)	13.7	16.0	15.8
Value added in industry (% of GDP)	43.4	38.7	38.5
Value added in services (% of GDP)	42.8	45.3	45.7
Exports of goods and services (% of GDP)	76.8	101.5	106.7
Imports of goods and services (% of GDP)	76.0	94.6	98.5
Gross domestic investment (% of GDP)	19.6	12.3	12.9
Central government revenues (% of GDP)	33.5	..	..
Overall budget deficit (% of GDP)	0.0	..	..
Money and quasi money (annual % growth)	0.6	12.9	15.6
Technology and infrastructure			
Telephone mainlines (per 1,000 people)	17	30	31
Cost of 3 min local call ($)	0.05	..	0.05
Personal computers (per 1,000 people)	..	..	..
Internet users (thousands)	..	1	5
Paved roads (% of total)	54	..	..
Aircraft departures (thousands)	1	2	1
Trade and finance			
Trade as share of PPP GDP (%)	42.7	46.6	47.4
Trade growth less GDP growth (average %, 1989-99)			-3.1
High-technology exports (% of manufactured exports)	..	..	..
Net barter terms of trade (1995=100)	116	82	..
Foreign direct investment ($ millions)	30	124	33
Present value of debt ($ millions)			212
Total debt service ($ millions)	47	23	31
Short term debt ($ millions)	5	28	53
Aid per capita ($)	70	31	28

Population (millions)	9	Population growth (%)	0.1
Surface area (1,000 sq km)	450	Population per sq km	22
GNI ($ millions)	236,940	GNI per capita ($)	26,750

	1990	1998	1999
People			
Life expectancy (years)	78	79	79
Fertility rate (births per woman)	2.1	1.5	1.5
Infant mortality rate (per 1,000 live births)	6	4	4
Under 5 mortality rate (per 1,000 children)	6	5	4
Child malnutrition (% of children under 5)	..	..	..
Urban population (% of total)	83	83	83
Rural population density (per km^2 arable land)	51	53	..
Illiteracy male (% of people 15 and above)	..	..	..
Illiteracy female (% of people 15 and above)	..	..	..
Net primary enrollment (% of relevant age group)	100	102	..
Net secondary enrollment (% of relevant age group)	85	99	..
Girls in primary school (% of enrollment)	49	50	..
Girls in secondary school (% of enrollment)	50	54	..
Environment			
Forests (1,000 sq. km.)	271	..	271
Deforestation (% change 1990-2000)			0.0
Water use (% of total resources)	..	..	1.5
CO$_2$ emissions (metric tons per capita)	5.8	5.5	..
Access to improved water source (% of urban pop.)	100	..	100
Access to sanitation (% of urban population)	100	..	100
Energy use per capita (kg of oil equivalent)	5,579	5,928	..
Electricity use per capita (kWh)	14,061	13,955	..
Economy			
GDP ($ millions)	237,928	237,765	238,682
GDP growth (annual %)	1.4	3.0	3.8
GDP implicit price deflator (annual % growth)	8.8	1.3	0.5
Value added in agriculture (% of GDP)	3.0	2.0	..
Value added in industry (% of GDP)	28.1	26.5	..
Value added in services (% of GDP)	68.9	71.5	..
Exports of goods and services (% of GDP)	30.1	43.8	43.8
Imports of goods and services (% of GDP)	29.5	37.5	38.2
Gross domestic investment (% of GDP)	23.7	16.7	16.9
Central government revenues (% of GDP)	42.7	39.0	40.1
Overall budget deficit (% of GDP)	1.0	-0.5	0.1
Money and quasi money (annual % growth)	..	..	..
Technology and infrastructure			
Telephone mainlines (per 1,000 people)	681	674	665
Cost of 3 min local call ($)	0.03	0.13	..
Personal computers (per 1,000 people)	104.8	395.5	451.4
Internet users (thousands)	100	2,960	3,666
Paved roads (% of total)	71	78	..
Aircraft departures (thousands)	208	223	237
Trade and finance			
Trade as share of PPP GDP (%)	71.6	80.8	76.5
Trade growth less GDP growth (average %, 1989-99)			4.6
High-technology exports (% of manufactured exports)	14	21	22
Net barter terms of trade (1995=100)	97	99	96
Foreign direct investment ($ millions)	..	..	..
Present value of debt ($ millions)			..
Total debt service ($ millions)	..	..	..
Short term debt ($ millions)	..	..	..
Aid per capita ($)			..

SWITZERLAND

Population (millions)	7	Population growth (%)	0.4
Surface area (1,000 sq km)	41	Population per sq km	180
GNI ($ millions)	273,856	GNI per capita ($)	38,380

	1990	1998	1999
People			
Life expectancy (years)	77	79	80
Fertility rate (births per woman)	1.6	1.5	1.5
Infant mortality rate (per 1,000 live births)	7	5	5
Under 5 mortality rate (per 1,000 children)	8	6	5
Child malnutrition (% of children under 5)	..	..	
Urban population (% of total)	60	68	68
Rural population density (per km^2 arable land)	692	553	..
Illiteracy male (% of people 15 and above)		..	
Illiteracy female (% of people 15 and above)		..	
Net primary enrollment (% of relevant age group)	84	90	..
Net secondary enrollment (% of relevant age group)	80	84	..
Girls in primary school (% of enrollment)	49	49	..
Girls in secondary school (% of enrollment)	47	47	..
Environment			
Forests (1,000 sq. km.)	12	..	12
Deforestation (% change 1990-2000)			-0.4
Water use (% of total resources)	..	..	4.9
CO_2 emissions (metric tons per capita)	6.7	6.0	..
Access to improved water source (% of urban pop.)	100	100	100
Access to sanitation (% of urban population)	100	..	100
Energy use per capita (kg of oil equivalent)	3,724	3,742	..
Electricity use per capita (kWh)	6,997	6,980	..
Economy			
GDP ($ millions)	228,415	262,110	258,550
GDP growth (annual %)	3.7	2.1	1.5
GDP implicit price deflator (annual % growth)	4.3	0.2	0.7
Value added in agriculture (% of GDP)	..	..	..
Value added in industry (% of GDP)	..	..	..
Value added in services (% of GDP)	..	..	..
Exports of goods and services (% of GDP)	36.3	40.2	..
Imports of goods and services (% of GDP)	35.7	36.4	..
Gross domestic investment (% of GDP)	28.3	21.2	..
Central government revenues (% of GDP)	20.8	24.8	..
Overall budget deficit (% of GDP)	-0.9	0.5	..
Money and quasi money (annual % growth)	0.8	5.1	13.3
Technology and infrastructure			
Telephone mainlines (per 1,000 people)	574	686	699
Cost of 3 min local call ($)	0.14	0.13	0.13
Personal computers (per 1,000 people)	87.3	421.3	461.9
Internet users (thousands)	40	853	1,427
Paved roads (% of total)	..		
Aircraft departures (thousands)	152	250	276
Trade and finance			
Trade as share of PPP GDP (%)	82.0	84.9	82.7
Trade growth less GDP growth (average %, 1989-99)			2.0
High-technology exports (% of manufactured exports)	16	19	22
Net barter terms of trade (1995=100)	..	..	..
Foreign direct investment ($ millions)	..	..	..
Present value of debt ($ millions)			..
Total debt service ($ millions)	..	..	..
Short term debt ($ millions)	..	..	..
Aid per capita ($)	..	..	..

204

SYRIAN ARAB REPUBLIC

Population (millions)	16	Population growth (%)	2.6
Surface area (1,000 sq km)	185	Population per sq km	85
GNI ($ millions)	15,172	GNI per capita ($)	970

	1990	1998	1999
People			
Life expectancy (years)	66	..	69
Fertility rate (births per woman)	5.3	..	3.7
Infant mortality rate (per 1,000 live births)	39	28	26
Under 5 mortality rate (per 1,000 children)	..	32	30
Child malnutrition (% of children under 5)	..	..	..
Urban population (% of total)	50	54	54
Rural population density (per km^2 arable land)	124	151	..
Illiteracy male (% of people 15 and above)	18	13	12
Illiteracy female (% of people 15 and above)	53	42	41
Net primary enrollment (% of relevant age group)	98	..	..
Net secondary enrollment (% of relevant age group)	46	..	..
Girls in primary school (% of enrollment)	..	47	..
Girls in secondary school (% of enrollment)	41	..	..
Environment			
Forests (1,000 sq. km.)	5	..	..
Deforestation (% change 1990-2000)			..
Water use (% of total resources)	..	..	32.2
CO_2 emissions (metric tons per capita)	3.1	..	..
Access to improved water source (% of urban pop.)	..	..	..
Access to sanitation (% of urban population)	..	..	..
Energy use per capita (kg of oil equivalent)	985	1,133	..
Electricity use per capita (kWh)	683	838	..
Economy			
GDP ($ millions)	12,309	17,412	19,380
GDP growth (annual %)	7.6	5.0	5.3
GDP implicit price deflator (annual % growth)	19.3	7.0	5.8
Value added in agriculture (% of GDP)	28.5	..	..
Value added in industry (% of GDP)	23.9	..	..
Value added in services (% of GDP)	47.6	..	..
Exports of goods and services (% of GDP)	27.7	29.0	28.9
Imports of goods and services (% of GDP)	27.4	40.2	40.2
Gross domestic investment (% of GDP)	15.4	29.5	29.5
Central government revenues (% of GDP)	21.9	21.7	..
Overall budget deficit (% of GDP)	0.3	-0.7	..
Money and quasi money (annual % growth)	26.1	10.5	13.4
Technology and infrastructure			
Telephone mainlines (per 1,000 people)	40	95	99
Cost of 3 min local call ($)	0.02	0.05	0.01
Personal computers (per 1,000 people)	..	13.1	14.3
Internet users (thousands)	0	10	20
Paved roads (% of total)	..	..	..
Aircraft departures (thousands)	11	10	11
Trade and finance			
Trade as share of PPP GDP (%)	22.0	11.8	10.4
Trade growth less GDP growth (average %, 1989-99)			-6.0
High-technology exports (% of manufactured exports)	..	..	..
Net barter terms of trade (1995=100)	131	90	..
Foreign direct investment ($ millions)	71	80	91
Present value of debt ($ millions)			21,913
Total debt service ($ millions)	1,269	339	370
Short term debt ($ millions)	2,151	6,107	6,227
Aid per capita ($)	56	10	15

TAJIKISTAN

Low income

Population (millions)	6	Population growth (%)	2.0
Surface area (1,000 sq km)	143	Population per sq km	44
GNI ($ millions)	1,749	GNI per capita ($)	280

	1990	1998	1999
People			
Life expectancy (years)	69	..	69
Fertility rate (births per woman)	5.1	..	3.3
Infant mortality rate (per 1,000 live births)	41	23	20
Under 5 mortality rate (per 1,000 children)	..	..	34
Child malnutrition (% of children under 5)	..	..	..
Urban population (% of total)	32	28	28
Rural population density (per km^2 arable land)	..	583	..
Illiteracy male (% of people 15 and above)	1	1	1
Illiteracy female (% of people 15 and above)	3	1	1
Net primary enrollment (% of relevant age group)	..	..	..
Net secondary enrollment (% of relevant age group)	..	..	..
Girls in primary school (% of enrollment)	..	..	..
Girls in secondary school (% of enrollment)	..	..	..
Environment			
Forests (1,000 sq. km.)	4	..	..
Deforestation (% change 1990-2000)			..
Water use (% of total resources)	..	..	14.9
CO_2 emissions (metric tons per capita)	..	..	..
Access to improved water source (% of urban pop.)	..	..	..
Access to sanitation (% of urban population)	..	..	..
Energy use per capita (kg of oil equivalent)	..	532	..
Electricity use per capita (kWh)	..	2,045	..
Economy			
GDP ($ millions)	..	1,779	1,870
GDP growth (annual %)	..	5.3	3.7
GDP implicit price deflator (annual % growth)	..	54.1	26.5
Value added in agriculture (% of GDP)	..	22.1	18.7
Value added in industry (% of GDP)	..	22.2	24.6
Value added in services (% of GDP)	..	55.8	56.7
Exports of goods and services (% of GDP)	..	49.9	68.4
Imports of goods and services (% of GDP)	..	57.6	63.5
Gross domestic investment (% of GDP)	..	8.7	8.6
Central government revenues (% of GDP)	..	9.3	..
Overall budget deficit (% of GDP)	..	-2.5	..
Money and quasi money (annual % growth)	..	..	..
Technology and infrastructure			
Telephone mainlines (per 1,000 people)	45	37	35
Cost of 3 min local call ($)	0.00	0.00	..
Personal computers (per 1,000 people)	..	..	..
Internet users (thousands)	..	..	2
Paved roads (% of total)	72	..	..
Aircraft departures (thousands)	..	5	4
Trade and finance			
Trade as share of PPP GDP (%)	..	..	..
Trade growth less GDP growth (average %, 1989-99)			..
High-technology exports (% of manufactured exports)	..	..	..
Net barter terms of trade (1995=100)	..	..	..
Foreign direct investment ($ millions)	0	30	24
Present value of debt ($ millions)			684
Total debt service ($ millions)	..	83	48
Short term debt ($ millions)	..	147	91
Aid per capita ($)	..	17	20

Sub-Saharan Africa   **Low income**

Population (millions)	33	Population growth (%)	2.4
Surface area (1,000 sq km)	945	Population per sq km	37
GNI ($ millions)	8,515	GNI per capita ($)	260

	1990	1998	1999
People			
Life expectancy (years)	50	..	45
Fertility rate (births per woman)	6.3	5.6	5.4
Infant mortality rate (per 1,000 live births)	115	..	95
Under 5 mortality rate (per 1,000 children)	..	..	152
Child malnutrition (% of children under 5)	..	..	..
Urban population (% of total)	21	31	32
Rural population density (per km^2 arable land)	576	595	..
Illiteracy male (% of people 15 and above)	23	17	16
Illiteracy female (% of people 15 and above)	49	36	34
Net primary enrollment (% of relevant age group)	51	..	..
Net secondary enrollment (% of relevant age group)	..	..	..
Girls in primary school (% of enrollment)	50	..	..
Girls in secondary school (% of enrollment)	42	..	..
Environment			
Forests (1,000 sq. km.)	397	..	..
Deforestation (% change 1990-2000)			..
Water use (% of total resources)	..	..	1.3
CO_2 emissions (metric tons per capita)	0.1	..	..
Access to improved water source (% of urban pop.)	80	..	..
Access to sanitation (% of urban population)	97	..	..
Energy use per capita (kg of oil equivalent)	492	456	..
Electricity use per capita (kWh)	51	53	..
Economy			
GDP ($ millions)	4,259	8,591	8,760
GDP growth (annual %)	7.0	4.0	4.7
GDP implicit price deflator (annual % growth)	22.4	16.7	9.1
Value added in agriculture (% of GDP)	46.0	44.8	44.8
Value added in industry (% of GDP)	17.7	15.4	15.4
Value added in services (% of GDP)	36.4	39.8	39.8
Exports of goods and services (% of GDP)	12.6	12.8	13.3
Imports of goods and services (% of GDP)	37.5	26.9	28.0
Gross domestic investment (% of GDP)	26.1	16.5	17.0
Central government revenues (% of GDP)	..	..	..
Overall budget deficit (% of GDP)	..	..	..
Money and quasi money (annual % growth)	41.9	10.8	18.6
Technology and infrastructure			
Telephone mainlines (per 1,000 people)	3	4	5
Cost of 3 min local call ($)	0.01	0.09	0.08
Personal computers (per 1,000 people)	..	1.7	2.4
Internet users (thousands)	..	3	25
Paved roads (% of total)	37	..	..
Aircraft departures (thousands)	8	6	5
Trade and finance			
Trade as share of PPP GDP (%)	12.4	13.9	14.3
Trade growth less GDP growth (average %, 1989-99)			-2.9
High-technology exports (% of manufactured exports)	..	3	6
Net barter terms of trade (1995=100)	105	91	..
Foreign direct investment ($ millions)	0	172	183
Present value of debt ($ millions)			4,613
Total debt service ($ millions)	179	246	194
Short term debt ($ millions)	518	900	1,028
Aid per capita ($)	46	31	30

THAILAND

Population (millions)	60	Population growth (%)		0.8
Surface area (1,000 sq km)	513	Population per sq km		118
GNI ($ millions)	121,051	GNI per capita ($)		2,010

	1990	1998	1999
People			
Life expectancy (years)	69	..	69
Fertility rate (births per woman)	2.3	..	1.9
Infant mortality rate (per 1,000 live births)	37	..	28
Under 5 mortality rate (per 1,000 children)	41	..	33
Child malnutrition (% of children under 5)	..	..	..
Urban population (% of total)	19	21	21
Rural population density (per km^2 arable land)	258	281	..
Illiteracy male (% of people 15 and above)	5	3	3
Illiteracy female (% of people 15 and above)	11	7	7
Net primary enrollment (% of relevant age group)	..	..	..
Net secondary enrollment (% of relevant age group)	..	..	..
Girls in primary school (% of enrollment)	..	..	..
Girls in secondary school (% of enrollment)	48	..	..
Environment			
Forests (1,000 sq. km.)	159	..	..
Deforestation (% change 1990-2000)			..
Water use (% of total resources)	..	..	8.1
CO_2 emissions (metric tons per capita)	1.9	..	..
Access to improved water source (% of urban pop.)	83	..	..
Access to sanitation (% of urban population)	97	..	..
Energy use per capita (kg of oil equivalent)	784	1,153	..
Electricity use per capita (kWh)	690	1,345	..
Economy			
GDP ($ millions)	85,345	112,090	124,369
GDP growth (annual %)	11.2	-10.2	4.2
GDP implicit price deflator (annual % growth)	5.8	9.2	-2.6
Value added in agriculture (% of GDP)	12.5	11.9	10.5
Value added in industry (% of GDP)	37.2	38.8	40.0
Value added in services (% of GDP)	50.3	49.2	49.5
Exports of goods and services (% of GDP)	34.1	58.6	57.3
Imports of goods and services (% of GDP)	41.7	42.7	44.9
Gross domestic investment (% of GDP)	41.4	20.3	21.0
Central government revenues (% of GDP)	18.5	16.3	15.7
Overall budget deficit (% of GDP)	4.6	-7.7	-10.9
Money and quasi money (annual % growth)	26.7	9.7	5.4
Technology and infrastructure			
Telephone mainlines (per 1,000 people)	24	84	86
Cost of 3 min local call ($)	..	0.07	0.08
Personal computers (per 1,000 people)	4.2	21.6	22.7
Internet users (thousands)	0	200	800
Paved roads (% of total)	55	..	..
Aircraft departures (thousands)	70	94	95
Trade and finance			
Trade as share of PPP GDP (%)	26.3	27.9	29.4
Trade growth less GDP growth (average %, 1989-99)			-5.4
High-technology exports (% of manufactured exports)	21	34	32
Net barter terms of trade (1995=100)	103	93	..
Foreign direct investment ($ millions)	2,444	7,315	6,213
Present value of debt ($ millions)			94,341
Total debt service ($ millions)	5,295	12,763	16,380
Short term debt ($ millions)	8,322	29,660	23,418
Aid per capita ($)	14	12	17

Togo

Low income

Population (millions)	5	Population growth (%)	2.4
Surface area (1,000 sq km)	56.8	Population per sq km	84
GNI ($ millions)	1,398	GNI per capita ($)	310

	1990	1998	1999
People			
Life expectancy (years)	50	..	49
Fertility rate (births per woman)	6.6	..	5.1
Infant mortality rate (per 1,000 live births)	81	..	77
Under 5 mortality rate (per 1,000 children)	142	..	143
Child malnutrition (% of children under 5)	..	25	..
Urban population (% of total)	29	32	33
Rural population density (per km^2 arable land)	120	137	..
Illiteracy male (% of people 15 and above)	36	28	26
Illiteracy female (% of people 15 and above)	71	62	60
Net primary enrollment (% of relevant age group)	75	..	..
Net secondary enrollment (% of relevant age group)	18	..	..
Girls in primary school (% of enrollment)	..	42	..
Girls in secondary school (% of enrollment)	25	..	..
Environment			
Forests (1,000 sq. km.)	7	..	..
Deforestation (% change 1990-2000)			..
Water use (% of total resources)	..	..	0.8
CO_2 emissions (metric tons per capita)	0.3	..	..
Access to improved water source (% of urban pop.)	82	..	..
Access to sanitation (% of urban population)	71	..	..
Energy use per capita (kg of oil equivalent)	..	..	..
Electricity use per capita (kWh)	..	..	..
Economy			
GDP ($ millions)	1,628	1,414	1,405
GDP growth (annual %)	-0.2	-2.2	2.1
GDP implicit price deflator (annual % growth)	3.0	-2.6	1.5
Value added in agriculture (% of GDP)	33.8	39.0	41.3
Value added in industry (% of GDP)	22.5	22.1	21.0
Value added in services (% of GDP)	43.7	38.9	37.7
Exports of goods and services (% of GDP)	33.5	32.0	30.3
Imports of goods and services (% of GDP)	45.3	43.1	40.1
Gross domestic investment (% of GDP)	26.6	13.6	13.4
Central government revenues (% of GDP)	..	..	..
Overall budget deficit (% of GDP)	..	..	..
Money and quasi money (annual % growth)	9.5	0.1	8.4
Technology and infrastructure			
Telephone mainlines (per 1,000 people)	3	7	8
Cost of 3 min local call ($)	0.18	0.10	0.10
Personal computers (per 1,000 people)	..	6.8	17.7
Internet users (thousands)	0	75	15
Paved roads (% of total)	21	..	..
Aircraft departures (thousands)	1	2	2
Trade and finance			
Trade as share of PPP GDP (%)	17.3	13.9	13.0
Trade growth less GDP growth (average %, 1989-99)			-1.9
High-technology exports (% of manufactured exports)	..	1	1
Net barter terms of trade (1995=100)	127	125	..
Foreign direct investment ($ millions)	0	30	30
Present value of debt ($ millions)			1,126
Total debt service ($ millions)	86	40	40
Short term debt ($ millions)	113	52	154
Aid per capita ($)	74	29	16

TONGA

Population (thousands)	100	Population growth (%)	0.9
Surface area (1,000 sq km)	1	Population per sq km	138
GNI ($ millions)	172	GNI per capita ($)	1,730

	1990	1998	1999
People			
Life expectancy (years)	69	..	71
Fertility rate (births per woman)	4.2	..	3.8
Infant mortality rate (per 1,000 live births)	25	..	21
Under 5 mortality rate (per 1,000 children)	27	..	24
Child malnutrition (% of children under 5)	..	..	..
Urban population (% of total)	33	37	37
Rural population density (per km^2 arable land)	381	366	..
Illiteracy male (% of people 15 and above)	..	..	..
Illiteracy female (% of people 15 and above)	..	..	..
Net primary enrollment (% of relevant age group)	..	..	..
Net secondary enrollment (% of relevant age group)	..	..	..
Girls in primary school (% of enrollment)	48	..	..
Girls in secondary school (% of enrollment)	48	..	..
Environment			
Forests (1,000 sq. km.)	0	..	..
Deforestation (% change 1990-2000)			..
Water use (% of total resources)			..
CO_2 emissions (metric tons per capita)	0.8	..	..
Access to improved water source (% of urban pop.)	..	..	..
Access to sanitation (% of urban population)	..	..	..
Energy use per capita (kg of oil equivalent)	..	..	..
Electricity use per capita (kWh)	..	..	..
Economy			
GDP ($ millions)	113	173	160
GDP growth (annual %)	-2.0	-1.5	3.5
GDP implicit price deflator (annual % growth)	11.1	5.6	4.7
Value added in agriculture (% of GDP)	35.1	38.3	..
Value added in industry (% of GDP)	14.4	11.5	..
Value added in services (% of GDP)	50.4	50.2	..
Exports of goods and services (% of GDP)	31.8	..	..
Imports of goods and services (% of GDP)	60.9	..	..
Gross domestic investment (% of GDP)	18.5	..	..
Central government revenues (% of GDP)	27.1	..	..
Overall budget deficit (% of GDP)	-1.3	..	..
Money and quasi money (annual % growth)	20.6	14.7	11.9
Technology and infrastructure			
Telephone mainlines (per 1,000 people)	46	86	93
Cost of 3 min local call ($)	0.07	..	..
Personal computers (per 1,000 people)	..	..	..
Internet users (thousands)	..	1	1
Paved roads (% of total)	..	..	..
Aircraft departures (thousands)	4	3	4
Trade and finance			
Trade as share of PPP GDP (%)	..	..	..
Trade growth less GDP growth (average %, 1989-99)			..
High-technology exports (% of manufactured exports)	..	..	..
Net barter terms of trade (1995=100)	..	..	..
Foreign direct investment ($ millions)	0	2	2
Present value of debt ($ millions)			38
Total debt service ($ millions)	2	4	4
Short term debt ($ millions)	9	1	0
Aid per capita ($)	309	250	213

Latin America & Caribbean | **Upper middle income**

Population (millions)	1	Population growth (%)	0.6
Surface area (1,000 sq km)	5	Population per sq km	252
GNI ($ millions)	6,142	GNI per capita ($)	4,750

	1990	1998	1999
People			
Life expectancy (years)	71	73	73
Fertility rate (births per woman)	2.4	1.8	1.8
Infant mortality rate (per 1,000 live births)	18	16	16
Under 5 mortality rate (per 1,000 children)	24	19	20
Child malnutrition (% of children under 5)	..	..	..
Urban population (% of total)	69	73	74
Rural population density (per km^2 arable land)	507	460	..
Illiteracy male (% of people 15 and above)	6	5	5
Illiteracy female (% of people 15 and above)	11	8	8
Net primary enrollment (% of relevant age group)	91	88	..
Net secondary enrollment (% of relevant age group)	65	..	..
Girls in primary school (% of enrollment)	49	49	..
Girls in secondary school (% of enrollment)	50	..	..
Environment			
Forests (1,000 sq. km.)	3	..	3
Deforestation (% change 1990-2000)			0.8
Water use (% of total resources)	..	..	
CO$_2$ emissions (metric tons per capita)	14.1	17.4	..
Access to improved water source (% of urban pop.)	..	83	..
Access to sanitation (% of urban population)	100	97	..
Energy use per capita (kg of oil equivalent)	4,970	6,964	..
Electricity use per capita (kWh)	2,553	3,478	..
Economy			
GDP ($ millions)	5,068	6,113	6,869
GDP growth (annual %)	1.5	4.8	6.8
GDP implicit price deflator (annual % growth)	15.5	-0.1	5.2
Value added in agriculture (% of GDP)	2.6	1.9	1.9
Value added in industry (% of GDP)	46.5	38.8	39.7
Value added in services (% of GDP)	51.6	62.2	58.3
Exports of goods and services (% of GDP)	45.4	48.1	49.6
Imports of goods and services (% of GDP)	28.6	53.4	43.9
Gross domestic investment (% of GDP)	12.6	28.0	21.0
Central government revenues (% of GDP)	..	27.9	..
Overall budget deficit (% of GDP)	..	0.2	..
Money and quasi money (annual % growth)	6.2	14.5	4.2
Technology and infrastructure			
Telephone mainlines (per 1,000 people)	141	206	216
Cost of 3 min local call ($)	0.05	0.03	0.04
Personal computers (per 1,000 people)	4.2	46.9	54.2
Internet users (thousands)	..	20	30
Paved roads (% of total)	46	51	..
Aircraft departures (thousands)	22	13	21
Trade and finance			
Trade as share of PPP GDP (%)	45.3	54.6	44.6
Trade growth less GDP growth (average %, 1989-99)			0.9
High-technology exports (% of manufactured exports)	..	1	2
Net barter terms of trade (1995=100)	117	105	..
Foreign direct investment ($ millions)	109	730	633
Present value of debt ($ millions)			2,509
Total debt service ($ millions)	449	313	454
Short term debt ($ millions)	127	553	833
Aid per capita ($)	15	11	20

TUNISIA

Population (millions)	9	Population growth (%)		1.3
Surface area (1,000 sq km)	164	Population per sq km		61
GNI ($ millions)	19,757	GNI per capita ($)		2,090

	1990	1998	1999
People			
Life expectancy (years)	68	72	73
Fertility rate (births per woman)	3.5	2.2	2.2
Infant mortality rate (per 1,000 live births)	37	25	24
Under 5 mortality rate (per 1,000 children)	52	..	30
Child malnutrition (% of children under 5)	..	..	..
Urban population (% of total)	58	64	65
Rural population density (per km^2 arable land)	118	116	..
Illiteracy male (% of people 15 and above)	28	21	20
Illiteracy female (% of people 15 and above)	54	42	41
Net primary enrollment (% of relevant age group)	94	..	..
Net secondary enrollment (% of relevant age group)	..	..	..
Girls in primary school (% of enrollment)	..	47	..
Girls in secondary school (% of enrollment)	43	..	..
Environment			
Forests (1,000 sq. km.)	5	..	..
Deforestation (% change 1990-2000)			..
Water use (% of total resources)	..	..	69.0
CO_2 emissions (metric tons per capita)	1.8	..	..
Access to improved water source (% of urban pop.)	94	..	..
Access to sanitation (% of urban population)	97	..	..
Energy use per capita (kg of oil equivalent)	694	812	..
Electricity use per capita (kWh)	604	824	..
Economy			
GDP ($ millions)	12,291	19,847	20,944
GDP growth (annual %)	8.0	4.8	6.2
GDP implicit price deflator (annual % growth)	4.5	3.2	3.5
Value added in agriculture (% of GDP)	15.7	12.5	12.8
Value added in industry (% of GDP)	29.8	28.2	28.1
Value added in services (% of GDP)	54.5	59.2	59.0
Exports of goods and services (% of GDP)	43.6	42.6	41.9
Imports of goods and services (% of GDP)	50.6	45.9	44.1
Gross domestic investment (% of GDP)	32.5	26.9	26.6
Central government revenues (% of GDP)	30.7	31.2	28.9
Overall budget deficit (% of GDP)	-5.4	-0.4	-2.3
Money and quasi money (annual % growth)	7.6	5.4	18.9
Technology and infrastructure			
Telephone mainlines (per 1,000 people)	38	81	90
Cost of 3 min local call ($)	0.07	0.02	0.03
Personal computers (per 1,000 people)	2.6	14.8	15.3
Internet users (thousands)	..	10	30
Paved roads (% of total)	76	..	..
Aircraft departures (thousands)	13	20	20
Trade and finance			
Trade as share of PPP GDP (%)	28.4	27.1	25.5
Trade growth less GDP growth (average %, 1989-99)			-4.7
High-technology exports (% of manufactured exports)	2	2	3
Net barter terms of trade (1995=100)	103	101	..
Foreign direct investment ($ millions)	76	650	350
Present value of debt ($ millions)			11,783
Total debt service ($ millions)	1,431	1,430	1,532
Short term debt ($ millions)	634	1,040	1,538
Aid per capita ($)	48	16	26

TURKEY

Lower middle income

Population (millions)	64	Population growth (%)	1.6
Surface area (1,000 sq km)	775	Population per sq km	84
GNI ($ millions)	186,490	GNI per capita ($)	2,900

	1990	1998	1999
People			
Life expectancy (years)	66	..	69
Fertility rate (births per woman)	3.0	..	2.4
Infant mortality rate (per 1,000 live births)	58	38	36
Under 5 mortality rate (per 1,000 children)	67	..	45
Child malnutrition (% of children under 5)	..	8	..
Urban population (% of total)	61	73	74
Rural population density (per km^2 arable land)	88	70	..
Illiteracy male (% of people 15 and above)	11	7	7
Illiteracy female (% of people 15 and above)	33	25	24
Net primary enrollment (% of relevant age group)	89	..	..
Net secondary enrollment (% of relevant age group)	41	..	..
Girls in primary school (% of enrollment)	..	47	..
Girls in secondary school (% of enrollment)	37	..	..
Environment			
Forests (1,000 sq. km.)	100	..	..
Deforestation (% change 1990-2000)			..
Water use (% of total resources)	..	..	17.4
CO_2 emissions (metric tons per capita)	2.8	..	..
Access to improved water source (% of urban pop.)	82	..	..
Access to sanitation (% of urban population)	98	..	..
Energy use per capita (kg of oil equivalent)	935	1,144	..
Electricity use per capita (kWh)	801	1,353	..
Economy			
GDP ($ millions)	150,721	201,154	185,691
GDP growth (annual %)	9.3	3.1	-5.1
GDP implicit price deflator (annual % growth)	58.2	75.7	56.2
Value added in agriculture (% of GDP)	18.3	18.5	15.8
Value added in industry (% of GDP)	29.8	25.0	24.3
Value added in services (% of GDP)	51.9	56.5	60.0
Exports of goods and services (% of GDP)	13.3	24.3	23.2
Imports of goods and services (% of GDP)	17.6	27.9	26.9
Gross domestic investment (% of GDP)	24.3	24.2	23.3
Central government revenues (% of GDP)	14.0	24.2	25.6
Overall budget deficit (% of GDP)	-3.0	-8.4	-13.0
Money and quasi money (annual % growth)	53.2	89.7	98.3
Technology and infrastructure			
Telephone mainlines (per 1,000 people)	121	254	278
Cost of 3 min local call ($)	0.06	0.08	0.10
Personal computers (per 1,000 people)	5.3	25.5	33.9
Internet users (thousands)	..	450	1,500
Paved roads (% of total)	..	28	34
Aircraft departures (thousands)	44	104	111
Trade and finance			
Trade as share of PPP GDP (%)	13.0	17.4	16.2
Trade growth less GDP growth (average %, 1989-99)			-4.0
High-technology exports (% of manufactured exports)	1	2	4
Net barter terms of trade (1995=100)	104	102	..
Foreign direct investment ($ millions)	684	940	783
Present value of debt ($ millions)			97,483
Total debt service ($ millions)	7,422	14,900	13,787
Short term debt ($ millions)	9,500	21,217	23,472
Aid per capita ($)	22	0	0

TURKMENISTAN

Europe & Central Asia   Low income

Population (millions)	5	Population growth (%)		1.3
Surface area (1,000 sq km)	488	Population per sq km		10
GNI ($ millions)	3,205	GNI per capita ($)		670

	1990	1998	1999
People			
Life expectancy (years)	66	..	66
Fertility rate (births per woman)	4.2	..	2.8
Infant mortality rate (per 1,000 live births)	45	33	33
Under 5 mortality rate (per 1,000 children)	..	..	45
Child malnutrition (% of children under 5)	..	..	..
Urban population (% of total)	45	45	45
Rural population density (per km^2 arable land)	..	160	..
Illiteracy male (% of people 15 and above)	..	..	..
Illiteracy female (% of people 15 and above)	..	..	..
Net primary enrollment (% of relevant age group)	..	..	..
Net secondary enrollment (% of relevant age group)	..	..	..
Girls in primary school (% of enrollment)	..	..	..
Girls in secondary school (% of enrollment)	..	..	..
Environment			
Forests (1,000 sq. km.)	38	..	..
Deforestation (% change 1990-2000)			..
Water use (% of total resources)	..	..	52.3
CO_2 emissions (metric tons per capita)	..	..	..
Access to improved water source (% of urban pop.)	..	..	..
Access to sanitation (% of urban population)	..	..	..
Energy use per capita (kg of oil equivalent)	..	2,357	..
Electricity use per capita (kWh)	..	859	..
Economy			
GDP ($ millions)	..	2,642	3,204
GDP growth (annual %)	0.7	7.0	16.0
GDP implicit price deflator (annual % growth)	6.3	17.7	5.9
Value added in agriculture (% of GDP)	32.2	26.0	27.1
Value added in industry (% of GDP)	29.6	44.1	45.0
Value added in services (% of GDP)	38.2	29.9	27.9
Exports of goods and services (% of GDP)	..	29.7	41.6
Imports of goods and services (% of GDP)	..	64.5	61.9
Gross domestic investment (% of GDP)	40.1	45.5	46.3
Central government revenues (% of GDP)	..	..	..
Overall budget deficit (% of GDP)	..	..	..
Money and quasi money (annual % growth)	..	82.2	22.6
Technology and infrastructure			
Telephone mainlines (per 1,000 people)	60	82	82
Cost of 3 min local call ($)	..	..	..
Personal computers (per 1,000 people)	..	..	..
Internet users (thousands)	..	..	2
Paved roads (% of total)	74	..	..
Aircraft departures (thousands)	..	17	3
Trade and finance			
Trade as share of PPP GDP (%)	..	14.2	16.8
Trade growth less GDP growth (average %, 1989-99)			6.6
High-technology exports (% of manufactured exports)	..	..	..
Net barter terms of trade (1995=100)	..	..	..
Foreign direct investment ($ millions)	0	130	80
Present value of debt ($ millions)			1,730
Total debt service ($ millions)	..	311	465
Short term debt ($ millions)	..	521	322
Aid per capita ($)	..	4	4

UGANDA

Sub-Saharan Africa   **Low income**

Population (millions)	21	Population growth (%)	2.7
Surface area (1,000 sq km)	241	Population per sq km	108
GNI ($ millions)	6,794	GNI per capita ($)	320

	1990	1998	1999
People			
Life expectancy (years)	47	..	42
Fertility rate (births per woman)	7.0	..	6.4
Infant mortality rate (per 1,000 live births)	104	..	88
Under 5 mortality rate (per 1,000 children)	165	..	162
Child malnutrition (% of children under 5)	..	..	..
Urban population (% of total)	11	14	14
Rural population density (per km² arable land)	290	357	..
Illiteracy male (% of people 15 and above)	31	24	23
Illiteracy female (% of people 15 and above)	57	46	45
Net primary enrollment (% of relevant age group)	..	..	..
Net secondary enrollment (% of relevant age group)	..	..	..
Girls in primary school (% of enrollment)	44	..	..
Girls in secondary school (% of enrollment)	..	..	..
Environment			
Forests (1,000 sq. km.)	51	..	..
Deforestation (% change 1990-2000)			..
Water use (% of total resources)	..	..	0.3
CO_2 emissions (metric tons per capita)	0.1	..	..
Access to improved water source (% of urban pop.)	80	..	..
Access to sanitation (% of urban population)	96	..	..
Energy use per capita (kg of oil equivalent)	..	..	..
Electricity use per capita (kWh)	..	..	..
Economy			
GDP ($ millions)	4,304	6,777	6,411
GDP growth (annual %)	6.5	5.6	7.4
GDP implicit price deflator (annual % growth)	44.4	10.7	4.4
Value added in agriculture (% of GDP)	56.6	44.6	44.4
Value added in industry (% of GDP)	11.1	17.6	17.8
Value added in services (% of GDP)	32.4	37.8	37.8
Exports of goods and services (% of GDP)	7.2	10.3	11.3
Imports of goods and services (% of GDP)	19.4	19.7	22.9
Gross domestic investment (% of GDP)	12.7	15.0	16.4
Central government revenues (% of GDP)	..	..	..
Overall budget deficit (% of GDP)	..	..	..
Money and quasi money (annual % growth)	60.2	22.9	13.6
Technology and infrastructure			
Telephone mainlines (per 1,000 people)	2	3	3
Cost of 3 min local call ($)	..	0.18	0.15
Personal computers (per 1,000 people)	..	1.9	2.5
Internet users (thousands)	..	15	25
Paved roads (% of total)	..	..	..
Aircraft departures (thousands)	2	3	3
Trade and finance			
Trade as share of PPP GDP (%)	3.0	8.4	7.4
Trade growth less GDP growth (average %, 1989-99)			-7.1
High-technology exports (% of manufactured exports)	..	5	11
Net barter terms of trade (1995=100)	74	78	..
Foreign direct investment ($ millions)	0	210	222
Present value of debt ($ millions)			1,748
Total debt service ($ millions)	145	165	184
Short term debt ($ millions)	140	135	141
Aid per capita ($)	41	23	27

215

UKRAINE

Europe & Central Asia   **Low income**

Population (millions)	50	Population growth (%)		-0.7
Surface area (1,000 sq km)	604	Population per sq km		86
GNI ($ millions)	41,991	GNI per capita ($)		840

	1990	1998	1999
People			
Life expectancy (years)	70	..	67
Fertility rate (births per woman)	1.8	..	1.3
Infant mortality rate (per 1,000 live births)	13	..	14
Under 5 mortality rate (per 1,000 children)	..	..	17
Child malnutrition (% of children under 5)	..	..	..
Urban population (% of total)	67	68	68
Rural population density (per km^2 arable land)	..	49	..
Illiteracy male (% of people 15 and above)	0	0	0
Illiteracy female (% of people 15 and above)	1	1	1
Net primary enrollment (% of relevant age group)	..	..	..
Net secondary enrollment (% of relevant age group)	..	..	..
Girls in primary school (% of enrollment)	..	49	..
Girls in secondary school (% of enrollment)	..	..	..
Environment			
Forests (1,000 sq. km.)	93	..	..
Deforestation (% change 1990-2000)			..
Water use (% of total resources)	..	..	18.6
CO$_2$ emissions (metric tons per capita)	..	..	..
Access to improved water source (% of urban pop.)	..	..	..
Access to sanitation (% of urban population)	..	..	..
Energy use per capita (kg of oil equivalent)	..	2,842	..
Electricity use per capita (kWh)	..	2,350	..
Economy			
GDP ($ millions)	91,327	43,079	38,653
GDP growth (annual %)	-6.4	-1.9	-0.4
GDP implicit price deflator (annual % growth)	16.4	12.0	24.4
Value added in agriculture (% of GDP)	25.6	14.2	12.8
Value added in industry (% of GDP)	44.6	35.4	38.4
Value added in services (% of GDP)	29.9	50.4	48.8
Exports of goods and services (% of GDP)	27.6	41.9	52.8
Imports of goods and services (% of GDP)	28.7	44.2	51.7
Gross domestic investment (% of GDP)	27.5	20.8	19.8
Central government revenues (% of GDP)	..	..	..
Overall budget deficit (% of GDP)	..	..	..
Money and quasi money (annual % growth)	..	22.3	41.3
Technology and infrastructure			
Telephone mainlines (per 1,000 people)	136	191	199
Cost of 3 min local call ($)	..	0.01	0.00
Personal computers (per 1,000 people)	1.9	13.9	15.8
Internet users (thousands)	..	150	200
Paved roads (% of total)	94	97	97
Aircraft departures (thousands)	..	29	28
Trade and finance			
Trade as share of PPP GDP (%)	..	16.2	13.6
Trade growth less GDP growth (average %, 1989-99)			10.7
High-technology exports (% of manufactured exports)	..	..	..
Net barter terms of trade (1995=100)	..	..	..
Foreign direct investment ($ millions)	0	743	496
Present value of debt ($ millions)			12,832
Total debt service ($ millions)	..	2,027	2,800
Short term debt ($ millions)	..	479	316
Aid per capita ($)	6	8	10

UNITED ARAB EMIRATES

High income

Population (millions)	3	Population growth (%)	3.3
Surface area (1,000 sq km)	84	Population per sq km	34
GNI ($ millions)	..	GNI per capita ($)	..

	1990	1998	1999
People			
Life expectancy (years)	74	75	75
Fertility rate (births per woman)	4.1	3.5	3.3
Infant mortality rate (per 1,000 live births)	20	8	8
Under 5 mortality rate (per 1,000 children)	..	11	9
Child malnutrition (% of children under 5)	..	7	..
Urban population (% of total)	81	85	85
Rural population density (per km^2 arable land)	1,006	1,017	..
Illiteracy male (% of people 15 and above)	29	27	26
Illiteracy female (% of people 15 and above)	30	23	22
Net primary enrollment (% of relevant age group)	94	78	..
Net secondary enrollment (% of relevant age group)	59	71	..
Girls in primary school (% of enrollment)	48	48	..
Girls in secondary school (% of enrollment)	50	50	..
Environment			
Forests (1,000 sq. km.)	2	..	3
Deforestation (% change 1990-2000)			-2.8
Water use (% of total resources)	..	..	1,055.0
CO_2 emissions (metric tons per capita)	33.9	32.0	..
Access to improved water source (% of urban pop.)	100	98	..
Access to sanitation (% of urban population)	100	..	..
Energy use per capita (kg of oil equivalent)	9,411	10,035	..
Electricity use per capita (kWh)	7,780	9,892	..
Economy			
GDP ($ millions)	34,132	47,234	..
GDP growth (annual %)	17.5	-5.7	..
GDP implicit price deflator (annual % growth)	5.8	1.6	..
Value added in agriculture (% of GDP)	1.6	2.2	..
Value added in industry (% of GDP)	63.7	57.5	..
Value added in services (% of GDP)	34.7	40.3	..
Exports of goods and services (% of GDP)	65.4	65.9	..
Imports of goods and services (% of GDP)	40.4	65.4	..
Gross domestic investment (% of GDP)	20.2	25.5	..
Central government revenues (% of GDP)	1.6	3.4	..
Overall budget deficit (% of GDP)	0.4	-0.3	..
Money and quasi money (annual % growth)	-8.2	4.2	11.5
Technology and infrastructure			
Telephone mainlines (per 1,000 people)	206	389	332
Cost of 3 min local call ($)	0.00	0.00	0.00
Personal computers (per 1,000 people)	29.4	106.4	102.1
Internet users (thousands)	..	200	400
Paved roads (% of total)	94	100	..
Aircraft departures (thousands)	19	40	44
Trade and finance			
Trade as share of PPP GDP (%)	85.3	106.7	..
Trade growth less GDP growth (average %, 1989-99)			..
High-technology exports (% of manufactured exports)	0	1	..
Net barter terms of trade (1995=100)	174	98	..
Foreign direct investment ($ millions)	..	..	..
Present value of debt ($ millions)			..
Total debt service ($ millions)	..	..	..
Short term debt ($ millions)	..	..	..
Aid per capita ($)	2	1	1

217

UNITED KINGDOM

High income

Population (millions)	60	Population growth (%)	0.4
Surface area (1,000 sq km)	245	Population per sq km	246
GNI ($ millions)	1,403,844	GNI per capita ($)	23,590

	1990	1998	1999
People			
Life expectancy (years)	76	77	77
Fertility rate (births per woman)	1.8	1.7	1.7
Infant mortality rate (per 1,000 live births)	8	6	6
Under 5 mortality rate (per 1,000 children)	9	7	6
Child malnutrition (% of children under 5)	..	..	..
Urban population (% of total)	89	89	89
Rural population density (per km^2 arable land)	95	100	..
Illiteracy male (% of people 15 and above)	..	..	..
Illiteracy female (% of people 15 and above)	..	..	..
Net primary enrollment (% of relevant age group)	97	99	..
Net secondary enrollment (% of relevant age group)	79	92	..
Girls in primary school (% of enrollment)	49	49	..
Girls in secondary school (% of enrollment)	50	52	..
Environment			
Forests (1,000 sq. km.)	24	..	26
Deforestation (% change 1990-2000)			-0.8
Water use (% of total resources)	..	..	6.4
CO_2 emissions (metric tons per capita)	9.9	8.9	..
Access to improved water source (% of urban pop.)	100	100	100
Access to sanitation (% of urban population)	100	..	100
Energy use per capita (kg of oil equivalent)	3,702	3,930	..
Electricity use per capita (kWh)	4,768	5,327	..
Economy			
GDP ($ millions)	987,641	1,410,433	1,441,787
GDP growth (annual %)	0.7	2.6	2.1
GDP implicit price deflator (annual % growth)	7.7	3.0	2.5
Value added in agriculture (% of GDP)	1.7	1.1	1.0
Value added in industry (% of GDP)	31.4	26.0	25.2
Value added in services (% of GDP)	66.9	72.9	73.7
Exports of goods and services (% of GDP)	24.0	26.5	25.8
Imports of goods and services (% of GDP)	26.6	27.4	27.5
Gross domestic investment (% of GDP)	20.2	18.0	17.6
Central government revenues (% of GDP)	36.2	37.3	36.5
Overall budget deficit (% of GDP)	0.6	0.6	0.0
Money and quasi money (annual % growth)	..	..	..
Technology and infrastructure			
Telephone mainlines (per 1,000 people)	441	557	567
Cost of 3 min local call ($)	0.26	0.19	0.19
Personal computers (per 1,000 people)	107.6	269.9	302.5
Internet users (thousands)	100	8,000	12,500
Paved roads (% of total)	100	100	..
Aircraft departures (thousands)	671	802	906
Trade and finance			
Trade as share of PPP GDP (%)	42.3	46.9	44.8
Trade growth less GDP growth (average %, 1989-99)			3.5
High-technology exports (% of manufactured exports)	24	29	30
Net barter terms of trade (1995=100)	101	103	104
Foreign direct investment ($ millions)	..	..	..
Present value of debt ($ millions)			..
Total debt service ($ millions)	..	..	..
Short term debt ($ millions)	..	..	..
Aid per capita ($)	..	..	..

218

Population (millions)	278	Population growth (%)		1.2
Surface area (1,000 sq km)	9,364	Population per sq km		30
GNI ($ millions)	8,879,500	GNI per capita ($)		31,910

	1990	1998	1999
People			
Life expectancy (years)	75	76	77
Fertility rate (births per woman)	2.1	2.1	2.1
Infant mortality rate (per 1,000 live births)	9	7	7
Under 5 mortality rate (per 1,000 children)	10	9	8
Child malnutrition (% of children under 5)	..	1	..
Urban population (% of total)	75	77	77
Rural population density (per km^2 arable land)	33	36	..
Illiteracy male (% of people 15 and above)	..	..	..
Illiteracy female (% of people 15 and above)	..	..	..
Net primary enrollment (% of relevant age group)	96	95	..
Net secondary enrollment (% of relevant age group)	86	90	..
Girls in primary school (% of enrollment)	48	49	49
Girls in secondary school (% of enrollment)	49	50	..
Environment			
Forests (1,000 sq. km.)	2,221	..	2,260
Deforestation (% change 1990-2000)			-0.2
Water use (% of total resources)	..	..	18.1
CO_2 emissions (metric tons per capita)	19.4	20.1	..
Access to improved water source (% of urban pop.)	100	..	100
Access to sanitation (% of urban population)	100	..	100
Energy use per capita (kg of oil equivalent)	7,719	7,937	..
Electricity use per capita (kWh)	10,558	11,832	..
Economy			
GDP ($ millions)	5,750,800	8,699,200	9,152,098
GDP growth (annual %)	1.8	4.4	3.6
GDP implicit price deflator (annual % growth)	3.9	1.2	1.6
Value added in agriculture (% of GDP)	..	..	..
Value added in industry (% of GDP)	..	..	..
Value added in services (% of GDP)	..	..	..
Exports of goods and services (% of GDP)	9.7	11.1	..
Imports of goods and services (% of GDP)	10.9	12.8	..
Gross domestic investment (% of GDP)	17.6	20.1	..
Central government revenues (% of GDP)	18.9	20.8	20.8
Overall budget deficit (% of GDP)	-3.8	0.8	1.3
Money and quasi money (annual % growth)	4.9	10.1	8.2
Technology and infrastructure			
Telephone mainlines (per 1,000 people)	545	661	664
Cost of 3 min local call ($)	0.09	0.09	..
Personal computers (per 1,000 people)	216.8	455.9	510.5
Internet users (thousands)	3,000	60,000	74,100
Paved roads (% of total)	58	59	..
Aircraft departures (thousands)	6,849	7,825	8,512
Trade and finance			
Trade as share of PPP GDP (%)	15.5	19.4	19.8
Trade growth less GDP growth (average %, 1989-99)			4.9
High-technology exports (% of manufactured exports)	34	34	35
Net barter terms of trade (1995=100)	98	104	101
Foreign direct investment ($ millions)	..	..	..
Present value of debt ($ millions)			..
Total debt service ($ millions)	..	..	..
Short term debt ($ millions)	..	..	..
Aid per capita ($)	..	..-	..

URUGUAY

Population (millions)	3	Population growth (%)	0.7
Surface area (1,000 sq km)	177	Population per sq km	19
GNI ($ millions)	20,604	GNI per capita ($)	6,220

	1990	1998	1999
People			
Life expectancy (years)	73	..	74
Fertility rate (births per woman)	2.5	..	2.3
Infant mortality rate (per 1,000 live births)	21	16	15
Under 5 mortality rate (per 1,000 children)	24	..	17
Child malnutrition (% of children under 5)	..	..	..
Urban population (% of total)	89	91	91
Rural population density (per km^2 arable land)	28	24	..
Illiteracy male (% of people 15 and above)	4	3	3
Illiteracy female (% of people 15 and above)	3	2	2
Net primary enrollment (% of relevant age group)	..	..	..
Net secondary enrollment (% of relevant age group)	..	..	..
Girls in primary school (% of enrollment)	49	..	..
Girls in secondary school (% of enrollment)	..	..	..
Environment			
Forests (1,000 sq. km.)	8	..	..
Deforestation (% change 1990-2000)			..
Water use (% of total resources)	..	..	7.1
CO$_2$ emissions (metric tons per capita)	1.3	..	..
Access to improved water source (% of urban pop.)	..	..	..
Access to sanitation (% of urban population)	..	..	..
Energy use per capita (kg of oil equivalent)	719	910	..
Electricity use per capita (kWh)	1,220	1,788	..
Economy			
GDP ($ millions)	9,287	22,205	20,805
GDP growth (annual %)	0.3	4.6	-3.2
GDP implicit price deflator (annual % growth)	106.8	9.8	4.8
Value added in agriculture (% of GDP)	9.2	7.1	5.7
Value added in industry (% of GDP)	34.6	28.7	27.2
Value added in services (% of GDP)	56.1	64.1	67.2
Exports of goods and services (% of GDP)	23.5	19.8	18.0
Imports of goods and services (% of GDP)	18.1	20.5	19.6
Gross domestic investment (% of GDP)	12.2	15.6	15.2
Central government revenues (% of GDP)	23.9	30.0	28.1
Overall budget deficit (% of GDP)	0.3	-0.8	-3.7
Money and quasi money (annual % growth)	118.5	26.8	13.1
Technology and infrastructure			
Telephone mainlines (per 1,000 people)	134	250	..
Cost of 3 min local call ($)	0.03	0.18	0.18
Personal computers (per 1,000 people)	..	91.2	99.6
Internet users (thousands)	..	230	300
Paved roads (% of total)	74	..	..
Aircraft departures (thousands)	5	10	11
Trade and finance			
Trade as share of PPP GDP (%)	15.8	22.1	19.0
Trade growth less GDP growth (average %, 1989-99)			-3.7
High-technology exports (% of manufactured exports)	..	2	2
Net barter terms of trade (1995=100)	100	103	..
Foreign direct investment ($ millions)	0	164	229
Present value of debt ($ millions)			7,507
Total debt service ($ millions)	987	1,135	1,059
Short term debt ($ millions)	1,201	2,009	1,794
Aid per capita ($)	17	7	7

Europe & Central Asia — Low income

Population (thousands)	24,406	Population growth (%)		1.8
Surface area (1,000 sq km)	447.4	Population per sq km		59
GNI ($ millions)	17,613	GNI per capita ($)		720

	1990	1998	1999
People			
Life expectancy (years)	69	..	70
Fertility rate (births per woman)	4.1	2.8	2.7
Infant mortality rate (per 1,000 live births)	35	..	22
Under 5 mortality rate (per 1,000 children)	..	..	29
Child malnutrition (% of children under 5)	..	..	..
Urban population (% of total)	40	38	37
Rural population density (per km^2 arable land)	..	335	..
Illiteracy male (% of people 15 and above)	10	7	7
Illiteracy female (% of people 15 and above)	23	17	16
Net primary enrollment (% of relevant age group)	..	..	..
Net secondary enrollment (% of relevant age group)	..	..	..
Girls in primary school (% of enrollment)	..	..	..
Girls in secondary school (% of enrollment)	..	..	..
Environment			
Forests (1,000 sq. km.)	19	..	..
Deforestation (% change 1990-2000)			..
Water use (% of total resources)	..	..	356.1
CO_2 emissions (metric tons per capita)	..	..	..
Access to improved water source (% of urban pop.)	..	..	..
Access to sanitation (% of urban population)	..	..	..
Energy use per capita (kg of oil equivalent)	..	1,930	..
Electricity use per capita (kWh)	..	1,618	..
Economy			
GDP ($ millions)	..	17,555	17,705
GDP growth (annual %)	1.6	4.4	4.4
GDP implicit price deflator (annual % growth)	4.0	38.9	38.5
Value added in agriculture (% of GDP)	32.8	31.3	32.9
Value added in industry (% of GDP)	33.0	26.2	24.5
Value added in services (% of GDP)	34.3	42.5	42.6
Exports of goods and services (% of GDP)	28.8	22.3	19.3
Imports of goods and services (% of GDP)	47.8	22.7	18.6
Gross domestic investment (% of GDP)	32.2	16.9	15.1
Central government revenues (% of GDP)	..	..	..
Overall budget deficit (% of GDP)	..	..	..
Money and quasi money (annual % growth)	..	..	..
Technology and infrastructure			
Telephone mainlines (per 1,000 people)	69	65	66
Cost of 3 min local call ($)	0.00	..	..
Personal computers (per 1,000 people)	..	..	..
Internet users (thousands)	..	5	8
Paved roads (% of total)	79	..	..
Aircraft departures (thousands)	..	31	31
Trade and finance			
Trade as share of PPP GDP (%)	..	10.0	7.7
Trade growth less GDP growth (average %, 1989-99)			1.4
High-technology exports (% of manufactured exports)	..	..	..
Net barter terms of trade (1995=100)	..	..	..
Foreign direct investment ($ millions)	0	200	113
Present value of debt ($ millions)			4,161
Total debt service ($ millions)	..	370	567
Short term debt ($ millions)	..	147	626
Aid per capita ($)	..	6	5

VANUATU

Population (thousands)	193	Population growth (%)		3.7
Surface area (1,000 sq km)	12	Population per sq km		16
GNI ($ millions)	227	GNI per capita ($)		1,180

	1990	1998	1999
People			
Life expectancy (years)	61	..	65
Fertility rate (births per woman)	5.5	..	4.6
Infant mortality rate (per 1,000 live births)	56	..	36
Under 5 mortality rate (per 1,000 children)	70	..	44
Child malnutrition (% of children under 5)	..	..	..
Urban population (% of total)	18	20	20
Rural population density (per km^2 arable land)	402	499	..
Illiteracy male (% of people 15 and above)	..	..	..
Illiteracy female (% of people 15 and above)	..	..	..
Net primary enrollment (% of relevant age group)	..	..	..
Net secondary enrollment (% of relevant age group)	..	..	..
Girls in primary school (% of enrollment)	47	..	..
Girls in secondary school (% of enrollment)	..	..	..
Environment			
Forests (1,000 sq. km.)	4	..	..
Deforestation (% change 1990-2000)			..
Water use (% of total resources)	..		
CO_2 emissions (metric tons per capita)	0.4	..	..
Access to improved water source (% of urban pop.)		..	..
Access to sanitation (% of urban population)	..	..	..
Energy use per capita (kg of oil equivalent)	..	..	..
Electricity use per capita (kWh)	..	..	..
Economy			
GDP ($ millions)	153	248	247
GDP growth (annual %)	5.2	6.0	-2.5
GDP implicit price deflator (annual % growth)	4.0	2.2	3.3
Value added in agriculture (% of GDP)	20.0	..	..
Value added in industry (% of GDP)	13.5	..	..
Value added in services (% of GDP)	66.5	..	..
Exports of goods and services (% of GDP)	46.4	..	..
Imports of goods and services (% of GDP)	76.6	..	..
Gross domestic investment (% of GDP)	43.6	..	..
Central government revenues (% of GDP)	27.1	20.9	21.2
Overall budget deficit (% of GDP)	-7.8	-9.7	-1.2
Money and quasi money (annual % growth)	5.6	12.6	-9.2
Technology and infrastructure			
Telephone mainlines (per 1,000 people)	18	28	..
Cost of 3 min local call ($)	..	..	0.15
Personal computers (per 1,000 people)	..	..	..
Internet users (thousands)	..	2	3
Paved roads (% of total)	22	..	..
Aircraft departures (thousands)	0	2	1
Trade and finance			
Trade as share of PPP GDP (%)	27.9	20.2	..
Trade growth less GDP growth (average %, 1989-99)			..
High-technology exports (% of manufactured exports)	20	..	..
Net barter terms of trade (1995=100)	..	..	..
Foreign direct investment ($ millions)	13	20	20
Present value of debt ($ millions)			25
Total debt service ($ millions)	2	2	2
Short term debt ($ millions)	10	9	1
Aid per capita ($)	338	218	193

Latin America & Caribbean   **Upper middle income**

Population (millions)	24	Population growth (%)	2.0
Surface area (1,000 sq km)	912	Population per sq km	27
GNI ($ millions)	87,313	GNI per capita ($)	3,680

	1990	1998	1999
People			
Life expectancy (years)	71	..	73
Fertility rate (births per woman)	3.4	..	2.9
Infant mortality rate (per 1,000 live births)	25	..	20
Under 5 mortality rate (per 1,000 children)	27	..	23
Child malnutrition (% of children under 5)	8	8	..
Urban population (% of total)	84	86	87
Rural population density (per km^2 arable land)	105	120	..
Illiteracy male (% of people 15 and above)	10	7	7
Illiteracy female (% of people 15 and above)	12	9	8
Net primary enrollment (% of relevant age group)	88	..	..
Net secondary enrollment (% of relevant age group)	19	..	..
Girls in primary school (% of enrollment)	..	..	..
Girls in secondary school (% of enrollment)	57	..	..
Environment			
Forests (1,000 sq. km.)	517	..	..
Deforestation (% change 1990-2000)			
Water use (% of total resources)	..	..	0.5
CO$_2$ emissions (metric tons per capita)	6.0	..	..
Access to improved water source (% of urban pop.)	..	..	..
Access to sanitation (% of urban population)	..	..	..
Energy use per capita (kg of oil equivalent)	2,155	2,433	..
Electricity use per capita (kWh)	2,308	2,566	..
Economy			
GDP ($ millions)	48,593	95,450	102,222
GDP growth (annual %)	6.5	-0.1	-7.2
GDP implicit price deflator (annual % growth)	41.7	20.7	27.6
Value added in agriculture (% of GDP)	5.4	5.1	5.1
Value added in industry (% of GDP)	50.2	35.3	36.4
Value added in services (% of GDP)	44.4	59.6	58.5
Exports of goods and services (% of GDP)	39.4	20.0	22.0
Imports of goods and services (% of GDP)	20.2	20.9	15.4
Gross domestic investment (% of GDP)	10.2	21.2	15.6
Central government revenues (% of GDP)	23.7	17.2	17.4
Overall budget deficit (% of GDP)	0.0	-3.7	-2.3
Money and quasi money (annual % growth)	71.2	6.5	20.9
Technology and infrastructure			
Telephone mainlines (per 1,000 people)	82	117	109
Cost of 3 min local call ($)	0.01	0.06	0.09
Personal computers (per 1,000 people)	11.0	38.8	42.2
Internet users (thousands)	..	350	525
Paved roads (% of total)	36	..	..
Aircraft departures (thousands)	82	99	130
Trade and finance			
Trade as share of PPP GDP (%)	25.1	24.0	26.6
Trade growth less GDP growth (average %, 1989-99)			-2.3
High-technology exports (% of manufactured exports)	4	3	3
Net barter terms of trade (1995=100)	142	83	..
Foreign direct investment ($ millions)	451	4,495	3,187
Present value of debt ($ millions)			37,818
Total debt service ($ millions)	4,990	5,880	5,631
Short term debt ($ millions)	2,000	2,405	2,269
Aid per capita ($)	4	2	2

VIETNAM

Population (thousands)	77,515	Population growth (%)	1.3
Surface area (1,000 sq km)	331.7	Population per sq km	238
GNI ($ millions)	28,733	GNI per capita ($)	370

	1990	1998	1999
People			
Life expectancy (years)	67	..	69
Fertility rate (births per woman)	3.6	..	2.3
Infant mortality rate (per 1,000 live births)	40	..	37
Under 5 mortality rate (per 1,000 children)	54	..	42
Child malnutrition (% of children under 5)	..	40	37
Urban population (% of total)	20	20	20
Rural population density (per km^2 arable land)	996	1,080	..
Illiteracy male (% of people 15 and above)	6	5	5
Illiteracy female (% of people 15 and above)	13	9	9
Net primary enrollment (% of relevant age group)	..	..	..
Net secondary enrollment (% of relevant age group)	..	..	..
Girls in primary school (% of enrollment)	..	48	..
Girls in secondary school (% of enrollment)	..	..	..
Environment			
Forests (1,000 sq. km.)	93	..	..
Deforestation (% change 1990-2000)			..
Water use (% of total resources)	..	..	6.1
CO_2 emissions (metric tons per capita)	0.4	..	..
Access to improved water source (% of urban pop.)	81	..	..
Access to sanitation (% of urban population)	86	..	..
Energy use per capita (kg of oil equivalent)	373	440	..
Electricity use per capita (kWh)	94	232	..
Economy			
GDP ($ millions)	6,472	27,184	28,682
GDP growth (annual %)	5.1	.5.8	4.8
GDP implicit price deflator (annual % growth)	42.1	8.9	5.6
Value added in agriculture (% of GDP)	37.5	25.7	25.4
Value added in industry (% of GDP)	22.7	32.6	34.5
Value added in services (% of GDP)	39.9	41.7	40.1
Exports of goods and services (% of GDP)	26.4	..	..
Imports of goods and services (% of GDP)	33.4	..	..
Gross domestic investment (% of GDP)	13.0	28.7	25.4
Central government revenues (% of GDP)	..	18.4	16.9
Overall budget deficit (% of GDP)	..	-1.1	-1.0
Money and quasi money (annual % growth)	..	23.5	48.8
Technology and infrastructure			
Telephone mainlines (per 1,000 people)	1	22	27
Cost of 3 min local call ($)	..	0.08	0.08
Personal computers (per 1,000 people)	..	6.4	8.9
Internet users (thousands)	..	10	100
Paved roads (% of total)	24	..	..
Aircraft departures (thousands)	2	30	29
Trade and finance			
Trade as share of PPP GDP (%)	..	15.5	16.0
Trade growth less GDP growth (average %, 1989-99)			-8.0
High-technology exports (% of manufactured exports)	..	..	..
Net barter terms of trade (1995=100)			..
Foreign direct investment ($ millions)	16	1,972	1,609
Present value of debt ($ millions)			21,672
Total debt service ($ millions)	174	1,094	1,410
Short term debt ($ millions)	1,780	2,193	2,376
Aid per capita ($)	3	15	18

VIRGIN ISLANDS (U.S.)

High income

Population (thousands)	120	Population growth (%)	1.1
Surface area (1,000 sq km)	0	Population per sq km	352
GNI ($ millions)	..	GNI per capita ($)	..

	1990	1998	1999
People			
Life expectancy (years)	74	77	77
Fertility rate (births per woman)	2.6	2.5	2.4
Infant mortality rate (per 1,000 live births)	20	10	9
Under 5 mortality rate (per 1,000 children)	..	13	12
Child malnutrition (% of children under 5)			..
Urban population (% of total)	45	46	46
Rural population density (per km^2 arable land)	1,157	1,280	..
Illiteracy male (% of people 15 and above)	..	..	..
Illiteracy female (% of people 15 and above)	..	..	..
Net primary enrollment (% of relevant age group)	..	..	
Net secondary enrollment (% of relevant age group)	..	..	
Girls in primary school (% of enrollment)	40	47	..
Girls in secondary school (% of enrollment)	55	..	..
Environment			
Forests (1,000 sq. km.)	0	..	0
Deforestation (% change 1990-2000)			0.0
Water use (% of total resources)	..	..	
CO$_2$ emissions (metric tons per capita)	81.1	98.9	..
Access to improved water source (% of urban pop.)	..	..	..
Access to sanitation (% of urban population)	..	..	..
Energy use per capita (kg of oil equivalent)	..	..	..
Electricity use per capita (kWh)	..	..	..
Economy			
GDP ($ millions)	1,565	1,996	..
GDP growth (annual %)	7.1	..	..
GDP implicit price deflator (annual % growth)	4.1	..	..
Value added in agriculture (% of GDP)	..	..	..
Value added in industry (% of GDP)	..	..	..
Value added in services (% of GDP)	..	..	..
Exports of goods and services (% of GDP)	..	..	..
Imports of goods and services (% of GDP)	..	..	..
Gross domestic investment (% of GDP)	..	..	..
Central government revenues (% of GDP)	..	..	..
Overall budget deficit (% of GDP)	..	..	..
Money and quasi money (annual % growth)	..	..	..
Technology and infrastructure			
Telephone mainlines (per 1,000 people)	453	548	..
Cost of 3 min local call ($)	..	0.00	..
Personal computers (per 1,000 people)	..	..	
Internet users (thousands)	..	10	12
Paved roads (% of total)	..	..	..
Aircraft departures (thousands)	..	..	..
Trade and finance			
Trade as share of PPP GDP (%)	..	..	..
Trade growth less GDP growth (average %, 1989-99)			..
High-technology exports (% of manufactured exports)	..	..	..
Net barter terms of trade (1995=100)	..	..	..
Foreign direct investment ($ millions)	..	..	..
Present value of debt ($ millions)			..
Total debt service ($ millions)	..	..	..
Short term debt ($ millions)	..	..	..
Aid per capita ($)	54	17	..

WEST BANK AND GAZA

Middle East & North Africa   Lower middle income

Population (millions)	3	Population growth (%)	3.7
Surface area (1,000 sq km)	..	Population per sq km	..
GNI ($ millions)	5,063	GNI per capita ($)	1,780

	1990	1998	1999
People			
Life expectancy (years)	..	71	72
Fertility rate (births per woman)	..	5.9	5.8
Infant mortality rate (per 1,000 live births)	..	24	23
Under 5 mortality rate (per 1,000 children)	..	..	26
Child malnutrition (% of children under 5)	..	..	..
Urban population (% of total)	..	..	..
Rural population density (per km^2 arable land)	..	..	..
Illiteracy male (% of people 15 and above)	..	..	..
Illiteracy female (% of people 15 and above)	..	..	..
Net primary enrollment (% of relevant age group)	..	..	..
Net secondary enrollment (% of relevant age group)	..	..	..
Girls in primary school (% of enrollment)	..	..	..
Girls in secondary school (% of enrollment)	..	..	..
Environment			
Forests (1,000 sq. km.)			
Deforestation (% change 1990-2000)	..	..	..
Water use (% of total resources)			
CO_2 emissions (metric tons per capita)	..	..	..
Access to improved water source (% of urban pop.)	..	..	..
Access to sanitation (% of urban population)	..	..	..
Energy use per capita (kg of oil equivalent)	..	..	..
Electricity use per capita (kWh)	..	..	..
Economy			
GDP ($ millions)	..	4,078	4,222
GDP growth (annual %)	..	8.1	6.9
GDP implicit price deflator (annual % growth)	..	7.9	5.3
Value added in agriculture (% of GDP)	..	8.7	8.9
Value added in industry (% of GDP)	..	29.6	28.9
Value added in services (% of GDP)	..	61.7	62.2
Exports of goods and services (% of GDP)	..	17.8	17.1
Imports of goods and services (% of GDP)	..	78.3	75.1
Gross domestic investment (% of GDP)	..	39.2	39.2
Central government revenues (% of GDP)	..	..	..
Overall budget deficit (% of GDP)	..	..	..
Money and quasi money (annual % growth)	..	..	..
Technology and infrastructure			
Telephone mainlines (per 1,000 people)	..	..	72
Cost of 3 min local call ($)	..	0.04	0.05
Personal computers (per 1,000 people)	..	..	..
Internet users (thousands)	..	..	..
Paved roads (% of total)	..	..	..
Aircraft departures (thousands)	..	..	..
Trade and finance			
Trade as share of PPP GDP (%)	..	..	..
Trade growth less GDP growth (average %, 1989-99)			-3.7
High-technology exports (% of manufactured exports)	..	..	..
Net barter terms of trade (1995=100)	..	..	..
Foreign direct investment ($ millions)	..	..	..
Present value of debt ($ millions)			..
Total debt service ($ millions)	..	..	..
Short term debt ($ millions)	..	..	..
Aid per capita ($)	..	221	180

REPUBLIC OF YEMEN

Middle East & North Africa   **Low income**

Population (millions)	17	Population growth (%)	2.7
Surface area (1,000 sq km)	528	Population per sq km	32
GNI ($ millions)	6,088	GNI per capita ($)	360

	1990	1998	1999
People			
Life expectancy (years)	52	..	56
Fertility rate (births per woman)	7.5	..	6.2
Infant mortality rate (per 1,000 live births)	110	..	79
Under 5 mortality rate (per 1,000 children)	130	..	97
Child malnutrition (% of children under 5)	..	..	..
Urban population (% of total)	23	24	24
Rural population density (per km^2 arable land)	665	838	..
Illiteracy male (% of people 15 and above)	45	34	33
Illiteracy female (% of people 15 and above)	87	77	76
Net primary enrollment (% of relevant age group)	..	..	..
Net secondary enrollment (% of relevant age group)	..	..	..
Girls in primary school (% of enrollment)	..	..	..
Girls in secondary school (% of enrollment)	..	..	..
Environment			
Forests (1,000 sq. km.)	5	..	..
Deforestation (% change 1990-2000)			..
Water use (% of total resources)	..	..	71.5
CO_2 emissions (metric tons per capita)	..	..	..
Access to improved water source (% of urban pop.)	85	..	..
Access to sanitation (% of urban population)	80	..	..
Energy use per capita (kg of oil equivalent)	224	201	..
Electricity use per capita (kWh)	108	96	..
Economy			
GDP ($ millions)	4,660	6,302	6,825
GDP growth (annual %)	..	5.3	3.8
GDP implicit price deflator (annual % growth)	..	-4.7	19.7
Value added in agriculture (% of GDP)	25.1	20.4	17.5
Value added in industry (% of GDP)	27.6	34.5	40.5
Value added in services (% of GDP)	47.3	45.1	42.0
Exports of goods and services (% of GDP)	16.4	27.4	38.6
Imports of goods and services (% of GDP)	27.4	45.2	45.4
Gross domestic investment (% of GDP)	14.6	21.1	18.6
Central government revenues (% of GDP)	19.6	35.1	26.3
Overall budget deficit (% of GDP)	-9.1	-2.2	-3.8
Money and quasi money (annual % growth)	..	11.8	13.8
Technology and infrastructure			
Telephone mainlines (per 1,000 people)	11	15	17
Cost of 3 min local call ($)	0.01	0.02	0.02
Personal computers (per 1,000 people)	..	1.5	1.7
Internet users (thousands)	..	4	10
Paved roads (% of total)	9	..	..
Aircraft departures (thousands)	14	7	8
Trade and finance			
Trade as share of PPP GDP (%)	25.9	29.4	34.1
Trade growth less GDP growth (average %, 1989-99)			-3.2
High-technology exports (% of manufactured exports)	..	..	..
Net barter terms of trade (1995=100)	..	..	..
Foreign direct investment ($ millions)	-131	-210	-150
Present value of debt ($ millions)			3,552
Total debt service ($ millions)	169	125	157
Short term debt ($ millions)	1,192	215	473
Aid per capita ($)	34	19	27

YUGOSLAVIA, FR (SERBIA /MONTENEGRO)

Europe & Central Asia **Lower middle income**

Population (millions)	11	Population growth (%)		0.0
Surface area (1,000 sq km)	..	Population per sq km		..
GNI ($ millions)	..	GNI per capita ($)		..

	1990	1998	1999
People			
Life expectancy (years)	72	..	72
Fertility rate (births per woman)	2.1	..	1.7
Infant mortality rate (per 1,000 live births)	23	13	12
Under 5 mortality rate (per 1,000 children)	26	..	16
Child malnutrition (% of children under 5)	..	..	
Urban population (% of total)	51	52	52
Rural population density (per km^2 arable land)	74	..	..
Illiteracy male (% of people 15 and above)	..	..	..
Illiteracy female (% of people 15 and above)	..	..	..
Net primary enrollment (% of relevant age group)	69	..	..
Net secondary enrollment (% of relevant age group)	62	..	..
Girls in primary school (% of enrollment)	..	..	..
Girls in secondary school (% of enrollment)	..	..	..
Environment			
Forests (1,000 sq. km.)	29	..	..
Deforestation (% change 1990-2000)			..
Water use (% of total resources)	..	..	..
CO$_2$ emissions (metric tons per capita)	..	..	..
Access to improved water source (% of urban pop.)	..	..	..
Access to sanitation (% of urban population)	..	..	..
Energy use per capita (kg of oil equivalent)	..	..	..
Electricity use per capita (kWh)	..	..	..
Economy			
GDP ($ millions)	..	..	..
GDP growth (annual %)	..	..	..
GDP implicit price deflator (annual % growth)	..	..	..
Value added in agriculture (% of GDP)	..	..	..
Value added in industry (% of GDP)	..	..	..
Value added in services (% of GDP)	..	..	..
Exports of goods and services (% of GDP)	..	..	..
Imports of goods and services (% of GDP)	..	..	..
Gross domestic investment (% of GDP)	..	..	..
Central government revenues (% of GDP)	..	..	..
Overall budget deficit (% of GDP)	..	..	..
Money and quasi money (annual % growth)	..	..	..
Technology and infrastructure			
Telephone mainlines (per 1,000 people)	166	218	214
Cost of 3 min local call ($)	..	0.01	0.01
Personal computers (per 1,000 people)	..	18.9	20.7
Internet users (thousands)	..	65	80
Paved roads (% of total)	59	59	..
Aircraft departures (thousands)	57	..	..
Trade and finance			
Trade as share of PPP GDP (%)	..	..	..
Trade growth less GDP growth (average %, 1989-99)			..
High-technology exports (% of manufactured exports)	4	..	..
Net barter terms of trade (1995=100)	..	..	..
Foreign direct investment ($ millions)	67	0	0
Present value of debt ($ millions)			12,978
Total debt service ($ millions)	4,779	57	1
Short term debt ($ millions)	524	2,584	2,698
Aid per capita ($)	..	10	60

228

Sub-Saharan Africa — **Low income**

Population (millions)	10	Population growth (%)		2.2
Surface area (1,000 sq km)	753	Population per sq km		13
GNI ($ millions)	3,222	GNI per capita ($)		330

	1990	1998	1999
People			
Life expectancy (years)	49	..	38
Fertility rate (births per woman)	6.3	..	5.4
Infant mortality rate (per 1,000 live births)	107	..	114
Under 5 mortality rate (per 1,000 children)	..	..	187
Child malnutrition (% of children under 5)	..	..	..
Urban population (% of total)	39	39	40
Rural population density (per km^2 arable land)	90	111	..
Illiteracy male (% of people 15 and above)	22	16	15
Illiteracy female (% of people 15 and above)	41	31	30
Net primary enrollment (% of relevant age group)	..	..	..
Net secondary enrollment (% of relevant age group)	..	..	..
Girls in primary school (% of enrollment)	..	..	..
Girls in secondary school (% of enrollment)	..	..	..
Environment			
Forests (1,000 sq. km.)	398	..	..
Deforestation (% change 1990-2000)			..
Water use (% of total resources)	..	..	1.5
CO_2 emissions (metric tons per capita)	0.3	..	..
Access to improved water source (% of urban pop.)	88	..	..
Access to sanitation (% of urban population)	86	..	..
Energy use per capita (kg of oil equivalent)	671	630	..
Electricity use per capita (kWh)	503	539	..
Economy			
GDP ($ millions)	3,288	3,240	3,150
GDP growth (annual %)	-0.5	-1.9	2.4
GDP implicit price deflator (annual % growth)	106.4	19.6	21.7
Value added in agriculture (% of GDP)	20.6	21.2	24.6
Value added in industry (% of GDP)	49.1	29.1	24.5
Value added in services (% of GDP)	30.3	49.7	50.9
Exports of goods and services (% of GDP)	35.9	26.7	22.3
Imports of goods and services (% of GDP)	36.6	39.2	40.9
Gross domestic investment (% of GDP)	17.3	16.3	17.5
Central government revenues (% of GDP)	..	..	..
Overall budget deficit (% of GDP)	..	..	..
Money and quasi money (annual % growth)	47.9	25.6	27.7
Technology and infrastructure			
Telephone mainlines (per 1,000 people)	9	9	9
Cost of 3 min local call ($)	0.05	0.06	0.05
Personal computers (per 1,000 people)	..	6.8	7.2
Internet users (thousands)	..	3	15
Paved roads (% of total)	17	..	..
Aircraft departures (thousands)	7	1	1
Trade and finance			
Trade as share of PPP GDP (%)	38.7	19.8	18.7
Trade growth less GDP growth (average %, 1989-99)			-0.2
High-technology exports (% of manufactured exports)	..	..	..
Net barter terms of trade (1995=100)	131	84	..
Foreign direct investment ($ millions)	203	198	163
Present value of debt ($ millions)			5,154
Total debt service ($ millions)	202	202	439
Short term debt ($ millions)	1,414	329	111
Aid per capita ($)	62	36	63

Population (millions)	12	Population growth (%)	1.8
Surface area (1,000 sq km)	391	Population per sq km	31
GNI ($ millions)	6,302	GNI per capita ($)	530

	1990	1998	1999
People			
Life expectancy (years)	56	..	40
Fertility rate (births per woman)	4.8	..	3.6
Infant mortality rate (per 1,000 live births)	52	..	70
Under 5 mortality rate (per 1,000 children)	..	..	118
Child malnutrition (% of children under 5)	..	..	..
Urban population (% of total)	28	34	35
Rural population density (per km^2 arable land)	241	240	..
Illiteracy male (% of people 15 and above)	13	8	8
Illiteracy female (% of people 15 and above)	25	17	16
Net primary enrollment (% of relevant age group)	..	..	..
Net secondary enrollment (% of relevant age group)	..	..	..
Girls in primary school (% of enrollment)	50	..	..
Girls in secondary school (% of enrollment)	47	..	..
Environment			
Forests (1,000 sq. km.)	222	..	..
Deforestation (% change 1990-2000)			
Water use (% of total resources)	..	..	6.1
CO_2 emissions (metric tons per capita)	1.7	..	..
Access to improved water source (% of urban pop.)	99	..	..
Access to sanitation (% of urban population)	98	..	..
Energy use per capita (kg of oil equivalent)	932	861	..
Electricity use per capita (kWh)	933	896	..
Economy			
GDP ($ millions)	8,784	6,769	5,608
GDP growth (annual %)	7.0	3.7	0.1
GDP implicit price deflator (annual % growth)	14.8	35.5	48.1
Value added in agriculture (% of GDP)	16.5	22.1	20.1
Value added in industry (% of GDP)	33.1	24.3	24.6
Value added in services (% of GDP)	50.4	53.5	55.3
Exports of goods and services (% of GDP)	22.9	43.0	45.2
Imports of goods and services (% of GDP)	22.8	44.7	45.7
Gross domestic investment (% of GDP)	17.4	19.8	11.5
Central government revenues (% of GDP)	24.2	..	..
Overall budget deficit (% of GDP)	-5.3	..	..
Money and quasi money (annual % growth)	15.1	11.3	35.9
Technology and infrastructure			
Telephone mainlines (per 1,000 people)	12	21	..
Cost of 3 min local call ($)	0.04	..	..
Personal computers (per 1,000 people)	0.2	11.4	13.0
Internet users (thousands)	..	10	20
Paved roads (% of total)	14	..	..
Aircraft departures (thousands)	10	17	13
Trade and finance			
Trade as share of PPP GDP (%)	15.5	14.6	14.4
Trade growth less GDP growth (average %, 1989-99)			-2.9
High-technology exports (% of manufactured exports)	2	..	2
Net barter terms of trade (1995=100)	100	105	..
Foreign direct investment ($ millions)	-12	444	59
Present value of debt ($ millions)			4,074
Total debt service ($ millions)	471	981	648
Short term debt ($ millions)	591	768	746
Aid per capita ($)	35	24	21

GLOSSARY

Access to improved water source — refers to the percentage of the population with reasonable access to an adequate amount of water from an improved water source, such as household connection, public standpipe, borehole, protected well or spring, and rainwater collection. (World Health Organization/ UNICEF Joint Monitoring Programme)

Access to improved sanitation — is the percentage of the urban population served by connections to public sewers or household systems such as privies, pour-flush latrines, septic tanks, communal toilets, and similar facilities. (United Nations)

Aid per capita — official development assistance and official aid received from members of the OECD Development Assistance Committee and other official donors. (Organisation for Economic Cooperation and Development)

Aircraft departures — the number of domestic and international takeoffs of aircraft. (International Civil Aviation Organization)

Central government revenues — all revenue from taxes and current nontax revenues (other than grants) such as fines, fees, recoveries, and income from property or sales. The data are for 1997. (International Monetary Fund)

Child malnutrition — the percentage of children under five whose weight for age is more than two standard deviations below the average for the reference population. The reference population, adopted by the WHO in 1983, is based on children from the United States, who are assumed to be well nourished. (United Nations, World Health Organization, UNICEF)

CO$_2$ emissions — emissions stemming from the burning of fossil fuels and the manufacture of cement. They include carbon dioxide produced during consumption of solid, liquid, and gas fuels and gas flaring. The data are for 1996. (Carbon Dioxide Analysis Center)

Cost of 3 minute local call — the cost of a three-minute call within the same exchange area using the subscriber's equipment (that is, not from a public phone). International Telecommunication Union)

Deforestation — the permanent conversion of natural forest areas to other uses, including shifting cultivation, permanent agriculture, ranching, settlements, and infrastructure development. Deforested areas do not include areas logged but intended for regeneration or areas degraded by fuelwood gathering, acid precipitation, or forest fires. Negative numbers indicate an increase in forest area. (Food and Agriculture Organization)

Electricity use per capita — the production of power plants and combined heat and power plants less transmission, distribution, and transformation losses and own use by heat and power plants. (International Energy Agency)

Energy use per capita — the apparent consumption of commercial energy, which is equal to indigenous production plus imports and stock changes, minus exports and fuels supplied to ships and aircraft engaged in international transportation. (International Energy Agency)

Europe EMU — is the 11 participating member countries of the European Monetary Union (EMU) comprising Austria, Belgium, Denmark, Finland, France, Germany, Greece, Ireland, Italy, Luxembourg, the Netherlands, Portugal, Spain, Sweden, anf the United Kingdom.

Exports of goods and services — the value of all goods and other market services provided to the world, including merchandise, freight, insurance, travel, and other nonfactor services. Factor and property income (formerly called factor services) such as investment income, is excluded. (World Bank, Organisation for Economic Co-operation and Development, United Nations)

Fertility rate — the number of children that would be born to a woman if she were to live to the end of her childbearing years and bear children in accordance with current age-specific fertility rates. (World Health Organization)

Foreign direct investment — net inflows of investment to acquire a lasting management interest (10 percent or more of voting stock) in an enterprise operating in an economy other than that of the investor. It is the sum of equity capital, reinvestment of earnings, other long-term capital, and short-term capital as shown in the balance of payments. (International Monetary Fund)

Forests — land under natural or planted stands of trees, whether productive or not. (Food and Agriculture Organization)

GDP (gross domestic product) — the gross domestic product at purchasers' prices is the sum of the gross value added by all resident and non resident producers in the economy plus indirect taxes and minus any subsidies not included in the value of the products. It is calculated without making deductions for depreciation of fabricated assets or for depletion and degradation of natural resources. (World Bank, Organisation for Economic Co-operation and Development, United Nations)

GDP growth — the one-year rate of growth in real gross domestic product. (World Bank, Organisation for Economic Co-operation and Development, United Nations)

GDP implicit price deflator — the average annual rate of price change in the economy as a whole for 1990-98. (World Bank, Organisation for Economic Co-operation and Development, United Nations)

GNI (gross national income - formerly Gross National Product or GNP) — the value of the final output of goods and services produced by the residents of an economy plus net primary income from non resident sources.

GNI per capita (gross national income per capita) — the gross national product divided by midyear population. Gross national product is equal to GDP plus net receipts of primary income (employee compensation and property income) from nonresident sources. (World Bank)

Girls in primary school — the number of female pupils enrolled in primary school as a percentage of total pupils enrolled in public and private schools. (United Nations Educational, Scientific, and Cultural Organization)

Girls in secondary school — the number of female pupils enrolled in secondary school as a percentage of total pupils enrolled in public and private schools. (United Nations Educational, Scientific, and Cultural Organization)

Gross capital formation — outlays on additions to the fixed assets of the economy plus net changes in the level of inventories. Fixed assets include land improvements; plant, machinery, and equipment purchases; and the construction of roads, railways, and the like, including commercial and industrial buildings, offices, schools, hospitals, and private residential dwellings. Inventories are stocks of goods held by firms to meet temporary or unexpected fluctuations in production or sales. (World Bank, Organisation for Economic Co-operation and Development, United Nations)

High technology exports — are products with high research and development intensity. They include high-technology products such as in aerospace, computers, pharmaceuticals, scientific instruments, and electrical machinery. (COMTRADE database)

Illiteracy, female — the percentage of females age 15 and older who cannot, with understanding, read and write a short, simple statement about their everyday life. (United Nations Educational, Scientific, and Cultural Organization)

Illiteracy, male — the percentage of males age 15 and older who cannot, with understanding, read and write a short, simple statement about their everyday life. (United Nations Educational, Scientific, and Cultural Organization)

Imports of goods and services — the value of all goods and other market services provided to the world, including merchandise, freight, insurance, travel, and other nonfactor services. Factor and property income (formerly called factor services) such as investment income, is excluded. (World Bank, Organisation for Economic Co-operation and Development, United Nations)

Infant mortality rate — the number of infants who die before reaching the age of one year of age, per 1,000 live births in the same year. (World Health Organization)

Internet users — are the number of people with access to the worldwide network. (International Telecommunications Union)

Life expectancy — the number of years a newborn infant would live if prevailing patterns of mortality at the time of its birth were to stay the same throughout its life. (World Health Organization)

Money and quasi money — the sum of currency outside banks, demand deposits other than those of the central government, and the time, savings, and foreign currency deposits of resident sectors other than the central government (frequently called M2). (International Monetary Fund)

Net barter terms of trade — the ratio of the export price index to the corresponding import price index measured relative to the base year 1995. (United Nations Conference on Trade and Development, International Monetary Fund)

Net primary enrollment — the ratio of total enrollment, regardless of age, to the population of the primary school age group. Based on the International Standard Classification of Education (ISCED). Net enrollment ratios exceeding 100 indicate discrepancies between the estimates of school-age population and reported enrollment data. (United Nations Educational, Scientific, and Cultural Organization)

Net secondary enrollment — the ratio of total enrollment, regardless of age, to the population of the secondary school age group. Based on the International Standard Classification of Education (ISCED). Net enrollment ratios exceeding 100 indicate discrepancies between the estimates of school-age population and reported enrollment data. (United Nations Educational, Scientific, and Cultural Organization)

Overall budget deficit — current and capital revenue and official grants received, less total expenditure and lending minus repayments. (International Monetary Fund)

Paved roads — those surfaced with crushed stone (macadam) and hydrocarbon binder or bituminized agents, with concrete, or with cobblestones, as a percentage of all the country's roads, measured in length. (International Road Federation)

Personal computers — the estimated number of self-contained computers designed to be used by a single individual, per 1,000 people. (International Telecommunication Union)

Population — based on the de facto definition of population, which counts all residents regardless of legal status or citizenship, except for refugees not permanently settled in the country of asylum. (World Bank)

Population growth — the one-year rate of growth in total population. (World Bank)

Population per square kilometer— the total population divided by land area in square kilometers. (Land area excludes areas under inland bodies of water.) (World Bank, Food and Agriculture Organization)

Present value of debt — the sum of short-term external debt plus the discounted sum of total debt service payments due on public, publicly guaranteed, and private nonguaranteed long-term external debt over the life of existing loans. (World Bank, International Monetary Fund)

Rural population density — the rural population divided by the arable land area. Rural population is the difference between the total surface area population and the urban population. (Food and Agriculture Organization)

Short term debt — all debt having an original maturity of one year or less and interest in arrears on long-term debt. (World Bank)

Surface area — a country's total area, including areas under inland bodies of water and some coastal waterways. (Food and Agriculture Organization)

Telephone mainlines — telephone lines connecting a customer's equipment to the public switched telephone network, per 1,000 people. (International Telecommunication Union)

Total debt services — the sum of principal repayments and interest actually paid in foreign currency, goods, or services on long-term debt, interest paid on short-term debt, and repayments (repurchases and charges) to the IMF. (World Bank)

Trade as share of PPP GDP — the sum of exports and imports of goods and services divided by the value of GDP converted to international dollars at purchasing power parity (PPP) rates. (World Bank)

Trade growth less GDP growth — the difference between annual growth in trade of goods and services and growth in GDP from 1988-1998. (World Bank)

Under 5 mortality rate — the probability that a newborn baby will die before reaching the age of five, if subject to current age-specific mortality rates. (United Nations, UNICEF)

Urban population — the midyear population of areas defined as urban in each country and reported to the United Nations. (United Nations)

Value added in agriculture — the net output of agriculture (International Standard Industrial Classification divisions 1-5 including forestry and fishing) after adding up all outputs and subtracting intermediate outputs. (World Bank, Organisation for Economic Co-operation and Development, United Nations)

Value added in industry — the net output of industry (includes mining, manufacturing, construction, electricity, water, and gas) after adding up all outputs and subtracting intermediate outputs. (World Bank, Organisation for Economic Co-operation and Development, United Nations)

Value added in services — the net output of services (International Standard Industrial Classification divisions 50-99) after adding up all outputs and subtracting intermediate outputs. (World Bank, Organisation for Economic Co-operation and Development, United Nations)

Water use — estimates from the World Resources Institute of domestic, industrial, and agricultural water use. (World Resources Institute)